Wisdom Anthology

◀ PLAYS AND SCREENPLAYS ▶
BY WOMEN OVER 50

ARTemis Arts

This anthology contains works of fiction.
All the characters, events, and organizations portrayed
in this work are either products of the authors'
imaginations or used fictitiously.

ISBN 13: 978-1-63489-495-1

Library of Congress Catalog Number has been applied for.
Printed in the United States of America
First Printing: 2022

26 25 24 23 22   5 4 3 2 1

Cover and interior design by Cindy Samargia Laun
Cover art by Kathryn Suavé Liu

Wise Ink Creative Publishing
807 Broadway St NE, Suite 46
Minneapolis, MN 55413
wiseink.com

This project was made possible with the generous support of Ronni Lacroute
and the following organizations:

Contents

2020–21 ARTEMIS ARTS BOARD OF DIRECTORS

President	**Diane Bearden-Enright**
Vice President and Founder	**Sam Hull**
Secretary	**Sarah Behr**
Treasurer	**Leslie Clark**
Funding Chair	**Mary Sauvé**
Curator	**Jaki King**
Corporate Giving Chair	**Kristi Plahn-Gjersvold**

Statement

From the ARTemis Arts Board of Directors

The ARTemis Arts Board is incredibly proud and lucky to have been able to work on the inaugural *ARTemis Arts Wisdom Anthology*. It has been the culmination of years of observations and outreach from the board and our extended community.

Over the last seven years, many of ARTemis Arts's clients have been women over the age of fifty—women who had worked their entire lives in an industry that had no love or respect for them, or women who, after postponing their dreams and creative lives, were not welcomed into the arts community during their retirement years. When we, as a board, had an opportunity to create an anthology, we unanimously agreed that a wisdom anthology should be where we begin this work.

For us, this project was never about finding tried-and-true plays. It was about finding the artists who haven't had the opportunity to test their plays, to have them performed, to see them in print or read by someone other than friends and family. We wanted to provide an opportunity for these "nameless" women to showcase works that they created after they turned fifty; after they reached an age which (let's be honest) most people don't see as useful or creatively relevant/necessary, but which absolutely is.

The *ARTemis Arts Wisdom Anthology* is meant to bring opportunity, recognition, and community to those who have never had this support, or who have seen their opportunities dwindle as they age.

We experienced pushback concerning our mission. Some of this pushback was understandable; some writers were uncomfortable with submitting work that had not yet been tested. Another pushback was based in fear, primarily the fear that there can only be so many successful women in artistic venues—that those opportunities are limited and should only go to those already in the mix. There was also a lack of confidence—confidence in the work and abilities of the writers and, surprisingly, confidence in being selected and then paid to participate in the project. As is our method, we gave room for these experiences, but held tight to our plans. All these reactions are part of what ARTemis Arts hopes to influence through our work and our guiding pillars: knowledge building, exposure, and support.

We strive to provide a community to those who feel isolated, an arena to showcase and recognize the incredible work that women all over the world are currently creating. We also continually demand that they receive the same compensation as their male counterparts. We help to educate both artists and allies. We ask to be part of the conversation in both corporate giving and organizational production. We provide resources to individual women, including mentorships. We work with lawyers to help artists when they or their art has been taken advantage of—all of this is within the mission of ARTemis Arts.

This is but the first of many anthologies that ARTemis Arts hopes to curate. We see prose, visual arts, and music anthologies showcasing women of all ages in our future. Each writer featured in this, our first anthology, continues to hold all rights to their work past our anthology series. Each writer received a stipend after their play was selected, and each will share equally in 20 percent of all profits. The remaining profits will go toward creating the next anthology in the series and helping more women, of all ages, as they pursue their art forms. We are currently looking to fund the entire anthology series, in both the Wisdom and open categories, should you or your organization be interested in sponsoring one or all of those publications.

What did we learn from this project? We learned that we all need to be allies in some form. That we all, as a community, need to be building each other up, holding space for those coming behind us, and not letting fear keep us from pursuing our dreams. The women showcased within this anthology have decades of experience, strength, tenacity, brilliance, and wisdom. The following plays prove that together we are stronger; that we have similar yet unique and individual stories to share; and that no matter the start date of our artistic adventures, there is a place for our work. Being of wisdom age and emerging-artist status brings no shame—it shows that the work was worth the wait, the information seasoned, and the artist fiercely determined.

The work included in these pages varies from workshop ready, to immediately producible, to pure experimental expression. The board would also like to acknowledge the hundreds of writers that submitted work to this anthology. We see you and appreciate you, please continue to write and be the incredible creative individuals you are.

It is our pleasure to introduce you to the *ARTemis Arts Wisdom Anthology*.

Anthology Patron	**Ronni Lacroute**
Anthology Manager	**Melissa Schmitz**
Anthology Readers	**Ithica Tell**
	Pat Lach
	Heather Parody
	Sally Wheeler-Maier
	Jaki King
	Sam Hull
	Melissa Schmitz
	Michael Susko
	Diane Bearden-Enright
	Janice Blixt
	Itanza Wooden
	Ronni Lacroute
	Carol Drummond Maresh
	Kimberli Green

About ARTemis Arts

ARTemis Arts serves self-identifying women artists across three artistic sectors: visual arts, performing arts, and literature. Whether art imitates life or life imitates art, ARTemis Arts believes that it is vital that women cease being the silent societal majority. ARTemis Arts uses three pillars—knowledge building, exposure, and support—to enable the woman artist to develop her stories and strengthen her voice. We advance the woman artist by increasing public awareness of and attendance for her artistic work as well as demanding improvements in the opportunities for women as artists in both profit and nonprofit experiences. In addition to corporations seeking to support the arts in their community relations endeavors, ARTemis Arts facilitates opportunities by providing necessary support, by networking like-minded professionals and male and female non-artesian allies, and by acting as a critical sounding board for artistic entities.

Facebook: ARTemisartsorg
Twitter: @ARTemisarts_org
Instagram: Artemisarts_org

FOREWORD

Theatre has, unfortunately, become more and more a young person's game. The word "emerging" looms over every initiative. Everywhere one looks, there is a search for the next "emerging" artist to break through. The default definition of "emerging" seems to be "young and unknown." But what of the writers over fifty who have yet to be discovered—who are young in spirit, full of passion, blessed with wisdom born of life's experience? These people should be admired and supported, but instead have been pushed into the shadows by our youth-obsessed culture. The matter gets further complicated when that writer is female.

The state of the field for female artists is not level. In fact, it is still an uphill battle to get work produced. Organizations like 50/50 in 2020, the Kilroys, and others are shining the light on female playwrights. The goal of these efforts is to hold producers accountable for increasing parity and to remove the excuse that producers don't know where to find plays by female writers. These efforts are making a difference, though there is still work to do. Efforts like this book go one step further, inviting female writers over fifty to come from the shadows and dance in the light.

This anthology lifts up and celebrates those fifty-plus female writers who have crafted stories about the world as they see it. Thoughtful, inspiring, and provocative, these works range from workshop-ready to fully producible. The writers represented remind us that creativity is a lifelong vocation. They leave a trail for younger writers to follow, encouraged that there is a place for them as they grow into the fullness of their maturity. That their usefulness to the field has no expiration date.

Valerie Curtis-Newton

Ten-Minute
Plays

YVETTE HEYLIGER

I am part of the 93.9% of American women of color whose work does not reach production in this nation. Fortunately, I realized early on that in order to grow as a playwright, I needed to see my work living and breathing on the stage. So, I took a partner and hung up my shingle as a producing artist. I slowly began to build a body of work while raising a family. On occasion, I worked outside of the home to raise the money to produce my plays. In an effort to gain greater visibility for said growing body of work, and to ensure that my grandson and future generations of theatre lovers knew I was here and had something to say, I turned to self-publishing.

This path has brought me street-cred and the respect of my peers, but not the nationally recognized awards and accolades that garner the attention of regional theatres and Broadway producers. Now, at sixty-one years of age, me thinkith I am probably too old to be the next "hot thing," "theatre-darling," or token black woman playwright lucky enough to get her foot in the door of a prestigious theatre.

So, what keeps me in the theatre?

I believe my longevity is due to how I measure success. I measure success in service. And this is not some new revelation or sudden turnaround in my thinking. Service alone has defined the trajectory of my life. Case in point: my play with music about family, church, sex, and HIV, called *What Would Jesus Do?*

A local producer who had picked up the show wanted me to cut words like "sex" and "penis" and "gay" from the play, lest I offend her bread-and-butter church-going audiences. But I held firm. I held firm because *What Would Jesus Do?* was a dramatic demonstration to me that God was guiding my hand as a playwright, shepherding the plot and speaking through me on behalf of the characters. I remember watching that producer's church-going audiences (many of them repeat customers!) selling out houses, commenting and talking back to the stage, shouting out favorite lines, singing along, laughing and crying with the characters—and some even declaring, "That's my story!" There was a lot of healing going on and a lot of HIV-prevention awareness being raised—all while entertaining.

Standing in that theatre, I knew my play was anointed. Any doubt I had about the calling I received to write for the theatre was silenced by the standing ovations. By the measure of my bootstraps, I was feeling as successful as the 6.1%* of my sisters of color who had "made" it.

*The Count 2.0, An Ongoing Study by The Lilly's in Partnership with the Dramatists Guild

YVETTE HEYLIGER is a playwright, producing artist and activist. Author of *What a Piece of Work is Man! Full-Length Plays for Leading Women*, she has contributed to various anthologies including: *Performer Stuff, The Monologue Project, Short Plays on Reproductive Freedom, Later Chapters: The Best Scenes and Monologues for Actors over Fifty, WE ARE THEATRE, 24 Gun Control Plays, The Best Women's Stage Monologues 2003* and *The Best Stage Scenes 2003*. Pending: *Performing #MeToo: How Not to Look Away, The Children of the People: Writings by and about CUNY Students on Race and Social Justice, She Persisted: 30 Ten-Minute Plays by Women Over 40*, and *She Persisted: Monologues from Plays by Women Over 40*. Other writings include various articles and blog posts: *The Dramatists Guild Blog, I Write about Playwrights: #1087 Yvette Heyliger, The Native Society: Personalizing Thought Leadership, The Dramatist, Continuum: The Journal of African Diaspora Drama, Theatre and Performance, Black Masks: Spotlight on Black Art*, and *HowlRound*.

Yvette is the recipient of the AUDELCO Recognition Award for Excellence in Black Theatre's August Wilson Playwright Award and Dramatic Production of the Year. She received a Best Playwright nomination from NAACP's Annual Theatre Awards. After many years in front of the footlights, Yvette returned to the stage as a solo artist in her one-woman show, *Bridge to Baraka*, which she performed in the United Solo Theatre Festival and the National Black Theatre Festival, among others. A producing artist, Yvette was the co-recipient of the first National Black Theatre Festival Emerging Producer Award.

Memberships: Dramatist Guild, AEA, SDC, and AFTRA-SAG. She currently serves as a Dramatist Guild NYC Ambassador and on the executive committee of Honor Roll. She is the former VP of Programming on the Board of the League of Professional Theatre Women.

Yvette lives in Harlem, USA.

A Better Wife

A TEN-MINUTE PLAY BY YVETTE HEYLIGER

CAST OF CHARACTERS

WIFE: Mrs. Earline Thompson is an attractive, middle-class, African American wife and mother in her mid-fifties who will be celebrating her upcoming wedding anniversary with her husband of thirty years.

CANDIDATE: Ms. Veronica Douglass is an attractive, professional, African American woman who has recently turned forty-one years of age and who, perhaps, is a younger version of WIFE.

TIME

Springtime in the new millennium.

PLACE

A pre-war apartment building in Harlem, USA.

SETTING

The Thompsons live in a spacious apartment complete with wood floors and high ceilings. The living room, which features an Afrocentric décor, is a tasteful mix of color, pattern, and texture. An original painting by an African American artist hangs over the couch. There are framed family photos on display, including one of Junior and his girlfriend. On the coffee table rests a letter opener, a pen holder with pens, a clipboard with a checklist, and a stack of applications with 4 x 6 photos of applicants paper clipped to each one. On the side table next to the armchair is a cordless landline telephone. Beneath that is a small wastebasket with a few discarded applications inside. There is a coat closet and an umbrella stand in the foyer, as well as an intercom on the wall near the front door.

(Lights up. WIFE is at the front door showing an unseen candidate out)

WIFE
Yes, yes, you did fine! As I said, I'll be making my decision in a couple of days. Again, thank you for coming. Now, I really must prepare for the next candidate, you understand. Please, good bye! *(She closes the front door; enters the living room)* Finally! She'll not talk my Senior into an early grave! *(WIFE throws the application into the waste bin and picks up the clipboard to see if there are any more appointments. The buzzer rings. She looks at her watch. It rings again. She returns to the foyer; speaks into the intercom)* Who's there? *(Offstage, CANDIDATE speaks into the intercom from the lobby)*

CANDIDATE
It's Veronica Douglass!

WIFE
You are fifteen minutes late, Veronica Douglass.

CANDIDATE
Yes, I know. I'm so sorry, but may I— *(WIFE cuts her off midsentence, buzzing her in. She returns to the living room, looking for the name on the clipboard. Finding it, she checks if off and notes the time. Taking CANDIDATE's application off of the top of the pile, she inspects the photo. Shortly, the doorbell rings. WIFE returns to the foyer to open the door)*

CANDIDATE (CONT'D)
Hello. And thank you for allowing me to come up.

WIFE
I was very specific on the telephone that I cannot interview candidates for the position after 4:00 p.m. Did I or did I not say, half-hour time slots?

CANDIDATE
Yes, but—

WIFE
If we run overtime, it will disrupt everything. This has all been very carefully timed. *(Beat)* Well, come in, before someone sees you! *(CANDIDATE enters the living room. She is wearing a trench coat and carrying a wet umbrella, a briefcase, and purse)*

CANDIDATE
Thank you. It's a pleasure to meet—

WIFE
Oh, you're dripping.

CANDIDATE
Yes, it started raining just as I came up from the sub—

(WIFE holds up photograph next to her face)

WIFE
Douglass, is it? Good picture. Looks like you. *(Checks "Looks like Photo" off on the list)* You'd be surprised how many don't.

CANDIDATE
Don't?

WIFE
Look like their picture. *(Extending her hand to shake)*

CANDIDATE
Oh, well, thank you. It's a pleasure to—

WIFE
(Ignoring the gesture) We'll get as far as we can. Just be prepared for the fact that we may have to stop and reschedule.

CANDIDATE
Of course. *(Withdrawing her hand)*

Please accept my apology. Someone was sick on the subway car ahead of mine and service was interrupt—

WIFE
Whatever. These things happen.

CANDIDATE
Thank you for selecting me.

WIFE
I haven't selected you.

CANDIDATE
I mean for the personal interview. Thank you for selecting me for the personal interview. My guess is that I must be in the running if I've made it to the face-to-face.

WIFE
Yes, well, let's get on with it, shall we? Time is of the essence. I'll just take that. *(WIFE takes the umbrella and places it in the umbrella stand)*

CANDIDATE
Wow! Look at this ceiling! *(Taking off her coat)* High ceilings are hard to find these days.

WIFE
Not in Harlem, as the white folks have discovered.

CANDIDATE
Most buildings are all chopped up—landlords trying to squeeze in as many units as they possibly can. *(Holding out her coat)*

WIFE
Enough with the chit chat. Have a seat there.

CANDIDATE
Don't you want to take my coat?

WIFE
Is it wet?

CANDIDATE
No, not rea—

WIFE

Might as well keep it then. You may not be here that long. *(Sitting in arm chair)* Let's begin, shall we.

CANDIDATE

Might I trouble you for the restroom and a glass of water first?

WIFE

Perhaps if you'd arrived on time that might have been possible.

CANDIDATE

I'm sorry, why don't we just reschedule, that way I can use the restroom, be on my way, and you won't run over time.

WIFE

Well, you're here now, aren't you? Might as well have a look-see if you're suitable. A second appointment may not even be warranted.

CANDIDATE

All right, then. *(Sitting on the couch)* I guess I can hold it.

WIFE

Congratulations. You just flunked the first test. You're desperate!

CANDIDATE

No, I'm not.

WIFE

Yes, you are.

CANDIDATE

No, I'm not. Because I can hold it, I'm desperate?

WIFE

Thank you for coming. *(Checks "Desperate" off of the list)* There's the door.

CANDIDATE

You're the one on a schedule. I'm just trying to comply.

WIFE

Obviously you must be younger than what you reported on your application.

No woman I know can "hold it," especially on a rainy day, and ask for a glass of water unless she's young. Fibbing about one's age is immediate cause for disqualification.

CANDIDATE

I am not fibbing! I can see I've made a mistake answering this ad. *(She stands and gathers her belongings)* I'll just be getting the hell out of here. *(The phone rings. WIFE checks the caller ID feature and sees it is her husband)*

WIFE

Hold it! I've changed my mind. You may use the powder room. It's just down the hall where you see the open door. *(Answering the phone)* Hello, Senior. Yes, hold on. *(CANDIDATE starts towards the bathroom with her purse. WIFE covers the mouthpiece and calls after her)* The only open door of all the closed doors in the hallway. Be sure you go through the open door. If you want a drink of water, there are some Dixie cups in the dispenser next to the sink. *(WIFE waits to hear the bathroom door close and then takes the call)* Hi, honey. No, I'm here. I was just talking to one of the neighbors. *(Beat)* What's that? *(Beat)* Late? Good. I mean, that's fine, Herman. *(Under her breath)* It's perfect actually. *(Beat)* What? *(Beat)* Of course I'll miss you. I can hardly hear you. Where are you? *(Beat)* Oh, the Knicks game. That's right, I forgot. *(Beat)* No, don't wait. Go ahead and eat there. We only have leftovers here. Only leftovers, I said! Yes, go ahead! Maybe they have a veggie burger or something on the menu. *(Beat)* Well, have pasta or pizza then. *(Beat)* I say have pas—can you go somewhere where it's a little quieter? *(Beat)* Me? Oh, nothing. I may just catch up on my reading or watch a little TV. *(Quickly)* Your new yoga mat came today. I said, your new yoga mat, it came today! Its lavender, just like you wanted. *(Beat)* What? No, I didn't open it. *(Beat)* Oh, alright, I peeked! *(CANDIDATE re-enters, her lipstick freshened and hair smoothed)* Okay, honey, have fun with the guys and do me a favor, get crazy and have a beer. *(Beat)* A! One beer is not going to kill you, Senior, for heaven's sake! *(Beat)* I love you too. Bye. *(WIFE hangs up the phone; turns to face CANDIDATE)* Well, it seems we have a little more time on our hands.

CANDIDATE
(Gathering her belongings, CANDIDATE heads for the door) You do. I don't.

WIFE
I'm sorry if I've been a little less than gracious. I've had quite a day screening candidates and you are the last one.

CANDIDATE
(Pausing) Of course, I understand.

WIFE
Perhaps we can start over?

CANDIDATE
Yes, I'd like that.

WIFE
I'll just take your coat…*(CANDIDATE hands it to her. WIFE hangs the coat in the coat closet and starts for the kitchen)* And get you that glass of water. *(Holding her full Dixie cup)*

CANDIDATE
Oh, no. That's OK. I'm fine.

WIFE
(Extending her hand to shake) Well, then, I'm Earline Thompson. Mrs. Earline Thompson. And you are—

CANDIDATE
(Shaking her hand) Veronica P. Douglass. Ms. Veronica P. Douglass.

WIFE
Is that Ms. as in "Miss" or Ms. as in "Mrs."?

CANDIDATE
(Taken aback by the question) Why, "Miss," of course.

WIFE
It wasn't a trick question, dear.

CANDIDATE
Wasn't it?

WIFE
The choice to use the title "Ms." I believe, reveals something about character—the need or desire perhaps to be purposefully ambiguous. *(Beat)* Well, surely, you agree?

CANDIDATE
(Slowly) No, most women use Ms.—

WIFE
One is either something or they're not. Let's take the guesswork out of it, shall we?

CANDIDATE
But, women fought for—I mean the Women's Liberation movement—

WIFE
Had its pluses and its minuses— especially if you were a woman, black, and poor. What does the "P" stand for?

CANDIDATE
The "P"? *(Beat)* Oh, the "P"! Pearl. That's my middle name. Pearl.

WIFE
Is it really? *(Considers the coincidence)* Humph…

CANDIDATE
What…is that significant?

WIFE
(Getting papers in order for the interview) We shall see.

CANDIDATE
OK…If you don't mind, what might our going longer have disrupted?

WIFE
Come again?

CANDIDATE
You said, "If we run overtime, it will disrupt everything." I asked what might—

WIFE
Oh, cooking dinner and the arrival of my husband from work.

CANDIDATE
I see. Well, shouldn't I meet him anyway?

WIFE
First things first. We haven't even completed Phase II.

CANDIDATE
What was Phase I?

WIFE
Screening you over the telephone. Well, technically I guess placing the ad was Phase I. Your answering the ad and me screening you over the telephone was Phase II. Congratulations, we're on to Phase III. If all goes well, the home visit will be next. Please, have a seat. *(THEY sit)* Now, I read on your application that you were married once before.

CANDIDATE
Yes, a long time ago.

WIFE
What happened?

CANDIDATE
It's not very interesting—a cliché, really.

WIFE
A cliché? Well, let's hear it.

CANDIDATE
We met in college, married right after graduation, he cheated and we divorced.

WIFE
No children?

CANDIDATE
No. Although, I would have liked—

WIFE
A clean break. That's a blessing.

CANDIDATE
Is it? It didn't feel like a—

WIFE
Children complicate matters. You brought the divorce decree?

CANDIDATE
Oh, yes. *(She retrieves the document from her briefcase)* I filed all the papers myself. The matter was settled and behind me before law school was over. *(She gives it to WIFE)* See? *(Beat)* A cliché. It's funny; I swore I would never be a cliché and here—

WIFE
Well, it's better than being a statistic.

CANDIDATE
A statistic?

WIFE
He could have cheated, given you HIV, and where would you be now, Miss Douglass? Certainly not sitting here with me.

CANDIDATE
That's not very nice.

WIFE
But it's what's true. Speaking of which, did you bring your test results?

CANDIDATE
Yes. They're in a signed, sealed envelope from my doctor, as you requested. *(SHE retrieves the envelope and hands it to WIFE who opens it with a letter opener and reads)*

WIFE
Non-reactive. Congratulations, you're negative. *(Checks this off her list)* Wait a minute. When was this test taken?

CANDIDATE
Yesterday. You said you wanted the most recent results.

WIFE
Well, what about last night? Did you have sex with anyone last night? Or today, on your lunch break?

CANDIDATE
My lunch break? Are you serious? That is none of your business!

WIFE
It most certainly is! Full disclosure, Miss Douglass! You signed an agreement to full disclosure. I have it right here along with your application. *(Holding up the document)* Is this or is it not your signature?!

CANDIDATE
Fine. Yes, I admit it. I had sex today at lunch! I made partner at the firm, so we had a party, right there in the law office. Actually, it was an orgy. In fact, we had a just-made-partner-office-orgy-lunch-party with guests that included the senior partners, the third-years, the secretaries, and a couple paralegals. We even invited a few clients whose cases I had won.

WIFE
Really?

CANDIDATE
No, of course not!

WIFE
Oh.

CANDIDATE
You sound disappointed.

WIFE
No, it's just that, unlike your Facebook page, your answer would have provided me with a more entertaining reason to disqualify you.

CANDIDATE
How did you see my Facebook page? But, my settings—you're not one of my friends! Only my friends can see what is on my page.

WIFE
I have my ways, MissDouglass. Honestly, don't you people realize that professionals in decision-making positions are looking at these Facebook pages—that we're Googling you? Now, do you have a condom?

CANDIDATE
A condom?! Look, can you please get up out of my bedroom?

WIFE
It's a new world, Miss Douglass. Spot check. Do you or don't you?

CANDIDATE
Yes, of course. Who doesn't carry condoms these days? *(CANDIDATE takes a female condom from her purse and gives it to WIFE)*

WIFE
You'd be surprised. *(Looking at the packaging)* What in the world?

CANDIDATE
It's a female condom. If he doesn't have one, makes excuses, or refuses to put a condom on, I have my own. *(Beat)* Wait a minute. You've never seen one before, have you?

WIFE
No, I can't say that I have.

CANDIDATE
It's very empowering.

WIFE
Yes, I can see how it would be.

CANDIDATE
Want to take a look? I can open it. *(Seeing WIFE is hesitant)* It's OK. I have plenty more.

WIFE
Maybe some other time. I'll just check the expiration date then…*(Inspecting the condom she sees it has not expired)* Still good. Well done, Miss Douglass!

WIFE (CONT'D)
(Checks this off her list) Congratulations, you've passed the spot check. Onward and upward then! Your assets. *(Reading down the checklist)* Did you remember to bring your credit report? Are you set for retirement? Do you have a will? 401K? Pension plan? Savings? Life insurance? Healthcare proxy? Burial plot? How old did you say you were again?

CANDIDATE
Yes; yes; yes; yes; yes; some savings; yes; yes; no, I want to be cremated and, I can't believe it but, yes, I just turned forty-one. Here. *(She pulls the document file from her briefcase and hands it to WIFE)* My dossier.

WIFE
And the essay question?

CANDIDATE
It's in there. But I'm happy to summarize. *(Looks through each document and checks it off on her list)*

WIFE
Yes, please do. I just hope it isn't a response I've heard already. Talk about cliché! "I answered this ad because there is a shortage of suitable black men due to insufficient education, unemployment and/or incarceration; the good ones are already taken or they're all on the down low; he doesn't make as much money as me…" let's see, what else? Oh, yes. "My biological clock is ticking; I want a monogamous relationship; I don't trust online dating…" Oh, and my personal favorite, "I answered this ad because, ain't no men in church." Tell me if I'm getting warm.

CANDIDATE
Still cold.

WIFE
Cold? Really? Then, let's hear it, Miss Douglass. Warm me up.

CANDIDATE
I'm not a back pocket girl.

WIFE
A "back pocket girl?"

CANDIDATE
A woman kept in a man's "back pocket" until he feels he's ready to settle down, share his life with one person; start a family.

WIFE
I see.

CANDIDATE
And until that day comes around, he checks that back pocket from time to time to see if she's still there. If she's there when he's ready, so be it. If she's not, she's not. No problem. Usually, he's got a couple of women back pocketed. Girlfriend is not the only one. So, you see, I'd rather be with an older man who is settled, stable; someone who has slowed down. I'm nobody's back pocket girl.

WIFE
Originality. I like it. You're a strong candidate, Ms. Douglass.

CANDIDATE
It's either that or join the ranks of the 42% of black women who have never been married—oh, but wait, I have been married. Then, I guess that means I've joined the ranks of 50% of American couples who have divorced. *(Beat)* Can I ask you something, Mrs. Thompson?

WIFE
Earline. You may call me Earline. We may as well dispense with the formalities now that we're getting into it.

CANDIDATE
Why did you place this ad, Earline? *(Reading from the classified advertisement section of a New York newspaper)*

WIFE
What do you mean?

CANDIDATE
"Spouse Seeks A Better Wife For Husband. Rigorous Vetting Process. Must Be Attractive, 40–50 Years Old, Middle Class, In Good Physical And Mental Health With Secure Job And Financial Future. No Artists, No Children And No Baggage. Good Homemaker And Lover A Plus. African American Candidates Preferred." Nice touch. "Minimum Of Three References, One Of Which Must Be From A Member Of The Clergy. Fingerprint Clearance Required." Does he know?

WIFE
No, of course not. If all goes as planned, he will never know. It's in the non-disclosure agreement you signed.

CANDIDATE
What's wrong with him?

WIFE
Nothing. Senior—that's my husband— is a good man, a good provider, a good father. You know, a good man is hard to find, but a good black man—

CANDIDATE
Amen, sister! I heard that! *(Offers a high-five but WIFE does not respond. SHE resumes a more professional demeanor)* So why would you want to give him up? *(Thinks)* Oh! He's not good in bed?

WIFE
I assure you, there are no problems there, Miss Douglass. He is amply endowed and everything works in that department. And if it doesn't, which happens on occasion with men his age, then oral sex it is—if that's what you're wondering.

CANDIDATE
I wasn't.

WIFE
You were. But, to be truthful, at fifty-nine, exercising and staying in shape takes precedence over sex. He's got a young man's body. You'll enjoy him. I mean, whoever moves on to the next phase—well, that would be down the line a bit…probably Phase VIII or IX— anyway, at that point, whomever will enjoy him, as I have.

CANDIDATE
If it's not sex, then what is it? You're not happy with him?

WIFE
Oh, no. I'm happy.

CANDIDATE
He's not happy with you?

WIFE
No, not really. I don't think so.

CANDIDATE
Well, what's wrong with you? Granted, you are a little strange, but from what I see, you keep a nice house and— *(Picking up a framed photo)* Hey, he looks familiar. Is this—

WIFE
My son. *(Snatching the framed photo before CANDIDATE recognizes him as a Facebook friend)* Junior. Herman, Jr.

CANDIDATE
He's handsome. Who's he got his arm around there?

WIFE
That's his girlfriend, Kimono— Kimunu—Kimiku…Oh, for heaven's sake—Kimiko. That's it, Kimiko. They met in college. Of course, I wished he'd found himself a nice African American girl, but what can you expect, there are more of them than there are of us on these college campuses now—Asians, I mean. I guess you can't help who you love. Well, as long as he's happy.

WIFE (CONT'D)
(Putting the framed photo back in its place) My Junior's a good catch. He didn't move back home like most graduates are doing these days. No, he found a good job right out of college and you know how difficult that is. And he has his own place. Yes, Senior and I are officially "empty nesters." Junior washes his own clothes, cooks, cleans, opens doors for the ladies…I've been blessed. Two for two: good man, good son.

CANDIDATE
You certainly don't look like you have a grown son.

WIFE
Well, you know how we black women are. We tend to hold up well—look younger than we really are…Are you sure you weren't born after 1978?

CANDIDATE
Yes. My birth certificate should be in there…*(She searches among the papers that WIFE is holding; pulls out her birth certificate and points to date of birth)* See?

WIFE
Oh. Thank you. *(WIFE checks this off on the list; moves on)*

CANDIDATE
So?

WIFE
So, what?

CANDIDATE
The ad?

WIFE
What about it?

CANDIDATE
Why did you place it?

WIFE
I believe I am the one conducting this interview, Miss Douglass. I will not be questioned.

CANDIDATE
(Intrigued; tries to guess) Let's see… You're having a mid-life crisis and you're bored. You've done the family thing and want to move on to a new phase of your life. Is that it?

WIFE
No, that is not it.

CANDIDATE
(Thinks) You're a wanna-be cougar trying to find a way to justify having a younger man—a boy toy.

WIFE
I don't want a boy toy.

CANDIDATE
Listen, there's nothing wrong with May/December relationships. Men have them.

WIFE
I am not a cougar!

CANDIDATE
Well, I don't understand. Why would… Oh! I'm sorry. You've got a terminal illness and only have a few months to live?

WIFE
Heavens no!

CANDIDATE
(Stumped; then a revelation) I've got it! Your arrow's moving!

WIFE
What?!

CANDIDATE
See, human sexuality, it falls along a spectrum—the Spectrum of Sexuality.

WIFE
That is preposterous!

CANDIDATE
Along this spectrum, no one is definitively straight or gay. Sexual orientation can change over one's lifetime, thus moving the arrow from heterosexual to bisexual to homosexual

to asexual…You just have to learn to go with the flow—

WIFE
I certainly will not! I am a Christian woman.

CANDIDATE
I hate to be the one to break it to you, but there are a lot of gay Christians.

WIFE
Not in this house!

CANDIDATE
Fine. Then I don't know what else it could be…*(It comes to her)* Of course! Why didn't I think of it before? You've fallen out of love! Why don't you just be honest and tell him?

WIFE
I do love Senior. It's because I love him that I'm doing all of this. You see, I believe I'm standing in the way of him finding true happiness. I am standing in the way of someone coming into his life that could truly make him happy— someone better; a better wife.

CANDIDATE
A better wife?

WIFE
Yes, you see when we were married— well, before we were married—he was so sure he wanted to marry me, but I wasn't sure at all. He was my best friend. Yes, I loved him. I mean, a black man on a yoga mat, what's not to love? But inside I knew I wasn't ready. On my wedding day I remember thinking, "There's always divorce if it doesn't work out." I mean, who is thinking about divorce as an option on their wedding day? As the years went by I grew to love him deeply and we've been happy for the most part—except for me not being a good housekeeper and all.

CANDIDATE
So that's why you've got all the doors closed! Girl, I'd do the same thing if I were you—*(Seeing that EARLINE is not amused)* I'm sorry, go on.

WIFE
We've been having the same fight, or different versions of it, for thirty years. But lately the harmonious times have lasted longer than the inharmonious times. It could be we just don't have the energy to fight like we used to. Or maybe we're more accepting of each other, I don't know…There's a lot that happens between a man and a woman, years of stuff, hard stuff, but basically he's a good person, and I'm a good person. In some ways, it would have been easier to split up if one of us weren't—if you could point to one or the other of us and say, "he or she is the bad one…" The foundation of friendship and goodwill that has kept us together, won't let us part.

CANDIDATE
Sounds like you have some regret.

WIFE
Well, as they say, "Youth is wasted on the young."

CANDITATE
What does that mean?

WIFE
Young people have everything going for them—health, vitality, a feeling of invincibility and "joie de vivre." But they lack wisdom, experience, hindsight—

CANDIDATE
I know that. I wasn't born yesterday.

WIFE
Yes, and that is to your advantage—if your documentation checks out.

CANDIDATE
Whatever. What I'm asking is what do you mean by "youth is wasted on the young" in this context?

WIFE
I mean I wish I had known when I was younger what I know now, that we—my husband, son, and I—could have survived divorce, and maybe even been better for it. As a young couple, it was hard to imagine breaking up the family unit. My husband and I both come from families where our parents had been married "for richer or poorer, in sickness and in health, till death do us part." Added up, there was like seventy-five or eighty years of marriage between them. Even though our marriage wasn't perfect, we had to ask ourselves if we really wanted to raise our son without the benefit of having both a mother and a father in the home. "For better or worse," we made the choice to keep the family together, but it wasn't easy. All of our married friends, one-by-one, were getting divorced. And yes, it was hard and even ugly at times for those families, but eventually they got over it. Custody arrangements were made and the children were fine—

CANDIDATE
Seemed fine. Take my word for it as a child of divorce. The children seemed fine.

WIFE
Well, fine or not, life goes on doesn't it? If I'd known this early on in the marriage, maybe it could have saved us both some heartache. But no—neither of us wanted to be the bad guy that breaks up the home; neither of us wanted to be the parent with visitation on the weekends; neither of us wanted to be the one that was alone at Christmas. So we stuck it out. And there's something to that—to sticking it out. I'm proud of us; proud of our thirty years of sticking it out. In a way, I love my Senior even more for it.

CANDIDATE
I know lots of women who'd be jealous; who'd take those thirty years of marriage and raise you one.

WIFE
I suppose they would indeed, Miss Douglass. *(With resolve)* But who knows how much time any of us has left on this earth? Who wants to spend the rest of it sticking something out? One of us has to have the strength to leave. I am strong. I can do it for both of us. We may as well try to find true happiness, or let it come find us, while we both still have some vitality left in us.

CANDIDATE
Hence the want ad.

WIFE
Yes. I believe there is a better cook, a better housekeeper, a better lover, a better wife for him. And she's out there, somewhere, waiting for him. I just don't want to continue to stand in the way of them finding one another. *(Beat)* The thirtieth wedding anniversary is the "pearl anniversary," That is my gift to Senior, a pearl.

CANDIDATE
A pearl? You mean like a pearl gift… for a man? How unusual. What, like a shell with a pearl in it? Or piece of jewelry—like a pearl ring or a pendant? Or pearl roses, perhaps? Or something made of mother of pearl, like a vase? Or something knitted with a pearl stitch?

WIFE
No, no, no, no and no. You seem to know a lot about pearls…

CANDIDATE
I've got it! A second honeymoon trip to go pearling!

WIFE
Pearling?

CANDIDATE
Yes. Diving or fishing for pearl oysters.

WIFE
Oh, for heaven's sake! Do I strike you as someone who would go diving for anything?

CANDIDATE
Wait a minute! Could it be "pearling" as in…no! It couldn't be!

WIFE
Couldn't be what?

CANDIDATE
Genital beading?

WIFE
Genital beading? I don't even know what that is. *(CANDIDATE starts to explain; she stops her)* And I don't want to know. For heaven's sake, the Better Wife! She's the pearl! *(On an impulse, CANDIDATE kisses her. Surprised, WIFE pulls away, horrified)*

WIFE
Why did you do that?!

CANDIDATE
Oh, Earline—

WIFE
Don't call me that!

CANDIDATE
I couldn't imagine loving someone so much I would give them up…and to go to such lengths!

WIFE
Who are you, Miss Douglass? LESBIANS NEED NOT APPLY FOR THIS POSITION!

CANDIDATE
I'm not a lesbian! I'm Q.

WIFE
Q?

CANDIDATE
As in LGBT…Q. Questioning.

WIFE
Questioning? Questioning what?

CANDIDATE
My sexual preference.

WIFE
Like I said, you either are something or you're not, Miss Douglass!

CANDIDATE
That's right, and I'm the pearl! Veronica Pearl Douglass! It's a sign!

WIFE
It is not. It's a mere coincidence at best; a cruel twist of fate!

CANDIDATE
I kissed you because it felt like something must be done or the moment would pass and never come again!

WIFE
You could have shaken my hand!

CANDIDATE
The generosity! The unselfishness!

WIFE
This interview is over! *(She gets CANDIDATE's coat and umbrella)*

CANDIDATE
Now, Earline—

WIFE
Don't call me that.

CANDIDATE
You told me to!

WIFE
Well, now I'm telling you not to. *(Holding out her belongings)* Thank you for coming, Miss Douglass. The position has been filled.

CANDIDATE
Earline, please!

WIFE
I said the position has been filled!

CANDIDATE
Filled by whom?

WIFE
Me! His first, but flawed, wife!

CANDIDATE
Oh, Earline! *(VERONICA takes the umbrella and throws it down. Then she takes the coat and throws it down. She takes EARLINE in her arms and at once, kisses her. Without understanding why, EARLINE kisses her back as the curtain falls)*

MARJORIE BICKNELL

I first developed an interest in working in the theatre at the age of six when I saw a high school production of *The Student Prince*. I hold a Bachelor of Arts in Theater from Mundelein College and an Interdepartmental Master's of Arts in Speech and Communications from Northwestern University.

I studied acting in Coventry, England, in a program run by Valparaiso University and Coventry Cathedral, where we also took our art out into the community, working with immigrants, deaf children, and Borstal boys (reform school inmates).

Following graduation, I worked in my hometown of Chicago, Illinois, where I became manager of Pary Production Company: a professional, nonprofit theater. I wrote my first play for Pary, an adaptation of *Frankenstein*, which won three Joseph Jefferson awards in its world-premiere production.

Since then, I have lived in Philadelphia, Harrisburg, Pennsylvania, and again in Philadelphia where I currently reside.

Throughout my life, I have felt compelled to write about both the need for family, and the frustration women feel when they are underestimated or disregarded. Sometimes these twin themes show up in the same play. I am also compelled to help other playwrights. I founded a playwrights' group, Playwrights Alliance of Pennsylvania, served as president of another, Philadelphia Dramatists Center, and am currently the Regional Representative in Philadelphia for the Dramatists Guild of America.

Carolee's Closet

A TEN-MINUTE PLAY BY MARJORIE BICKNELL

(It's early evening and CAROLEE's bedroom looks as though it has been hit by a tornado. There are open boxes littering the bed and floor, and shopping bags, some torn, are tossed hither and yon. Peeking out of the boxes and bags are household items: bathroom and kitchen towels, some pots and pans, a percolator coffee pot, spatulas, mixing spoons and cups, a canister set, a lamp, sofa pillows, etc. All of it is lit only by light from an unseen window, giving it an eerie, nightmarish cast. In the middle of this stands MOM holding a feather duster and surveying the damage. CAROLEE enters the room snapping on the light)

CAROLEE
Mom!!!

MOM
Carolee! You're home early!

CAROLEE
What have you done to my stuff? You don't come into my room. You don't go through my stuff! We set boundaries.

MOM
Dirt doesn't know boundaries. Dirt goes everywhere, and everywhere dirt goes, I follow.

CAROLEE
You can't follow it into my closet! I'm the one who decides what and who goes in there.

MOM
But you've been carrying in so many packages for so long. I just knew you'd need help organizing.

CAROLEE
You went snooping!
(CAROLEE angrily begins cleaning up. MOM trails after her)

MOM
What have you been buying all this stuff for? And why was it all packed away in your closet? Is it wedding season // or—?

CAROLEE
No! // It's not wedding season! All this stuff is for me. For my house. When I move out.

MOM
On your own? On your salary? You're a very picky person, Carolee. You like monogrammed towels and gourmet coffee. How are you going to afford them unless you stay here // with me!

CAROLEE
I'll get by! // Mom, it's time I start my own life—have my own home—even if I have to drink Maxwell House.

MOM
But, sweetie, you have everything you need here—a comfortable, clean house, a lovely bedroom. Nothing needs to change. Unless you'd like to add a rocking chair.

CAROLEE
I don't need a rocking chair.

MOM
You'll never last on your own, Carolee. You don't make friends easily. You'll get lonely. // Depressed.

CAROLEE
No. // I won't.

MOM
That's what you say, but //

CAROLEE
I // have friends!

MOM
Oh! That's why—!
(MOM rushes into the closet and comes out with HAROLD COLLIER, a middle-aged man in a suit and tie)

MOM (CONT'D)
Who's this, Carolee?

CAROLEE
That's my boyfriend. Harold Collier. Harold, I see you've met my mother.

HAROLD
I'm very pleased to be introduced, Mrs. Mooney. I've heard a lot // about you.

MOM
Where did // you get him?

HAROLD
Carolee and I have been seeing each other for months, Mrs. Mooney. I'm very interested in your daughter.

MOM
(To HAROLD) I know what men are interested in. (To CAROLEE) Carolee! Sneaking around with men and hiding them in your closet. I'm ashamed of // you.

CAROLEE
I // haven't been // sneaking!

MOM
It's // clear to me that you can't be trusted to live on your own. That's why—

CAROLEE
(Interrupting) Harold and I have been going out on dates like normal people.

MOM
Nonsense! You don't have the time. Your life is totally full with all the wonderful activities we do together.

HAROLD
Carolee and I see each other every weekend. We'd like to spend more time with each other, but Carolee knows how much doing things together means // to you—

MOM
(Interrupting) But I // do them to keep Carolee busy.

CAROLEE
I can find better things to do with my time then spend Monday at Book Club, Tuesday with the Altar and Rosary Society, Wednesday at Gardening Club, etc., etc., etc.! I'm tired of trying to make you happy.

HAROLD
Are you happy with me, Carolee?

CAROLEE
Yes, Harold. I am.
(HAROLD drops on one knee in front of CAROLEE and holds out a ring)

MOM
You can't just walk out of a closet and marry my // daughter!

CAROLEE
He // didn't walk out! You dragged him out!

HAROLD
(Ignoring the exchange) Carolee? Will you do me the honor of being my wife?

CAROLEE
Yes, Harold! I'd be proud to become your wife.
(HAROLD stands, places the ring on CAROLEE's finger and kisses her)

HAROLD
This is wonderful, sweetie.

MOM
Carolee, are you sure about this? Our life has been perfect. And men are so—

CAROLEE
Mom, I'm through! I've sewn my last quilt for the little "pagan babies" //

MOM
Nobody // calls them that // anymore.

HAROLD
I'll take // very good care of Carolee. Don't you worry. I've got my eye on a lovely house, and—

MOM
Harold, do you know what you're getting yourself into? I mean, have you tasted Carolee's meatloaf? And I can't praise her cleaning skills. She lets her things get so dusty.

HAROLD
I'm not marrying your daughter for her cleaning skills, Mrs. Mooney.
(HAROLD turns to CAROLEE and gives her a peck on the cheek)

HAROLD
Well, I must be going! I have a wedding to plan. *(Turns and leaves happily whistling a tune)*

MOM
You'll regret this day, Carolee. Men can't be trusted. He'll move you into that big, fancy house, but before you get it decorated, he'll be gone leaving you with a mortgage you can't afford.

CAROLEE
I'm getting married, Mom.

MOM
(Getting an idea) Well, if you have to marry him, why not move in here? You have a lovely room. And our house is just one short bus ride from your office.

CAROLEE
Harold drives to work.

MOM
(Surveying the room) Harold will just love this relaxing little room. I know the bed is a tad narrow, but newlyweds…

CAROLEE
Mom!

MOM
I know! I can switch beds with you. What do I need with a king size bed!! You won't even have to buy new sheets! Now all you need is that rocking chair.

CAROLEE
I have one. But it's for you.
(CAROLEE ducks into the closet and returns with a rocking chair)

MOM
What do I need with a rocking chair? I have plenty of furniture!

CAROLEE
But it's very comfortable—and relaxing! Best of all, it will look lovely in your new home.

MOM
Nobody's moving, Carolee. We have everything we need right here.

CAROLEE
Mom, I can't stay here anymore…and neither can you. I've been storing up everything I need right here in this closet for years. My hopes. My dreams. My future. And now it's finally time for me to bring them all out. I'm moving on.

MOM
Nonsense. You and Harold will live in my house with me! You know, a husband just might liven things up around here. *(Heads for the closet)* I'm excited! I'm sure I'll find a use for all the new things you have in here. Let's see—
(MOM ducks in and then backs right out with NURSE JUDY)

MOM
What's a nurse doing in your closet? Are you sick, Carolee?

CAROLEE
This is Nurse Judy, Mom. She's here to take care of you.
(NURSE JUDY takes MOM by the arm, leads her to the rocking chair and settles her in it. MOM, surprised, lets her do it)

NURSE JUDY
Now, Mrs. Mooney, isn't that better? Rocking is so relaxing, and you seem rather excited today. It never does anyone any good to become too excited.

MOM
(Excitedly) I am not excited! And I demand to know what's going on.

CAROLEE
I got Nurse Judy to take care of you.

NURSE JUDY
You've been taking care of others for so long. Now it's time for you to relax and let someone take care of you.

MOM
I don't need—

CAROLEE
(Interrupting) Yes you do. I've been taking care of you for a long time. But I can't do that anymore. You'll be very happy with Nurse Judy and all your new friends in your new home.

MOM
An old people's home? Not me.

NURSE JUDY
It's an active senior community.

CAROLEE
You'll still have all your activities— book club, garden club, sewing club. But you won't have to cook or clean for anyone. It'll be like vacation every day. And Harold and I will visit you on the weekend. We'll bring the kids.

MOM
Children? When did you find time to have children? You just got engaged!

CAROLEE
Little Harold and little Julia have been waiting in the closet with their father.
(HAROLD peeks his head out of the closet.)

HAROLD
Sweetie, are you ready to go?

CAROLEE
Almost. Well, Mom, it's time for me to leave. I'm sure you'll be very happy here with Nurse Judy.

NURSE JUDY
We'll get along fine.

HAROLD
We'll see you on Sunday, Mom! The kids are looking forward to it. Come on, Carolee.

(CAROLEE exits through the closet with HAROLD. NURSE JUDY turns back to MOM)

NURSE JUDY
Come along now, Mary. It's time for dinner. We're having ravioli—with a nice salad. And then it's book club night! And while you're chatting with your friends, I'll straighten up in here.

MOM
Danielle Steele, tonight. Right? Where's my book?

NURSE JUDY
In the closet. We'll pick it up on the way out.

LORETTA BOLGER WISH

Most of my career has been connected to writing, from journalism to textbooks to PR, but I don't simply work as a writer. I live as one. That's been true since grade school, when composition class was as much fun as recess. Seeking words to describe people, events, and ideas is second nature, and whatever my interests, writing permeates them. A passion for singing and guitar prompted me to write songs for my band and a love of movies fueled my blog, *Hollywood Castaway*. A book devotee, I happily finished a novel, *Bumpy Night on the Walk of Fame*, and eventually found a small but enthusiastic publisher. By then I was semi-retired, with more time for creativity. The ham in me liked performing comedy, so I wrote monologues. Then came the short leap to plays, a genre I'd been afraid to try. Right away, I was hooked by the immediacy. Free from exposition, I was amazed that characters came to life as rapidly as my fingers hit the keyboard. Before long, I had several works featured in theater festivals, with more chosen each year. My monologues have turned into plays, several of my short plays are growing, and one may become a musical. What's next? I don't know, but one of the joys of a writing life is that anytime I open my laptop or pick up a pen, I'm apt to find out.

I Didn't Do Anything

A TEN-MINUTE PLAY BY LORETTA BOLGER WISH

CAST OF CHARACTERS
MS. TYLER: School counselor
ELIZABETH: Sixteen year–old student

SETTING
Present, in a high school office.
(Lights up. Both are seated at a table. MS. TYLER is taking notes)

ELIZABETH
Look, Ms. Tyler, I don't know what you want me to say. Why am I here? I didn't do anything.

MS. TYLER
Maybe not, but I need to ask you a few questions. We're hoping to gain some insight into what happened last night.

ELIZABETH
Why are you asking me? I hardly know Casey.

MS. TYLER
You've been in class with her every day since the semester started. I'm sure you noticed she was having difficulties.

ELIZABETH
You know, I'm missing a history test and Ms. Johnson's a bitch about makeups.

MS. TYLER
Not a problem, Elizabeth. I'll write you an excuse. Were you aware that Casey was having trouble fitting in?

ELIZABETH
Maybe. I guess so. All I can tell you for sure is that I didn't do anything to her.

MS. TYLER
Someone else did. At least two girls, maybe more. *(Sips from a commuter mug and waits)*

ELIZABETH
Are you allowed to talk to me like this without my parents being here? I mean, am I being charged with something?

MS. TYLER
No, but in a situation like this, any information you have might be helpful to us.

ELIZABETH
You know, even a counselor can't just fire questions at me like this. My dad's a lawyer. He'll sue for harassment.

MS. TYLER
Do you feel as if I'm harassing you by asking about Casey?

ELIZABETH
Okay, maybe not harassing, but…look, I'm sorry she's in the hospital and I'm sorry she took those pills. But it's not my fault.

MS. TYLER
Did you have any reason to think she was unhappy?

ELIZABETH
I don't know! *(Her gesture knocks over the thermos)* Sorry about that. Should I clean it up?

MS. TYLER
No, let's leave it for now.

ELIZABETH
I hope it wasn't like an antique or anything.

MS. TYLER
Yes, travel mugs with #1 Mom written on them were big in the Victorian era. *(Laughs)* Apparently Casey has been unhappy for quite a while.

ELIZABETH
I could get you more coffee.

MS. TYLER
I'm good, thanks. *(Pause)* Elizabeth?

ELIZABETH
Okay, I guess Casey was pretty unhappy. But is it my fault she doesn't have any friends?

MS. TYLER
Most students don't have friends when they come to a new school.

ELIZABETH
I'm sorry, Ms. Tyler, but looking after her wasn't my job. I mean, I'm not the Chamber of Commerce.

MS. TYLER
No, but you are somewhat of a class leader.

ELIZABETH
Not really. I'm not super popular or anything. I'm not on the Student Council and it's not like I run all the clubs.

MS. TYLER
You are well-liked, though, and you take part in a lot of activities.

ELIZABETH
Isn't it your job to help new kids adjust?

MS. TYLER
Partly, but it means more if their peers extend a helping hand.

ELIZABETH
Casey sort of kept to herself. Maybe she liked it that way.

MS. TYLER
Would you say she was shy?

ELIZABETH
I don't think so. She wasn't too shy to go to the Red Robin with Jaden after school.

MS. TYLER
It sounds like that bothered you. Is Jaden someone you were dating?

ELIZABETH
Of course not! I've been with Ryan since ninth grade. But Vicky was going out with Jaden and they only broke up last month.

MS. TYLER
Was Vicky still interested in Jaden?

ELIZABETH
I doubt it. She's been going out with Trevor for weeks.

MS. TYLER
Then what was the problem?

ELIZABETH
I didn't say it was a problem…Okay, so it was kind of humiliating for Vicky. Seriously, you wouldn't want your ex to be into some random new girl just because she has big boobs.

MS. TYLER
Do you think that's the reason Jaden liked Casey?

ELIZABETH
How should I know? I'm not even sure he really liked her.

MS. TYLER
If they were meeting after school, he must have liked her pretty well. Do you remember what happened the next day?

ELIZABETH
I had nothing to do with that!

MS. TYLER
Someone wrote *"SLUT"* on Casey's locker in red paint. Do you know who it was?

ELIZABETH
Well, Vicky and Justine were laughing about it and Vicky kind of hinted that she did it. But I couldn't say for sure.

MS. TYLER
Vicky and Justine were the ones who suggested that Casey try out for cheer squad.

ELIZABETH
I think so.

MS. TYLER
Do you know why?

ELIZABETH
Um…yeah. Vicky said it would make Casey feel better about the locker thing.

MS. TYLER
And did it?

ELIZABETH
Ms. Tyler, why are you asking me stuff you already know the answer to? Of course it didn't make her feel better.

MS. TYLER
Because when Casey went out on the field, Vicky made fun of her. And everyone laughed.

ELIZABETH
I didn't. Not really.

MS. TYLER
Vicky said Casey could never be on the squad without breast reduction surgery.

ELIZABETH
Yeah, and a butt reduction. You know, Casey wasn't the only one Vicky made fun of. She says stuff like that to everyone. She told me I shouldn't wear my skirt too short because of my thighs.

MS. TYLER
Really?

ELIZABETH
Sure. She'll tell anyone they're too klutzy for the squad or they're too chunky for the uniform. That's just the way she is. She's the captain and she wants our squad to look good.

MS. TYLER
Vicky personally invited Casey to try out. Does she often do that?

ELIZABETH
I don't know. Why are you asking me about this?

MS. TYLER
Did Vicky and Justine tell you they planned to hide in the locker room while Casey was changing? And take pictures as Casey was getting into the shower?

ELIZABETH
No! I mean I wasn't sure. Not till I saw the photos at school the next day.

MS. TYLER
But the girls didn't just circulate the photos in this school, did they?

ELIZABETH
How do I know?… Yeah, I heard Vicky sent them to Casey's old school too.

MS. TYLER
And someone sent them to Casey's church group.

ELIZABETH
I didn't know that. But still, I didn't take the pictures and I didn't send them anywhere.

MS. TYLER
How about afterwards?

ELIZABETH
Afterwards?

MS. TYLER
After those pictures of Casey were distributed all over school. What did you do then?

ELIZABETH
Nothing! How many times do I have to tell you: I. Didn't. Do. ANYTHING!

MS. TYLER
What about your classmates?

ELIZABETH
What about them?

MS. TYLER
How did they react to the incident?

ELIZABETH
What do you mean, react?

MS. TYLER
Did anyone try to comfort Casey? Did any of you show her any sympathy or maybe tell Vicky she shouldn't have done it?

ELIZABETH
Right, like I was supposed to tell Vicky off. You don't know what she's like. Do you have any idea what she'd do to me?

MS. TYLER
I was talking about your classmates. But now that you mention it, how did you feel about what happened? You and Vicky have been friends for a long time.

ELIZABETH
Yeah, since middle school but I wouldn't ever want to cross her. Trust me, she wouldn't take it well at all.

MS. TYLER
So you didn't feel you could confront Vicky. Suppose you'd just said something to Casey.

ELIZABETH
Like what?

MS. TYLER
Maybe said you were sorry it happened or asked if she was doing okay. Or maybe sat with her in the cafeteria.

ELIZABETH
Seriously? I swear, Ms. Tyler, it's like you were never in high school!

MS. TYLER
Why do you say that, Elizabeth?

ELIZABETH
You know why. I mean you try being nice to someone your friends don't like. Do you know how pissed everyone on the squad would be if I ate lunch with Casey? Or even talked to her?

MS. TYLER
So your friends not only snubbed Casey, they expected you to do the same.

ELIZABETH
Hey, would you stop treating me like I'm some mean girl? I already went to your assembly last fall, so you don't have to repeat it all for me.

MS. TYLER
Which assembly?

ELIZABETH
The one you had for anti-bullying week or whatever you call it. Most of the school just laughed at your video, but I sort of got it. I never, ever make fun of those kids.

MS. TYLER
What kids?

ELIZABETH
You know the ones. The kids with acne or crappy clothes. Or the fat kids or the special ed students. Or that trans kid.

MS. TYLER
Do you hear people making fun of them?

ELIZABETH
Yeah, but mostly behind their backs. Vicky and Justine call them the LKs. That's short for Loser Kids. But I don't.

MS. TYLER
Did they consider Casey a Loser Kid?

ELIZABETH
Not exactly. I mean she's quiet and her accent's a little strange, but she's basically normal. She's pretty cute, actually. Cute enough that the guys noticed her.

MS. TYLER
Did the other girls resent that?

ELIZABETH
I don't think so. But even if they did, she should've been able to take care of herself.

MS. TYLER
Do you think you could have? If the other girls ganged up on you that way?

ELIZABETH
Yeah, I do think so. At least better than Casey did.

MS. TYLER
Are you sure about that? You just admitted you were afraid to go against Vicky and the rest of the squad. But you have other friends on the soccer team and in chorus. And you have a boyfriend. Casey had no one.

ELIZABETH
Look, none of this is my fault. I didn't do anything.

MS. TYLER
You're right, it appears you didn't. When Casey first got here you didn't say hi or walk to class with her. You didn't suggest that she join any of your clubs or invite her to Ray's Café or the Red Robin.

ELIZABETH
I meant I didn't make fun of her. Jeez!

MS. TYLER
But when other girls ridiculed her, you didn't try to stop it. And you didn't console her or say anything nice to her afterward. Not even when the bullying escalated.

ELIZABETH
I told you what would have happened if I sided with Casey. Vicky woulda put me through hell.

MS. TYLER
She might have. Do you realize you're so focused on you that you haven't asked how Casey is?

ELIZABETH
Well, her mother found her in time so I figured she's okay. Is she?

MS. TYLER
It was touch and go but yes, it appears she's out of the woods now.

ELIZABETH
Good. I'm glad it's over.

MS. TYLER
I didn't say that. When Casey's released from the hospital, she has to return to a school that's been very unfriendly to her.

ELIZABETH
You mean she's coming back here?

MS. TYLER
Of course. What did you think would happen?

ELIZABETH
I don't know. I guess I thought she'd change schools or something.

MS. TYLER
That's not an option. Her mother's a widow and they left Ireland two years ago. She worked in New York and when she was laid off, they moved here to stay with a cousin. Casey and her mother both waitress part time and they can't afford a private school.

ELIZABETH
Really? That's too bad, but I don't know what you want from me. I mean, it's not like Casey and I are friends.

MS. TYLER
No, but you're in school together and you know what an ordeal she's been through.

ELIZABETH
Okay, but what is it you want me to do? Should I send her a get-well card or a note in the hospital or something?

MS. TYLER
It would be a nice gesture. A word of encouragement from a classmate might help.

ELIZABETH
But why me, Ms. Tyler? I mean, why aren't you yelling at Vicky instead? Why don't you make her send a note to Casey?

MS. TYLER
Several reasons. For one thing, she already sent Casey a message.

ELIZABETH
Cool. What did she say?

MS. TYLER
(Picks up phone) Here's what Vicky wrote: "Next time try harder. I'll get you more pills so you can do it again. Only don't screw it up."

ELIZABETH
No way! Even Vicky would never say that.

MS. TYLER
The message came from her phone. We confirmed that and Vicky admitted it. We also learned she's been messaging Casey for a while.

ELIZABETH
If Vicky sent that text, then why aren't you talking to her instead of me?

MS. TYLER
Someone else is speaking to her right now. Someone from the police department.

ELIZABETH
Am I gonna have to talk to the police too?

MS. TYLER
That may depend on what I say in my report. But this incident is in the hands of the authorities now, so it's their decision.

ELIZABETH
Are you gonna tell them I didn't do anything?

MS. TYLER
I suppose I will. Because that's the sad truth.

ELIZABETH
Can I ask you something?

MS. TYLER
All right.

ELIZABETH
What do you think the police are gonna
do next?

MS. TYLER
I'm not sure. Can I ask you something?

ELIZABETH
Yeah, I guess.

MS. TYLER
What do you think you're going to
do next?

ANDREA TROTENBERG

I have always derived solace from and delighted in the magic of words, beginning as a young girl writing countless nonsense-rhyme poems to give as gifts to friends and family. I chose a career that allowed me to play with words by becoming a copywriter and creative director in Chicago ad agencies, working on numerous national and international brands. In my forties I stepped back from (paid) work to have children and raise my family. Now I have returned to writing once again. The transformative power of the theater drew me to playwriting. I am a member of Chicago Dramatists Network and have been writing plays for the past several years. *The July Effect* is greatly influenced by my own experiences in the Neonatal Intensive Care Unit, where I spent months with my son, Noah. This play is dedicated to him.

The July Effect

A TEN-MINUTE PLAY BY ANDREA TROTENBERG

CAST OF CHARACTERS

NORA BORMAN: Early forties, a grieving mother who's lost her only child.

DR. JOSH BRENNER: Mid –thirties, a neonatologist at a Chicago teaching hospital.

PLACE

A windowless hospital consult room in Chicago, Illinois.

TIME

January 17, 1994.

SETTING

A windowless hospital consult room dimly lit by a couple of floor lamps. Framed photos of infants line the walls. A TV in the corner plays a newscast of the Northridge, California, earthquake which just occurred that morning. A circular conference table surrounded by chairs sits in the middle of the room. NORA's winter coat and red scarf are draped over a chair. An oversized tote bag bulging with file folders sits on another.

(Lights up. NORA studies the photos, then her attention is drawn to the newscast. DR. BRENNER, dressed in scrubs, ENTERS quietly, startling her)

BRENNER

Tragic, isn't it?
(NORA, caught off guard, turns around)

NORA

What? Yes, yes. It is.

BRENNER

I heard about it on my way in this morning. I guess that's the price you pay for living in paradise. California, I mean. Earthquakes.

NORA

Mm.

BRENNER

As opposed to here in Chicago. I think they said it's ten below outside today, one of the coldest days on record.
(Chuckles) I'm not sure which is worse.
(He reaches out his hand; NORA doesn't take it)

BRENNER

I'm Dr. Brenner, by the way, Mrs. Borman. I understand you wanted to meet with me.

NORA

I was downstairs dealing with some billing issues, and I thought I'd stop by the NICU to say hello to some people. *(Looks about as if in a trance)* It's strange being back here. It feels like a lifetime ago, but it's only been six months.

BRENNER
Let me say how sorry I am for your loss.
I never got to speak with you after your
son, Jacob—

NORA
Jonah.

BRENNER
Right, Jonah. After Jonah died. Our
hearts go out to you and your family.

NORA
Thank you.

BRENNER
I should tell you we're getting an admit
from a community hospital any minute.
A baby with sepsis. It might be better if
you schedule an appointment, then I'd
have the time—

NORA
No. I don't want to come back here
again. I know I caught you on the fly,
but I'm glad I did.

BRENNER
All right, then. *(Gestures for her to sit)*
Let's hope I don't get paged right away.
So, what can I do for you? Usually
when a parent wants to meet, it's with
the director, not the chief resident.

NORA
I want to, I want to know, I—want—
you—to—tell me, what happened the
night Jonah died.

BRENNER
I thought that was all explained to you.
It wasn't?

NORA
I'd like to hear it directly from you.

BRENNER
I don't remember the details off hand.
I'd have to review his records—

NORA
I'd think you'd remember that night.
Thursday, July 17, 1993.

BRENNER
(Smiles) I know what year it was.

NORA
Exactly six months ago today in fact.
Huh. I didn't realize that before now.

BRENNER
Must be because of all the earthquake
news.

NORA
It was during the July staff transition.
You had just become chief resident.

BRENNER
(Cautious) Mhm.

NORA
Jonah was taken out of his isolette
to be weighed, which shouldn't have
happened.

BRENNER
Weighing infants is protocol.

NORA
Not for him. It was in his record.
He wasn't supposed to be handled
frequently.

BRENNER
Protocol is important in the NICU.
Without protocol—

NORA
Please. Stop saying that word.

BRENNER
There are procedures, processes. We
need to weigh infants every other day
to properly titrate medications, to know
if a baby is really growing or if it's just
fluid. Without that knowledge it's hard
to know if—

NORA
He was growing, he was developing.

BRENNER
He was a very sick baby.

NORA
He wasn't sick. He wasn't diseased.

BRENNER
That's a term we—he was born at, what, twenty-six weeks, weighing just over a pound?

NORA
You remember.

BRENNER
An infant with that kind of beginning would have a challenging road ahead. Statistically speaking, his chances of survival—

NORA
Everyone said if he lived to three months, he was going to make it. He was three months old in July.

BRENNER
People try to be optimistic, Mrs. Borman, but I think a dose of reality is always best. He was still on a ventilator—

NORA
He survived three surgeries, a staph infection, anemia, pneumonia. He defied the statistics.
(BRENNER is silent)

NORA
Why did you insist he be weighed? To show you were in charge?

BRENNER
I just explained—is this an ambush? If I need an attorney present, we need to reschedule.

NORA
His heart rate decelerated, and you didn't call in the attending physician.

BRENNER
Of course I called in the attending!

NORA
Not for eight hours. You let eight hours go by. You waited until it was too late.

BRENNER
Where are you getting your information from?

NORA
(In tears) You played God with my son, Dr. Brenner. Who gave you that right?

BRENNER
I understand you're grieving, but to accuse me of malpractice—

NORA
Your word.

BRENNER
If you believe this is remotely true, where were you six months ago?

NORA
I was barely putting one foot in front of the other, that's where I was. I'm still barely putting one foot in front of the other. It takes everything I have just to wake up in the morning and get out of bed. I spend my days combing through newspaper obituary pages looking for children who have died. You know how you can tell?

BRENNER
(Peeved) No. I don't.

NORA
First names. You look for first names that are current like Ashley and Brandon and they're always for a young person. It brings me comfort, in a perverse way, to know there are other parents out there like me who are grieving.

BRENNER
I know it's devastating, losing a child—

NORA
I'm forty-two years old, Dr. Brenner. There won't be another child for me.

BRENNER
There are women who conceive late in life—

NORA
Please. Don't. I know what happened that night.

BRENNER
What you believe is inaccurate.

NORA
No, it's accurate.
(NORA pulls an overstuffed file folder out of her tote. She pages through it and, with hand shaking, takes out a folded piece of paper)

NORA
It's all right here.

BRENNER
(Nervous) What's that?

NORA
It's a log. A fifteen-minute-by-fifteen-minute log of all of Jonah's readings from the night he died. His oxygen saturation levels, his respiratory rate, his heart rate. The respiratory therapist on duty that night kept it and sent it to me after he died. I couldn't bear to look at it back then. I just opened it a week ago.

(BRENNER is silent)

NORA (CONT'D)
She said she wanted me to know what happened because she was a mother too, and she'd want to know if it were her child. She details what you did, what you didn't do. She said I wouldn't find it in Jonah's medical records. Why is that?

BRENNER
These therapists, these nurses think they have all the answers. Have they ever worked a twenty-eight-hour shift? Do they know how exhausting it is being chief resident when the new interns start in July?

NORA
(Quietly) I would think they do.

BRENNER
They don't know what I know. You think an attending was going to run over in the middle of the night?

NORA
That would be protocol, wouldn't it?

BRENNER
Hmmm…

NORA
You didn't read the record. You made a mistake and that mistake cost me my son's life.

BRENNER
We're done.
(He pushes his chair back and stands)

NORA
Jonah was having a good day. His numbers were strong. He was doing so well.

BRENNER
Things can go awry in the NICU at any time. I'm sure you know that.

NORA
You're sure of so many things.
(Introspectively) No one asks about him anymore. People are afraid to say his name. It's like he was never here, but he was here—

BRENNER
I'm a good doctor. People respect me. Why do you think I was appointed chief resident?

NORA
I held him in my arms; I held him to my chest. I sang to him.

BRENNER
If you want to sue, I can't stop you.

(Pause)

NORA
Why do you even work with babies,
Dr. Brenner?

BRENNER
Because they don't talk back.

*(NORA recoils. BRENNER realizes
what he's said and is stunned into silence.
Very long pause)*

BRENNER
Why are you here? What do you want?

NORA
I want you to admit you made a
mistake.

BRENNER
I didn't.

NORA
Please.

BRENNER
I followed protocol.

NORA
Please.

BRENNER
Why does it matter?

NORA
Because I have to stop blaming myself!
I have to stop thinking every minute of
every day what I could have done, what
I should have done to save him. I can't
live with the fact that maybe because I
was too old, or because I worked too
long, or because I ate the wrong things,
or because I didn't pump goddamn
breast milk that I'm responsible for his
death. I have to stop blaming myself or
I don't know how I'm going to live.

(Pause)

BRENNER
You're not responsible.

NORA
I'm not?

BRENNER
No. You're not.

*(CODE BLUE is sounded on the
intercom. BRENNER'S pager goes off)*

One-Act Plays

IRENE AUBRY KELLOGG

Irene Aubry Kellogg was born in Port-au-Prince, Haiti, in 1943. She came to the United States in 1963 to go to college. She married an American and many years later became an American citizen. She lived in New York City for forty years and worked at the Board of Education throughout her adult life as a teacher, coordinator of bilingual and ESL programs, and staff developer. She was actively engaged in the struggle for Haitian Bilingual Education. Confronting sexism, racism, and elitism, she became a passionate feminist and anti-racist, squarely landing on the side of the working class in their struggle for survival against the devastation of the capitalist system. When she retired, she moved to the Catskills in upstate New York, but spends her winters with her family in the Bay Area in California. She studied acting and performed with The Comets in Woodstock and at the Open Eye Theater in Margaretville, New York. Out of curiosity, she joined a writing workshop in Oakland, California, led by American playwright Anthony Clarvoe, whose extraordinary teaching skills enabled her to discover the rich experience of writing plays. Two of her plays, *Gin Rummy* and *Happily Ever After* were read and/or performed in Oakland. The most influential person in Irene's life was her second husband, Stephan Kass, with whom she shared forty-three years of deep companionship and love. He died in 2015. She expresses her loss in the words of W. S. Merwin:

> *Your absence has gone through me*
> *Like thread through a needle.*
> *Everything I do is stitched with its color.*

The Arrangement

A PLAY BY IRENE AUBRY KELLOGG

CAST OF CHARACTERS

HANS: a white man in his late forties/later a man in his early seventies.

CARLA: his wife, a Hispanic woman in her late thirties.

ERMANCE: their servant, a Black woman in her early thirties/later a woman in her late fifties.

MADAN BELIZOR: a Black woman, a Mambo (a vodou priestess) in her forties.

MARCELIN: Ermance's son. A young Black man in his thirties.

ADRIENNE: Ermance's daughter. A young Black woman in her thirties. (MADAN BELIZOR and ADRIENNE can be played by the same actor)

JASMINE: a child's voice offstage.

SYNOPSIS

ERMANCE, a servant in HANS and CARLA's home, becomes pregnant with HANS' child. Everyone's life changes.

SCENE 1

(1970. HANS and CARLA's living room in a house in Petionville, Haiti. It's a spacious, comfortable, cool room. You can hear dogs barking and cicadas singing. ERMANCE is serving HANS a cup of coffee)

HANS
Are you sure?

ERMANCE
Yes.

HANS
When did you find out?

ERMANCE
Yesterday.

HANS
Are you sure?

ERMANCE
Yes, the test was positive.

HANS
Do you need some money?

ERMANCE
For what?

HANS
To take care of it.

ERMANCE
What do you mean take care of it?

HANS
You're not going to keep it, are you?

ERMANCE
Why not?

HANS
You already have four children.

ERMANCE
But you don't have any.

HANS
What do you think Carla will say?

ERMANCE
She doesn't have to know.

HANS
But she will know. Do you really think you can hide this?

ERMANCE
She doesn't have to know it's yours.

HANS
The child will be a mulatto! Is there another white man around here?

ERMANCE
Don't you want it? You don't have any children. This child will be yours.

HANS
But what do you think Carla will say?

ERMANCE
When the time comes, I'll leave. Then you can send me some money to take care of the baby.

SCENE 2
(Same room. CARLA is reading a magazine. ERMANCE is leaning on a mop)

CARLA
You want to go home early?

ERMANCE
No, I'll be OK.

CARLA
This is the second time you're not feeling well this week.

ERMANCE
Yes.

CARLA
What's going on?

ERMANCE
I don't know.

CARLA
Did you see a doctor?

ERMANCE
No.

CARLA
What is it exactly that you're feeling? Do you have a headache?

ERMANCE
No. I feel like throwing up.

CARLA
Is it something you ate?

ERMANCE
I don't think so, no.

CARLA
Well, you're not losing weight. In fact, you look like you've put on weight. Do you think you might be pregnant?

ERMANCE
Could be.

CARLA
Oh, so you're not sick. You're pregnant. How do you feel about that?

ERMANCE
If I'm pregnant, I'm fine with it.

CARLA
How does your husband feel? I know you already have four children. Isn't one more a financial burden?

ERMANCE
I haven't told him anything. I'm not even sure I'm pregnant. I'm just not feeling well. That's all.

CARLA
Well, I think you better go to a doctor and find out what's going on. If you're pregnant, he needs to know.

ERMANCE
I don't think he will care.

CARLA
I don't understand. He has no feelings about this one way or the other?

ERMANCE
No.

CARLA
This is beyond me. Anyway, I think you should go to a doctor. And if you need anything, let me know.

SCENE 3
(Same room. CARLA and HANS are about to go to bed)

CARLA
When were you going to tell me this?

HANS
I'm telling you now.

CARLA
Do you realize I offered to help her?

HANS
That was nice of you.

CARLA
You know, I don't mind her lying to me. I understand her position. She's a poor woman who wants to be taken care of. I've heard that's what poor Haitian women do. They have children for men, hoping that one of the men will take care of their family. But you! To do this behind my back!

HANS
Oh, please, Carla. Let's not talk about doing things behind each other's back. I know what goes on in this house when I'm at work.

CARLA
Do tell. What does go on?

HANS
Please. Don't make me say things I don't want to say.

CARLA
Say anything you want. You fucking Ermance would be like me fucking the yard boy.

HANS
Hopefully, you didn't do that.

CARLA
No. But I don't understand why it's OK for you to fuck the maid.

HANS
Please.

CARLA
Didn't it occur to you that the reason she got pregnant was to buy herself a retirement plan?

HANS
No. It was an accident.

CARLA
You're so naive. She's over thirty. She knows how to take care of herself. She knows what to do to avoid being pregnant.

HANS
I think it was an accident.

CARLA
Believe whatever you want. *(Silence)* How much money have you already given her?

HANS
I don't want to talk about it.

CARLA
Oh, you're going to have to talk about it, alright, because that concerns me. You're giving away what's mine. *(Silence)*

CARLA (CONT'D)
I don't want to see her in this house again. And I don't want to be the one to ask her to leave because I don't trust what I might say to her. So, you're going to tell her not to come back and

you're going to have to figure out what to do about that child. I'm going back to Chile and you will let me know when that problem is solved.

SCENE 4

(Same room. ERMANCE is sitting with her feet on the coffee table. She looks like she's six months pregnant. She's looking at a magazine. It's obvious that she's looking at the pictures because she doesn't know how to read. HANS walks in)

HANS
You're still here?

ERMANCE
I put your dinner on the dining room table.

HANS
You don't need to stay and wait for me to get back. You can go home.

ERMANCE
I know. But I enjoy being here.

HANS
You know, Ermance, this is not your home. This is my home.

ERMANCE
Yes, but I'm carrying your baby.

HANS
I told you I would take care of it, but you can't just install yourself in Carla's place. Carla is my wife.

ERMANCE
But she left.

HANS
She left because you're here.

ERMANCE
She left because I'm having a baby for you.

HANS
Having a baby is one thing. Thinking you can be my wife is another.

ERMANCE
Oh! So, I'm not good enough for you, huh?

HANS
I didn't say that.

ERMANCE
But that's what you mean, no? I'm good enough to have a child for you but not good enough to be your wife?

HANS
When we had sex, you knew I was married.

ERMANCE
I knew you were married, but I did not know you had such disrespect for me.

HANS
It's not about disrespect. But be realistic, do you really think I can take you to dinner to my friends' house? You don't even speak French.

ERMANCE
Neither do you.

HANS
But, I'm German. I speak German, English, and Creole.

ERMANCE
So? I am Haitian and I speak Creole.

HANS
You don't seem to get it, do you? Whatever you think, you cannot stay here like this.

ERMANCE
Huh! We'll see about that.
(ERMANCE leaves and HANS sits with his head in his hands)

SCENE 5

(MADAN BELIZOR's front porch. ERMANCE and MADAN BELIZOR are sitting close to the ground)

ERMANCE

…And that's the story. What can you do for me?

MADAN BELIZOR

Dear me. This man has no shame. Don't worry, we're going to take care of it. What is he called?

ERMANCE

Hans Muller.

MADAN BELIZOR

Good. Write his name on a piece of paper and put it in a matchbox. Place that box under your mattress and then, this is what you're going to do…

SCENE 6

(CARLA and HANS' living room. ERMANCE is sitting in a chair with a bundle in her arms. She's totally focused on the baby, cuddling it and cooing to it. CARLA and HANS are talking about her and the baby as if they aren't in the room)

CARLA

You aren't seriously asking me to accept this situation, are you?

HANS

What can we do? What's done is done.

CARLA

What is it with men? They just can't think farther than their dicks.

HANS

Please. (Beat) I can't explain it, Carla. But there's a child here now. And she's awfully cute. She looks a little like me. I can't watch her grow up in the street knowing that she's mine. We don't have any children. Can you find it in your heart to accept her into our lives?

CARLA

Look! I came back because you wrote me that everything was taken care of. I thought you meant that Ermance was out of your life. I even asked you if she was gone and you said yes. So, what is she doing here today?

HANS

I thought she was gone. The last time I saw her she was upset but she left and didn't come back. This is the first time I've seen her since she gave birth.

CARLA

So, what is she doing here?

HANS

I guess she wants me to see the child.

CARLA

And now that you've seen it. Now what?

HANS

It's a human being, Carla. A person. A girl who will grow up with no opportunity for a decent life if we choose to ignore her.

CARLA

I don't understand what you want. You want me to accept her, here, in our home, as if she were our child?

HANS

Well…

CARLA

But she isn't our child. She is your child and the maid's child.

HANS

You haven't been able to have children //

CARLA

// Oh! Now I'm to blame for this situation.

HANS

I'm sorry, I didn't mean it that way. I meant to say, we haven't had a child.

CARLA

Like Sarah in the Bible huh? Except you found your way to the servant's bed without my help. I didn't have to send her to you.

HANS
No, you didn't. Providence found its way.

CARLA
Providence has nothing to do with this.

HANS
Anyway, I hope you will not persecute Ermance like Sarah persecuted Hagar.

CARLA
Jesus, why are we talking about the Bible?

HANS
You brought it up. Perhaps you did because our story is as old as the Bible. *(Silence)*

CARLA
If, and I'm not saying I will, but if I accept this, there's a price to pay.

HANS
A price?

CARLA
Yes. A price.

HANS
You want to punish me?

CARLA
This isn't about punishing you. This is about protecting my interests. I'm in a bigamist situation //

HANS
// This is not bigamy.

CARLA
Maybe not technically, but you have two women in your life: the mother of your child and your wife. Ermance bought her insurance when she bore you a child. I want my insurance. Your house in Chile must be put in my name.

HANS
I didn't know you were so materialistic.

CARLA
I'm not. I'm just practical and cautious. I don't want to be fighting with your daughter at your death.

HANS
How do you know I will die before you?

CARLA
I don't know that, but just in case, I want protection from…providence.

SCENE 7
(Six years later. CARLA and HAN's living room. A six-year-old child is singing offstage. HANS is reading work-related reports. CARLA is putting some crackers and cookies in a shopping bag)

CARLA
Ermance tells me that her kids love these crackers and cookies. I packed up some evaporated milk for them too. I don't think those kids get enough calcium. *(Speaking to a child offstage)* Jasmine, are you getting ready? Your Mother will be picking you up soon.

JASMINE
(Offstage) Yes, Aunt Carla.

CARLA
(To the child offstage) Don't forget to take your painting with you to show it to your Mother.

JASMINE
(Offstage) I won't forget.

HANS
She's growing up fast.

CARLA
Yes, she's growing up to be quite a nice girl.

HANS
Did you see her latest report card?

CARLA
Yes, she's smart, really smart.

HANS
Just like her father.

CARLA
If you say so. *(Beat)* I'll have to get her that dress she liked so much. *(Louder, to JASMINE, who's still offstage)* Jasmine, when you come back next weekend, we'll go shopping for that blue dress you liked.

JASMINE
(Offstage) Thanks, Aunt Carla.

HANS
(Tenderly) Carla?

CARLA
Yes?

HANS
I want to thank you for taking care of Jasmine in such a nice way.

CARLA
She's easy to love. She's kind and she's beautiful. And she's not responsible for the circumstances of her birth. *(Trying not to tear up)* She turned out to be quite a nice girl.

HANS
Yes.
(Silence. CARLA is lost in thought)

CARLA
When we first got married, I wanted a child. Remember?

HANS
Yes. We did try to have one.

CARLA
Yes, we did. But it didn't happen. So, I gave up the yearning…I thought I had given it up until Jasmine came around. I was so surprised to feel what she stirred inside of me. At first anger and then a surge of love and longing. A little girl. Needing to be loved. And me. Aching to give it. What a surprise!

HANS
Yes. It was a surprise for me too.

CARLA
My love? Or yours?

HANS
Both.
(Silence. They are both lost in thought)

CARLA
Did you tell her mother we're going back to Chile?

HANS
I haven't told her yet.

CARLA
Don't you think she should be the first one to know?

HANS
Yes, I'll have to tell her.

CARLA
Are you afraid to tell her?

HANS
No, why?

CARLA
You've decided to take Jasmine with you. Don't you think Ermance will object?

HANS
I don't think she will. I don't know. It's not like we're going to the end of the world.

CARLA
I think you better tell her.

HANS
Yes, you're right.

CARLA
Soon.

HANS
Yes. *(Beat)* How do you think Jasmine will feel about it?

CARLA
She will probably be excited. She's very curious about things. She's a kid. It's an adventure. But then, you never know. She's never been away from her mother for more than a weekend.

SCENE 8
(CARLA and HANS's living room. ERMANCE and CARLA are sitting. HANS is standing)

HANS
Ermance, my contract hasn't been renewed.

ERMANCE
Oh!

HANS
We have to go back to Chile.

ERMANCE
That's not good.

HANS
No, it's not good.

ERMANCE
Jasmine will miss you.

HANS
What I want to tell you is, we are thinking of taking Jasmine with us.

ERMANCE
Taking Jasmine?

HANS
Yes.

ERMANCE
Taking her away from me?

HANS
She would come to visit you.

ERMANCE
Visit me?

HANS
Yes.

ERMANCE
She's my daughter.

CARLA
We know. We'll take good care of her.

ERMANCE
But I won't see her.

CARLA
She'll have a good life with us, Ermance. And she'll come and visit you.

ERMANCE
Visit me? I can't give up my daughter.

HANS
You wouldn't be giving up your daughter. She'd just be coming with us.

ERMANCE
Going with you? But when would I see her?

HANS
You will see her during the summer. She will be going to school so she will come to spend the summer with you.

ERMANCE
Jasmine doesn't speak Spanish.

HANS
She will be fine. She's smart. She will learn Spanish very quickly.

ERMANCE
I can't give her up like that. Can't you leave her here with me? Send me some money for her?

CARLA
We could, but you know that she would have a better life with us.

ERMANCE
She's not your daughter, Carla.

HANS
Ermance, that's not fair. Carla has been like a mother to Jasmine.

ERMANCE

(Speaking directly to CARLA) You didn't carry her in your stomach for nine months. You didn't give birth to her. She's not yours. You didn't even want her. Jasmine is my child.

CARLA

I'm not taking Jasmine away from you. I know she's your child. We're just proposing to take care of her and give her what she needs.

ERMANCE

I can give her what she needs. If you send her some money, I can give her what she needs.

HANS

You know it wouldn't be the same, Ermance.

ERMANCE

(Looks at them in disbelief and shakes her head vigorously) I can't give her up. I won't give her up. Jasmine is my child. *(Beat)* My mother abandoned me. She gave me up to this old lady who needed a caretaker. Mme. Lafontant. I was only six years old. That woman was supposed to send me to school. She never did. I took care of her and when she died, I had to become a servant in someone else's house. I remember wanting my mother so badly that I thought my insides were going to spill out of my body. I cried and cried and cried. But I cried behind everybody's back. That old woman beat me whenever she saw me crying. "I'll give you something to cry about." Eventually, my grief turned to anger. I never forgave my mother. I don't want my daughter to carry in her heart the hate that I carry in mine.

CARLA

Ermance, your child will not be a servant. She will be our daughter.

ERMANCE

But how will I explain to her that I gave her up?

HANS

You're not giving her up. She will be back to visit you.

ERMANCE

You keep saying VISIT, VISIT, VISIT. When does a daughter VISIT her mother? A daughter LIVES with her mother.

SCENE 9

(The front porch of MADAN BELIZOR's house. ERMANCE is crying)

ERMANCE

Madan Belizor, how can I let my child go? How can they ask me to do something like that?

MADAN BELIZOR

It's a hard thing to ask a mother to do. I understand your grief, my child.

ERMANCE

My God! My master! Misery sticks to us poor people like glue. All my life I have gone around like a scavenger. Refusing to accept that I was born to have nothing. Worse, to know nothing but pain and suffering. Every time I felt beat down, I would reach out for some hope. When my mother left me in that old woman's house, I felt such despair. One person felt sorry for me. Matante Saintclus. She was Mme. Lafontant's cook. She would give me sweets and tell me that someday I would grow up and be able to have my own family. Whenever I felt despair, I would hold on to that dream. She taught me to pray. God is good, she said. He will not leave you like this forever. God heard me and he didn't leave me like this. I met Wilson when I turned eighteen. We decided to live together until we could

ERMANCE

He just refuses to accept the reality. He has no right calling Hans a moocher. He doesn't realize if we survived in Haiti, it was thanks to Hans who kept sending me money.

ADRIENNE

You didn't tell us, Ma.

ERMANCE

Hans didn't want me to tell you. He didn't just take care of Jasmine. Even when Jasmine was with him, he sent me some money for you all. It's thanks to him that we didn't starve.

HANS

I wish I could have done more for you.

ERMANCE

You did what you could. With God's help, we all do what we can.

ADRIENNE

How is Jasmine?

ERMANCE

(Shrugs, resigned, sad) Hans hears from her more often than I do.

HANS

She's fine. She likes the army but she talks about leaving soon. She wants to go back to school to study psychology. Doesn't she write you?

ADRIENNE

She hardly ever sends us a letter.

ERMANCE

(Sadly) She's so far away. Once in a blue moon, we talk on the phone. She's always nice but she doesn't seem to need me. Thank God, she has no bitterness in her heart. But she doesn't seem to need her mother. It's as if I don't exist for her as a mother. I have a daughter who does not recognize her mother. *(Beat)* I knew something like that would happen. I guess that's life. I've resigned my head to it.

ADRIENNE

(Taking her mother's hand) Mommy, we all need you, back in Haiti. In fact, we miss you. We talk about you all the time. We sit around the dining room table and tell stories about you. How you used to have us read the Bible to you. How proud you were of us. How you used to chase us around the house when we were bad. And how you almost burst with pride when Beatrice graduated from nursing school.

ERMANCE

(Patting her daughter's hand) I know, my child. I know. I miss you all too. *(Beat)* I keep having this dream. We are all living in a big house. You and your sisters and Marcelin, your spouses and your children, my grandchildren. We're all living together in Haiti, in this beautiful house. We're sitting at a big table, telling stories, laughing, and waiting for the food. The plates arrive…but they're empty, there's no food on them.

ADRIENNE

What happens then?

ERMANCE

I don't know. I just wake up.

MARJORIE BICKNELL

I first developed an interest in working in the theatre at the age of six when I saw a high school production of *The Student Prince*. I hold a Bachelor of Arts in Theater from Mundelein College and an Interdepartmental Master of Arts degree in Speech and Communications from Northwestern University.

I studied acting in Coventry, England, in a program run by Valparaiso University and Coventry Cathedral, where we also took our art out into the community, working with immigrants, deaf children, and Borstal boys (reform school inmates).

Following graduation, I worked in my hometown of Chicago, Illinois, where I became manager of Pary Production Company, a professional, non-profit theater. I wrote my first play for Pary, an adaptation of *Frankenstein*, which won three Joseph Jefferson awards in its world-premiere production.

Since then, I have lived in Philadelphia, Harrisburg, Pennsylvania and again in Philadelphia where I currently reside.

Throughout my life, I have felt compelled to write about both the need for family, and the frustration women feel when they are underestimated or disregarded. Sometimes these twin themes show up in the same play. I am also compelled to help other playwrights. I founded a playwrights' group, Playwrights Alliance of Pennsylvania, served as president of another, Philadelphia Dramatists Center, and am currently the Regional Representative in Philadelphia for the Dramatists Guild of America.

Carmageddon

A MODERN FARCE BY MARJORIE BICKNELL

CAST OF CHARACTERS
MAN—somewhere between twenty and thirty, any race or ethnicity
WOMAN—somewhere between twenty and thirty, any race or ethnicity

SETTING
The Service Desk and Office of the Continental Car Club

SYNOPSIS
When a young woman wants an oil change before driving off to her discount luxury vacation, she turns to her car club, the most trusted provider she knows. What could possibly go wrong?

(A chest-high service counter stands just right of center stage. Signs above read "Continental Car Club," "CCC-Authorized Service. Nothing like it on the planet!" and "15% off our rates—just for our members." On the counter is a telephone, a computer monitor, a number dispenser, and a coffee machine and cups. A television is mounted near high-top tables and chairs face a MAN wearing a golf shirt with the CCC logo and a Velcroed name tag reading "Mike" standing behind the counter. The WOMAN enters)

WOMAN
Hello! I have an appointment for an oil change at 2 p.m.

MAN
Take a number, please.

WOMAN
But I have an appointment—

MAN
I heard you. Take a number and someone will be right with you.

WOMAN
I am in a bit of a hurry. And Bill, the man I spoke to on the phone, said I'd be taken right away, if I made an appointment for 2 p.m.

MAN
Bill isn't here today. It's his day off.

WOMAN
I spoke to Bill yesterday, and said I wanted an oil change because I'm going on vacation. I wanted to bring the car in yesterday because I'm leaving today, but Bill said you're never busy at 2 p.m. on Tuesdays and I should come now for faster service.

MAN
How would Bill know if it's busy at 2 p.m. on Tuesday? Tuesday is his day off.

WOMAN
I didn't…He could still…What difference does it make? I have an appointment at 2 p.m. for an oil change, and it's 2 p.m.

MAN
(Checking his computer screen) No, it's not!

WOMAN
It most certainly is! My watch says it's 2 p.m. exactly.

MAN
This computer is equipped with the latest atomic clock. It is accurate to one one hundredth of a nanosecond. And this clock says it is only 1 and 59 minutes and 23 seconds p.m. So kindly take a number and wait your turn!
(The WOMAN presses the button on the dispenser. It makes a noise, but no ticket appears)

WOMAN
Sir! Sir! Mike? Can you help me? Hey! Mike! Please—

MAN
Do you have a number?

WOMAN
No. This machine—

MAN
I'm sorry. I can't help you without a number.

WOMAN
The machine won't give me one.

MAN
That's ridiculous! There's nothing wrong with this machine! (The MAN reaches for the machine and pushes the button. Nothing happens. He replaces it with a wire rack that has numbered cards hanging off it. He speaks to the WOMAN as though there has been no intervening action)

MAN
I don't understand why you had a problem, ma'am. There are plenty of numbers here right here. Please take one and have a seat. I'm sure your number will be called shortly.

(The WOMAN hesitates then takes a number, and sits at a table. The television set suddenly goes on and the MAN appears on screen)

MAN (ON TELEVISION)
Hello, members! Welcome to Continental Car Club TV, where you learn how we make our members the happiest drivers on the planet! Today, I am talking about Continental Car Club–authorized service. Need an oil change? A tune-up? A new transmission or even an engine replaced? Just leave it to us! Our technicians are the most highly trained and responsible mechanics we could find! And our service personnel will never make you wait or take a number. That makes our service as convenient as it is reliable.
(The television clicks off. The WOMAN returns to the counter carrying her number)

WOMAN
Excuse me, sir, uh, Mike. How come I have a number when you just said that members will never be told to wait or to take a number?

MAN
I never said that!

WOMAN
You did too! On the television.

MAN
That wasn't me. I haven't said a word. Besides, we always tell people to take a number. First come, first served is the only way to be fair to our members.

WOMAN
But I have an appointment. I told you.

MAN
What's your number?

WOMAN
43.

MAN

Oh, lady! I called your number ages ago. In fact, I called it several times and you never said a peep. I just called 44 and he was ready right away, so I am afraid your spot is lost.

WOMAN

Well, you didn't call very loud because I was right over there, and I didn't hear a thing. If you skipped me I think you should help me now—especially since I have an—

MAN

(Interrupting) Since you couldn't be bothered to pay attention, I'm afraid you're going to have to wait until we get back to 43 again. We are extremely busy today and it wouldn't be fair to the other members to take you out of turn.

WOMAN

But you are not being fair to me! I had an appointment. I made that appointment for 2 p.m. because I was told I'd be taken promptly…and I have to leave on my vacation today—or I won't have a place to stay. *(Pause. She asserts herself)* I think it's time for me to speak to a manager.

MAN

Bill's the manager, but Tuesday is his day off. So today I'm empowered to help you.

WOMAN

Then help me! I really need this oil change. I'm supposed to go on vacation today. I have a discount on a luxury vacation at the New Jersey shore. If I don't get there by 6 p.m., I won't get the discount, and if I don't get the discount, I won't get a luxury vacation. And I need this luxury vacation!

MAN

Don't worry, lady. I will help you. Just as soon as your number is called.

WOMAN

Aren't these numbers for members who don't have appointments? I have an appointment and I can prove it. *(Produces a sheet of paper)* Here's my reminder with my appointment number: CCC-82-4343.

MAN

Let me see that!

WOMAN

You're not touching it!

MAN

But I need to check your name and number.

WOMAN

I'll read it to you.

MAN

You don't trust me! And after everything I've done to try and help you!

WOMAN

You're not helping at all. Here's the information. Appointment number: CCC-82-4343. Time: Tuesday, 2 p.m. Car Make and Model: Toyota Prius. Name: Emily Smith.

MAN

(Writing furiously)…Prius…Emily Smith. Okay, let me check.
(The MAN pulls out a book and shuffles through pages until he finds a page he likes)

MAN (CONT'D)

Tuesday. *(The MAN draw his finger slowly down the list)*

WOMAN

What are you doing?

MAN

Checking The Book to see if you have an appointment.

WOMAN
The book? But my appointment should be right there in your computer!

MAN
My computer?

WOMAN
Yes. Your computer. Right there on the counter. You know. The one with the atomic clock.

MAN
Why would I look there?

WOMAN
Because that's where you keep your list. Because you used it to send me this computer-generated email with my computer-generated confirmation number.

MAN
You can't trust computers. We write everything down in The Book. It's the only way to keep things straight. *(Pause. He glares)* Now, if you don't mind, I will TRY to help you by looking up your name in The Book. *(Draws his finger down the list)* Bacon…Schreiber… O'Hara…Williams…Sikorsky… Mattuso…Olivetti…hmmm. What's your name again?

WOMAN
Emily Smith.

MAN
I have an Emile Smythe with a Prius at 2 o'clock.

WOMAN
That's me!

MAN
Emile is a man's name. Is that your husband?

WOMAN
No. I don't have a husband. I was supposed to, but my fiancé broke up with—

MAN
(Interrupting) Lady, please! We don't make mistakes. Not in The Book. It's always perfect. Of course, sometimes our customers make mistakes. But not us. Could it be your father?

WOMAN
No.

MAN
Brother?

WOMAN
No.

MAN
Uncle? Cousin? Brother-in-law?

WOMAN
No, No, and No! It's me! Here's my driver's license. With my photo. See? Looks just like me. And heres my appointment reminder with my name on it. I'm Emily Smith and that's my appointment! Do you really think It's possible that you have both an Emily Smith and an Emile Smythe as members?

MAN
It's a big club. And I wouldn't want to accidentally give Emile's appointment to you. After all, we want // to be—

WOMAN
"Fair to // all our members." I know. But that's my appointment! Even the appointment number is the same. I can read it from here.

MAN
Okay, maybe you're right, but you're very late. I don't know if we can handle you now.

WOMAN
I am not late.

MAN
Oh, but you are. It's 2:02 p.m. You should have been here on time at 2. I'm afraid we've had to give your appointment time away.

WOMAN
Well, you better find another one for me because I was here at 2 p.m. In fact, you told me I had to wait because I was early.

MAN
Well, you should have spoken up at 2 p.m. I'm afraid you're going to have to come back tomorrow.

WOMAN
I can't come back tomorrow, because I am leaving on vacation today. I will be driving my car, which has just had an oil change—even if I have to go to Jiffy Lube.

MAN
You'd take your car to Jiffy Lube? Do you know what happens to cars at Jiffy Lube?

WOMAN
No, but I bet you're going to tell me!
(Before the MAN has a chance to answer, the television snaps back on)

MAN (ON TELEVISION)
You can drop in for Continental Car Club–approved service anytime, and be back on the road the same day. But if you call ahead and make an appointment, we guarantee that work will start on your vehicle within thirty minutes of your appointment time or it will be done for free. If you have to come back, both this service and the next will be free. It's how we keep our members the happiest drivers on the planet! *(The television snaps off)*

WOMAN
Well, Mike? What are you going to do about that?

MAN
Who are you talking to?

WOMAN
You.

MAN
My name is Larry. Mike doesn't work here anymore.

WOMAN
What? I've been talking to you since 1:58 p.m. and your name is Mike. It says so, right there on your shirt.

MAN
Really? My shirt says "Larry."
(The MAN looks down and notices that his name tag reads "Mike". He quickly pulls out another tag and slaps it on his shirt)

MAN
See! Larry! L-A-R-R-Y.

WOMAN
You just switched it!

MAN
What?

WOMAN
Your name tag. You just switched it. Right in front of me!

MAN
That's ridiculous. I'm Larry. I've always been Larry. And I plan to continue being Larry for a long time. It's who I am, and you can't blame me for anything that Mike may have done. Now, what can I do for you?

WOMAN
You can change the oil in my car!!!! I am going on vacation today. I don't want to have any trouble while I am on vacation. Not even car trouble. I need this vacation very badly!

MAN
Do you have an appointment?

WOMAN
What?

MAN
Do you have an appointment?

ONE-ACT PLAYS

WOMAN
Yes! My appointment number is
CCC-82-4343, and unless I'm mistaken,
you have…*(She checks her watch)* Exactly
eight minutes to start my service or It's
free!

MAN
Who told you that?

WOMAN
You did.

MAN
I did? Never!

WOMAN
You said it on that TV. We were both
standing here, so I know you heard it.

MAN
I was on TV and standing here at the
same time. Lady, that's impossible!

WOMAN
You were in the recorded commercial
on that TV and you said, "We start your
service within thirty minutes of your
appointment time or it's free."

MAN
No. I never said that. That was some
random actor reading cue cards. And
everybody knows you can't trust actors.
They lie for a living. Now if you'll just
excuse me for a minute. *(The MAN
turns to go. The WOMAN reaches and
grabs him holding on for dear life)*

WOMAN
No! You're not going anywhere. Not
until you take my car for an oil change
so I can take my discounted, trouble-
free vacation. If I don't get to go, I don't
know what I'm going to—

MAN
(Gasping) Calm down, lady, calm down.
I'm not going anywhere. I am here to
help you. Honest! Honest! Please let me
go. *(The WOMAN releases the MAN.
The MAN becomes very conciliatory)*

MAN
There was no reason for you to get
so upset. I just wanted you to wait
for one little minute while I check
the computer to see whether we have
any openings to service your car this
afternoon. Okay? Can I do that? Can I
check a time for you?

WOMAN
But you don't need to check! I already
have a—Wait! You're checking the
computer? Don't you have to look it up
in The Book?

MAN
The Book? Nobody writes things down
in a book anymore. Everything has been
computerized for years. Why would you
write things in a book when you can
look them up on a computer in just a
second?

WOMAN
Just what I was thinking.

MAN
Now…Just hold on a minute. I think
I may…Yes! A Mr. Emile Smythe
never showed up for his 2 o'clock
appointment, so I am able to give you
his slot. Now, what type of a car are you
having serviced?

WOMAN
A Prius.

MAN
Well, that's something! Mr. Smythe had
a Prius too. And what are we having
done today?

WOMAN
Just an oil change.

MAN
I'm flabbergasted. Mr. Smythe was due
for an oil change! What a small world!
Well, just let me call back and have one
of our technicians get started. What
color is your car?

WOMAN
Green.

MAN
Really? A GREEN Prius? You're quite the jokester, aren't you? *(The MAN speaks into the phone)*

MAN (CONT'D)
Jeff, we got a Prius—a GREEN Prius—for an oil and lube. *(Pause. He listens)* Yeah, I know. These tree-huggers think they're hilarious. *(He listens again)* Yeah, just an oil and lube.

WOMAN
Did you say oil and lube?

MAN
Yeah. So?

WOMAN
You can't give my car a lube! It's got a sealed system.

MAN
(Into the phone) Hang on, Jeff. *(To the Woman)* What? What are you talking about?

WOMAN
The Prius's system is sealed. You can change the oil, but you can't lubricate the engine.

MAN
How do you know that? Are you a mechanic?

WOMAN
No, I'm not. But my boyfriend is… was…I mean my ex-boyfriend… And I work at a Toyota dealership…I mean, used to work there…so I know something about Priuses…and you don't lube them!

MAN
Look, we got a Prius specialist back in the shop, and he'll be doing the oil and lube.

WOMAN
Oil change! No lube! You can't lube a Prius!

MAN
(Into the phone) Jeff, this lady here is an expert on the Prius. She says no lube. *(Pause.)* Hilarious! *(Pause)* And Jeff, don't forget the 52-point inspection. You forgot to do Father O'Hara's Caddy and he's threatening us with hell.

WOMAN
Excuse me. About that 52-point inspection. How long will that take?

MAN
Not long.

WOMAN
How long is "not long"?

MAN
It depends.

WOMAN
On what?

MAN
On the make and model, the mechanic's experience, the patience of the member—

WOMAN
Did you just say, "The patience of the member"?

MAN
What? Huh! No! I would never say that!

WOMAN
Well, you just—Look! I don't care how long a 52-point inspection takes because I'm not getting one. Just give me an oil change and ONLY an oil change. Okay? I'm not Father What's-his-name. I won't condemn you to hell. I'm just going to sit down over there, and calmly read a magazine while my car gets an oil change. Okay?

MAN
Whatever you say, ma'am! *(The WOMAN sits down. The MAN turns away from her and picks up the phone)*

MAN (CONT'D)
Hey, Jeff, the crazy lady with the Prius says she doesn't want a lube. *(Pause. He listens)* I know! Who ever heard of not getting a lube when you get an oil change? *(Pause. He listens)* You're right! She will be sorry. If you want your car to run forever you have to keep it lubricated. *(Pause. He thinks)* Look. I think you should lube the engine regardless. What's going to happen anyway? Is it going to freeze the engine and set off all the idiot lights? Of course not! She'll thank us—if she ever figures out what we've done for her! I know. Women know nothing about cars. Okay, I have to go. It's just about time for my break. *(He starts to hang up then remembers)* Say Jeff? I almost forgot. She said to skip the 52-point inspection. Whaddaya think? *(Pause. He listens)* Oh yeah, that's right. It's company policy. Do it. She'll never notice. I don't want to get in trouble, do you? *(The MAN hangs up the phone, gets himself a cup of coffee, then turns to the WOMAN)*

MAN (CONT'D)
Hey, lady! We've got hot coffee on the counter if you want some. I'll be back in a minute. *(The MAN exits. The WOMAN, goes to the counter and pours a cup of coffee. Just then, the television snaps on. The WOMAN is onscreen dressed in a muumuu with a large flower behind her right ear. Hawaiian music begins to play)*

WOMAN (ON TELEVISION)
Continental Car Club members aren't just the happiest drivers on the planet, they're also the happiest travelers! I'm here in Hawaii at the fabulous Kaumakani Beach Resort to show you how easy it is to afford the best vacation of your life. For just $1,499 we'll fly you direct to the Garden Isle and your own private cottage. This all-inclusive luxury vacation in one of the most romantic spots in the world is better than any Jersey shore vacation and it's sure to make you forget all your troubles. Even if you lost your job. Even if your fiancé dumped you. Even if he stole your dog—*(The WOMAN turns to watch, then does a huge double take as she sees herself on television. She looks around to discover who is responsible. Then, as her personal problems are revealed, she screams and throws her cup at the screen and drenches the TV, which shuts off. The MAN comes racing through the door)*

MAN
Call 911! Call 911! What happened? Who screamed? Who's hurt? *(Coffee drips on his head from the TV)* What? What's this? Where's this coffee coming from?

WOMAN
(Very upset) You did this! You! You put me in your television. Are you trying to drive me crazy? First there's no appointment. Then there is. Then you don't call my number but say that you did. Then you look me up in The Book and claim there's no Book. Then you try to make me think I'm a man named Emile Smythe. But I'm not a man. I'm a woman. A woman named Emily Smith. A woman who just wants an oil change so she can drive her car to the beach and take a nice discounted luxury vacation before she goes crazy. But I guess I am crazy because I'm in your TV wearing a flower behind my ear. My right ear! Which means I'm looking for a man! Which means that Buddy is never coming back.

MAN
Buddy your fiancé?

WOMAN
No! Buddy, my dog! Bradley is my fiancé. Was my fiancé! Buddy is my dog! Was my dog! But Bradley took Buddy when he broke up with me! So now I've got nobody!! *(The WOMAN sobs. The MAN comes around the corner and attempts to comfort her)*

MAN
Gee lady, I'm sorry. We'll have your car around in a few minutes. Can I get you some more coffee? I guess you spilled yours, huh?

WOMAN
I didn't spill it. I threw the cup at her!

MAN
Who?

WOMAN
Her! The woman in the TV who looked like me. Was me. Is me. The one who said that if I went to Hawaii, I would forget all about losing my job and my fiancé and my dog. But I can't afford Hawaii. I won't be able to afford my beach vacation at the Jersey Shore if I'm not checked in before six o'clock when the higher rates kick in!

MAN
Lady, please. Calm down. You'll scare the other members. You couldn't have been in the TV. You're right here.

WOMAN
You were in the TV. I saw you. Twice. Once when you were Mike. And once when you were Larry.

MAN
You've got to calm down. You're going batty. You've never been on TV and I've never been on TV. What you saw were just some actors.

WOMAN
No! It was you, Larry. And me. I saw both of us.

MAN
Together?

WOMAN
Not together. In separate commercials. *(Pause. She calms herself)* Look, Larry.

MAN
Larry? I'm not Larry. I'm Bill. The supervisor. I'm the one who booked your car in yesterday.

WOMAN
No! First you were Mike. Then you switched your name tag right in front of me and became Larry.

MAN
And what does my name tag say now?

WOMAN
It says, "Bill."

MAN
And what does it say underneath "Bill"?

WOMAN
It says "Supervisor."

MAN
That's right.

WOMAN
But today's Tuesday, and that's your day off.

MAN
Who told you that?

WOMAN
Mike…or Larry…or both of them!

MAN
They couldn't have.

WOMAN
Why not?

MAN
Because they don't work here anymore.

WOMAN
I should have gone to Jiffy Lube. Bradley always says, "If you can't take the car to the dealer, take it to Jiffy Lube."

MAN
So why didn't you take it to the dealer?

WOMAN
Because they fired me!

MAN
And why didn't you take it to Jiffy Lube?

WOMAN
Because Bradley works there…and he dumped me!

MAN
See? You really did bring it to the best place. And you really can't blame us for one little mix up with your appointment. I mean…nobody's perfect. We're all human right? *(The phone on the counter rings)* Oh! And there's Tony telling me your car is ready, I'll bet.

WOMAN
Tony? What happened to Jeff?

MAN
Tony's our Prius specialist. Jeff's not here. Tuesday is his day off. *(The MAN answers the phone and listens)* Thanks! That's just what I wanted to hear. *(Pause. Looks all around the room as he speaks but not at the woman)* Emile Smythe, your car is ready.

WOMAN
Good! If I really put the pedal to the metal, I can still make to the beach before 5.

MAN
Your name is Emile Smythe?

WOMAN
Yes! No! Yes! I'm Emily Smith. I'm the one with the green Prius—not Emile Smythe. That's the mistake, remember?

MAN
We don't make mistakes like that, and even if we did, I can't go giving you that car. What will I tell Emile Smythe

when he wants to drive his Prius home and you've got it?

WOMAN
It's MY green Prius. Here's my appointment confirmation. See, Emily Smith. Here's my registration. Emily Smith again. Here's my driver's license with a photo of me, Emily Smith. Now give me my goddamn car!

MAN
Well, you certainly have a lot of documentation. And your name is certainly similar to Mr. Smythe's. But I still think we should wait for him. Just in case.

WOMAN
But we straightened all this out before you took my car in back for the oil change. You understood everything perfectly.

MAN
But that was Larry. And he doesn't work here anymore.

WOMAN
It's my car. It's my oil change. Please! Let me pay and get out of here. I need to check in to my discounted hotel, drink the half-priced wine I've packed and cry myself to sleep.

MAN
Okay, Okay! Just let me copy down your address and telephone number in case Mr. Emile Smythe comes looking for his car! *(The MAN grabs her paperwork begins writing. The WOMAN snatches each piece of paper back as quickly as possible)*

WOMAN
Now, may I please have my bill?

MAN
Coming right up. One oil change. One lube. One 52-point inspection.

WOMAN
No, no, no! I just had an oil change and nothing else.

MAN
You sure?

WOMAN
Of course, I'm sure. Now how much?

MAN
With your discount, that will be $32.95.

WOMAN
Here's $35. Keep the change. I'm getting out of here. *(The WOMAN races, rushes out the door. We hear a car engine star, quickly followed by a loud thumping noise. A moment passes. Then the MAN looks quickly to the outside door. He races to the back door and exits just as THE WOMAN marches to center stage, throws down her purse, and yells)*

WOMAN (CONT'D)
What the hell did you do to my car? *(The television clicks on revealing the WOMAN)*

WOMAN (ON TELEVISION)
All Continental Car Club service is guaranteed. From a simple oil change or annual inspection to a complete overhaul of your car's engine, we won't be satisfied until you're satisfied. If anything about your recent service isn't absolutely perfect, just speak to a member of our service team right here at the service counter.

WOMAN
Not this again! I am not on that TV! You people want me to think I'm nuts. But I'm not nuts and you're not going to drive me nuts. There's nobody here! And. You're. Not. Real.

WOMAN (ON TELEVISION)
Don't see anyone around? Then call us at 1–800-CAR-CLUB or visit us on the web at www dot continental car club dot com. *(The WOMAN screams in frustration, picks up another coffee cup and winds up to throw. The WOMAN on the television speaks)*

WOMAN (ON TELEVISION) (CONT'D)
Uh, uh, uh! Throwing that cup won't get you anywhere. Pick up the phone and dial 1–800-CAR-CLUB. That's 1–800-227-2582. What are you waiting for? Do it! Pick up that phone and call. *(The WOMAN spots the phone on the counter)*

WOMAN (ON TELEVISION) (CONT'D)
Yes, that one, right there on the counter. Go ahead!

WOMAN
Yeah. Okay! I can pick up the phone on the counter and throw it right at you! *(The WOMAN picks up the phone, yanks until the cord comes out and winds up to throw. Just then the MAN comes through the door wearing a blazer with no name tag on it. The woman stops. The television clicks off)*

MAN
What are you doing with that phone?

WOMAN
What phone? *(Feigns a double take)* Oh, this phone! I was just about to call customer service…but look! The cord isn't attached. Somebody should call maintenance.

MAN
That phone is for staff only. You shouldn't be using it.

WOMAN
(Pointing at the television monitor) Well, that woman told me to call 1–800-CAR-CLUB for service.

MAN
What woman?

WOMAN
The one who was there—up on the TV—a minute ago. My car is stalled out in the parking lot with all the idiot lights blinking—

MAN
Oh, you're here for service! Then you'll have to wait for Tom. He's the Customer Service Supervisor on duty today.

WOMAN
Tom? What happened to Bill?

MAN
Bill's on vacation.

WOMAN
But I just spoke to him.

MAN
Not possible. Even if he weren't on vacation, he wouldn't be here today. Wednesday is his day off.

WOMAN
Today is Tuesday.

MAN
Tuesday, Wednesday. It doesn't matter because today is Bill's day off. Except that he's not here because—as I told you—Bill's on vacation.

WOMAN
Can you help me?

MAN
Help you with what?

WOMAN
(Getting more upset as she speaks) I just came in for an oil change, and when I went to drive away, my car stopped dead, and all the idiot lights started blinking. I'm supposed to leave on my vacation right now and my car's dead. I can't lose my dog, my job, my fiancé, my car, and my vacation! It's not fair.

MAN
Now, now. There's no need to get upset. Somebody will help you. But that somebody is not me. I don't work in service. I work in personnel. I'm here to conduct job interviews.

WOMAN
With whom? There's nobody here but me.

MAN
That's not possible. We're hiring new Customer Service Reps and we always have a large turnout. People love working here.

WOMAN
You don't have a large turnout today. As you can see, I'm the only one here.

MAN
Then I have one applicant already.

WOMAN
But—

MAN
Didn't you just say you lost your job? I'll bet that's why you came in today. To get an oil change for your car and a new job for you. Wednesday is the day I always hold interviews. That's very smart of you. Killing two birds with one stone.

WOMAN
But today is Tuesday.

MAN
(Interrupting) It's Wednesday. We had this conversation before. You remember? When you asked why Bill wasn't here today? (Looks around, surprised that no one else is there) Well, it looks like you're the first.

WOMAN
The first?

MAN
For the interview, of course. I'm sure you're eager to begin.

WOMAN
I don't have time to interview for some stupid job. I need to get my car fixed now! I'm going to lose my hotel discount and my vacation if I don't leave…*(She checks her watch)* in the next five minutes.

MAN
You poor dear! We can't fix your car that fast. Tom, our Prius expert, is at lunch!

WOMAN
Lunch? It's after three!

MAN
He likes to take a late lunch. He says it makes his afternoon fly by…and he's a slow eater, so I wouldn't expect him back before 4:30. So it looks like you'll have plenty of time for an interview.

WOMAN
I don't want to interview. I want to go on vacation!

MAN
But you haven't even heard about all the great benefits we offer. They're irresistible.

WOMAN
Irresistible? Nobody has benefits that are irresistible.

MAN
The Continental Car Club does.

WOMAN
Really? Just what kind of benefits do you offer?

MAN
Three weeks' vacation after six months, a Cadillac health insurance policy, and of course, free service and repair visits for your car as long as you work here. And then there's—

WOMAN
Did you say free service and repair visits? As in free?

MAN
Well, of course. We are the Continental Car Club.

WOMAN
If I work here, you'll fix anything that goes wrong with my car—for free.

MAN
Absolutely.

WOMAN
Even if it's sitting dead in the parking lot with all the idiot lights blinking?

MAN
Of course! It's all part of the package.

WOMAN
Where do I sign up?

MAN
Oh, thought you just wanted to go on your discount vacation.

WOMAN
What time is it now?

MAN
It's 3:15.

WOMAN
I'll never make it there in time—even if I could leave, which I can't because my car's engine is dead and all the idiot lights are blinking.

MAN
(Opens his folder and runs his finger down the list of names on the paper inside) So, let's see. As I said, It's 3:15 p.m., and you obviously have an appointment because you're here, so… *(He runs his finger down the list)* You must be…Emile Smythe.

WOMAN
Who?

MAN
Emile Smythe—but wait! Isn't Emile a man's name?

WOMAN
(Thinking quickly) Oh! You're pronouncing it wrong! *(She laughs)* It's all my parents' fault. They just love "original" spellings. My name isn't pronounced Emile. It's Emily. There's an accent on the E. Oh, and the E in Smythe is silent, so it's pronounced "Smith."

MAN
Ah, I see. "Emily Smith!" Very clever. And did you have a 2 p.m. appointment here at Continental Car Club to get your Prius serviced?

WOMAN
You know I did.

MAN
Great! Then we're both on the same page. Why don't we get started? *(He leads the WOMAN to a nearby table and offers her a seat. Then sits himself. He looks through the folder for her resume)*

MAN
Hmmm, I don't seem to see your resume—Oh! Here it is. Emile—I mean Emily Smith.

WOMAN
My resume? Oh! Of course, my resume. I certainly hope you find it impressive.

MAN
Oh, I do. I certainly do! Looking at this very impressive resume, I think that you have all the qualifications we need in a service representative, and this interview certainly reinforces my first impression. Apart from exhibiting a bit of a temper regarding the current state of your car, I think you are perfect for this position. As soon as we channel all that energy into enthusiasm for the Continental Car Club way of doing business, you'll be a real asset to the team.

WOMAN
So, I've got the job?

MAN
You've got the job.

WOMAN
Can I start today?

MAN
Well, that is a little fast.

WOMAN
Great! Since I'm starting today, can I get my car fixed for free today? It's the green Prius sitting dead in the parking lot with all the idiot lights flashing. I think the problem was caused by the 52-point inspection that Bill and Jeff—or was it Larry and Tony—gave it today.

MAN
I can see you're a little confused about who we have on staff. But that will straighten itself out after you've been working here awhile. And yes, all employees get vehicle maintenance and repairs for free. So if you're working here today, we'll fix your Prius for free.

WOMAN
I won't have to wait for service?

MAN
Never.

WOMAN
Or be told my appointment was given to someone else.

MAN
Nope! Can't happen.

WOMAN
And some woman on TV who looks just like me won't be able to tell me "Just call 1–800-CAR CLUB," when there's nobody around to help me?

MAN
Absolutely not!

WOMAN
Then hand me that uniform. I'm a size Medium. I can change in the Ladies' Room.

MAN
Wait! Didn't you say that your fiancé left you and took your dog. So you were going on vacation to recover?

WOMAN
Screw my boyfriend, screw the dog, and screw my vacation!

MAN
Well, we're pretty short-handed with Mike and Larry out. How about first thing in the morning?

WOMAN
How about now! My car isn't going anywhere in its present condition, so I might as well do something constructive with my time. And you did say "free repairs," didn't you, uh—*(She hesitates, looking for a name tag)* Say, you never told me your name. *(The MAN looks down. Sure enough. There's no name tag on the pocket of his blazer. He reaches into the front pocket of the blazer and looks surprised. There are multiple name tags inside. He pulls the pocket down, so that he can read the names without pulling them out…maybe his lips move. He finds one he likes, pulls it out, attaches it to his blazer, smiles and holds out his hand)*

MAN
Hi! I'm Bob, the supervisor.

WOMAN
I thought Bill was the supervisor. He even had a tag that said supervisor. Yours doesn't.

MAN
Bill's the service supervisor. I'm the personnel supervisor. But everyone who works here knows that, so there's no need for my name tag to say supervisor. See? *(As he speaks the MAN ushers the WOMAN around the counter and opens the door)*

MAN (CONT'D)
Now you just go on in there, and Emily will help you find a uniform that fits.

WOMAN
Emily?

MAN
Emily. She's the assistant personnel supervisor. You saw her on TV. *(He pushes the WOMAN through the door)* There you go. I'll be back in a few minutes to see how you are getting on. *(The WOMAN exits to the back. The MAN straightens up the counter. He plugs the phone back in. He straightens the coffee cups, sugar, and creamer. He puts The Book in the very center of the counter. Then he turns and leaves through the rear door. The television suddenly comes on. The MAN wearing his Continental Car Club jacket smiles out of the monitor)*

MAN (ON TELEVISION)
Planning a trip to a far-away spot… or just an overnighter to Grandma's house? Either way, you'll want to pack in Continental Car Club luggage. Our suitcases are lightweight, roomy, and oh so sturdy. Why I just kicked this suitcase down a flight of stairs and the fall actually rubbed away the scuffs on the luggage left from running my car over it… *(While the television plays, the WOMAN enters in a Continental Car Club T-shirt and wearing a badge that says, "Emily." The instant she sees that the television is on, she finds a switch on the back of the counter and turns it off)*

WOMAN
That's enough out of you! *(The door to outside opens and the MAN enters dressed in a tweed jacket and wearing a matching driving cap. He walks up to the counter)*

MAN
Hello! I'm here for an appointment to have my car serviced.

WOMAN
Take a number.

MAN
But I have an appointment.

WOMAN
(Obviously doing nothing) You have to take a number. It's policy.

MAN
(Looking around) Where do I get the number? *(The WOMAN notices the machine is missing, reaches under the counter and pulls the ticket machine)*

WOMAN
Right there!

MAN
But—

WOMAN
Take a number and have a seat. We'll call you when It's your turn.

MAN
But I have an appointment. For 3:30 p.m.

WOMAN
Sorry, you missed it.

MAN
That's not possible. It's 3:30 now.

WOMAN
Nope. It's not. According to the atomic clock on my computer, which is accurate to one one-hundredth of a nanosecond, it's 3:30 p.m. and nineteen seconds. You've missed your time. You'll have to wait.

MAN
Look! You're not going to refuse to service my car because I am 19 seconds late, are you?

WOMAN
Of course not. We'll service your car when it's your turn. We just won't be able to honor a 3:30 appointment because it's no longer 3:30. You'll

have to take a number and wait. *(The WOMAN types madly on the computer. The MAN pushes the button on the machine several times but gets no ticket)*

MAN
Excuse me. *(The WOMAN continues typing madly)*

MAN (CONT'D)
Excuse me, miss! *(The WOMAN continues typing madly)*

MAN (CONT'D)
Hey, you! *(The WOMAN looks up)*

WOMAN
What?

MAN
Your machine is broken. *(WOMAN quickly grabs the machine an substitutes the rack with the numbers on it)*

WOMAN
Machine? We don't have a machine. You just take a number off the hook.

MAN
I am not taking a number off the hook and waiting when there is no one else here. I expect you to honor my appointment.

WOMAN
How do I know you have an appointment? I've only got your word for it. You haven't shown me any proof of an appointment. Have you?

MAN
Proof? You want proof! There's my name. Right there. In your book! *(The MAN jabs his finger angrily on the page in the book where his name appears. The WOMAN looks, shocked)*

MAN (CONT'D)
Emile Smythe!

WOMAN
Emile Smythe? *(The lights black out*

*on the MAN and the WOMAN and
simultaneously the television pops on)*

MAN (ON TELEVISION)
Thanks for visiting the Continental Car
Club and watching Continental Car
Club TV! It's how we show you all the
ways we're making our members the
Happiest Drivers on the Planet. We'll be
back tomorrow during business hours
with more great news about all our
products and services. Be sure to watch
the next time you stop by to pick a
map, make some travel plans, buy some
luggage, or get an oil change… *(The
WOMAN appears with the MAN on
screen)*

MAN
So until then…

WOMAN
Happy driving!

MAN
Happy driving!

VITA PATRICK MORALES

I have always wanted to be a writer. When I was twelve, a very long time ago, I decided to write. That was an odd decision because I was the world's worst speller. In addition, I tended to speak in a distorted poetic meter that everyone found strange, but charming. My learning disabilities made my writing something of a curiosity, and so I stuck with it, writing on anything I could find, including napkins and paper towels. In college, at NYU, I decided to major in journalism—a kind of writing—and one through which I might actually be able to make a living. I did not last long as a journalism major because it was not the type of writing I was meant to pursue. Instead, I discovered that I had an ear for languages and I decided to major in Italian. I studied in Italy and when I returned, I took classes in Spanish as well. At this point, I was the world's worst speller in several languages.

When I was older, a year or two after my second child was born, I decided to take a writing course. I needed to get away from my husband and kids, even if only for an hour a week. The professor who taught the class was a playwright and screenwriter. He taught the course as if we all were budding dialogue builders. I wrote a script for him, and that's how I started writing plays. I was living in New York City at the time, because that's where writers lived in the 1970s. My husband and I were working-class kids from Hell's Kitchen, so I started my Master's Degree in Playwriting at Hunter College. There, I was fortunate to study with Romulus Linney. Hunter was very supportive, and I needed that because I was working nights and taking care of my kids during the day. Eventually, I was asked to join the Professional Playwrights Unit of the Puerto Rican Traveling Theatre. Later, I helped start a theater company in the basement of our church on the fabled 42nd Street, just a block from Broadway. We left New York for the wilds of Northwestern New Jersey in 1999. It was there that I met Catherine Rust, a promoter of women playwrights, and John Pietrowski, who became my mentor.

Because I speak several languages, I feel as if I'm a participant in the cultures where those languages are spoken. I am Italian-American but my husband is Cuban. He is in his seventies and I am in my late sixties. We raised our four children in a multicultural neighborhood, and the two eldest are completely bilingual. I have taught ESL, Spanish, and Italian at all levels, including at our local community colleges. My knowledge of different languages has inspired my writing and is inextricable from all that I do. I consider myself lucky to be able to continue teaching and writing, and I hope to do so for a very long time.

Esmeralda of the Pacific Vortex

AN ECOLOGICAL CAUTIONARY PLAY BY VITA PATRICK MORALES

CAST OF CHARACTERS

ESMERALDA: A seventeen year-old Peruvian girl. She has a scar from a burn on her face. She is dressed in rags.

SANTA ROSA: A very beautiful thirty-one year-old woman dressed in a light brown cassock and a traditional Indian cape. She has roses in her long, braided hair. She has a hand-carved cross around her neck.

FORESTER: A very handsome Anglo man of any race. His white, linen pants and his shirt have been torn up by the surf.

PLACE

Along the coast of Peru near the salt pits of Salinas there are two beaches, side by side. One is pristine with immaculate white sand and the other, just over a stony hill, is covered with garbage. The garbage, mostly plastics, is deposited there by the currents in the Pacific Ocean. All the countries along the Pacific Rim have contributed to this collection of waste.

CULTURAL NOTES

Santa Rosa de Lima is the patron saint of Peru and all of South America. St. Martin de Porres, also known as Papa Candela, and she were friends and neighbors. Both ministered to the sick and the poor. Mamacha de Belen is the name given to a representation of the Virgin Mary that is popular in Peru. Saint Peter's cactus (San Pedro cactus) is a powerful hallucinogenic cactus that grows all over Peru. The Spanish called it Saint Peter's cactus because it made them feel as if they were meeting St. Peter at the gates of heaven.

Sisma and terremoto = earthquake
maremoto = tsunami
los lobos (Marinos) = sea lions
El Hogar de San Francisco de Asis = an orphanage for abandoned children with disabilities

This play should be done without an intermission.

SCENE 1

(One side of the stage is strewn with detritus that has come ashore on a Peruvian beach somewhere north of Lima. The other side of the stage is a beautiful, pristine white sand beach. [it is possible to stage this with just the clean beach, a high mound of rocks, without showing the garbage on the other side.] The Pacific Ocean is where the public sits in the theater. The theater is filled with the sounds of the sea. [Nature Sounds for Babies: Relaxing Ambiance for Bedtime, 2010, Spotify])

(Lights up low. We see a seventeen-year-old girl, ESMERALDA, motionless, face-down in the sand. Her hands are bound behind her and she is tied to the remnants of an uprooted tree. The LIGHTS come up slowly as if dawn is breaking and ESMERALDA moves, but she is barely able to lift herself up)

(As ESMERALDA rises to face the audience, we see that she has a slight facial disfigurement. Her clothes are torn, dirty, and full of sand. SHE manages to free herself from the cloth that binds her to the tree)

(All speeches in the first scene are made by ESMERALDA, but many times she doesn't say much of anything. Her movements must reveal her feelings. The other sounds we hear as she rises are the sounds of coastal lands)

(A silence)

ESMERALDA

Awww. Get away from me. (Bats the flies away from her face) Stop! Go away. (She gets up and hops around, all the time batting insects away from her. She pulls her long hair over her face to protect her from the bugs)

ESMERALDA

There. I can't see you and you can't see me. Owww. (ESMERALDA swats the flies that land on her legs. She sits up and covers her legs with sand. She seems to settle down. Slowly, she moves the hair from her face, then quickly replaces it as the buzzing of the insects increases. She stays very still and the buzzing stops. She gets up and starts to climb the rocks that separate the two sides of the beach. She reaches the top and looks out over what should seem to be a great expanse. She climbs down the rocks and disappears from the view of the audience. After a few beats, the stage is filled with the sounds of the seaside. ESMERALDA returns, dragging behind her a kayak. She pushes it down the rocks to the sand below and then climbs down herself. She picks the kayak up with the bottom facing the audience and we should clearly see that the boat has a huge hole in it and is no way seaworthy)

ESMERALDA

No worries. I can use you as a bed. I can sleep in here and the bugs won't eat me alive. (She puts the kayak down and climbs into it completely prone. It fits her like a coffin. Beat. She pops up out of it and wiggles free. She then goes back over the pile of rocks, looks out, as before, and disappears to the other side. She now returns with wire mesh, as one would find in window screens. She gets back in the kayak and puts the wire mesh on top of the opening)

ESMERALDA

(From inside the boat) You can't eat me now. (Beat. ESMERALDA pops up from the kayak)

ESMERALDA

I'm hungry. (*She gets out of the kayak and climbs the rocks once again. Again, she disappears from our view. Beat. She returns with cans of food that have no labels. She throws one of these cans on the rocks, picks it up, and throws it again. When she sees it did not open, she takes it down to the water's edge, picks up a rock, and starts pounding it until it opens. She eats the contents with her fingers. When she is done, she again climbs to the top of the rocks and throws the empty can to the other side. She then comes down again and washes her hands in the water*)

ESMERALDA

(*Making the sign of the cross*) Dear Father in heaven. Forgive me, please, for eating without your blessing. I was so hungry. I thank you now for the gift you left for me in the garbage on the beach. It was very tasty. Amen. When you made the earth move, we all thought we would die. I tried to save the baby but Joaquin took him from me and gave him to his wife. When he tied me to the tree, he said you would protect me and I should protect la casa. Please forgive me, but la casa went into the sea, just as I did. I'm sorry I could not save it. Please don't let Joaquin be mad at me. Please keep the baby safe. (*She makes the sign of the cross and climbs into the kayak. The lights fade to black. End of scene*)

SCENE 2

(*We hear the sounds of the OCEAN coming up on the shore. The LIGHTS come up slowly and after a BEAT, ESMERALDA rises from the kayak. She stretches and tries to get out of the kayak but it tips over and she ends up with her face in the sand. With some difficulty, she flips the kayak over and is able to get out*)

(*We see the SHADOW OF AN ALBATROSS fly across the stage and*

ESMERALDA looks up to watch it as its huge wingspan blocks out the sun. From the shadow, we can see that THE BIRD has landed on the other side of the rocks. ESMERALDA runs to the top of the rocks and searches for it on the other side)

ESMERALDA

Don't eat that! You stupid bird! You want to die? (*ESMERALDA runs down the other side and disappears from our view. We hear the whimpering of a BIRD and the flapping of many huge wings.*)

ESMERALDA

(*Offstage*) Stop! Stop! I'm trying to help your baby. (*She screams*) Stop! Look. He's free. Don't eat that. (*We hear the FLAPPING OF WINGS once again and the SQUAWKS of the sea birds. ESMERALDA appears again on top of the rocks. This time she appears with a full sixpack of Japanese beer. She scampers down to a rock that serves her as a seat and she unpacks the beer, one can at a time. She lines them up in a cool place in the rocks.*)

ESMERALDA

Dear Holy Father, I will not forget this time to thank you for this gift you left for me in the garbage. Thank you and if you could please let me know one way or another what it is I am about to drink, I would be forever thankful. Amen. (*She opens a can and drinks all of the beer it contains in one breath. Then she burps like a sailor. She opens another and chugs that as well. The SHADOW OF THE ALBATROSS flies across the stage and we can hear the sounds of SEABIRDS as they populate the sky. ESMERALDA is tipsy and slides off the rocks on her backside. She lands feet-first in the sand but falls to her knees because she is so intoxicated. She finds her way back to the kayak and climbs in. Blackout. End of scene*)

SCENE 3

*(The LIGHTS become bright and
the sounds of the birds become almost
deafening. ESMERALDA rises once
again, out of the kayak. SHE starts
screaming at the birds)*

ESMERALDA

Get out of here! Stop! Stop! Go over to
the other side. I don't have anything to
give you. *(She rushes up the side of the
rocks and peers over to the other side. She
rushes down the other side and disappears
from our view. When she returns she is
carrying two large eggs. She puts the eggs
down on the rocks and goes to get twigs
to make a nest. She uses what's left of
the branches on the log to which she had
been tied. She builds a nest at the top of
the rocks and puts the eggs in it. Then she
clamors to the other side. This time she
returns with three damaged religious icons,
either household pictures or statues of St.
Martin de Porres and La Mamacha de
Belen. She is now wearing unmatched and
very large athletic shoes with no laces. She
carries a plastic shopping bag that is filled
with many other plastic shopping bags.
She awkwardly climbs down the rocks
with all her treasures. She sets the saints
in nooks in the rocks and steps back to
admire them. They are broken and worn,
obviously unceremoniously discarded. St.
Martin has no head and Mamacha is
covered in seaweed)*

ESMERALDA (CONT'D)

Mamacha. Look at what has happened
to you. When I saw you last Christmas
you were dressed like Shakira, only
with more clothes. Who threw you into
the garbage? You must forgive them,
you know that. I'll fix you up and you
can live here with me. And you Papa
Candelo, you are a stinking mess, and
what happened to your head? Your little
girlfriend, Santa Rosa, will not like it if
we don't clean you up.

*(ENTER SANTA ROSA from the
other side of the rocks. She sits atop the
hill and looks down at ESMERALDA.
SANTA ROSA, thirty-one, is beautiful.
She is dressed in a brown cassock with a
traditional Peruvian cape)*

SANTA ROSA

I am not his girlfriend.

ESMERALDA

(Still tipsy) Who are you and where did
you come from?

SANTA ROSA

I'm Rose of Lima. I come from the
garbage pile, over there. You took my
friends so I came to take them back.

ESMERALDA

To the garbage pile?

SANTA ROSA

To our final resting place. Yes, to the
garbage pile. The people no longer need
us, so they throw us in the garbage.
Thanks to the Pacific Vortex, we end up
here. There are many of us on the other
side of the rocks. After all, what do you
do with an old, beat up Madonna?

ESMERALDA

I don't know. I guess you bury her, like
everybody else.

SANTA ROSA

In the real world, my head is yet to be
buried. It's sitting in some gaudy church
somewhere. I guess being driven by the
Vortex to a beach in the desert is not
quite so bad. Him too. His head still
makes the rounds like Juana la Loca.

ESMERALDA

Where is it?

SANTA ROSA

Somewhere in the garbage. You'll never
find it.

ESMERALDA
Papa Candelo. He is my closest friend. He loves me even though my face looks like mud and is scarred from the time my father tried to burn down our house.

SANTA ROSA
You, my precious girl, are the most beautiful star in the sky. The most beautiful planet of our universe.

ESMERALDA
Our universe is a desert that falls into the sea, surrounded by garbage.

SANTA ROSA
Our universe is you and me and so be it. Nice shoes.

ESMERALDA
I keep cutting myself on the rocks.

SANTA ROSA
What will you do with all those plastic bags?

ESMERALDA
I'm going to braid them together and then make something. I don't know. A rug, a blanket. Something to keep the bugs away from me. Look. Behind you. It's water. *(ESMERALDA goes to drink the water trickling down from the rocks)*

SANTA ROSA
Don't drink that.

ESMERALDA
Why? I'm dying of thirst.

SANTA ROSA
Drink the beer.

ESMERALDA
Really?

SANTA ROSA
Drink the beer and then go over to the other side and bring back as many empty water bottles as you can find. *(ESMERALDA goes to grab the bags)*

SANTA ROSA (CONT'D)
No. There are thousands of those over there. Fill as many as you can with clear water bottles and make sure they have tops. Go.

(EXIT ESMERALDA over the top of the rocks to the other side. ROSA begins to tidy up the area and when she finishes, she starts weaving together the plastic bags. She sings as she weaves)

(ENTER ESMERALDA with several plastic bags filled with water bottles. She calls to ROSA from the top of the rocks)

ESMERALDA
Look. I think I have about fifty.

SANTA ROSA
Good. Now let's get some of the water from the spring.

ESMERALDA
Hardly anything's coming out.

SANTA ROSA
Wait. *(ROSA takes a few rocks out of the pile and water starts to flow more freely)*

ESMERALDA
Was that a miracle?

SANTA ROSA
No. Common sense.

ESMERALDA
Sometimes common sense is a miracle.

SANTA ROSA
You're right. Now fill the bottles up but not all the way. Put the caps on tight. You'll see.

ESMERALDA
What are you doing with my bags?

SANTA ROSA
Braiding them, as you said. See.

ESMERALDA
Nice.

SANTA ROSA

When you are finished filling the bottles, we'll take them over to the salt ponds and leave them there in the sun.

ESMERALDA

And then you'll make a miracle.

SANTA ROSA

And then the sun will heat them hopefully enough to kill any microbes. That way, you'll have water to drink. It might take all day, but the sun is very strong over there. A full day in the summer's sun with no shade will heat the water enough to purify it. If we have to, we'll stay there overnight and come back tomorrow.

ESMERALDA

So you don't do miracles?

SANTA ROSA

Every day is a miracle. Every breath, every plant, every person. Everything has a purpose and all of us together make the miracle of creation.

ESMERALDA

What happened to my baby?

SANTA ROSA

You should ask Mamacha. She watches over babies. I never had children.

ESMERALDA

Mamacha won't answer me, I'm sure. She looks very disgusted that someone would throw her into the garbage.

SANTA ROSA

Maybe she wasn't thrown into the garbage, maybe she came here like you in the maremoto. Complete towns were washed into the sea. You are lucky to end up here. We are very close to Salinas. There are people who come here to work in the salt ponds. Eventually, one of them will see you and will save you.

ESMERALDA

Joaquin said that he was tying me to the tree to save me.

SANTA ROSA

You're alive.

ESMERALDA

I'm alive, but barely.

SANTA ROSA

Do you want to go home?

ESMERALDA

No.

SANTA ROSA

You want to live on the edges of the Gyre?

ESMERALDA

What's that?

SANTA ROSA

It's where we are.

ESMERALDA

This is the Gyre?

SANTA ROSA

It is the edge of the Gyre. Some people call it the Vortex. The currents of the Vortex spin in the sea like vegetables in a soup and eventually they carry whatever is floating in the water to beaches like that one.

ESMERALDA

Then I belong here. It's fits my life.

SANTA ROSA

Why?

ESMERALDA

Why not? I'm garbage too.

SANTA ROSA

No human is garbage.

ESMERALDA

You don't think so?

SANTA ROSA

Don't say such things.

ESMERALDA

We are all garbage, especially if we are unloved.

SANTA ROSA

You are never unloved if you love yourself.

ESMERALDA

My father sold me to Joaquin when I was eleven. I was supposed to help his wife keep his house. Instead, Joaquin made babies with me.

SANTA ROSA

Babies?

ESMERALDA

Well, if the earth and sea hadn't revolted, I would have made more babies for him and his fat wife.

SANTA ROSA

Don't speak unkindly.

ESMERALDA

I can say worse but I won't because you are a saint and Papa Candelo and Mamacha will crumble.

SANTA ROSA

One way or another, time will punish Joaquin. You think you were cast aside, but really you've been saved.

ESMERALDA

No, I ended up where I belong. With the garbage.

SANTA ROSA

If that's so, then you must make this a place where you will thrive.

ESMERALDA

You'll stay here with me, won't you?

SANTA ROSA

Well, I for one, am very happy you saved me from the Gyre. Who knows where I'd have ended up if not here with you. For all my knowledge of herbs and healing, I am now just a forgotten saint in a pile of garbage.

ESMERALDA

No. Everybody loves you. Little girls want to be just like you. They want to dress up like little nuns and walk around with roses on their heads.

SANTA ROSA

I know. They are so precious.

ESMERALDA

Do you think I can become a saint too? Saint Esmeralda…

SANTA ROSA

Saint Esmeralda of the Pacific Vortex. Why not? Even beaches filled with garbage need a patron saint. I will put in a good word for you. Now are you finished with those bottles?

ESMERALDA

Yes.

SANTA ROSA

Well then, we need to walk. It will be a long, tiring walk and at times you'll want to just sit down and die. But you won't. You'll keep going and we'll leave the bottles in the sun and bring them back tomorrow before dark. Then, at least you'll have some water.

ESMERALDA

I don't know.

SANTA ROSA

You don't have to know. I'm here now and I'm telling you what we have to do. Maybe if we're lucky, we'll find people who can take you home.

ESMERALDA

I still don't know.

SANTA ROSA

Come on. (*The two WOMEN go over the hill of rocks and disappear from view. We hear the sounds of the sea pierced by the squawking of birds and the sound of the arid wind. Fade to black. End of scene*)

SCENE 4

(We can hear the sounds of the sea and beach. It is nighttime but there is a full moon so a beautiful light fills the scene. A MAN with a dark complexion climbs to the top of the rocks. He is dirty and unshaven but he has sandals on so he can walk comfortably. This is FORESTER. He jumps down from the top of the rocks onto the beach below. He starts examining Esmeralda's collection of items. He finds the two eggs and he eats them. He finds the beer and downs a can in noisy gulps. He goes over to the statues and begins to address the saints)

FORESTER
Mamacha, how lovely you look this fine summer's night. And you, my brother, Papa Candelo, do you think you can find me another beer? At least tell me who was here. *(The bugs start to torment him. He goes to the kayak and climbs in. Beat)*

ESMERALDA
(Offstage) I am so tired and my feet are still burning.

(She appears at the top of the rocks carrying her bundles of water. She kicks off the sneakers and hurries to the edge of the sea. She coos with relief as we hear the sound of WAVES gently coming to shore. SANTA ROSA appears at the top of the rocks and watches. She says nothing)

ESMERALDA
Aren't you coming? The water is warm but cool all the same.

SANTA ROSA
I'll stay up here tonight and watch over you. Don't be afraid if you can't see me. I'll be around somewhere. Just call.

ESMERALDA
I'm hungry.

SANTA ROSA
I know.

ESMERALDA
I'm tired too.

SANTA ROSA
I'll try to find you something to eat.

ESMERALDA
In the garbage?

SANTA ROSA
Of course. There are treasures in the garbage.

ESMERALDA
All right.

(EXIT SANTA ROSA. ESMERALDA goes to the kayak and turns it over. She kicks it)

FORESTER
What in the devil's name?

ESMERALDA
There's a devil in there. Mamacha. Help me. Santa Rosa!

FORESTER
Get me out. Turn me over.

ESMERALDA
No. Go back to where you came from. Santa Rosa, come quick, I've trapped a devil in my kayak.

FORESTER
I am not a devil. Let me out.

ESMERALDA
No!

FORESTER
Let me out. I'm going to suffocate in here.

ESMERALDA
Then suffocate. What do I care?

FORESTER
I don't care if you care. I care. Now turn me over.

ESMERALDA
No! Not until Santa Rosa comes back.

FORESTER
Santa Rosa? You like saints, do you?

ESMERALDA
She's here. I saved her from the garbage. Papa Candela is here too but he's missing his head.

FORESTER
I have his head. Let me out and I'll give it to you.

ESMERALDA
Why did you take his head?

FORESTER
I'm Papa Candela. Now let me out.

ESMERALDA
Are you Santa Rosa's boyfriend?

FORESTER
Yes.

ESMERALDA
Then I'm not letting you out.

FORESTER
Why?

ESMERALDA
She said you were not her boyfriend, so you must be the devil.

FORESTER
I am Papa Candela. Let me out. I can help you. Please. Just turn the boat over. (*ESMERALDA tries to turn the kayak over but she's having difficulty*)

FORESTER
Push a little harder and I'll roll from the inside.

ESMERALDA
It's hard.

FORESTER
I know. I'll help. I'll count to three and then we'll move together. One, two, three. (*On three, ESMERALDA pushes the kayak and it starts to roll, but it rolls over 360 degrees and ends up in a similar position*)

ESMERALDA
I can't.

FORESTER
Si' se puede. Try again. Uno, dos, tres. (*She manages to roll it over and stop it before it turns again*)

ESMERALDA
You don't look like Papa Candela.

FORESTER
Because I have sand all over my face. Help me up. (*She extends her hand and helps him sit up. She wipes the sand from his face with her hands. SANTA ROSA appears at the top of the rocks but says nothing*)

ESMERALDA
Look, it's Papa Candela.

(*SANTA ROSA shakes her head no and walks away, out of sight*)

ESMERALDA
You're not Papa Candela.

FORESTER
No, I'm not. But maybe I can be of more help to you than he can.

ESMERALDA
You're going to hurt me.

FORESTER
No. I am not. How did you get here?

ESMERALDA
(*Motioning to what is left of the tree*) I was tied to that tree and it carried me here in the maremoto. I know about men.

FORESTER
What's that supposed to mean?

ESMERALDA
I'm not a little girl. I know about men and what they do to women when they want them.

FORESTER
Look, you're just a kid. I don't want you,

not now, not ever. All I want is some
water and someone who can get me out
of here. How old are you anyway?

ESMERALDA
Seventeen. I have water.

FORESTER
May I have some?

ESMERALDA
Do you promise not to hurt me?

FORESTER
I promise.

(ESMERALDA goes to get some bottles
of water. She gives him one)

FORESTER
Thank you. Gracias.

ESMERALDA
Who are you?

FORESTER
I'm not Papa Candela.

ESMERALDA
No. You are not. Are you Captain America?

FORESTER
What?

ESMERALDA
You're not from around here.

FORESTER
No one is from around here. This is hell.

ESMERALDA
So you are the devil.

FORESTER
No. I was out there fishing when the
water started foaming like it was the
end of the world. I got out just in time
but my Jeep was washed off the road
and the last I saw it, it was floating in
the water. I need to find someone who
can get me out of here. That won't be
you, I'm sure.

ESMERALDA
No.

FORESTER
No. Of course not.

ESMERALDA
Maybe the saints can help you.

FORESTER
Have you been eating St. Peter's cactus,
because you, my little friend, are talking
like a loquita.

ESMERALDA
I saved the saints from the garbage and
they—well, at least Santa Rosa—have
been helping me. Maybe it was Papa
Candela who sent you here.

FORESTER
Why would he send me here?

ESMERALDA
To help me get home.

FORESTER
Right.

ESMERALDA
Of course.

FORESTER
Well, he has to help me so I can help
you, right?

SANTA ROSA
(From on top of the rocks) Tell him to go
to the garbage.

ESMERALDA
Go to the garbage.

FORESTER
What?

SANTA ROSA
Take him. I'll watch over you, don't
worry.

ESMERALDA
Maybe we can find your Jeepe
(Pronounced Yeep-y) in the garbage.

FORESTER
Right.

ESMERALDA
No. Really.

SANTA ROSA
He has never seen the garbage. He's a stranger here.

ESMERALDA
I'll show you. Come. We have to climb over the rocks, but the saints will watch over us.

FORESTER
You are one strange little girl.

ESMERALDA
Woman. I have a baby.

FORESTER
Where?

ESMERALDA
Joaquin took him. But he's mine.

FORESTER
Is that your man?

ESMERALDA
No. I take care of his house. His wife can't have babies so he made one with me and gave it to her. Then in the sisma, he tied me to the tree and he and his wife took the baby.

FORESTER
Where did they go?

ESMERALDA
I don't know. *(Beat)* The sun is low in the sky and it's cool now. Let's go to the garbage. You'll see. There are miracles in the garbage.

FORESTER
Is that where you got that beer?

ESMERALDA
Yes.

FORESTER
Well, then, I guess there are miracles in the garbage. Let's go.

(They start up the rocks. SANTA ROSA helps ESMERALDA to the top by giving her a hand)

(ESMERALDA extends her hand to Forester and they disappear over the rocks. End of scene)

SCENE 5
(FORESTER appears at the top of the rocks with a large fish he is carrying by its gills and a bag filled with garbage. He sets the bag down and covers his eyes as he looks out on the horizon. The sun is setting)

FORESTER
Do you need help?

ESMERALDA
No. I'm coming. *(Beat)* I think the wind is changing.

(SANTA ROSA comes up behind ESMERALDA)

SANTA ROSA
It will rain tonight. You must set up containers to catch the water.

FORESTER
It's going to rain.

SANTA ROSA
Tell him to make fire.

ESMERALDA
Make fire.

FORESTER
Well, I'll try. You may have to ask your saints for help. Everything is damp. Bring me some rocks, not big ones.

(ESMERALDA gathers rocks from the hill and brings them to FORESTER)

FORESTER
Build a pit. You know how to do that?

ESMERALDA
Yes.

SANTA ROSA
I'll help you. *(SANTA ROSA tosses stones down the hill. It should look as if they tumbled down on their own. ESMERALDA digs a shallow hole with her hands and lines it with the stones. FORESTER is hunched over a small pile of dried seaweed and sticks. He is trying to start a fire with two rocks)*

ESMERALDA
Is it fire yet?

SANTA ROSA
It's going to take a little while, but he'll do it.

ESMERALDA
Do you need help?

FORESTER
No. Go make yourself useful somewhere else.

ESMERALDA
You found a knife on the beach.

FORESTER
Yes.

ESMERALDA
Give it to me and I'll clean the fish.

FORESTER
It's in the bag. *(ESMERALDA goes to his bag and starts to remove the items inside. She holds them up and examines them. The first is a wrench)*

ESMERALDA
What is this?

FORESTER
A wrench.

ESMERALDA
What good will this do for us?

FORESTER
Us? Not much. I can use it to fix the Jeep.

ESMERALDA
I think your Jeepe will not go very far.

FORESTER
At least it's there.

ESMERALDA
If you fix it, you will go back to where you are from.

FORESTER
I will go back to Lima. That's where I work.

SANTA ROSA
Ask him what he needs to make the Jeep go.

ESMERALDA
What else do you need to make it go?

FORESTER
Gas, probably. I don't know what else. The keys are gone.

SANTA ROSA
We can look for the keys.

ESMERALDA
Can we look for the keys?

FORESTER
Sure, we can look. There are probably 1,000 square tons of garbage on that beach. Do you really think we will find a bunch of car keys?

(ESMERALDA looks mournfully at SANTA ROSA who just shakes her head and looks out over the garbage)

FORESTER (CONT'D)
But don't worry. If we can find someone who can charge the battery, we'll be able to start it without the key. Any fisherman with a motor boat will be able to help us.

ESMERALDA
The Jeepe is heavy.

FORESTER
Yes. Yes, it is. Thanks for helping me push it onto the beach. We are lucky it didn't get carried out to sea by the currents.

ESMERALDA
That was fun. But hard.

FORESTER
You did good, kid. Real good.

ESMERALDA
Woman. I'm a real woman. I'm not a kid.

FORESTER
Yeah. I understand.

(SMOKE starts to rise from the pile of debris. FORESTER starts puffing on it)

FORESTER (CONT'D)
Come here. Can you do this?

(SANTA ROSA motions for her to go over to him and to kneel down by the fire)

ESMERALDA
I can do it.

FORESTER
Good. I'm going to look for some dry wood. Don't let it go out.

(FORESTER clamors up the hill and disappears. SANTA ROSA goes to where Esmeralda is kneeling and kneels down next to her. She takes a kerchief from her pocket and tears it into threads. The two of them feed the little fire until it grows)

SANTA ROSA
Tonight you will eat well.

ESMERALDA
And tomorrow?

SANTA ROSA
Tomorrow it will rain and you will not be able to do much of anything.

ESMERALDA
And the next day?

SANTA ROSA
And the next day will bring what it brings. We will deal with it when it comes.

(FORESTER reappears with seaweed and driftwood. SANTA ROSA recedes into the shadows and the sunlight fades. ESMERALDA helps FORESTER with the logs)

ESMERALDA
I'll clean the fish.

FORESTER
Are you sure? I can do it.

ESMERALDA
I can do it.

(She starts to clean the fish with the knife. When FORESTER is satisfied with the fire, He leans back and goes through the contents of his bag)

FORESTER
So you can cook.

ESMERALDA
I am a very good cook. I was famous for my pan de comote.

SANTA ROSA
Put out the pots for water. The rain is coming.

ESMERALDA
The rain is coming. Put out the pots.

FORESTER
You are getting a little bossy.

SANTA ROSA
It has to be done.

ESMERALDA
It has to be done.

FORESTER
Okay, boss.

(ESMERALDA puts the fish on the stones in the fire. FORESTER pulls out of his

bag a small collection of cans and pots.
He puts them on the rocks to catch water)

FORESTER
We will have to protect the fire from
the rain.

SANTA ROSA
After you cook the fish, move the fire
over there under the rocks.

ESMERALDA
We will move it. First, we eat.
(BIRD NOISES increase as their forms
cast shadows from overhead)

SANTA ROSA
The birds came for your cooking.

FORESTER
Even the birds want some of your fish. I
think it's ready.

ESMERALDA
We need plates. There, in my bag.

(FORESTER goes through her bag and
finds two broken dishes. He rinses them
with water from the water bottles and sets
them on the rocks)

FORESTER
Madame. Right this way to your table.

ESMERALDA
Here. Give me your plate.

(She takes the knife and serves the fish,
first to him and then to herself. They eat
in silence, smiling at each other)

FORESTER
This is good.

ESMERALDA
Do you have a wife?

FORESTER
Why do you ask?

ESMERALDA
I want to know.

SANTA ROSA
Be careful.

ESMERALDA
Do you?

FORESTER
No. No, I do not have a wife.

ESMERALDA
Why not?

FORESTER
You eat and then you get nosy?

ESMERALDA
I want to know.

FORESTER
Because I don't want one.

ESMERALDA
Why?

FORESTER
Because.

ESMERALDA
That is not a reason. Don't you like
women?

FORESTER
That's very personal.

ESMERALDA
Then why don't you have a wife?

FORESTER
Because I don't want one.

ESMERALDA
All men want a wife.

FORESTER
No. Men want women, not necessarily
a wife.

SANTA ROSA
You are leading him somewhere he
doesn't want to go. I won't warn you
again. Be very careful.

ESMERALDA
Your Jeepe is your wife.

FORESTER
No. My job is my wife.

ESMERALDA
Where?

FORESTER
All over.

ESMERALDA
You can't take a wife with you?

FORESTER
I won't take a wife with me.

ESMERALDA
Who takes care of you?

FORESTER
I take care of myself.

ESMERALDA
A woman would take better care of you.

FORESTER
What are you getting at?

SANTA ROSA
There is no place for me here.

(*SANTA ROSA EXITS. It starts to rain and ESMERALDA and FORESTER quickly pull logs out of the fire and take them under an overhang in the rocks. The space is small so they must huddle together*)

ESMERALDA
Owww.

FORESTER
You burned yourself.

ESMERALDA
I did.

(*FORESTER takes her hand and holds it out in the rain*)

FORESTER
Let the rain fall on it.

(*She pulls away from him. He recedes deep into their dry space*)

FORESTER
Tomorrow, I'll work on the Jeep.

ESMERALDA
It will rain all day tomorrow.

FORESTER
That's okay. I can work on it in the rain. You want to get out of here, don't you?

ESMERALDA
Why?

FORESTER
You're joking with me.

ESMERALDA
No. Why?

FORESTER
You want to stay here?

ESMERALDA
Yes.

FORESTER
In the garbage?

ESMERALDA
Why not? I am garbage.

FORESTER
What?

ESMERALDA
I am, you know. No one wants me.

FORESTER
You won't ever find out if you stay here, will you?

ESMERALDA
I will never find out for certain that no one wants me?

FORESTER
Or that someone does want you.

ESMERALDA
No. I'll stay.

FORESTER
We'll both be staying if I can't fix the Jeep.

ESMERALDA
Fishermen will come. Not right away because everything on Earth is upside down but when the world is right again, they will come. They will help you.

FORESTER
Until then, you and I will just live off garbage and whatever I can catch. I'm not so sure we can pull it off. I'm not used to chaos.

ESMERALDA
It will be all right. You'll see. The saints will take care of us.

FORESTER
Maybe.

ESMERALDA
The saints stay the same. They hold the world together, you'll see. We are here, but we are alive.

FORESTER
For now.

ESMERALDA
Yes, you're right. *(Beat)*

FORESTER
So when the fishermen come and I fix the Jeep, you and I will go back together.

ESMERALDA
Where?

FORESTER
Lima. That's where my apartment is.

ESMERALDA
I don't know Lima.

FORESTER
It's big, it's dirty, well, not all of it. You can get a job there. You can work in someone's house. If not, I'll take you to the Hogar. You can work for them.

ESMERALDA
I can work in your house for you.

FORESTER
No. I didn't say that.

ESMERALDA
I can clean and cook and if you want a baby of your own, I can make you one.

FORESTER
You're serious.

ESMERALDA
I am.

FORESTER
No, that's not going to happen.

ESMERALDA
Then I won't go back with you.

FORESTER
Come here.

(ESMERALDA looks around for SANTA ROSA, but she is nowhere to be found)

ESMERALDA
No.

FORESTER
Come here. You're getting wet.

ESMERALDA
I will not.

FORESTER
I won't touch you. Come here.

(The sounds of the WAVES hitting the beach increase in force and volume. She looks out towards the sea. The BIRDS start to screech above her and she looks up at the sky. He gets up and goes over to her)

ESMERALDA
You said you wouldn't touch me.

FORESTER
I just want to help you. I want to protect you. Come here, please.

(She allows him to gently take her hand and guide her to the sheltering rock)

ESMERALDA
No.

FORESTER
I don't want anything from you.

ESMERALDA
Why won't you take me home with you?

FORESTER
Why do you want to come home with me?

ESMERALDA
I have nowhere to go.

FORESTER
I'll take you to the Hogar, there are lots of children there.

ESMERALDA
I know the Hogar. Parents leave their damaged children there. Joaquin said he would take me to the Hogar too if I didn't obey him. I don't want to go there. I'm not a child anymore. I know how to work and I know how to take care of myself.

FORESTER
I'll take you back to your house.

ESMERALDA
I have no house. I have no home. I don't want to live with Joaquin and his wife.

FORESTER
I'll take you back to your baby.

ESMERALDA
He's not my baby. He belongs to them.

FORESTER
He'll always be your baby.

ESMERALDA
No. He won't.

FORESTER
What's his name?

ESMERALDA
Somac.

FORESTER
Somac. Beautiful.

ESMERALDA
How do you know?

FORESTER
I speak Quechua. I was a teacher once. I speak several languages.

ESMERALDA
Teach me.

FORESTER
I'm not a teacher anymore. Now I work for an agency of a group of nations that are trying to solve problems.

ESMERALDA
Teach me anyway. Teach me what the world is like.

FORESTER
No. You teach me. I want to know what you know.

ESMERALDA
I never went to school. I don't know anything.

FORESTER
I want to know what you learned without going to school.

ESMERALDA
I learned about the world and how it's divided into the earth and the sea. The sky is divided into the light and the dark; people are male and female, father and mother, husband and wife. The world is divided into pairs. If we cannot find our pair, we are doomed.

FORESTER
That's sad.

ESMERALDA
That's sad for you.

FORESTER
Why?

ESMERALDA
Because you do not want to find your other self.

FORESTER
But I do.

ESMERALDA
No. That's why you have no wife. You don't want to be complete.

FORESTER
You believe that a person—a man, needs another person—a woman to be complete?

ESMERALDA
People need people to be safe.

FORESTER
Maybe so. Do you feel safe with me?

ESMERALDA
I don't know.

FORESTER
I'm not going to do anything to you. I'm not going to rape you, if that's what you think.

ESMERALDA
I didn't say that.

FORESTER
If you weren't so innocent, so young and so sad, I would make love to you, but not here. Understand that. We'll get out of here and soon. Just believe me, all right?

(ESMERALDA *turns her back to him and cries*)

FORESTER (CONT'D)
Please don't cry. *(Beat)*

ESMERALDA
The pairs are made by fate: Joaquin and his wife. His wife and my baby. I am left to the side to be discarded like garbage.

I have no one to complete me and you have no one to complete you. If you won't let me stay with you, I'll stay here.

FORESTER
So that's what you want?

ESMERALDA
Of all the people who could be brought here to this place by the movements of the sea and the earth, why you and why me?

FORESTER
I don't believe in fate. *(Beat)* What's your name? You have a name, right?

ESMERALDA
Esmeralda.

FORESTER
Esmeralda of the Pacific Vortex. Nice.

ESMERALDA
So I do belong here.

FORESTER
I'm not saying that. I just like the sound of it. You know, like Saint Rose of Lima. You can be Saint Esmeralda of the Pacific Vortex.

ESMERALDA
That's not funny.

FORESTER
Yes. Yes, it is. *(He laughs)*

ESMERALDA
No. Stop laughing at me.

FORESTER
All right. I won't laugh at you anymore.

ESMERALDA
Is that why I'm here?

FORESTER
I think it's less complicated than that.

ESMERALDA
What's your name?

FORESTER
I'm Papa Candela.

ESMERALDA
No, you're not. You don't want to tell me your name.

FORESTER
Why do you need to know?

ESMERALDA
You know my name.

FORESTER
Esmeralda. It is a very beautiful name. I like it very much.

ESMERALDA
And you don't like your name?

FORESTER
Call me Captain America.

ESMERALDA
I will.

FORESTER
Good. I like that.

ESMERALDA
Why do you think you ended up here with me?

FORESTER
I ended up here with you because I wanted to do some fishing and the waves picked up my little boat, turned it upside down and deposited me on the beach. No car, no cell phone, no wallet, nothing. It was all washed out to sea.

ESMERALDA
You don't think you ended up here so you could meet me and take me home?

FORESTER
No. I don't.

ESMERALDA
Everything happens for a reason.

FORESTER
Everything happens because of the rules of physics.

ESMERALDA
Why didn't I drown in the sea? There is some reason. There is always a reason that things happen to us. You'll see.

FORESTER
No. Things just happen. They happen because of the stars and the currents. The push and pull of the forces that control nature. They happen because something makes contact with something else.

ESMERALDA
The earth moves. The sea moves. The sky darkens. All these things happen for a reason.

FORESTER
Yes, but those reasons are due to science. The Earth moves because of instability in *(He looks at her, changing his mind)*. You're right. The Earth moves and the sea swells up and creates giant waves that carry people away.

ESMERALDA
That's why we're here.

FORESTER
I guess you're right.

ESMERALDA
You are here and I am here and we make a pair.

(He takes her hand and brings her closer to him. He is squatting but she remains upright)

ESMERALDA (CONT'D)
You said you wouldn't touch me.

FORESTER
Come here. Stop talking.

ESMERALDA
I'm cold.

FORESTER
Come here and I'll keep you warm. Come.

ESMERALDA
I will not go back with you unless I
have a place to go.

FORESTER
We'll talk about it tomorrow. Now, I'm
tired and we need to sleep.

(He snuggles back into the rocks and curls
up to sleep. She stays awake. ENTER
SANTA ROSA carrying driftwood for
the fire)

ESMERALDA
Where did you go?

SANTA ROSA
Don't worry. I didn't go far.

ESMERALDA
I won't go back with him.

SANTA ROSA
You can't stay here.

ESMERALDA
He won't take me to his home and
I will not go back to Joaquin.

SANTA ROSA
We will talk about it when things change.

ESMERALDA
What things?

SANTA ROSA
When the world is put right again.
Not now. Now you will go to sleep. Go.

(ESMERALDA gets into the kayak.
Lights fade to black, the rain continues)

SCENE 6

(The LIGHTS come up slowly and
the overall effect is gray. SANTA
ROSA is sitting on top of the rocks and
ESMERALDA is moving around the
camp, tidying up. We hear the sounds of
the waves hitting the shoreline and light
RAIN. The WATER seems to calm down
slowly and the BIRDS start to hover
overhead, making their presence known to
the actors and the audience)

ESMERALDA
These birds.

SANTA ROSA
They are upset.

ESMERALDA
Why?

SANTA ROSA
Listen.

(Off in the distance, but getting closer, we
can hear the sound of SEA MAMMALS
as they beach themselves on the other side
of the rocks)

ESMERALDA
What is that?

SANTA ROSA
Look.

(ESMERALDA climbs to the top of
the rocks)

ESMERALDA
How many are there?

SANTA ROSA
Several hundred. Maybe more. Maybe
close to a thousand.

ESMERALDA
Los lobos.

SANTA ROSA
Sea lions, whales, and dolphins. So sad
and terrifying.

ESMERALDA
That sound.

SANTA ROSA
They're crying.

ESMERALDA
What's wrong with them?

SANTA ROSA
The world has been turned upside down.

ESMERALDA
We have to do something?

SANTA ROSA
What would you do?

ESMERALDA
We'll call the man. He'll know.

SANTA ROSA
I'm a saint and I don't know what to do.

ESMERALDA
Why? Why don't you know?

SANTA ROSA
Because only the Earth knows what she wants. And she will win.

ESMERALDA
What do you mean?

SANTA ROSA
No matter what we do to hurt her, she will win. She will punish us.

(FORESTER rushes over the rocks)

FORESTER
Do you hear that?

ESMERALDA
Yes. Look.

FORESTER
There are hundreds of them.

ESMERALDA
Hundreds, maybe more, maybe a thousand.

FORESTER
What the hell is going on? The whole world is falling apart.

ESMERALDA
You should know.

FORESTER
I should know. Why?

ESMERALDA
Aren't you a teacher? What can we do to save them?

FORESTER
Nothing. They're too big and we are just two people. There's nothing we can do.

ESMERALDA
Los lobos y sus bebes.

FORESTER
Most of them probably died days ago in the earthquake and tsunami. Their bodies are just washing up on shore now. The others are crying because they are sick or injured.

ESMERALDA
The smell is unbearable.

FORESTER
We have to get out of here. There is no way we can stay here now. Once they start to rot, the contamination will kill us.

ESMERALDA
Did you fix the Jeepe?

FORESTER
The Jeep? I think so, but the battery's dead, ruined, and we still need gas.

ESMERALDA
Maybe Santa Rosa will help us.

FORESTER
All right, loquita, you just pray on that. Meanwhile, we should pack as much water as we can carry and we should head out of here.

ESMERALDA
Where are we going to go?

FORESTER
We'll follow the road and hope we meet someone on their way here. If not, we'll camp and continue in the morning. Now get ready.

ESMERALDA
I told you. I'm not going.

FORESTER
Don't be a stupid girl.

ESMERALDA
I'm a woman.

FORESTER
Then think like a woman and not a superstitious little peasant girl. We have to be smart here. You know, usar las cabezas. We have to save ourselves because no one is going to come looking for us.

ESMERALDA
I'm not going back. I have nothing and no one to go back to. I don't care if I die like one of the lobos or one of the birds who strangles on fishing line and plastic rings. I will not go back there to live like garbage. I will live here and this will be my home.

FORESTER
I'm not going to argue with you. Stay here. I'll come back. But when I come back you are going with me, do you understand? Stay away from the salt pits and don't go anywhere near those dead animals. Move to the other side of the garbage beach, close to the Jeep. Keep an eye on it. If any fishermen come, tell them to give you some gas. Or ask them to get you out of here. Don't wait for me. Go with them. Promise me.

SANTA ROSA
Say yes.

ESMERALDA
Yes.

FORESTER
Promise?

ESMERALDA
I said yes.

FORESTER
And talk like you have some sense. Don't mention your collection of saints. Do you understand me?

(She nods. He grabs what he can find and the knife. He ties a kerchief around this mouth and nose and EXITS up over the rocks)

SANTA ROSA
You must do as he says.

ESMERALDA
Will he come back?

SANTA ROSA
We'll see.

ESMERALDA
He'll come back for his Jeepe.

SANTA ROSA
We'll see. Get the water and whatever else you need and let's go.

(ESMERALDA gathers a few items and the two women EXIT up and over the rocks. Blackout)

SCENE 7
(ESMERALDA stands on top of the rocks with the sun behind her. She is frightened and angry. At times she cries and other times she screams)

ESMERALDA
Where am I? Where is this place? Why don't I have anywhere to go? Why is there no home for me except here in this garbage? Where is the man? He said he would come back for me.

(SANTA ROSA stands in the shadows at a distance)

ESMERALDA (CONT'D)
I'm hungry.

SANTA ROSA
Eat this.

ESMERALDA
What is it?

SANTA ROSA
Saint Peter's cactus.

ESMERALDA
It will make me sick.

SANTA ROSA
It will take away your pain.

ESMERALDA

It will make me want to fly off the rocks. Is that what you want?

SANTA ROSA

Eat it. It will take away your hunger. Eat it.

(ESMERALDA takes the chunks of cactus from SANTA ROSA's hands. ESMERALDA hesitates)

SANTA ROSA (CONT'D)

Eat it. I'll stay here with you.

(ESMERALDA savagely eats the cactus. The juice colors her lips and hands and she smears it all over her body)

SANTA ROSA (CONT'D)

You should sit. Drink some water.

ESMERALDA

The water is almost gone.

SANTA ROSA

Drink.

(ESMERALDA drinks voraciously and then cries hysterically. She hallucinates)

ESMERALDA

He said he'd come for me.

SANTA ROSA

You told him not to come.

ESMERALDA

I didn't mean it. I don't want to die here in the garbage like the birds and the lobos.

SANTA ROSA

But that's not what you said.

ESMERALDA

I thought you would help me.

SANTA ROSA

I have.

ESMERALDA

Make him come back. Tell him I was foolish. A foolish little girl.

SANTA ROSA

But you told him you were a woman.

ESMERALDA

I'm not. I have no soul left.

SANTA ROSA

You will always have a soul. Your body will disintegrate, but your soul will go on.

ESMERALDA

Like you? Wandering around in the garbage?

SANTA ROSA

I came to help you but if you want me to go, I will.

ESMERALDA

Go. Go and find him. Tell him to come back for me.

SANTA ROSA

The roads were ruined in the earthquake. There were landslides and the bridges were washed away. He had to walk around the mountains into the desert.

ESMERALDA

Then he's dead.

SANTA ROSA

I didn't say that.

ESMERALDA

Help him.

SANTA ROSA

You should have told him to come back for you. You could have given him a reason to return.

ESMERALDA

Go away. Go away. I don't need your help anymore. He needs you.

SANTA ROSA

He doesn't want my help.

ESMERALDA

Oh, no. I see his soul. He's dead.

SANTA ROSA
That's just the cactus. It will make you
see things.

ESMERALDA
He's in the water. He's in my kayak
but the kayak has a hole in it and he's
sinking. Help him.

SANTA ROSA
You are seeing things that don't exist.

ESMERALDA
I see you.

SANTA ROSA
I exist.

ESMERALDA
Then he exists.

SANTA ROSA
We will wait for him. If he comes, you
have to promise to go with him.

ESMERALDA
Yes, yes, I promise.

SANTA ROSA
If he doesn't come back, your body will
die and your soul will come with me.
Do you see your soul?

ESMERALDA
No.

SANTA ROSA
Yes, you do. Look at your hands.

ESMERALDA
No. No. No.

SANTA ROSA
Look at your feet. Hold your head in
your hands. Can you feel it?

ESMERALDA
No. Help me.

SANTA ROSA
Sit down. Wait until this passes. If it
does, you will live another day and if it
doesn't, you'll come with me and we'll
leave this place.

*(ESMERALDA cries herself to sleep.
SANTA ROSA watches over her as the
lights fade to darkness)*

SCENE 8
*(We hear the birds screeching as
if someone has disturbed them.
ESMERALDA is still asleep on the
rocks. The screeching of the birds wakes
her. Slowly, she moves one body part at
a time, examining each hand as if she
is making sure she still exists. SANTA
ROSA stands off in the distance)*

SANTA ROSA
Get up now.

ESMERALDA
I can't.

SANTA ROSA
You can. Get up.

ESMERALDA
My body is dead.

SANTA ROSA
No. Your body lives.

ESMERALDA
Then my soul is dead.

SANTA ROSA
No. It is not.

*(The BIRDS and the OCEAN create a
deafening din)*

ESMERALDA
What is happening?

SANTA ROSA
Look.

*(ESMERALDA stands and looks out in
the direction of the sea. She tries to block
out the sun with her hands. It takes a
few beats for her to recognize what she is
looking at)*

ESMERALDA
It's a boat.

SANTA ROSA
It is.

ESMERALDA
(Ecstatic) It's a boat. Thank you. Thank you. It's coming here. It's coming to the beach. It's him. He came back for me.

SANTA ROSA
And if it's not him?

ESMERALDA
But it is. He said he was coming for me.

SANTA ROSA
He told you that if fishermen should come, you were to go with them. He did not want you to wait for him.

ESMERALDA
Why are you being so mean to me?

SANTA ROSA
I'm not. I'm just reminding you what he said. You should not wait for him to come back.

ESMERALDA
Go away. I won't listen to you anymore. Go away.

(ESMERALDA clamors to the top of the rocks and runs down out of sight. SANTA ROSA watches her. Then turns away. The birds screech and we see their shadows as they fly over the rocks. Long beat. SANTA ROSA starts to collect the garbage from the camp. She picks up the cans and bottles and puts them in plastic bags. She is about to collect the saints on the rocks when FORESTER enters from the opposite side of the stage wearing a backpack and carrying a metal gas container. He is out of breath and turns to address the saints on the rocks. SANTA ROSA speaks but FORESTER does not hear or see her)

FORESTER
Esmeralda? *(Beat, as he looks around)* So my little saints where did she go? You're

still here, so she must be around here somewhere. Can you at least give me a clue?

(BIRDS squawk. He looks out to sea but sees nothing. Finally, He climbs the rocks. He looks for her but doesn't see her)

FORESTER (CONT'D)
Okay, now this isn't funny anymore. Where is she?

(He kicks over the kayak half expecting to find her lifeless body inside)

FORESTER (CONT'D)
Esmeralda! Answer me.

(SANTA ROSA remains motionless watching him)

FORESTER (CONT'D)
Where is she? Esmeralda! Esmeralda! I came back for you. Where are you? Answer me! Answer me, you foolish, foolish little girl.

SANTA ROSA
She was waiting for you.

FORESTER
Esmeralda! Where the hell did you go?

(He kicks the ashes of the dead fire and turns to look out to sea again)

SANTA ROSA
She was almost dead. You took too long.

FORESTER
Even if you were dead, I thought I would find you.

SANTA ROSA
You told her to go with the fishermen if they should come. One came. He was young and simple, like her. He needs a wife and she needs a home. They complete each other.

FORESTER
I should have taken you with me.

SANTA ROSA
No. It all happened for a reason, just as she said. Take your gas and your car and go back to your life but don't forget what you've seen here. Don't forget the little saint of the Pacific Vortex. Don't forget this waste, this ugliness and death. Do something when and if you can.

(The BIRDS start their screeching once again. He looks up at them and then climbs the rocks. He looks out to sea shading his eyes with his hands)

FORESTER
Oye! Hey out there. Hey. Have you seen a girl? A woman—on the beach? Hey. Wait! Esmeralda! I told you I would come back.

(He stands at the top of the rocks, resigned that she has left. He kneels on one knee and throws pebbles towards the sea)

SANTA ROSA
It's all right to let her go.

FORESTER
Esmeralda!

(He receives no answer and gives up. He stands up, still looking out to sea)

FORESTER (CONT'D)
I hope your saints go with you, little girl. I hope they are enough to protect you.

SANTA ROSA
But you don't believe in miracles.

(She looks at him like a mother looking at a naughty child)

FORESTER
I wish I had that kind of faith. After this, I don't see anything except the end of the world.

SANTA ROSA
You live on a ball of blue glass that circles around a ball of fire and between the two is a smaller piece of stone that controls

all the oceans of the world, and you still don't believe in saints and miracles, do you? Who is the foolish one?

FORESTER
Pray for me, Saint Esmeralda of the Pacific Gyre.

SANTA ROSA
Would you like me to do a miracle for you…even though you don't believe in anything, not even your own soul? I will help you find peace. There.

(She takes a set of car keys out of the pocket of her tunic and throws them on the beach near the water's edge. He continues looking out to sea as the BIRDS screech louder and louder. The SHADOW of a large bird flies above him and lands by the keys)

FORESTER
Well look at that. I don't believe it.

(He scrambles down the rocks and gets down on one knee. He picks up the keys and looks up to the sky)

FORESTER (CONT'D)
Well, well, well. My keys. Impossible. Impossible and incredible. Ha.

(He grabs the gas tank and the backpack and runs up the rocks. His shape becomes a silhouette against the sky that is now almost black with the shadows of the screeching BIRDS flying above his head. He descends the rocks and disappears to the other side. The BIRDS screech even louder and then suddenly stop)

(SANTA ROSA looks up at the sky and starts to collect the saints on the rocks. She puts them in plastic bags and EXITS over the rocks toward the garbage. Blackout)

DANA SCHWARTZ

I started my theater career as an actress, and when I first had kids I decided to spend my time in other ways. I started directing, which was fun, but I missed the creative outlet that acting had always provided me. One night, after a particualarly brutal PTA meeting, I came home and wrote a script about a mom who was secretly a black-ops spy. I cracked myself up, submitted it to a theater company I knew, it cracked THEM up, and I've been writing ever since. I love writing about strong, real, interesting women of all ages, but I especially love my middle -aged Gen X badasses. Even when they don't quite realize yet that they are badasses.

DANA SCHWARTZ is a writer, director, actress working in her adopted home of Los Angeles for the past couple of decades. Her award-winning play *Early Birds* had its world premiere in 2019, and is also being produced at the Curtis Theater. Her play *@Playaz* was a 2019 O'Neill Finalist. *Perspective* enjoyed its World Premiere at *THEATER AT THE MUSEUM* at LACMA. *The PTA* and *That Time She Proposed* were in several productions of the internationally renowned Car Plays, notably at REDcat LA, Disney Hall, Segerstrom Arts and Costa Mesa. *Undead* will be produced at Theater Roulette in Cleveland in 2021, and her newest play *O My Days* is published by Montag Press. She is co-creator, writer and appearing in the new Zoom series *Isolation Inn*, currently airing online. As a director, Dana has worked with many theaters including Moving Arts, Sacred Fools, Offending Shadows, Actors Theater NoHo, Victory, and Lyric. As an actor, she trained in New York at AADA and HB Studios, and has appeared in productions all over the world. She is the co-creator and Producer of Theater at the Museum at LACMA, and is currently the Producer of the MADlab New Play Development Program at Moving Arts, where she is also a company member.

The Poppy Party

A PLAY BY DANA SCHWARTZ

CAST OF CHARACTERS

Enid: A lovely hostess
Sharon: SUPER into it
Anita: The great friend
Marion: The dorky one
Dorothy: The cool one
Emerson: THAT guy

SETTING

Enid's beautiful home

SCENE 1

(ENID, on her phone)

ENID

Sunday. No, like, happy hour. Five? Bloodys, of course. Please. Perfect. Okay, no, it will be fun! Yep. Okay, bye.

(Phone rings. ANITA, on her phone)

ANITA

What time? Should I bring anything, what are you making? I'll bring those things we had at the thing! I can't believe you are doing this! Oh, gotta go—

(A different ring tone. MARION, on her phone)

MARION

Five? I guess we can go to the early church service…No, I'm not…I'm NOT. It's fine. What can I bring? Oh, hmm. Well, it will be tricky to try and do anything hot if we…I'm NOT! Let me just check with Benji. I'm NOT!

(A different ring tone. DOROTHY, on her phone)

DOROTHY

Fuck no. No. No fucking way. Bloodys? *(Sigh)* Fine.

SCENE 2

(ENID'S living room. Clean. Lovely. Everything in its place. Several dining room chairs have been brought in for extra seating. A groovy bar cart is ready to go for Bloody Marys with all the fixings. ENID is surveying the room, final prep. SHARON enters from the kitchen)

SHARON
Looks terrific, Enid!

ENID
Oh, well, thank you, Sharon. I just— *(Flicks some invisible dust off a chair)* Yes, well, thank you. I like having people over; it's always fun for me.

SHARON
And it WILL be fun! That's what I love most about a Poppy Party—everyone always has so much FUN!

ENID
Yes, you mentioned that earlier.

SHARON
And when I met you at Dee's Poppy Party, I just KNEW you would throw a lovely one for your group!

ENID
After three of my mother's mimosas I'll agree to almost anything.

SHARON
That's what I heard!

ENID
What?

SHARON
So what time are your guests scheduled to arrive, 5:00?

ENID
Yes.

SHARON
Is that five with drinks or should I plan to start right at five?

ENID
Oh, well, I suppose—five with drinks?

SHARON
Wonderful.

ENID
Can you run me through the—

SHARON
Of course! A Perfect Poppy Party has three phases. Phase One—meet, greet, and treats! You have taken care of that part. Do you need any mixer game ideas or are you all set?

ENID
Uh, you know, I mean, we all know—

SHARON
No problemo, I have a bag of mixers I'll just grab from my Prius when we're done. Phase Two—Poppy Presentation! That's when I do my thing, a small self-narrated fashion show featuring the famous Poppy Convertible Dress, a display of additional items and accessories, and the big brochure available for browsing. That will only take me eight minutes to set up, and eighteen to present, so I'll plan to start that around 5:32.

ENID
Wow, you really have this down to a science, don't you?

SHARON
I'll tell you a secret. This is my hundredth Poppy Party! It's kind of a big deal.

ENID
Wow.

SHARON
And then we move to Phase Three— the Ups. Pay Up, Clean Up, and Close Up! I like to pop the champagne just before the Ups, help keep the party going, do you know what I mean?

ENID
I didn't get any...I mean, we had talked about Bloody—

SHARON
No champagne? At all? Huh. Well, that's a first! How funny, after ninety-nine of these bad boys you don't think anything can surprise you and then BAM! Well, not to worry, not to worry at all, I have a few emergency bottles in my Prius. We'll just subtract them from your hostess cut.

ENID
Great.

SHARON
Great! So you finish up in here and I'll just pop out to the Prius and we can get started. *(SHARON exits)*

ENID
Holy fuck.

(Doorbell rings)

ENID (CONT'D)
It's open!

(ANITA enters carrying a pink bakery box, a huge purse, and a bottle of vodka)

ANITA
Am I late?!

ENID
Right on time!

ANITA
Take something!

(ENID takes the vodka, ANITA exits to the kitchen with the box)

ANITA (CONT'D) (Offstage)
I can't believe you're doing this! It's so retro!

ENID
It's going to be fun. Want a drink?

ANITA (Offstage)
Uh, yeah.

(ENID goes to the bar cart with the Vodka and starts making two very fancy Bloody Marys)

ENID
Heads-up, wait until you meet the Poppy Lady.

(ANITA enters)

ANITA
Oh no, is she here already??

ENID
She "popped out to her Prius" to get more stuff. Just wait.

ANITA
This is hilarious! Who else is coming?

ENID
Dorothy and Marion. I asked some people from work too. I'm supposed to have at least twelve, counting me.

ANITA
Fun!

ENID
It's so old-school. I think it will be cute. And the clothes aren't terrible.

(Doorbell rings)

ANITA
It's open!

(MARION and DOROTHY enter, each with a bottle of Vodka. MARION's is small. DOROTHY's is from Costco)

MARION
Technically, I am not late because I picked up Dorothy.

DOROTHY
Thank you. Again.

MARION
And Benji wants to know if he is allowed to come in and have some food or if this is a hen party.

ANITA
A what??

MARION
A hen party. Just ladies.

ENID
Wow, Marion, I don't think that's a
thing people say anymore—

MARION
No, a HEN party!

DOROTHY
You saying it over and over is not
making it less misogynistic.
(Pause)

MARION
So, he shouldn't come in?

(DOROTHY goes to door and yells out)

DOROTHY
It's a hen party, Benji, bye!

ANITA
He's from another planet.

MARION
Oh, hush, he's just sometimes a bit—

ENID
Can I get you two a drink?

MARION
Just a tiny little one for me, please.

(ENID goes back to the bar cart for two
more fancy drinks)

DOROTHY
So listen, real quick, I quit my job
yesterday.

ENID
What??

DOROTHY
It's done. People cried. Not me, but
people. And it's over.

ANITA
Well, good for you. I'm proud of you,
it's about time.

MARION
What are you going to do?

DOROTHY
I don't know. I've been unemployed for
like eighteen hours.

MARION
You don't have a plan?!

ENID
Marion.

DOROTHY
I don't want to talk about it anymore. I
only wanted to tell you all that it's done.
Okay, moving on, what the hell are we
doing?

ANITA
It's a Poppy Party!

ENID
Clothes. And necklaces. Stuff like that.

MARION
Also, it's a pyramid scheme.

ANITA
Here we go.

MARION
What? It is! Benji says things like this
are pyramid schemes to make money.
Like Tupperware.

DOROTHY
He's such a douche—

ENID
Stop. Seriously. This is going to be a nice
evening and the two of you will act like
grown ups. Marion, if you don't want
to buy a statement necklace, don't buy a
statement necklace. I don't care. Dorothy,
we are absolutely going to talk more
about your job later, so be ready. Anita,
we need snacks. Stat. All of you, there
are about to be a ton of people here and
I need you to get it together, okay?

(SHARON enters breathlessly, carrying a
large tote. She seems slightly off her game)

SHARON
I'm sorry that took so long. Ooh, those stairs are a bear! Hello! Hello, everyone, welcome to the Poppy Party! You're a tad early I think but no problem! You're beautiful! I see you have drinks, lovely, thank you, Enid. Enid, may I speak to you privately for one moment?

(SHARON leads ENID a few steps away but does not lower her volume in any way)

SHARON (CONT'D)
I have horrifying news. I am completely out of champagne. I'm so, so sorry.

ENID
It's not a big deal! We have plenty of vodka, as usual, and—

SHARON
My daughter Britney and her friends took my Prius out last night, and I am now sickened to learn that they drank my—well, anyway, I hope you don't feel like this has in any way ruined your—Or that my personal failing has caused—

ENID
Seriously, Sharon, it's not a problem. I'll just call one of the other guests and see if she can bring some with her!

SHARON
Oh my goodness, that would be perfect. Thank you!

ENID
So. Kids, right? I remember sneaking some champagne when I was younger, don't you? How old is your daughter?

SHARON
Twenty-seven.

ENID
Oh.

SHARON
She lives in my garage.

ENID
Huh.

SHARON
With her children.

ENID
Okay! Well, I better make those phone calls, so—

SHARON
Fantastic, I'll get set up!

(ENID grabs her phone and exits to the kitchen. SHARON begins to set up her display. This should happen quickly, seamlessly, almost magically, things fold out and pop up and spread out in a precise and practiced way. This ritual soothes her and by the time it is done she is right as rain)

SHARON (CONT'D)
Ahhhh. That's good. Yeah! Okay, ladies, thank you for your patience. Welcome to the Poppy Party!

(She pauses, waits for applause. Receives none. Carries on gamely)

SHARON (CONT'D)
Great! So I'll do the formal speech when the rest of the guests arrive, but in the meantime, please feel free to start browsing. There will be a short fashion presentation in just a bit so if you want to see anything on just let me know.

(ENID enters and SHARON heads her way)

SHARON (CONT'D)
(To the others) Please help yourself to food and libations! *(To ENID)* Good news, I hope?

ENID
Well, actually. Uh, that is—So it looks like a few people aren't going to make it.

SHARON
(Fake brightly) Oh. How few?

ENID
Four?

SHARON
(Darkly) Oh. (Brightening) Well, that's
not too terrible, I guess. (SHARON
feels her phone buzz, she takes a peek)
Please excuse me for a quick second!
(on phone as she exits) Britney??

DOROTHY
Who bailed?

ENID
A bunch of those bitches from work.
I always go to their stupid crap, but the
minute they have to come to this side of
town they freak out! God, I hate that job.

DOROTHY
You know what you should do?

ENID
I'm not going to quit.

DOROTHY
Telling you, it changed my life.

ENID
It's been eighteen hours!

DOROTHY
And look, I'm a completely new person.

(A knock at the door)

DOROTHY (CONT'D)
Ooh, new blood!

(DOROTHY goes to open the door.
She sees EMERSON, a young man,
in full-on hipster regalia and man-bag,
standing at the door)

DOROTHY (CONT'D)
Hi.

EMERSON
Hi. (Pause)

DOROTHY
What's up?

EMERSON
I'm Emerson.

DOROTHY
Okay.

EMERSON
I'm here for the party?

DOROTHY
Why?

EMERSON
What?

DOROTHY
Wait. (She calls to ENID) Enid?
Someone is here. For the party.

ENID
God, Dorothy, let her in!

DOROTHY
Him.

ENID
Huh?

DOROTHY
God, Dorothy, let HIM in.

ENID
What?

(ENID goes to the door)

ENID (CONT'D)
Emerson! Hi! What are you doing here?

EMERSON
I'm here for the party.

ENID
The party.

EMERSON
There was a flyer in the break room.
Poppy Party. Food, drinks, clothes.
At Enid's. I like all those things.

ENID
But I—they're mostly—You're
welcome, of course. But you should
know it's, like, ladies.

EMERSON
I like ladies too.

ENID
Ladies' clothes.

EMERSON
I have no problem with that.

ENID
You know what, sure! Okay. Great. The more the merrier. Everyone? This is Emerson. From work. He's here for the party.

DOROTHY
Nice to meet you.

ANITA
Can I get you a drink?

EMERSON
Sure! Whatever you're having.

ANITA
Okay!

EMERSON
I love your house! I didn't realize anyone lived on this side of town.

ENID
It's, like, twenty-five minutes from work.

EMERSON
I'm glad I made it before the cement thing.

MARION
Cement thing?

EMERSON
Oh, do you not get cell reception over here?

MARION
What are you talking about?

EMERSON
A truck flipped over on the freeway. Dumped wet cement across all six lanes. It's a mess!

ENID
Fuck.

ANITA
(To ENID) Don't panic. I'm sure they're coming. There are 500 ways to get here.

ENID
No one is coming.

DOROTHY
Wayz it from your work and see what it says.

EMERSON
(Holding up his phone) It says "don't even bother."

(ENID starts to answer, exits instead)

SCENE 3
(Outside patio. SHARON is on her phone)

SHARON
—because it's not very ladylike. No, you listen, Britney, I can NOT leave this Poppy and come get you! For the love of god, honey, I've literally done one hundred of these, you have to know what I—No. No. Absolutely—no. Don't you dare. No!

(ENID enters. SHARON senses someone behind her. Pretending she doesn't, she continues)

SHARON (CONT'D)
And that's what one would say in that situation. Gotta go, sweetheart, okay, bye! *(She hangs up)* Enid! Hello, I didn't see you there. Everything all right? The rest of the group arrive okay? *(ENID lights a joint)* Oh my! I'll just pretend like I don't see a thing!

ENID
We have another—guest. Emerson.

SHARON
The rest are late?

ENID
Uh. Late. Yes. And also…

SHARON
Also what?

ENID
Also possibly not coming.

SHARON
I'm sorry, what?

ENID
I guess there was an accident on the freeway. A cement truck flipped over.

SHARON
So. It's just you four and the new gal.

ENID
Yes. And also.

SHARON
Also what?

ENID
Emerson is not a gal.

SHARON
Hmm?

ENID
He's a male. A guy. A man.

SHARON
You said her name was Emerson.

ENID
Yes.

SHARON
Ohh. A millennial?

ENID
For sure.

SHARON
That's okay then, he'll buy.

ENID
Really?

SHARON
They like the belts. They think they're ironic.

ENID
Great!

(SHARON sighs and motions for the joint. ENID passes it SHARON takes one hit)

SHARON
It doesn't matter anyway. This Poppy was doomed from the start.

ENID
What??

SHARON
Yes. Sorry. Doomed. Your mom referred you, which means she's either trying to get back at you for something, or trying to run your life. Either way, bad. There's no champagne. Bad. You picked a Sunday, so your crowd either has no church or no one to brunch with. Sad bad. And it's my hundredth. That's unknown territory. Rarified Air, as they say. No one besides the founder has done over one hundred Poppys. I have become a legend. That's not conceited or anything, it's true. I am legendary. On the website. I'm trending!

ENID
That's great. Right?

SHARON
Apparently, not so much.

(EMERSON enters)

EMERSON
What's happening out here?

ENID
Have you ever thrown a party and no one came?

EMERSON
I came.

ENID
Yes. Yes, you did.

(They have a silent moment)

SHARON
Okay! We're going to carry right on with this party, so if you two will excuse me, I'll see you inside in just a bit! *(SHARON exits)*

ENID
Why are you here?

EMERSON
Why not?

ENID
You have nothing better to do on a Sunday afternoon than come to some work lady's party?

EMERSON
You know you're not some work lady.

ENID
Don't be stupid.

EMERSON
You know how I feel about you.

ENID
You're insane.

EMERSON
Remember Alan's retirement? "I'll stop the world and melt with you"—

ENID
Drunk karaoke.

EMERSON
Was it?

ENID
Wasn't it?

(EMERSON gets very close to her, and takes the joint)

EMERSON
You don't scare me.

ENID
I'm old enough to be your mother.

EMERSON
Not even close.

ENID
Your older sister, then.

EMERSON
I'm an only child.

ENID
I thought you were with Trina.

EMERSON
I have no feelings for Trina.

ENID
I do. I hate her.

EMERSON
No, you don't!

ENID
You don't know what I hate.

EMERSON
You're smart. You're funny. You're good at your job. It's incredibly hot.

ENID
I have to go back in.

EMERSON
You're so beautiful.

ENID
Stop saying that!

EMERSON
Can't help it.

ENID
Try harder, please.

EMERSON
Now you sound like Bob.

ENID
Ugh. He's a horrible boss.

EMERSON
That should be your job.

ENID
Probably.

EMERSON
Everyone thinks so.

ENID
Well. I'm going back in. The Poppy must go on, all that.

EMERSON
I'm going to keep trying Enid. Until you tell me no. Okay?

(Pause. ENID takes EMERSON'S hand and they exit)

SCENE 4

(Bedroom. ANITA, MARION, and DOROTHY are trying on the Poppy Convertible Dress. They each have one in a different color. They are trying to make the straps do what they are supposed to do. They are failing. They are also a few Bloody Marys in)

DOROTHY
I'm going to strangle myself with this thing!

ANITA
You're doing it wrong!

DOROTHY
Fuck you!

MARION
Wait, I think I'm trapped.

ANITA
Here, I'll—

DOROTHY
Just put that thing—

MARION
That tickles!

ANITA
Your boob is out again.

MARION
No, it's not!

DOROTHY
Your OTHER boob—

ANITA
Okay, okay. Time out!

MARION
Can I put my clothes back on now?

DOROTHY
No.

ANITA
Just wear the stupid dress.

MARION
I AM wearing the—

DOROTHY
Drink break. *(She sits down and pulls the small vodka bottle out and takes a sip)*

MARION
You stole that.

DOROTHY
I moved it. From there to here.

ANITA
Pass it over.
(She takes a sip and hands it to MARION)

MARION
No, thank you. Benji likes for me to stop at two. I've already had two, so—

DOROTHY
Oh, well, if DADDY says stop!

MARION
Don't be gross.

ANITA
Marion, don't you ever worry about the example you're setting for the boys?

MARION
I'm a good example!

DOROTHY
You're showing them they should find a woman who has no balls.

MARION
That's not fair!

ANITA
You know they told Hailey to "suck it" the last time she babysat. That's why she won't watch them anymore.

MARION
My boys??

DOROTHY
They're punks. Sorry. But they are.

ANITA
They're still little! They aren't punks. Yet.

MARION
Yet? They're fine! They're boys. Boys will be—

DOROTHY
Don't fucking say it.

MARION
Well, it's true.

ANITA
Is it, though?

MARION
What do you mean?

ANITA
It's kind of—not okay. A lot not okay actually.

DOROTHY
And Benji is not helping you out here at all.

MARION
Twins are hard.

DOROTHY
The twins are awful. I'm sorry, but I love you and someone has to say it.

MARION
Anita?!

ANITA
They're—a handful.

MARION
Boys will be—

DOROTHY
I'm not fucking kidding. Don't.

MARION
You're mean.

DOROTHY
I hate when you're a dishrag. "Boys will be boys" is not a valid excuse for shitty behavior.

MARION
They're boys!

DOROTHY
They don't have to be ASSHOLES!

MARION
Stop YELLING AT ME!

ANITA
She's not—

MARION
SHUT UP! Both of you SHUT UP! You have NO IDEA what's it like. NO IDEA. They are like a little gang. They speak their own language. They have their own rules. They play these games I don't even understand. And my house smells like pee ALL THE TIME! Do you know I can go for DAYS without someone making eye contact with me? Sometimes, I'll "forget" to make their breakfast just to see if they'll come look for me. But they don't! They sit in their underwear and play video games and don't even notice if I'm there or not. Unless I'm not. Then they SCREAM! MOM? MOM? MOOOOOOOOOOOOOM??? You and Enid have no kids. Anita has Hailey. Who's perfect. And QUIET! I have a sister! I have no idea what boys do. Or are supposed to do. Or WHY! Why do they do these things? I don't get it! And Benji, who has two brothers, and IS a boy, just sits there on his computer and never looks up and laughs at me when I ask! I'm a maid. Who cooks. And drives. And gives blowjobs.

DOROTHY
I'm sorry, honey. Can't you just—

MARION
NO. I can't "just." I hate that so much.
"Can't you just" people think they're
being so helpful. "Can't you just limit
their screen time?" "Can't you just
provide healthy alternatives?" "Can't
you just come up with a schedule?"
Can't you just FUCK OFF?! I can't just.
I can't. It's hard and I have no help and
I'm doing my best.

ANITA
You should talk to your husband!

MARION
Can't I just?

ANITA
Oh, shit.

MARION
I said the F-word.

ANITA
Yes, you did.

DOROTHY
And blowjob. I'm so proud of you.

MARION
It felt good.

DOROTHY
I bet!

ANITA
I'll make you a deal. You tell me when
you want my advice. Otherwise I'll
listen, and say "you are doing exactly
the right thing."

MARION
That would be great.

DOROTHY
Me too.

MARION
Not you. I want you to keep telling me
what I don't want to hear. It's good for me.

DOROTHY
Okay. You should stop all blowjobs until
he helps out.

ANITA
That.

MARION
Now that is good advice! Give me that
bottle. (She takes a big sip)

MARION (CONT'D)
Okay, so. Let's talk about Dorothy's job now.

DOROTHY
Ugh.

ANITA
What happened?

DOROTHY
They wanted to promote me.

ANITA
Again?

DOROTHY
I know! Look, this is not a big deal.
It was supposed to be temporary. It's
not like I need the money. After Sam
died, I needed a distraction. You were
there! You know. They needed help, I'm
fantastic at what I do, and I couldn't
be in our home office all by myself. I
ignored their pretentious dart boards
and stand up desks as long as I could.
I'm done. I'm good. Next.

MARION
What did they say?

DOROTHY
One of them really did cry.

ANITA
Which one?

DOROTHY
I don't know, all those nerds look alike.

MARION
I think you're full of it.

DOROTHY
Wow.

MARION
I do. I think you're going to miss them.

DOROTHY
Maybe. But I miss Sam more. And she would want me to move on. And she would be right. As always. So there you go. Onward and forward, as my mother used to say.

ANITA
Sam also would have known how to work these stupid dresses.

DOROTHY
And looked beautiful in them.

MARION
Oh. She was so beautiful.

ANITA
I miss her too.

MARION
Me too.

DOROTHY
She loved you guys.

MARION
You're so lucky you're gay.

DOROTHY
The fuck?

MARION
No, I know it's, whatever, challenging. But the thought of living with another woman, just—gardening. Watching shows where nothing explodes. It sounds so lovely.

ANITA
Hailey thinks she's gay.

MARION
Lucky!

ANITA
Marion!

DOROTHY
What? When did this happen?!

ANITA
Two weeks ago. She sat us down, made us tea. Did a powerpoint. It was beautiful. I'm so scared for her.

DOROTHY
Why didn't you tell me!

ANITA
Because then it would be real.

MARION
Yeah.

DOROTHY
I hope you didn't cry in front of her.

ANITA
Of course I did! I'm a crier. It's not a bad thing.

MARION
Which?

ANITA
Neither! Gay or crier! Right?

DOROTHY
Of course.

ANITA
I want her to talk to you, please.

DOROTHY
I'll text her the minute I find my phone.

ANITA
God, what did your mother do when you told her? Was she cool?

(DOROTHY snorts)

ANITA (CONT'D)
See, I can't do that. I want to be cool. For her. Hailey is so cool. She is. She's confident and strong and so easy about it all. Like she's always been. Shit, she's twelve and she has it all together! I have NO idea where she gets that. I'm soggy ball of emotion, and Mike is an inappropriate laugher, as you all know.

DOROTHY
He's my favorite.

ANITA
I'm so terrified that her life is going to
be harder than it needs to be. But she's
fearless.

MARION
That was definitely not me at twelve,
that's for sure. It's not even me now.

DOROTHY
Me neither. Different world I guess.

ANITA
She said being gay was really just more
of an adjective now. She said it's because
of people like you and Sam, by the way.

DOROTHY
Okay, now she's my favorite.

MARION
I think it's the internets.

ANITA
Oh, god.

MARION
There's so much information now. And
little groups. For everything. It's great,
really.

DOROTHY
It is great, really!

MARION
Did you tell Enid?

ANITA
Not yet. She's been distracted.

MARION
If that Emerson worked at my work I'd
be distracted too!

DOROTHY
Right?

ANITA
Wait, is he the guy from the office
party?!

DOROTHY
Oh my god. Is he Drunk Karaoke?

ANITA
He's got to be!

MARION
Oh, yes! Oh, yay! Oh no, we have to get
back out there!

(*They pass around the bottle and run off,
trying to keep all the boobs where they
belong*)

SCENE 5
(*Living Room. SHARON is wearing the
hell out of a Poppy Convertible Dress.
EMERSON is sitting with the Catalog
on his lap, listening to her pitch*)

SHARON
—as well as a wide range of accessories
and enhancements for those special
occasions when one wants to look their
very best!

EMERSON
Awesome!

SHARON
I'm sorry, I'm not sure where the rest of the—

EMERSON
No, this is great, keep going!

SHARON
You seem like a very nice young man.

EMERSON
Thanks!

SHARON
Are you?

EMERSON
Well, yeah. Usually. I think so.

SHARON
Is that unusual?

EMERSON
I hope not.

SHARON
I've just about given up trying to understand your generation.

EMERSON
Talk to me. What's wrong?

SHARON
I'm very confused by the Millennials. I just don't get it. Sometimes you all seem very, what? Organized? Able to work together? With your Ubers and your Kickstarters and whatnot. Hive mind. It's really something. Socially relevant. It's great. But then, you have no drive, no work ethic, and you think everything should be handed to you on a plate. Entitled. It just makes not one lick of sense.

EMERSON
You're stereotyping of course, but I know what you're saying. My dad says we have the luxury of bad manners.

SHARON
That's it! exactly!

EMERSON
We are the trophy generation. Huge prizes for middling success. It's pathetic.

SHARON
We wanted you to feel good about yourselves.

EMERSON
Indeed.

SHARON
No trophies for you?

EMERSON
Tons. But my parents were Peace Corps Volunteers. So, yes, I got a Tae Kwon Do trophy for splitting a piece of balsa wood in half, but I also learned how to install a drip irrigation system in a third-world village. I'm well-rounded and well-adjusted. And I was never allowed to have bad manners.

SHARON
I see. A rare bird.
(ENID enters wearing most of a Poppy Convertible Dress, and her tank top.)

SHARON (CONT'D)
Oh, Enid, there you are, aren't you lovely! And you almost have it on correctly!

ENID
This is insane! I can't even figure out which part is the top!

EMERSON
You look amazing.

ENID
Shut up.

SHARON
Come over here, Enid, I'll demonstrate the—

(ANITA, MARION, and DOROTHY come crashing in, wearing their Poppys. With their vodka)

ANITA
Sorry! Sorry, here we are!

ENID
Where have you been??

MARION
Putting on our Poppys!

(DOROTHY starts to laugh)

MARION (CONT'D)
No, stop it! Look, here we are in our dress things. Keep going!

DOROTHY
Yes! Fashion show time!

ANITA
Ooh, fashion show!

SHARON
I see you took some of the refreshments with you.

ANITA
Yes, we're super refreshed.

DOROTHY
(*In a loud whisper*) I think Enid did it wrong.

MARION
(*In a loud whisper*) Go help her!

ANITA
(*In a loud whisper*) Seriously, Marion, fix your boob!

SHARON
I will help Enid with her dress. Come here, Enid.

DOROTHY
No I'll help her!
(*DOROTHY and SHARON have a tug of war with Enid, who is not amused*)

ENID
No! No, I'm sorry, but this is just not going to work out. I'll make sure you get your cut or whatever, but this dress is ugly and horrible and I look like an idiot and no one can wear this thing!

SHARON
Calm down. I understand. The stress of hosting a Poppy can sometimes be a little—

ENID
I'm a great host! I love hosting! I hate this. This was a horrible idea. I got drunk at my mother's party and she got all mad and did this to me as a punishment! And this dress is NOT MY STYLE!

SHARON
The Poppy Convertible Dress looks good on everybody because it works on Every Body!

ENID
Stop quoting your horrible catalog at me!

DOROTHY
That's awesome.

MARION
SHH!

ANITA
I'm pretty sure it actually doesn't work on Every Body.

SHARON
YES IT DOES!

ANITA
She yelled at me!

MARION
You are just a little drunk.

DOROTHY
Every Body! Get it??

EMERSON
Let's see.

(*He goes to the display table where there is one last Poppy Convertible Dress. He looks straight at ENID, takes off his flannel and his pants. He pulls on the Poppy Convertible Dress. Slowly. It's a very hot and strange strip show. He takes the straps and ties them around his waist, so he's wearing it as a skirt*)

EMERSON (CONT'D)
What do you think?

ENID
Oh my god.

EMERSON
Let me help you now.

(*He drapes his flannel around her. Then he does a thing where the dress comes up, the tank goes off, the straps are tied perfectly, and he removes the shirt to reveal a beautifully done dress*)

ANITA
That is the sexiest thing I've ever seen.

MARION
What a gentleman.

EMERSON
A wise man once said, "Being a male is a matter of birth, being a man is a matter of age, but being a gentleman is a matter of choice."

DOROTHY
Nice.

EMERSON
I believe it was Vin Diesel.

ANITA
I think I need to sit down.

(ANITA, MARION, and DOROTHY sit in a pile on the couch. DOROTHY goes to take a sip from the bottle, but it's empty)

DOROTHY
Booooo.

MARION
There's more, but I can't get up.

ENID
I can't stay up. *(She joins their pile)* Now I really do wish we had some champagne.

EMERSON
I brought you some! *(He goes to his man-bag and pulls out a bottle)*

SHARON
And just in time for the ups!

ENID
Okay, Sharon. Thank you. I think we're done. We'll take all the dresses.

EMERSON
And that belt.

SHARON
See?

ANITA
Great party.

MARION
Let's do this again!

DOROTHY
I'm going to.

ANITA
What?

DOROTHY
This is what I'm doing next. It's a great concept. Needs a marketing genius. Which I am. And a manager. Which Enid is.

ENID
Enid is.

DOROTHY
We'll tweak the process a little. We'll need a little start up capital. But yeah, I think this is it.

ENID
I'm in.

EMERSON
You're going to leave?

ENID
Just that job. Not you.

EMERSON
Really?

ENID
You do look very nice in that skirt. *(EMERSON kisses ENID)*

SHARON
Ok! I hope you have had a Perfect Poppy Party today. Invoices are here next to the champagne. Please take your time and you all look very beautiful in your— *(Her phone rings)*

SHARON (CONT.)
—excuse me. *(She answers the phone as she exits)* Britney? I don't CARE if your Uber is stuck in cement, you cannot leave those children alone in my house!

Full-Length Plays

NANCY TEMPLE

Nancy Temple lives in Boston. She has written both short and full-length plays. Her short plays have been produced in a number of festivals, including Playwrights Platform, Theatre One's Slice of Life, Acme Theatre's New Works Winter Festival, Image Theatre's Fem Noire Festival, Flush Ink Productions, Fifth Avenue Theatre, and Eden Prairie. Her full-length *The Caregivers* will have a staged reading at North Shore Readers, Newburyport, MA, in December 2020. *Victoria for President! 1872*, a play written for high school drama clubs, was published by Next Stage Press. Nancy is currently enrolled in the MFA program in Creative Writing at Lesley University, Cambridge, Massachusetts.

The Caregivers

A PLAY BY NANCY TEMPLE

CAST OF CHARACTERS

RUTH: A woman in her mid to late eighties, mother of Louise.
LOUISE: A woman in her mid sixties, daughter of Ruth.
PATTI: A woman in her mid fifties.

SETTING

Ruth's house, comfortable but a little worn, the house of someone living perhaps on a fixed income. The set can be more or less elaborate, fully or very schematically furnished.

The set should be divided into two sections. On one side (stage left), a living room. This may be represented simply by a couch, coffee table, chair, a wall of books that may be simply painted, or simply labeled "books." On the other side, a kitchen with a table; the kitchen may be simply represented by a tall table with a few kitchen items, coffee pot, etc.

Exits and entrances are important. Offstage left is the exit to the outside world. Offstage right is Patti's bedroom and bathroom. Backstage is Ruth's bedroom.

The play takes place in a lower-middle-class town, anywhere, in the present.

SCENE 1

(Lights up. The stage is empty and silent for a few moments. There is a large crossword puzzle dictionary on the coffee table. We hear the sound of footsteps in the hallway backstage. RUTH appears in the kitchen, carrying the newspaper crossword puzzle with her. She hobbles with difficulty towards the couch, holding on to furniture as she goes, looking around for something)

RUTH
(Looking around) Where the hell is that cane?!

(She sits on the couch and begins to study the puzzle. After a moment, we hear knocking from offstage. After a few knocks, we hear a voice)

LOUISE
(Calls from offstage) Mom! Open the door!

(RUTH looks up briefly towards the sound and then returns to studying the puzzle. More knocking, voice calling offstage)

LOUISE
Mom!

(RUTH ignores this. Suddenly, she figures out a part of the puzzle)

RUTH
(Fills in the word) Eclipse! I knew it!

(We hear the sound of the door offstage bursting open, and LOUISE comes in with a pile of sheets and towels, using her chin to support the pile. RUTH doesn't look up.

LOUISE *watches RUTH as she carries the pile to the kitchen counter. She watches RUTH for a moment over the pile)*

LOUISE
I know you heard me knocking—I can see your hearing aids.

RUTH
(Pointedly, still not looking up) I heard you kicking, Louise. It didn't sound like knocking to me. *(Beat)* Where's your key?

LOUISE
(Exasperated) Jeez, Mom, look at me! *(Beat; she drops the pile on the kitchen counter)* You forgot to lock the door. Anyone could've come in.

RUTH
Well, anyone didn't, did they? It was just you.

LOUISE
It's not safe, forgetting to lock the door. You really shouldn't be here by yourself.

RUTH
You worry too much, Louise. *(Beat)* Did you get to the dry cleaner? I need that dress.

LOUISE
No. I didn't have time. I'll go tomorrow. *(She rummages in her bag as she walks to the living room)* Here, I got your mail—your check came.

RUTH
It's about time.

(As LOUISE puts the mail on the coffee table, RUTH notices something on LOUISE's arm and grabs it in order to look closely. LOUISE is forced to sit)

RUTH (CONT'D)
Wait a minute. That's a new one, isn't it? What is it? Some kind of bird?

LOUISE
(Tries to pull her arm away) Yes, it's a bird. It's not new. You've seen it before, Mom.

RUTH
What are you doing over there? Are you still answering the phone? You're turning into their best customer. How many of these do you have now?

LOUISE
(Pulls her arm away) Stop! I'm not counting. Five.

RUTH
Five?

LOUISE
Six. I don't know. What difference does it make?

RUTH
(Peers again at LOUISE's left arm) It's two birds. Is that water? What is that? Some kind of big…oh, I get it! What kind of person calls himself "Heron," anyway?

LOUISE
It was from his vision quest. *(Beat)* Never mind.

RUTH
You had to get involved with a shaman.

LOUISE
Mom, we're just friends now, okay? And I wish you'd stop calling him that.

RUTH
(Indicating the tattoo) You know, there are people who make a living taking those off.

LOUISE
Okay, Mom. Let's see your puzzle.

(LOUISE leans over RUTH and studies her puzzle) "Greek cheese." Four letters. Easy.

RUTH
(Leans close to LOUISE to look) What do you think it is?

LOUISE
Not "feta"?—wait, that doesn't work. "Goat"? "Brie"?

RUTH
(Takes the puzzle and puts it on the coffee table) Oh, come on. You're not paying attention.

LOUISE
You're the crossword champ, anyway.

RUTH
(Puts her head back and closes her eyes) Can you get me a cup of tea? *(LOUISE gets up)* Oh, and would you get my cane? I think I left it in the car.

LOUISE
Honestly, what would you do if I weren't here?

(LOUISE exits stage left into the garage. There is a moderately long silence. Then we hear the car door open, slam, and LOUISE comes back into the house, holding the cane. RUTH opens her eyes)

LOUISE (CONT'D)
For God's sake—what happened?! There's a big—gouge on the side of the car.

RUTH
Oh, that. Well, it's not my fault. Someone—banged into me—yesterday—a couple of days ago… I don't know!! *(Vague)* It's nothing… a little scratch.

LOUISE
A scratch! What about the dent in the rear bumper?!

RUTH
I didn't do that. Fran did it.

LOUISE
Fran? When was Fran ever driving your car?

RUTH
I lent her the car—I don't know, it was last year. She must have backed up into something. Don't nag me, Louise.

LOUISE
Oh, Mom…the bumper was fine last week.

RUTH
Listen, there's something wrong with that car, Louise. The other day, the key got stuck in the ignition. That's not normal! I had to go out and find someone—and that man next door… isn't he the fire chief?

LOUISE
You mean Joe?

RUTH
Joe. That's right. Thank God he was outside. He came and got the key out.

LOUISE
Oh my God. You forgot how to get the key out of the car!

RUTH
I did not forget how to get the key out! I said—there is something wrong with the car! I've got to get it fixed. I hope it's not too expensive. *(Beat)* Oh, and right after he got the key out, it happened again. He said…something about parking…I don't know.

LOUISE
He said something about parking? Mom—you have to put the car in park to take out the key!

RUTH
Well, no.

LOUISE
Yes. You do. The car's a mess. And now this. You really shouldn't be driving.

RUTH
At my age, is that what you mean?

LOUISE
Yes, at your age. *(She gets up and digs around in RUTH's handbag)* I'm taking the car keys.

RUTH
(Angry) I wish you would remember that I'm eighty years old, and I'm doing just fine! Just fine!

LOUISE
Eighty-seven. And you're not doing just fine! Last week the whole fire department was here—you could've burned the house down!

RUTH
A burned egg, that's all. Louise, that could happen to anyone. You're not the most—organized—person in the world. I'm sure it's happened to you.

LOUISE
Oh, don't start, please. Just don't. Listen. Mom. I want you to meet someone.

RUTH
(Alarmed) Meet someone?! What do you mean?

LOUISE
She could stay in the downstairs bedroom—she'd be out of your way.

RUTH
Why? I don't understand!

LOUISE
(Feeling her way) She needs a place to stay. It's temporary. A month…a couple of months. *(Beat)* Till she finds an apartment.

RUTH
Who is this person?

LOUISE
Her name's Patti. She's a friend.

RUTH
I never heard you talk about a Patti. Why doesn't she stay with you? *(LOUISE is silent)* Louise? How do you know this person? I hope this isn't another one of your schemes!

LOUISE
No, Mom. Heron knows her.

RUTH
Oh, Heron! For God's sake!

LOUISE
He's known her forever—since before he opened the shop. He says she's so tuned into, like, people's cosmic energy.

RUTH
Cosmic energy. Really. You're such a smart girl, Louise. I don't know how you ended up like this…your father and I always had such hopes for you. I'm glad he isn't alive to see you covered with tattoos. I mean, you and all your crazy schemes—are you still thinking about starting that organic juice farm? Perma—perma…what is it?

LOUISE
Permaculture. It's about sustainable agriculture and responsible farming and not wrecking the soil, and…you know.

RUTH
I don't know—I never heard of it. It sounds crazy to me. How much did I give you for that? And what about the money I gave you for that gallery? Weren't you going to rent looms to quilters?

LOUISE
Weavers, Mom, not quilters.

RUTH
Well, either way, that never happened. I thought you would've paid me back by now. I do have medical bills, Louise! You'll understand when you get to be my age.

LOUISE
I'm sorry, Mom. I gave the money to Heron…for the juice farm. I mean I lent it to him. I'll pay you back, I promise. *(Brief pause)* Look. There's some—problems. Heron says we have to go to Kentucky to talk to some guy about the project—about the money, and—it's really important! Right now everything's on hold.

RUTH
(Sighs) Oh, surprise, everything's on
hold! Meanwhile, you're doing—
whatever—at that—place—and—
(RUTH pokes LOUISE's arm)—and
that damned shaman—is poking you
with needles!

LOUISE
He's an artist. Would you stop?

RUTH
(After a short, cold silence) Well, Louise, I
worked one steady job my whole life. I
paid my own bills and I own my house.
(Beat) I'm just saying. I can take care of
myself.

(LOUISE rummages in her own bag and
hands RUTH a bottle of pills)

LOUISE
Here. I almost forgot…I brought your
pills. Don't say it, Mom.

RUTH
(Gets up with great difficulty) You almost
forgot! I need water. Where's that
damned cane?!

(She sees the cane next to her chair, grabs
it, takes a few wobbly steps, and sits down
again. LOUISE meanwhile has gone into
the kitchen to get water for RUTH)

RUTH (CONT'D)
Shit! Old age is nothing but suffering,
Louise. I don't know why God lets
people live this long. (LOUISE hands
her a glass of water) It's just—if I were
God, I could design the world a whole
lot better. (RUTH swallows a pill)

LOUISE
You should do that breathing thing.
Let's do it together.

(LOUISE folds her hands in her lap,
closes her eyes, then audibly takes in a
deep breath, holds it, and exhales. RUTH
watches her with irritation)

RUTH
(Cranky) I know how to breathe,
Louise. (There is a brief silence. LOUISE
opens her eyes) Did you bring my milk?

LOUISE
No, and don't say it. (RUTH is pointedly
silent. LOUISE is defensive, frustrated,
flustered) Look, I can't do everything!
I'm just one person! I cook and bring
the laundry and the mail and—your
pills! And I take you to the hospital for
those shots!

RUTH
Those shots never help. My back still
hurts. (Beat) And if it's too much for
you, I'll go next door and ask Fay.

LOUISE
When the dishwasher broke, who got
you the new one? It wasn't Fay! Jesus!
(Short silence; RUTH looks away, sullen)
Listen, Patti's smart. You'll like her.
You'll see. You should keep an open
mind. Anyway, I told you, she's a friend!

RUTH
I don't care who she is. I don't want her
or anyone living in my house!
(There's a brief silence)

LOUISE
I'm sorry I didn't get the milk. I'll bring
it next time, okay?

RUTH
(Rummages in her handbag) I can't eat
cereal without milk. I'll go over to
Honey Farms. (She pulls out her wallet
and peers in; after a moment) Louise, lend
me a five. (LOUISE is silent. RUTH
looks up) What? (She puts her bag in her
lap, remembering) You took my car keys.

LOUISE
(Upset) I don't want you to get hurt, okay?

RUTH
(Plaintive) How will I get to the park?

LOUISE
I know. I'm sorry.

RUTH
(*Softens, remembering*) The ducks...
I like watching them.

LOUISE
Me too. They're funny.

RUTH
The way they sit on the edge of the
dam grooming their feathers...

LOUISE
They look like they're going to fall off,
but they never do.

(*They sit in short silence, contemplating
the ducks with pleasure. RUTH taps her
own arm, gestures at LOUISE's tattoo*)

RUTH
You know—that new thing—that big—
you could've gotten a duck. You know
how their heads are green. You've always
looked good in green, Louise.

LOUISE
(*Smiles*) I could have. You're right.

RUTH
Didn't we have a picnic there?

LOUISE
We did.

(*The doorbell rings, loud, sharp. RUTH
is startled*)

LOUISE (CONT'D)
Mom. Here's the thing. I asked Patti to
come meet you.

RUTH
(*Alarmed*) What?! Oh, no, I'm not
meeting her or anyone. Do you hear
me, Louise?! Don't answer that door!
(*The doorbell rings again. They are frozen
for a moment*) You go tell her there's
been a misunderstanding!

LOUISE
(*Frazzled*) But she can get groceries.
The dry cleaning!

RUTH
Oh, for God's sake—!

LOUISE
She could take you to the pond—

RUTH
I want you to take me to the pond.

LOUISE
And dinner—she can make dinner!
She's a fantastic cook.

(*RUTH looks away, frowns. The doorbell
rings again*)

LOUISE
Plus she can pay you for the room!
Didn't I say that? Maybe fifty a week—
seventy-five a week.

(*Pause; there is knocking on the door.
RUTH and LOUISE watch each other*)

RUTH
Seventy-five a week?

(*RUTH considers this. Then, sly*)

RUTH (CONT'D)
I might agree just to meet her. (*Beat*)
I want my car keys back, though.

LOUISE
No, Mom.

PATTI
(*Offstage*) Hello?

RUTH
A hundred a week—a hundred and
twenty-five a week!

(*The doorbell rings yet again, loud.
LOUISE gets up and walks to the door
as RUTH watches. At the door, LOUISE
turns to look at RUTH*)

RUTH
And I want that money up front!

(Slow fade on LOUISE and RUTH looking at each other—part way through fade—blackout)

SCENE 2

(Lights up; the stage is empty. The lighting is dim. After a few moments, PATTI wanders in from her bedroom, in childlike red pajamas [Decorated perhaps with hearts or puppies], yawning and stretching; she is relaxed. Lights become slowly brighter, as she putters around the kitchen, gets coffee. She looks for something to eat, gets a bowl and spoon, rummages in cabinets. She finds a box of Toasted O's cereal and shakes it over the bowl—what little is left she empties into the bowl)

PATTI
Oh, damn…

(She puts the empty cereal box back into the cabinet, gets milk from the fridge, makes herself a cup of coffee, closes her eyes, stretches, etc. She wanders off stage right towards her bedroom. After a moment, RUTH appears from the upstairs bedroom and enters the kitchen. She hobbles around the kitchen and living room, looking for something)

RUTH
Where's that newspaper! *(Shouts towards PATTI's room)* Did you take it into your room? *(Turns back)* I'll just bet it's in her room.

(Music now comes from PATTI's room. It is a ballad, perhaps by Norah Jones. RUTH goes to the door stage right and peers in the direction of PATTI's room)

RUTH (CONT'D)
Turn off that music!

(The music stops. RUTH hobbles towards the back bedroom. We hear the following lines from offstage)

RUTH (CONT'D)
You thought I couldn't hear that? I'm not deaf! You're not allowed to play music in there!

(After a moment, RUTH reappears in the kitchen. She sees that there is coffee in the coffeemaker, takes milk out of the fridge, makes a cup of coffee, leaves the milk on the counter, opens the cabinet, takes out the box of cereal, peers in, sees it is empty. She puts the empty box on the counter. She goes back to the door stage right and shouts)

RUTH (CONT'D)
You better do some shopping. You ate my Toasted O's! *(No response)* Are you hiding in the bathroom? Have you got my newspaper in there?

PATTI
(From offstage) I don't have it, Ruth— just a minute, okay?

RUTH
(Bangs her cane on the floor) You'd better not be smoking in there—that's not allowed. Do you hear me?

(RUTH turns back to the living room. She sits on the couch and folds her hands. She closes her eyes, puts her hands on her knees and hums audibly once, then concentrates on her breathing. PATTI reappears, dressed. She looks around, notices the cereal box, puts it in the trash, notices the milk is out and puts it in the fridge)

PATTI
(Perhaps referring to RUTH's mess) Hard to get organized some days, right?

RUTH
(Eyes still closed) Did you take my newspaper?

PATTI
Relax. It's probably outside.

(She comes to sit in the chair next to RUTH and watches her. RUTH continues her breathing)

PATTI (CONT'D)
What're you doing? Is that some kinda Chinese prayer? *(Brief pause)* Aren't you Jewish?

RUTH
It's mindful breathing. It's for my back. And my nerves. *(She opens her eyes)* Louise says I should just sit…and breathe slowly…when I get nervous. Although I'm not usually nervous. I'm a very strong person! I've always been very capable. *(Beat)* Anyway, I don't pray.

PATTI
You don't pray? Ever? I knew a Jewish person—*(Pause)*—I'm pretty sure he was Jewish. He prayed all the time.

RUTH
Well, there's no one up there listening, so what's the point!

PATTI
That's not true. It's not. I have a personal relationship with Jesus.

RUTH
Then you can give him a message from me—he needs to do a better job if he wants me to pray to him. Tell him to fix my back!

PATTI
You shouldn't talk like that, Ruth.

RUTH
(Cranky) My back still hurts! That breathing thing doesn't help. Louise took me to the hospital for those shots and they never helped either.

PATTI
Ruth—do you know the Lord's prayer?

RUTH
Everyone knows it. That's not the same as believing it.

PATTI
(Puts her hands on RUTH's) Ruth. Listen.

RUTH
(Pulls her hands away) Don't touch me.

PATTI
(Earnest) Jesus works through me. I'm a pastoral healer.

RUTH
A pastoral healer—that's a good one. I guess all the doctors can close up shop now that you're in town!

PATTI
Jesus is real. And he's the one that sent Louise.

RUTH
(Firmly) Oh, I think not.

PATTI
So I could help her, you know? Help you, is what I mean.

RUTH
I don't need help! And if I did, I could ask Louise. But I don't. I'm very independent!

PATTI
Okay, I know, Louise told me. Relax. *(She looks around the house)* I know you're not—*(Pause)*—some people say Jewish people are all rich. Your place is all right, though. I mean, it's really nice. *(Beat)* I love my room…I never woulda thought of painting the walls like that, different colors. And where the bed is I can see the moon out my window. Not always, you know. Right like through the branches of that whatever it is tree—if I was a painter, I'd do that picture. So pretty. I never had a room that nice before. I never had my own room before! Me and my sisters had to sleep on the porch—in our coats in winter! We were so cold.

RUTH
You slept on a porch?

PATTI
Yup. One of those ones with glass, you know? We had a little house out near Zoar—bet you never heard of it. Up in the mountains. Population, like, maybe fifty. They're all related. *(She gets up and goes over to the bookcase, gazes at the books, scanning titles)* So many books! Have you read them all?

RUTH
(Points at book on bookcase) I wrote one of them—that red book.

PATTI
Yeah…Louise told me you wrote stories. Wow, a book with your name on it!

RUTH
I got a prize. The O. Henry award.

PATTI
An award—no kidding! She didn't tell me that.

(She goes to the window and looks out. As she stands there, she reaches into her pocket and takes out a pill bottle, removes and swallows two pills. RUTH watches)

RUTH
What're you doing? Are you sick?

PATTI
(Turns to RUTH) Oh, no. No. Just, you know, aches and pains—you know what that's like. I've got a bum knee. How's your back?

RUTH
(Cranky) It always hurts—I can hardly walk!

PATTI
(Gesturing to the pill bottle) These really work, and I could give you some.

RUTH
No. The doctor gave me Tramadol.

PATTI
Yeah? You have Tramadol? Where—in your room?

RUTH
I can get it if I want to, and don't you go up there!

PATTI
Okay, jeez. *(She looks out the window again)* I love that little garden by the back door. Lou did that, right? *(Beat)* Having my own room—it's amazing. And my own bathroom!

RUTH
Well, it's not free.

PATTI
I know…I told Louise—whatever you need, you know? I'm so grateful—not many people would take a chance on me, to be honest.

RUTH
Louise took a chance?

PATTI
Yeah. *(Beat)* No, I mean, she trusts me! She's a trusting person. That's good, you know? Anyone can turn their life around. Start over again, put things right. Everyone makes mistakes. She gets that.

RUTH
Louise is good at that…making mistakes…starting over.

PATTI
It's the Lord's work.

RUTH
(Noticing tattoo on PATTI's arm) That tattoo. That's like the one Louise got.

PATTI
(Regarding the tattoo) Oh, yeah, I know. Heron did mine too…a couple of years ago. Lou saw it and wanted the same one. He designed this one specially for me. It's—old style. He said…what'd he say…it's like—art…nouveau? Right?

RUTH
I don't know about that.

PATTI
Well, he's a real artist.

RUTH
If he was, he'd know that's a Haida design.

PATTI
A what?

RUTH
Haida. Indians from Canada. Western Canada. Two big bird profiles facing each other *(She points at the tattoos)*— they look like mirror images, see? That's what they do. Blue water. Black and red. They do that too. Obviously, he copied it from a book.

PATTI
No, he didn't. It's from his vision quest!

RUTH
You and Louise—the two of you— gullible! You'll believe anything that shaman tells you. What is it? He's handsome? He's rich?

PATTI
(After a moment) One thing, he's actually fun to talk to.

RUTH
Well, I guess that was directed at me! I don't need to listen to insults! *(RUTH tries to rise; she clutches her back and sits down again)* Ow.

PATTI
Why don't I get your Tramadol?

RUTH
I don't have any.

PATTI
You just said you did—you said it's up in your bedroom. I can get it easy.

RUTH
No. I told you I don't.

PATTI
Why don't I look just to make sure?

RUTH
You stay out of my room! Don't you ever go in my room! That's not allowed!

(Short pause while they regard each other)

PATTI
Okay. I was just asking—just tryin' to be nice. Jeez. *(She regards RUTH)* I've got something. Wait a sec.

(PATTI goes out. RUTH grabs her cane, rises, begins to follow PATTI, who reappears holding a large pill bottle. The bottle is of the type in which pharmacies store pills. She pours one out into her hand, hesitates, looks deep into the bottle, then adds a second)

PATTI (CONT'D)
Here—*(Holds them out to RUTH)*— take these.

RUTH
I don't know. What are they?

PATTI
Just take them. For your back. *(RUTH hesitates)* They work way better than Tramadol—you'll see. *(PATTI goes to the kitchen and gets RUTH a glass of water)* Go on. You'll feel a lot better. Trust me.

RUTH
I don't know. *(She pushes PATTI's hand away)* No.

PATTI
They won't hurt you. Really.

RUTH
(Suspicious) I'm not supposed to take pills if I haven't eaten.

PATTI
(Puts the pills into RUTH's hand) You'll be fine. I'll get you something to eat. Go on.

(RUTH hesitates but swallows the pills)

RUTH
Were you really a nurse?

PATTI
Oh, yeah…Tufts, Boston…the ICU, surgical, you name it. I worked at the VA too. But that—didn't work out. D'ja ever hear of Pheonix House? I'll be working there afternoons. Counseling.

RUTH
That place is for addicts! It was on the news. Somebody died.

PATTI
Yeah, really sad. But I'm good with addicts. I'm like totally empathic. *(Beat)* It's just till I get on my feet, you know? Anyway, you and me are gonna get along really great. *(She peers into the pill bottle. It's empty. She looks at RUTH)* I gave you my last pill—can I look for yours? My knee's killing me. *(RUTH, feeling an effect from the pills, does not answer)* Hey, your back's better, isn't it?

RUTH
…Maybe…a little…*(Short pause; she considers her back)* No, it's not!

PATTI
I gave you two pills—you shouldn't be feeling anything. Where's your Tramadol?

RUTH
My head feels funny. You shouldn'da given me those pills. *(She feels her back)* My back doesn't hurt, though.

PATTI
Praise Jesus.

RUTH
My head feels really weird… I feel sick. I think I might throw up.

PATTI
If you eat, you'll feel better. It'll settle your stomach.

RUTH
I told you—I feel sick! And if I want something to eat, I can cook!

PATTI
(Dismissive) You don't cook!

RUTH
Well, I do cook! Look in the fridge— I've got tons of food.

PATTI
(Smirks) Fine, but you didn't cook it. Louise made that chicken thing.

RUTH
(Voice raised) Wipe that smile off your face! This is my house, and if I said I cooked that food, it's not your place to say I didn't!

PATTI
I wasn't smiling. Jeez.

(PATTI turns away, goes to the kitchen. RUTH gets up and starts to follow her, but only manages a few steps. As she is walking, PATTI goes to the fridge, takes out a beer, opens it, and swigs from the bottle. She turns and sees RUTH watching her. They exchange a look)

PATTI (CONT'D)
What?!

RUTH
(Aggressive) Drinking beer in the morning? First thing—outta the bottle—you're a wino. I've seen them. They lie around on the Common, and they steal, and then they get arrested and end up in prison. Where they rot! And that's what's gonna happen to you.

PATTI
(Tone is controlled but threatening) Oh! Now, Ruth, you better not talk to me like that. Didn't I just give you pills for your back? Wasn't I gonna get you something to eat? *(PATTI and RUTH confront each other for a few moments)*

Nobody talks to me that way. Nobody! I've been places. You talk like that where I've been, you'd be dead by now. *(PATTI approaches RUTH, who backs up and sits on the couch, leaning away from PATTI, who stands above her looking down on her. RUTH looks up. PATTI is falsely conciliatory)*

PATTI (CONT'D)
All right. I forgive you. This time.

RUTH
(Nervous) I'm not scared of you.

PATTI
I'm not scared of you either.
(RUTH puts her head back and closes her eyes; she doesn't answer. PATTI watches RUTH, then goes upstairs to RUTH's room. Short silence, then RUTH opens her eyes and sits up. She looks around for PATTI. PATTI reappears, grabs her bag and jacket, ignores RUTH, who is watching her. PATTI puts on her jacket)

RUTH
You can get me something to eat now. I got kind of hungry. *(RUTH becomes suspicious)* Did you go into my room?

PATTI
(To RUTH) I'll be back in half an hour, okay?

(PATTI exits, slamming the door. RUTH hobbles to the door, opens it and looks out)

RUTH
(Shouts after PATTI) I'll tell Louise you didn't give me anything to eat! And you took my newspaper! Where's my newspaper? *(Beat)* You made me take those pills—and they made me sick! *(RUTH slams the doors shut, and, banging her cane on the floor for emphasis, she hobbles back to PATTI's room. We hear her as she disappears stage right)*

RUTH (CONT'D)
And I'll tell her you were snooping around in my room!

(There is a short silence as lights fade, then blackout)

SCENE 3
(Lights up. RUTH enters from stage right, hobbles slowly towards the kitchen table and sits. As she does, LOUISE enters from the door center stage. She is carrying the NY Times and a small bag. She puts the Times on the table)

LOUISE
I found your paper stuck under the fence. That paper guy is such a jerk. Half the time he doesn't even deliver it. Or he throws it on someone else's steps…maybe Fay's reading your paper…I brought your milk.

(She hands the newspaper to RUTH, who opens it and begins to turn the pages. LOUISE takes the milk out of the bag and puts it in the refrigerator. RUTH sees something compelling in the paper, stops turning the pages, reads)

RUTH
(Peers at the paper) Listen to this. "Giraffe is dissected for Danish schoolchildren."

LOUISE
What?!

RUTH
(Peers again at the small print) I need better light. *(She moves the paper closer to the hanging lamp over the table, then reads slowly)* "In the chilly…dawn of Sunday morning…a healthy young giraffe…in a Danish zoo was given its favorite meal of rye bread—" *(Looks up, surprised!)*—rye bread? Giraffes eat rye bread?

LOUISE
Everybody in Denmark eats rye bread.

RUTH

(Peers, reads with difficulty) "Rye bread…by a keeper—and then shot in the head by a vet"—shot in the head! By a vet?! Oh my God! (She hands the paper to LOUISE) You read it.

LOUISE

(Reads) "The death of Marius, an 18-month-old giraffe considered useless for breeding because his genes were too common, was followed by his dissection in front of a large crowd, including fascinated-looking children…"

RUTH

(Puzzled) They let children watch? (LOUISE is reading silently) Well, go on.

LOUISE

(Reads) "The zoo's decision to conduct the public dissection, and the disclosure that the animal was shot"—(LOUISE pauses and gazes at RUTH) I don't want to read it, Mom.

RUTH

Read.

LOUISE

"…The zoo's scientific director said he never considered cancelling the killing…We can't all of a sudden change…because of some emotional events happening around us." (She puts the paper down) That's it. I'm not reading any more.

RUTH

An innocent animal! I think it's appalling! And—what did that man say? Something about being factual—proper—Louise, read that to me again.

LOUISE

It's too depressing.

(RUTH grabs the paper and scans it)

RUTH

"Can't change because of emotional events!" That's what he said. (She puts the paper down) Disgusting! It's the holocaust all over again!

LOUISE

Mom! The holocaust didn't happen in Denmark.

RUTH

Vets exterminating helpless young animals for the entertainment of children. What do you call it?

LOUISE

It's horrible, but it's not the holocaust, for God's sake.

(RUTH picks up the paper and scrutinizes it, with her face close to the paper, peering and tracing the words with her finger as she reads. She puts the paper down forcefully)

RUTH

Useless giraffes! Useless people! Just shoot them—burn them—push them onto the ice! People killing people! Doctors killing people! For no reason! Callous indifference.

LOUISE

Mom—stop.

RUTH

And the Eskimos do it too. When someone gets old, they just push them off the sled and leave them to freeze. Just leave them—abandon them— (Beat) If I were God, I certainly would've designed the world a helluva lot better.

LOUISE

I know. You've told me.

RUTH

Have I? Well, it bears repeating. Old age is nothing but suffering, Louise.

LOUISE

You've told me that too.

(They sit in silence for a moment. LOUISE hesitates)

LOUISE (CONT'D)
Listen, Mom…about the farm project.

RUTH
What about it?

LOUISE
The thing is…

RUTH
The thing is what? Don't say it, whatever it is.

LOUISE
I really do have to go to Kentucky—kind of soon. *(She holds up her hand to stop RUTH, who is about to interrupt)*—A week, ten days at most. Maybe a little longer…

RUTH
Oh, with that shaman!

LOUISE
Stop calling him that.

RUTH
Leaving me behind with that awful woman.

LOUISE
There's a lot of money involved. Mom, it's your money. I have to go. You'll be fine here with Patti. Nothing's gonna happen, I promise.

RUTH
(Leans forward, intense) She's lazy, Louise. Lazy! Doesn't get out of bed. Sleeps all morning.

LOUISE
Come on.

RUTH
I looked in her room, what d'ya think? It was ten o'clock and she was still sleeping! And you wouldn't believe what a mess it is in there.

LOUISE
I know. She has a lot of stuff. So what?

RUTH
Have you seen that big teddy bear?! What kind of grown woman has a teddy bear? It takes up half the bed. And that huge rubber ball!

LOUISE
It's an exercise ball, Mom.

RUTH
It's a goddamn mess, that's what it is—a bunch of crap!

LOUISE
Well, don't look at it. You don't need to go in there. It's none of your business anyway. I'm gonna make some tea.

(LOUISE gets up and busies herself in the kitchen, making tea. She stops to look at RUTH periodically as they talk)

RUTH
And then she comes in late and goes straight to her room, walks right by me—she doesn't even say hello! What am I, invisible? *(Beat)* Louise, are you listening? *(Beat)* She hides in the bathroom all the time. I don't like it! She goes in and…she just— she's just in there. In the dark. Not making any noise. Like you'd think, you know…you'd hear water running, or something…what's she doing, anyway? *(LOUISE brings tea to the table. RUTH grabs her arm)* She gave me some pills—a whole bunch of them. They made me really sick. I thought I was gonna throw up. You know I'm afraid of throwing up, Louise, I've always been like that.

LOUISE
Oh, for God's sake, Mom! It was probably your Tramadol.

RUTH

(Gestures towards bathroom) It was not my Tramadol. They never make me sick. Go look in the bathroom. She's got big bottles of pills—they're like those big ones in the drug store. *(LOUISE glances towards bathroom, hesitates)* Well, go on, look—you don't seem to believe me.

LOUISE

(To RUTH as she heads towards PATTI's room) Okay, just because you're nagging me, and then you have to stop complaining!

(LOUISE exits. RUTH drinks tea, glancing towards PATTI's room. LOUISE returns, sits at table)

RUTH

Well?

LOUISE

(Worried but covering it up) You're right…they're big.

RUTH

A lot of them! Why does she need all those pills, anyway?

LOUISE

(After a moment) I don't know. Stop worrying about it.

RUTH

I think you should be worrying about me, Louise. And you know what—she was taking those pills and she said it was for her "bum knee." How come they didn't make her sick? Maybe she gave me—some kind of poison. I don't trust her.

LOUISE

Some kind of poison—that's crazy. She's not gonna give you poison! She'd end up in prison. *(Beat)* She does not want to end up in prison.

RUTH

Well, of course, nobody wants to. I don't think serial killers want to end up in prison.

LOUISE

All right. Stop.

RUTH

She's not normal, Louise. She's got some kind of a drinking problem. The fridge is full of beer—she starts drinking first thing in the morning. And she works at that awful place…that place—with addicts!

LOUISE

(Tired of arguing) Yes, she works there. She's some kind of social worker.

RUTH

(Rubs a spot on the table) Social worker—you said she used to be a nurse. Look at this! *(Points to the spot)* It's filthy—disgusting!

LOUISE

(Looks) I don't see anything.

RUTH

Well, all right. That's because I rubbed it off already. *(She peers again at the table, points)* You don't see this? It's some kind of crap. It's sticky! What the hell is it? I thought nurses were supposed to keep things clean! She's not a nice person, Louise. She called me a piece of shit!

LOUISE

Come on, Mom, she wouldn't talk like that—to anyone.

RUTH

I'm scared of her!

LOUISE

(Exasperated) Oh my God—I really don't like what you're doing. I know you don't want her here, okay? You've made that clear and I get it. But you're telling me these ridiculous stories about how she's calling you a piece of shit and giving you poison! I don't want to hear any more. Pull yourself together.

RUTH

You always defend her! Whose side are you on? And you're the one who tells lies, Louise. What about that fancy gallery— and then you gave my money to that—I don't even want to say his name. You didn't tell me a thing about it. And this— Patti—did you know she's a *(Air quotes)* "pastoral healer"? She's either sleeping or praying. And what about the rent? She hasn't paid any of it. *(Beat)* You think you know her, but you don't.

LOUISE

Okay, fine. I don't know her. I'm just a fool. I'm sorry. But Mom, I have to make this trip, and I can't leave you alone here…I won't.

RUTH

Give me back my car keys. I'll be fine.

LOUISE

No. You said you'd give her a chance. It'll work out, I promise. I'll talk to her—she'll take you to the pond, and she won't play loud music. I'll ask her not to pray in front of you. I'll tell her to get out of bed before ten o'clock. Be a little patient, okay? Just try…please.

RUTH

I can see my feelings don't matter to you. You've never thought about anyone but yourself, ever since you were a little girl. Maybe it's because you're an only child—spoiled is what they say—I guess it's true. People say you can depend on a daughter to take care of you—look out for you when you're old. They never imagined a daughter like you. I should have had more children— more daughters. You can go live up— *(Gesture)*—up where the Eskimos throw the old people away. I won't miss you. You're selfish, Louise, just plain selfish.

(There is a moment of silence; LOUISE is stunned)

LOUISE

You stuck Dad in that awful place. Reminiscence Room—what a joke— and him asking when he could come home/

RUTH

/ How dare you! You weren't around when he got in the car and just vanished—vanished! They found him on Route 9 and called me—come get him, take him home. And the time I found him in the middle of the night— tying his shoes. He was going to see you, Louise—he said, it's a nice day, I'll walk over to visit her. In the middle of the night!

LOUISE

(Teary) You moved him right before Thanksgiving. Everyone missed him. You could have waited.

RUTH

Don't judge me, Louise. You don't know how it was. I had no choice.

LOUISE

You had a choice. Of course you had a choice.

(There are a few moments of silence)

RUTH

I'll never forgive you for this. Any of it.

LOUISE

(Mood clearly depressed) Yes, you will. You always forgive me. Why don't you just do it now and get it over with? *(There is another silence; LOUISE wipes her eyes)*

RUTH

If I thought I could kill myself, I'd do it.

LOUISE

Oh, don't say that.

RUTH

I just don't want to fail…and end up in the hospital. I've thought about it.

LOUISE
(Puts her head in her hands in despair)
For God's sake…

RUTH
I'll put stones in my pockets and walk
into the river.

LOUISE
(Looks up, almost amused) Really? That's
very dramatic, Mom, but it's not exactly
original. *(Short pause)* Virginia Woolf?
(Beat) Are you planning to call a taxi
and have him drop you off? I guess you
won't ask him to wait. *(Beat)* There
are easier ways, you know. If you were
serious.

RUTH
(Hurt) That's not nice, Louise.

LOUISE
Sorry. *(Beat)* Look at me. Things aren't
that bad.

RUTH
Oh, you don't know! What the hell do
you know!

*(LOUISE goes to sit next to RUTH and
puts her arms around her)*

LOUISE
(With empathy) Don't talk like that. I
can't stand it.

RUTH
I've been saving my sleeping pills too.
For when I'm ready.

*(RUTH puts her head on LOUISE's
shoulder. Slow fade to black)*

SCENE 4
*(RUTH's kitchen. LOUISE is alone
at the kitchen table with a cup of coffee.
There is a text-ping. She looks at her
cellphone, reads, and puts it away. She gets
up, goes to door center stage and calls up
"Mom?" She exits to go upstairs to check
on RUTH. While she is gone, PATTI
enters stage left, crosses stage to disappear
stage right in the direction of her room.
The stage is empty for a little while.
LOUISE reappears in the kitchen and
sits. A few moments later, PATTI comes
into the kitchen. She stops in surprise
when she sees Louise)*

PATTI
(Happy to see LOUISE) Hey, there!
(Gestures) Welcome to my abode!

LOUISE
Where were you? I've been here for
over an hour. I need to talk to you. *(She
indicates the stairs to RUTH's room, worried)*
She's still sleeping. It's after noon.

PATTI
So what? She's old.

*(PATTI sits and shows LOUISE a tattoo
on her arm. LOUISE stares)*

PATTI (CONT'D)
Well? What d'ya think?

LOUISE
Nice. I can tell it's his.

PATTI
I know, he's so good.

LOUISE
When'd you see him?

PATTI
Why? Are you jealous?

LOUISE
Of you and Heron? No.

PATTI
Good. 'Cause you know we had a really deep thing for a long time. And after you guys got together, I really missed him…even though it was over. But when you broke up, he called me, and… you know.

LOUISE
It's okay. Really.

PATTI
But as far as him and me getting back like before?—no way. Not gonna happen. I've got other plans. *(Beat)* Hey, I truly would not want me and Heron being friends again to mess up anything between you and me. At all. Ever.

LOUISE
I told you. I'm not worried. *(Brief pause)* He called me the other day.

PATTI
Yeah?

LOUISE
You know about Kentucky?

PATTI
No. *(Beat)* Yeah. I mean, I know you and him are doing–that hybrid juice thing—sweet potato kiwi or something.

LOUISE
I gave him five thousand dollars! Patti, five thousand! Now he's not even sure it's gonna happen. I don't know. He got somebody else into this.

PATTI
Somebody else? Who? He didn't tell me that.

LOUISE
(Cranky, frustrated) I think his name is like, Hank? Frank? I don't know. I'm really worried. Heron just does stuff …now he says we've gotta go down there…work something out with this— Frank. What do you mean, he didn't tell you?

PATTI
Oh. Well, he wanted my advice. He asked me about it, what I thought. I've always had a good head for business. I told him the whole idea was stupid. A juice farm? In Kentucky? Gimme a break.

LOUISE
You knew about it and you thought it was stupid. You could've told me!

PATTI
Look. I thought you were, like, really into it. You and your *(She makes air quotes)* "crazy schemes," right? Sorry. He's not the most—reliable…you know?

LOUISE
I'm such an idiot.

PATTI
I think he was prob'ly looking for somethin' new because he might be closing the shop.

LOUISE
Close the shop! But why? It's always busy!

PATTI
Shit. I guess he didn't tell you about that either. *(Beat)* I mean, people don't always know what they're doing, right? Heron's a good man…but he's a dreamer. So he tells you some big story, and you believe it because—maybe he does too. Or maybe he just wants the money. You gotta watch out for yourself, Lou. People will take advantage, you know?

LOUISE
(Gets up and paces) Oh, God, it's just one more thing.

PATTI
Yeah. Everything is just one more thing…all the time.

LOUISE
I have to make this trip. Patti, listen— I've got to talk to you…about what's going on here. She's miserable.

PATTI
Oh. Great. Of course.

LOUISE
The thing is—like last night—she didn't know you were back till she saw the car. She wants to know where you are.

PATTI
I have to clock in every time I make a move? It was late. I figured she was sleeping.

LOUISE
I don't know. You're smart, you figure it out.

PATTI
Cut me some slack. Your mom complains about everything.

LOUISE
Not everything. But she calls me every day! Patti this. Patti that. It's driving me crazy.

PATTI
You have caller ID—don't answer the phone. That's easy.

LOUISE
I can't do that. Listen. You were gonna take her out, watch TV with her, cook dinner—that meatloaf she likes—all that stuff—we talked about it, right? This was supposed to work out for everyone, make everything easier.

PATTI
Oh, really? Easier for who?

LOUISE
That's not funny.

PATTI
Look, I'm doin' the best I can. You wanted this, Lou. If she's not happy, don't blame me.

LOUISE
You know, you wanted it too. A new start, a new life. Now you've got a room—no rent—you've got your job.

So sometimes you have to talk to an old lady, cook a meal. Come on. She's traveled, she's a writer—you can have a conversation with someone like that. And she's got a good sense of humor, by the way, if you'd give her a chance. So what the hell is going on? *(Beat)* Say something. *(Beat)* You ate her Toasted O's. *(She holds up her hand to stop PATTI from speaking)* I know. But she made a big deal about it.

PATTI
She's lying. I never touched it. I don't even like it—that crap tastes like dust.

LOUISE
You keep her up all night with your music, that's another thing.

PATTI
(Scoffing) Oh, please—I keep her up at night! Oh, my God! She opens my door in the middle of the night. And she's screaming—"Turn off that damned music!" What music? Even if there was music, she can't hear anything without her hearing aids! You know that. I didn't tell you she called me a piece of shit. Eighty-whatever—you'd never hear me talk like that! "Where's the fucking music?!"

LOUISE
(Uses air quotes) Come on, she wouldn't say that—"fucking music," she doesn't talk like that.

PATTI
Man, you don't know—you're not here. And you think I don't hear her on the phone? "When's that woman leaving my house!" That woman, she calls me. Like I don't have a name. Listen. She breaks my stuff! You know that cute little pot my daughter made me? Remember—I showed it to you. The one with the handprints. I kept my Q tips in it and it was like a precious heirloom! Well, it's in pieces now. She was poking around

in my bathroom—and she busted it! Why's she in my bathroom all the time, anyway? It's my space, okay? She doesn't respect my boundaries. It's my bathroom.

LOUISE
Actually…it's not your space. It's hers.

PATTI
Who the hell's side are you on, anyway, Lou?

LOUISE
That's not a fair question. *(Brief pause. PATTI shifts to turn the tables)*

PATTI
Did you tell your mother about me?

LOUISE
Of course not!

PATTI
You did—that's why she hates me! I didn't give you permission to talk about me. What I told you—that was private.

LOUISE
I didn't tell her anything—what's the matter with you?!

PATTI
(On a rant) You know how people treat me when they find out! And I totally turned my life around, and you know that too! I thought you trusted me.

LOUISE
You're here, aren't you?

PATTI
You know what? I'm sick of this. I've been looking for another place…I could be out by…maybe this weekend. There's an apartment for rent over near the bridge.

LOUISE
(Startled) Oh—what—you've been looking? *(Beat)* Were you gonna tell me? *(Beat; suspicious)* What're you gonna do for rent?

PATTI
(Defensive) You think I can't pay! Well, you don't know everything.

(PATTI gets up and goes to the fridge for another beer; LOUISE watches her)

LOUISE
(Trying to appease) Sorry. Look, I came over to talk. My mom's—difficult. I told you that.

PATTI
(Sits) Yeah, you did. I didn't expect her to be this fucked up, though. I can't imagine what it's like having her for a mother. *(Beat; she drinks)* I know you were hoping it would work out.

LOUISE
I told you she'd be impossible. *(Beat)* Listen. Remember telling me about your cellmate?

PATTI
What about her?

LOUISE
You said if you could get through that, you could deal with anything.

PATTI
I did say that.

LOUISE
You're a really strong person. I know that. You went through so much shit. And then you pulled yourself together.

PATTI
With God's help.

LOUISE
You're like, practically a role model.

PATTI
(Flattered) Yeah?

LOUISE
Yeah. Six years in federal prison? I wouldn't last a day.

PATTI
True. And I've been clean ever since.
No matter what you've done, God
always forgives you.

(There is a silence)

LOUISE
I can't believe how she controls—both
of us. She has a will of iron.

PATTI
Nobody controls me.

LOUISE
No. I know that. (Brief pause) I don't
get why she hasn't come down. I'm
gonna check on her.

(LOUISE exits stage center. While she
is gone, PATTI exits to her room. After
a moment, she reappears, gets water, and
swallows two pills. She sits down, puts her
head in her hands. The sound of LOUISE
coming down the stairs. PATTI sits up.
LOUISE enters and sits at the table)

LOUISE (CONT'D)
Still dead asleep. Amazing. (Beat, then,
unhappy) She was so upset the other
day. She started talking about killing
herself again.

PATTI
She probably won't.

LOUISE
It's my fault. I do everything wrong.

PATTI
What are you talking about? Don't say
that. She doesn't know how lucky she is
to have you.

LOUISE
(Depressed) Now this thing—with
Heron! He talked me into this bullshit
farm. I'm an idiot.

PATTI
You made a mistake. Come on—you're
like the smartest person I know.

LOUISE
No, I'm not.

PATTI
Yeah, you are. Heron's the idiot.

LOUISE
I know that's not true, but thanks,
anyway. (Beat; hesitant) Patti, listen.
What if there's a storm? And the lights
go out?

PATTI
(Sensing the shift) You're right—she's
not safe here alone, that's for sure! She
almost set the place on fire the other
day. Started cooking eggs, went upstairs,
and next thing the pan's in flames,
smoke everywhere.

LOUISE
Oh, my God, you didn't tell me that.

PATTI
Yeah. Lucky I was here. Oh, and this
morning she said her back was killing
her, so I gave her a couple of my pills,
you know, the ones for my knee.

LOUISE
You shouldn't give her your pills. Old
people are, like, really sensitive to drugs.
Patti, just don't, okay?

PATTI
Well, then you better call the doc about
her meds—she's out.

LOUISE
She is? That's weird. I just brought them
over. I could check her room.

PATTI
Nope, nothin' in her room.

LOUISE
Huh, weird. (Brief pause, then hesitant)
Hey, look. You haven't found a place
yet. I mean…you could save more…you
know…?

PATTI
True, I could...I haven't...committed to anything.

LOUISE
You want to try—another month?

PATTI
(Without hesitation) I'm okay with it if you are.

LOUISE
Really?

PATTI
Yeah. I can deal with anything, remember?

LOUISE
(Grateful) We'll deal with it together. (Beat) We'll do that dinner thing, the three of us, like we talked about, okay?

PATTI
Sure. Everything'll be fine.

LOUISE
Everything'll be fine. That's great. (She gets a text on her cell, reads it) I gotta go. Heron's waiting. What a mess.

PATTI
Do what you have to. We'll do that dinner another time. (LOUISE goes to center stage door, looks towards stairs and hesitates)

LOUISE
(Worried) Maybe I should go up. She never sleeps this long. (She turns to PATTI) I hate leaving like this. I might be gone, I don't know, a couple of weeks? You think I should go up and wake her?

PATTI
No, you go. Let her sleep. I'll wake her later and make that meatloaf you guys are always talkin' about.

LOUISE
Tell her I'll call as soon as I get there.

PATTI
Don't worry about her, okay?

(LOUISE picks up her things and exits, waving to PATTI. After she leaves, PATTI pulls out and lights a cigarette. She puts her head back, closes her eyes, and drags on the cigarette, releasing a cloud of smoke with obvious pleasure. After a few moments, we hear RUTH's cane as she comes down the stairs. RUTH appears at the kitchen doorway. She stares at PATTI, who looks over at RUTH as she takes another drag on the cigarette)

RUTH
Where's Louise?

(PATTI doesn't answer, and they look at each other. Blackout)

SCENE 5
(Lights up. RUTH and PATTI are sitting at the kitchen table eating dinner. There is a period of silence at first. PATTI watches RUTH, but RUTH looks at her dinner plate. RUTH, being alone with PATTI while LOUISE is traveling, is tense. When they first begin talking, it is with pauses in between. The dinner consists of meatloaf, a bowl of potatoes, both on the kitchen counter, and bread on the table)

PATTI
(Eating meatloaf) I followed your recipe...with the egg. What'dya think? (Brief pause) I could spice it up with a little chili paste. You can get that stuff at Trader Joe's. D'ja ever buy that? (RUTH doesn't respond) You traveled a lot—d'ja ever go to like Thailand or Korea? They use a lot of that chili paste. You lived in India, right? Indian food's the best.

RUTH
(After a moment) I've never been in India. I don't know where you got that idea.

PATTI
I guess I got it wrong. Was it Africa?
(Beat) Not Africa? *(RUTH shakes her
head no. There's a short silence as they
eat)* You think it needs salt?

RUTH
It's fine. It's a little dry.

PATTI
(Regards RUTH's plate) Go on, finish it.

RUTH
I don't eat fast these days.

PATTI
When I used to take these classes in
cooking Indian food? The teacher was
from…somewhere in India, I forget
where. Doesn't matter. All her recipes
had six, maybe eight chili peppers, those
little green ones, what're they called…
anyway, so hot! Everything tasted like
fire! People think if your mouth's
burning from that kind of pepper
you're supposed to eat bread or drink
water. But that's not true. That doesn't
work at all! Milk, you drink milk. Did
you know that—about milk? *(RUTH
doesn't respond)* One time I was with
someone in a Chinese restaurant, and
he ate one of those big red peppers—
you're not supposed to eat those! He,
like, swallowed it practically whole. He
starting choking—coughing—everyone
was looking at him—the waiter brought
him some milk from the kitchen, and
he was, like, one sip, totally fine. Me,
I got to where I really like those hot
peppers. *(Beat)* You can get used to just
about anything. Don't you think?

*(RUTH is silent. PATTI gets up and gets
a beer from the fridge, popping the top
off. She keeps her eye on RUTH as she
drinks. She walks to the window, looks
out, peers at the sky)*

PATTI (CONT'D)
It better not rain…*(She returns to the
table and sits)* You want some bread?
(RUTH ignores this) Hey, I'm tryin'
here. Louise said you've got a really
great sense of humor and you're
interesting to talk to. So you gonna talk
to me, or what? *(Brief pause)*

RUTH
(Prods a tattoo on PATTI's arm) You
didn't have that one yesterday.

PATTI
(Pokes tattoo; peers) Ow! Well, what d'ya
think? You like it?

RUTH
(Peers) How much does something like
that cost?

PATTI
I designed it. Well, Heron helped. See
these? They're Chinese letters.

RUTH
They're not letters. They're called
logograms.

PATTI
He went to China, he knows all about
it. I almost went with him, actually,
but then—anyway, I would've gone,
I wanted to. I asked him to do the
Chinese for love and god.

RUTH
(Points to one of the characters) That's the
Chinese character for soul. Your soul
that goes up to heaven. If you believe
that kind of thing.

PATTI
He's been to China, he knows what he's
doing.

RUTH
Well, I'm afraid your friend has made a
mistake.

PATTI

Fine. Have it your way. *(She prods RUTH's plate)* You better finish that so I can wash the dishes. I gotta go out tonight.

RUTH

You're going out again?

PATTI

I have to meet someone. I don't wanna be late.

RUTH

You're always meeting someone. Who're you meeting? *(She pushes her plate away)* I can't eat any more. It's dry.

PATTI

It's not dry, what're you talking about?

RUTH

When I make it, it's not all…crumbly like this. It's probably overcooked. Anyway, I use better meat…and Louise said she gave you money for groceries. You don't have to skimp on the meat. *(Beat)* Are you giving my rent to Louise?

PATTI

I could make it jucier with a little pepper sauce. You'd be surprised, you might like it. I might just try it next time I make it. I think I will. Or maybe I won't. I could put something else in the middle instead of an egg. Maybe a hand grenade. Surprise! Don't worry, I'm just kidding. *(PATTI points at RUTH's plate)* Well, eat the potatoes, then.

RUTH

(Takes a tiny bite of potatoes, makes a face) They taste funny. *(She pushes them around on the plate, peers)* What did you put in them?

PATTI

(Picking up the dishes, etc) Oh, for god's sake! There's nothing wrong with the damned potatoes! Lou loves my potatoes. I ate everything—look! You're

gonna tell Lou you're hungry and it's my fault, and then I'll get in trouble.

RUTH

I told you, don't call her Lou, that's not her name. She doesn't like it when people call her Lou. She doesn't love your cooking, either—I don't believe it—and, anyway, when did you ever cook for her?

PATTI

(Working in the kitchen to clean up, exasperated) Okay. She doesn't love my cooking. Whatever. I don't wanna have an argument, so just be quiet about the cooking. Don't be complaining to Lou about it. Sorry. Louise. *(There is the sound of thunder)* Fuck. I knew it.

RUTH

Has she called again?

PATTI

I don't remember. Did she call? Maybe. Hmmm, yeah, she did. She wanted to talk to you too. But you were asleep. Too bad.

RUTH

(Distressed) You should've woken me up!

PATTI

You know, I tried, I did. You were conked out, zonked, out like a light. But I told her how everything's going good, and you're fine and I'm fine and we're doing great.

RUTH

(Trying to rise) Did she say when she'd be home? I put her cell phone number someplace.

PATTI

Just sit down, okay? She left her cell at home. It won't do any good to call, you'd get her message—she's prob'ly using Heron's phone. *(There is the sound of heavy rain, as the storm starts. The lights flicker, go out)* Whoa!

(The lights come on again)

RUTH

(Upset) I want his number. Give me his number.

PATTI

Yeah, sure, I'll try to find it later—I gotta get outta here now. Someone's waiting for me out on the street. In this shit weather!

(RUTH gets up with difficulty, hobbles towards PATTI's bathroom)

RUTH

I'm going to the bathroom. I feel sick again. I think maybe there was something in the potatoes. You better not go out if I'm sick!

PATTI

(Puts out an arm to stop her) Not that way. *(She points towards the stairs)* Up. Your bathroom is upstairs.

RUTH

I can't climb the stairs right now—my back is broken!

PATTI

(Taking RUTH's arm and steering her to the stairs) Come on. You can do it.

RUTH

Oh, my God.

(The stage is empty for a few moments; the sound of RUTH clumping up the stairs, and then PATTI reappears. She exits towards her bathroom and is gone for a few moments. When she reappears, she has a duffle into which she is shoving one of the huge pill bottles. She sits at the table. Sound of RUTH's footsteps. After a moment RUTH appears)

RUTH (CONT'D)

I didn't feel good before, but I'm kind of hungry now.

PATTI

Well, for Christ's sake, why didn't you eat your dinner!

(PATTI stands and picks up her bag, swings it over her shoulder, preparing to leave)

RUTH

You're going out? What if the lights go out again? *(Beat)* I don't feel good, and I'm hungry.

PATTI

If you're hungry, you can do some of that cooking you're always braggin' about. I gotta go.

RUTH

(Distressed) When Louise calls, I'll tell her you made a terrible dinner that I couldn't eat!

PATTI

Now listen. You don't want Louise to worry about you all the time, do you? When she takes a trip, she doesn't need to worry about leaving you, 'cause she knows you're in good hands. Right? She can have a little peace of mind. You want her to have a little peace of mind, I know you do. *(Beat)* Because you love her. *(Ruth, feeling pressured, is silent, sullen, looks away)* Come on, Ruth…we're doing okay here, you and me. I mean, think about it. I got a nice room—with a—that whats-it tree in the window…with the flowers, lots of light, peaceful. And you've got me to take care of stuff—hey! I'll plant tomatoes— or whatever—next summer—you like tomatoes? *(They regard each other; brief silence)* Why'd you bust my little pot, Ruth?

RUTH

I don't know what you're talking about.

PATTI

I saw you! I've got cameras watching you, understand? So stay out of my rooms.

RUTH
(Uncertain) You're a liar.

(PATTI's cell phone rings. She listens)

PATTI
(Into phone) Okay. Take it easy. Relax. I'll see what I can get. *(She puts away the phone. She looks at Ruth)* Hey—Ruth—does your back still hurt?

RUTH
It always hurts. It's broken.

PATTI
What about your Tramadols? You got some, like maybe you forgot about?

RUTH
No.

PATTI
Louise said you do.

RUTH
(Suspicious) Well, I don't.

(PATTI and RUTH regard each other for a moment)

PATTI
I'm meeting a friend—so you just sit quiet till I get back. *(PATTI gets ready to leave, turns, and points at RUTH. She says the following in such a way that although she means to intimidate RUTH, a stranger listening might think she is joking. RUTH is not fooled)* Now remember—I'm watching you! I see everything you do, even when I'm not here. Got it? *(She prepares to go)* About—dinner. Just—find—something to eat, I'll cook when I get back. Or tomorrow. Whatever you want. You do cereal tonight, okay? I gotta go.

(PATTI exits. RUTH stands and stares, watching her go. Her expression changes. She turns with determination and hobbles in the direction of PATTI's bedroom, banging her cane as she goes. After she has disappeared offstage, we hear unidentifiable sounds of things

being pushed around. This goes on for several moments. We hear something break in PATTI's room. The crash is loud. Blackout)

SCENE 6
(It is silent and the stage is dark. Slowly, a light comes up on RUTH, sitting on the couch and looking steadily in the direction of the audience. After a few moments, we hear the sound of a key in the lock and PATTI enters from stage right. She turns around as she enters and calls out the door to someone. She is in fact high. Her balance is affected more than her speech)

PATTI
See ya!

(She closes the door and comes into the room. She does not notice RUTH sitting on the couch, but as she throws her jacket over a chair and puts her bag on the kitchen table, she is unstable. As she does a quiet little boogie, singing "Get Down Tonight" softly, she opens cabinets, taking out boxes and cans, reading their labels and putting things on the counter. The words she reads from the labels are interjected as she continues to sing. She peers in the dim light. RUTH is watching her in silence)

PATTI (CONT'D)
Corn syrup— *(Beat; she examines something new)* Yellow five. *(Beat)* Ye Butylated…hydroxy—what the hell? *(She stops singing, puts things back in the cabinet)* Nothing, nothing, nothing. *(She shimmies to the refrigerator and gets a beer, then goes to sit at the kitchen table, drinks. She picks up her bag, takes out a pill bottle and takes a pill with the beer. RUTH, who has been watching her, speaks)*

RUTH
You don't have any cameras.

(PATTI, startled, knocks over her beer, puts her hand on her heart)

PATTI

Jesus! You scared me! *(She quiets her heart and looks at RUTH. She gets up and turns up the lights)* How long have you been sitting there?

RUTH

I guess your cameras don't work.

PATTI

My cameras! What the hell are you talking about? *(RUTH doesn't respond; she is stony. PATTI senses trouble, feels her way)*

Did you eat? *(Beat)* I got tied up, okay? Don't look at me like that. *(RUTH doesn't respond)*...want me to fix you— *(She goes to the fridge and looks in)*—I could make an omelette. *(RUTH doesn't respond. PATTI closes fridge and gestures towards the cabinets)*—what happened to the food I bought?

RUTH

(After a moment) Sergeant McCauley came here looking for you. Sergeant McCauley from the police.

PATTI

Excuse me?

RUTH

He said you're not fit to drive.

PATTI

(Staggers slightly to sit at kitchen table) That's bullshit. This is another one of your weird dreams. Like when you thought your dead husband was sleeping in my bedroom.

RUTH

He said to call him when you got back. And I'm not stupid. I know you don't have any cameras!

PATTI

Are you gonna call the cops to tell 'em I don't have any cameras? Like they give a shit. Anyway, you don't know.

RUTH

(Bangs her cane on the floor for emphasis) I know a lot more than you think! You get out!

PATTI

(Nasty) I said so many prayers for you. I really did. I tried. I hoped you'd...You shouldn't of always said you could do a better job than God. That's why he sends you all that pain, Ruth.

(There is a brief silence)

RUTH

(Attempting to rise) I've had enough of you—your evil God—you get out! I'll call Louise right now!

PATTI

(Vicious) "I'll call Louise! I'll call Louise!" Good luck! You don't know her phone number! Fuck you! I'm sick of you, Ruth! I woulda gotten outta this a long time ago, but she begged me to stay! That's right—I guess she didn't tell you. She begged me. She wanted to have a good time for a change. She didn't even wanna say goodbye! She just left. She said she had enough of you!

RUTH

Oh, you liar—Louise would never say that!

PATTI

Yeah, well, she did. She said plenty! I can't stand being with her. That's what she said. She was just, like—"somebody else deal with my mom, 'cause I don't wanna be around her anymore. She stuck my dad in that awful place where he kept asking when he could come home," and you wouldn't let him—

RUTH

Oh!

PATTI

Right before Thanksgiving—you had him locked up! You know what that's like?

(PATTI *lights a cigarette, folds her arms, and stares at RUTH during the following speech*)

RUTH
(*In great distress*) It wasn't my fault!

PATTI
You were ashamed of him—just like you're ashamed of her.

RUTH
(*In agony, gasps*) I'm very proud of Louise!

PATTI
I've heard the way you talk to her. "I've always had a steady job, I pay my bills, and I have this wonderful house." You think you're the queen of Natick, living here in this fucking mansion! "Take me to the pond, Louise. Do my laundry! Cook my dinner!" Jesus!

RUTH
(*Agitated*) I helped her out lots of times. Lots of times. Louise is my best friend!

PATTI
(*Scoffs*) She told me you were difficult. Actually, she called you pathological.

RUTH
You vile, wicked woman! She never did!

(*RUTH begins to weep quietly*)

PATTI
Lou just wanted some good things, you know? Someone to treat her nice. I feel sorry for her. You don't really care about her anyway. You only care about yourself. And money. "Where's my money! Where's the rent! Where's the fucking rent?" Money, money—that's all you think about! "When are you gonna pay me back, Louise? I need my money, Louise!"

(*RUTH gathers her inner and outer strength. She stands with difficulty*)

RUTH
Don't talk to me about money! I saw plenty in your room. Plenty!

PATTI
(*Freezes*) Don't you fuck with me!

RUTH
If you think I'm stupid, you'd better think again!

(*PATTI runs back into her room. She is gone for a few moments and returns, running, into the kitchen, stops, stares at RUTH*)

PATTI
(*Hysterical*) You trashed everything! My stuff is wrecked! You crazy old bitch! (*She grabs RUTH by the shoulders and shakes her, shouts*) Where's the money?! (*RUTH pushes weakly against PATTI, resisting*) Where is it?!

RUTH
(*Shouts*) You owed me!

PATTI
(*Screaming*) I never fuckin' owed you anything! (*She stands back from RUTH for a moment, speaks threateningly*) You've been crazy, mean, selfish from the beginning. Now you stole my money, and that makes you a thief. You can go to jail for that. (*Beat*) You don't wanna provoke me. Trust me, you don't. Where is it?

RUTH
(*Raised voice*) The police are looking for you, and I know why—I saw your pills! You think I don't know why you had all those bottles?! All that money?!

(*They stare at each other for a moment. PATTI raises her voice*)

PATTI
Tell me where it is!

RUTH
Well, I put it in the bank!

PATTI
(Shouts; grabs RUTH again; they push
each other) That's crap! You don't got
the car keys! I'll find it—

(PATTI tries to pull away to go upstairs,
RUTH, using what strength she has, pulls
at PATTI to prevent her from leaving,
they struggle; RUTH sticks her cane in
front of PATTI and trips her. PATTI
falls, shouting as she does so)

RUTH
(Shouts amid the physical struggle) And
I already called the police—I told them
about the money—and the pills—they
know everything!

(RUTH is holding one end of the cane;
Patti, lying on the floor, grabs the other
end and, yanking hard, pulls RUTH off
balance. As RUTH falls, her head hits the
coffee table. She lies, possibly unconscious.
PATTI gets up, holding her injured knee.
She stares at RUTH)

PATTI
Get up! (RUTH is unresponsive and does
not move until after PATTI exits) Is it
upstairs? Is it? I'm gonna shred every
goddamn thing in your room!

(PATTI runs, limping, occasionally
grabbing her knee, offstage through the
center door, and we hear her running up
the stairs. A door bangs as she enters
RUTH's bedroom. There is the sound
of furniture moving, perhaps something
breaking PATTI is looking for her money
in Ruth's room. This should go on for a
little while. Sound of PATTI's footsteps
running down the stairs and she appears
in the living room again, out of breath.
She sees that RUTH is still lying on the
floor without having moved. She pauses.
She walks over and pushes RUTH with
her foot)

PATTI (CONT'D)
Where the fuck is it? Get up!

(RUTH remains still. PATTI stares at
her and goes to the fridge and gets a beer.
She limps back, drinks, looking down at
RUTH. She pushes again with her foot)

PATTI (CONT'D)
You think you can steal my money?
You don't fool me, lying like that. (Beat)
Listen. You give it to me, I'm outta here.
Okay? Tell me where it is!

(RUTH is still motionless, and PATTI
is getting worried. She bends down and
stares closely at RUTH, then gently
pushes RUTH by the shoulder)

PATTI (CONT'D)
Come on, Ruth. Open your eyes. I'm
not gonna do anything to you. (She
puts her fingers on the pulse in RUTH's
throat) Damn, what's the matter with
you?! (She pushes RUTH by the shoulder
again to try and "wake" her. When
RUTH remains motionless, she gets
scared. She stands up) You in a fuckin'
coma or what? (She remembers what
RUTH yelled; she pushes RUTH roughly
with her foot) Listen, you little bitch,
did you really call the cops? Did you?
(PATTI stares at RUTH for a moment)
Fuck!

(PATTI turns and runs, limping, back to
her room. We hear sounds from PATTI's
room, a dresser drawer banging, a suitcase
slamming onto the floor. After a few
moments, PATTI reappears, still limping,
dragging a large suitcase. As she passes
RUTH lying on the floor, her suitcase
catches against RUTH's leg. PATTI looks
back and yanks it free. She exits through
the door stage left. After a few moments,
we hear the car engine roar and the sound
of the car driving away. The lights fade
slowly to black, with only a small spotlight
that travels around the set, moving here
and there, slowly, occasionally passing
over the figure of RUTH lying on the
floor, illuminating her face or limbs. This
continues for a little while, after which the

spotlight settles on RUTH, and we see her shift one leg. We hear a car drive up, come to a stop, a car door slams and the lights come up very slowly, dimly lighting the entire stage. We hear a key in the lock. LOUISE enters, holding her handbag in one hand and balancing a cake box. In the dim light, she does not see RUTH but closes the door with her foot. She goes into the kitchen and puts the cake box down. She goes to the door center stage and peers up towards RUTH's bedroom)

LOUISE
(Calls) Mom…you there? …come down, I'm back—I brought something special! *(Louise goes through the door and from offstage we hear her calling up to Ruth)* Hello?

(She reappears. She looks around and goes to turn up the lights. As she does so, the lights come up and she sees RUTH on the floor. LOUISE runs over to RUTH and kneels)

LOUISE (CONT'D)
Oh, God. What happened? Did you fall? *(RUTH rolls over very slowly to look up at LOUISE)*

LOUISE (CONT'D)
Can you get up? *(She looks around)* Where's Patti? *(Beat)* Where is she? *(RUTH is silent. LOUISE looks at her for a moment, then gets up and goes quickly back to PATTI's room, some moments of silence, then she reappears)*

LOUISE (CONT'D)
What happened? The room. It's a mess…she's gone!

(She goes to RUTH, sits beside her and embraces her. RUTH lifts her arm and puts it around LOUISE's shoulder. They hold each other)

LOUISE (CONT'D)
You'll be okay. You'll see.

RUTH
(Weak) She pushed me, Louise. She got angry and pushed me.

(LOUISE buries her face in RUTH's shoulder. She is ashamed)

LOUISE
Oh, Mom. No.

RUTH
I found those empty pill bottles…all over the room…

LOUISE
(After a moment) I know…I saw them.

RUTH
But I found her money! I took it, Louise. She owed me. *(Beat; she speaks with some agitation)* A lot of money—I hid it! *(There is a short silence, while Louise strokes RUTH's arms)*

LOUISE
Don't worry…I'm here. I won't leave.

RUTH
She said terrible things. Things I can't tell you. *(Beat)* She said you hate me.

LOUISE
(Looks away) That's not true. I never said that.

(Brief pause)

RUTH
I forgive you, Louise. *(Beat)* I'm going to give you all the money. It's for you. *(Short silence, then LOUISE kisses RUTH's cheek)*

LOUISE
I brought that pie you like—with the applesauce. Remember? *(Beat; she is worried)* But, Mom, can't you get up now?

RUTH
(Strains briefly and sinks back) Oh, it hurts!

(There is another silence as LOUISE and RUTH hold each other. LOUISE begins to rock RUTH in her arms)

LOUISE
It'll be okay. You'll get up soon...

RUTH
I don't know... *(Beat)* Will I?

LOUISE
Yes. But right now, let's practice our breathing, okay, Mom? Just breathe.

(Silence, as LOUISE continues to rock RUTH slowly in her arms. Slow fade... halfway through the fade, blackout)

BRENDA KENWORTHY

Brenda Kenworthy (playwright, *Dragonfly*) has a BFA in Fine Art from UCLA and an MA in Theatre from the California Institute of Arts. She recently appeared as Lotty Wilton in Newport Theatre Arts Center's production of *Enchanted April* and, just before that, as Williamina Fleming in the Long Beach Playhouse production of *Silent Sky*. She has also directed works at Santa Paula Theatre Center, Hunger Artists, and Stages Theatre. As a playwright, her shorter plays have been produced in California, Utah, and New York, and include *Godzone*, *Leather Jacket*, and *Daddy's Girl*. Most recently, her play *Vagina Blue, Vagina Green* was presented at Breath of Fire Theatre Company's 2018 New Works Festival.

Dragonfly

A PLAY BY BRENDA KENWORTHY

CAST OF CHARACTERS
NAOMI: Adult, older sister
LILLIAN: Adult, younger sister
MRS. LIBELLULE: Mom
MR. LIBELLULE: Dad
DR. CHAVEZ: Female doctor
DR. SUBRAMANIAN
(NOTE: LIBELLULE is pronounced
"Lee'–buh–lull")

SETTING
Room in a Southern California hospital.

TIME
Now.

(LIGHTS UP on a hospital room. The blinds are closed, making the room dark. MR. LIBELLULE, an older man, lies sleeping in the bed. The soft SOUND of BUZZING rises up, then dies down before actors speak)

NAOMI
(Offstage) Is this it?

MRS. LIBELLULE
(Offstage) I think so.

NAOMI
(Offstage) Weren't you here before?

MRS. LIBELLULE
(Offstage) No. Not this room.

NAOMI
(Offstage) It says forty-one thirty.

MRS. LIBELLULE
(Offstage) That's what they told me.

NAOMI
(Offstage) I'll just peek…

(NAOMI pops her head into the room and looks around)

MRS. LIBELLULE
(Offstage) Naomi! What if it's not…

NAOMI
It's him.

(NAOMI enters the room. She crosses to the other side of the room, passing the foot of MR. LIBELLULE's bed. MRS. LIBELLULE enters cautiously until she sees it is, indeed, MR. LIBELLULE)

MRS. LIBELLULE
It is.

NAOMI
It is what?

MRS. LIBELLULE
Him. It is him.

NAOMI
Yes. It's so dark in here.

MRS. LIBELLULE
We can turn on the light.

NAOMI
No. I'll just…

(NAOMI crosses to window and opens
the blinds a little)

MRS. LIBELLULE
Oh.

NAOMI
There we go.

(The two women stand looking at
MR. LIBELLULE as he sleeps)

MRS. LIBELLULE
See how yellow he is?

NAOMI
(Close to MR. LIBELLULE) Yeah, he is
kind of…ochre. Kind of mustardy.

MRS. LIBELLULE
His eyes too.

NAOMI
So what did they just do to him?

MRS. LIBELLULE
Some kind of procedure. Taking
biopsies, I think.

NAOMI
Here, Mom. (Indicating a chair in the
back corner) Sit down.

MRS. LIBELLULE
No, no, you go ahead.

NAOMI
Mom.

(MRS. LIBELLULE crosses the room.
NAOMI moves some wires and a
computer screen, then draws the chair out
into the room. MRS. LIBELLULE sits)

NAOMI (CONT'D)
How long has he been yellow?

MRS. LIBELLULE
A few days.

NAOMI
A few days. Since when?

MRS. LIBELLULE
Monday? Yes, Monday.

NAOMI
It's Saturday, Mom. That's almost a week.

MRS. LIBELLULE
I know…

NAOMI
That's too long.

MRS. LIBELLULE
I know. He wouldn't let me take him to
the hospital.

NAOMI
How did you finally get him to come?

MRS. LIBELLULE
We were at my physical therapy. My
therapist took one look at your daddy
and said, "I'm calling the hospital."

NAOMI
He was driving you around to
appointments looking like this?

MRS. LIBELLULE
Yes.

NAOMI
Jesus.

MRS. LIBELLULE
You know how he is.

NAOMI
Yes, I do. Was he in pain?

MRS. LIBELLULE
No. His knee was hurting. There's a
bump on it again.

NAOMI
You told me that on the phone. But
from his stomach, was that hurting him?

MRS. LIBELLULE
No.

NAOMI
Lil said his pee was the color of Coke.

MRS. LIBELLULE
Yeah, it was dark like Coca-Cola. Not good.

NAOMI
No.

(DR. CHAVEZ enters. She wears blue
scrubs and seems out of breath)

DR. CHAVEZ
(To MRS. LIBELLULE) Hello.

MRS. LIBELLULE
Hello.

DR. CHAVEZ
So Mr. Lee…

MRS. LIBELLULE
Lee'-buh-lull. It's French. It means…

NAOMI
Mom.

DR. CHAVEZ
Mr. Libellule. He did fine during
the procedure. Since he has a
history of sensitivity to the contrast
dye, an allergy, we gave him some
antihistamine. Like Benadryl.

NAOMI
He's allergic?

MRS. LIBELLULE
Yes.

NAOMI
You knew that?

MRS. LIBELLULE
Yes.

DR. CHAVEZ
And you are?

NAOMI
I'm the daughter. His daughter.

DR. CHAVEZ
I'm Dr. Chavez. I just performed the
procedure on your father.

NAOMI
What was the procedure?

DR. CHAVEZ
Ah.

(DR. CHAVEZ goes to the WHITE
BOARD on the wall next to the head of
MR. LIBELLULE'S BED and picks up
a marker)

DR. CHAVEZ (CONT'D)
We went in through his esophagus to
his stomach…

(DR. CHAVEZ draws a tube running
down to the stomach, then little blobs
representing the liver and the pancreas,
drawing a line through the tube and into
the organs)

DR. CHAVEZ (CONT'D)
…in through here. (Points to a small
passage) This leads into the pancreas,
here. (Taps on the pancreas blob) There
was a lot of mucus built up in this
area here, so we put in a stint to hold
it open. That will help it drain more
efficiently.

MRS. LIBELLULE
Oh, good.

NAOMI
So that's unusual, right? The mucus
building up? It's not supposed to do
that, is it?

DR. CHAVEZ
No.

(DR. CHAVEZ puts down the marker
and leads MOM and NAOMI to the foot
of the bed)

DR. CHAVEZ
It's not a good sign. That amount of mucus is indicative of a more serious problem.

NAOMI
Like cancer?

DR. CHAVEZ
Like cancer.

MRS. LIBELLULE
Oh.

DR. CHAVEZ
Yes. I'm sorry. There's about an eighty percent chance that this is cancer.

NAOMI
Of the pancreas?

DR. CHAVEZ
Yes. We'll need to do more tests to be certain.

NAOMI
Can you tell what stage it's at?

DR. CHAVEZ
Further tests will tell us that.

MRS. LIBELLULE
And you'll do those? When?

DR. CHAVEZ
No, I don't handle those tests. I'm going to send you to Dr. Newsome.

MRS. LIBELLULE
Here?

DR. CHAVEZ
No, she's down in LA. She's a specialist.

MRS. LIBELLULE
She's good?

DR. CHAVEZ
One of the best. Mr. Libellule will be in good hands.

MRS. LIBELLULE
Okay, okay. We'll do that.

DR. CHAVEZ
I must tell you, in your husband's present condition, surgery may not be an option.

MRS. LIBELLULE
You don't think so?

DR. CHAVEZ
Mrs. Libellule, he's lost a lot of weight.

MRS. LIBELLULE
(To NAOMI) He's down to 130 pounds.

NAOMI
What?

DR. CHAVEZ
He's pretty fragile, he's older. The infection in his knee needs to be addressed. If he were in better condition…

NAOMI
What about chemo?

DR. CHAVEZ
I would say chemo and radiation may be possibilities, but that infection needs to be cleared up first. Dr. Newsome will let you know your options once more tests are run.

NAOMI
Okay. Thank you.

MRS. LIBELLULE
Yes, thank you very much.

DR. CHAVEZ
You're welcome.

(DR. CHAVEZ exits)

MRS. LIBELLULE
Cancer.

NAOMI
It's okay, Mom. It's a high possibility, but we don't know for sure yet. Let's just get him feeling better, schedule the tests, then we'll find out.

MRS. LIBELLULE
You're right. Yes. Yes.

NAOMI
Has Lillian already been here today?

MRS. LIBELLULE
Lil? Yes, she was here this morning.

NAOMI
Here, Mom, go ahead and sit down.

MRS. LIBELLULE
She had to go home and see about Shasta.

NAOMI
Is she coming back?

MRS. LIBELLULE
I don't know. It probably depends on what Shasta is doing.

NAOMI
We can call her later, no worries.

(NAOMI stands, MRS. LIBELLULE sits quietly for a moment. NAOMI goes to MR. LIBELLULE)

NAOMI (CONT'D)
He is really, really yellow. Maybe it's the bilirubin. When your liver can't filter the bilirubin out, you turn yellow. More daffodil than…butterscotch, though.

MRS. LIBELLULE
Your liver?

NAOMI
Yeah. They put people under lamps, give them photo-something therapy. Like a fake sun. The light's absorbed through the skin and blood. Wonder if that would help Dad.

MRS. LIBELLULE
So maybe it's liver cancer?

NAOMI
What? No, I don't know. It might not be cancer. Let's just wait. I hope he's okay for Halloween.

MRS. LIBELLULE
Me too. He loves handing out the candy.

NAOMI
I know. Does he still count all the trick-or-treaters, making those hash marks on a piece of paper?

MRS. LIBELLULE
Sometimes. If Shasta is over, she likes to hand out the candy and Daddy loses track.

NAOMI
I thought Shasta was going up to Santa Barbara for Halloween. A party or something.

MRS. LIBELLULE
Is she?

NAOMI
I thought so. That's what Lil said. Some place around Hope Ranch. You know, upper State Street, by that restaurant we'd go to after Dad and I rode our bikes up there?

MRS. LIBELLULE
Where we met up with Grandma and Grandpa?

NAOMI
Yeah, the one that looked like a bottle green barn, by where they used to live.

MRS. LIBELLULE
That was fun. Your daddy loved riding bikes up there with you.

NAOMI
It was very nice.

(LIGHTS go down on MRS. LIBELLULE and MR. LIBELLULE. NAOMI enters a spotlight downstage)

NAOMI
At first, I went by myself. Not all the way to Santa Barbara alone. Maybe Carpinteria or Summerland. Montecito a couple of times. The section just past the

fairgrounds was always my favorite, the way it swept around the hills and then BAM!, there was the ocean, that same deep blue it always is, the sky the same blue it always is. By the time I got out to that point, the marine layer was gone, and always, every day, those blues. It was nice alone, but being with Dad was…

(MR. LIBELLULE, in cycling gear, pushes two BIKES into the spotlight and comes to stand next to NAOMI. NAOMI is younger than she was in the first scene. She takes her bike and checks the back tire and pumps it with air)

NAOMI (CONT'D)
…good.

MR. LIBELLULE
Good you had a spare.

NAOMI
Yeah. Seems like I get a flat every time.

MR. LIBELLULE
That's why you're so quick fixing them.

NAOMI
Where's Mom? Did you see her drive by?

MR. LIBELLULE
(Checking his watch) No. It's only been ten minutes since we passed her.

NAOMI
Ten minutes? I am quick.

MR. LIBELLULE
Look at that.

NAOMI
Where?

MR. LIBELLULE
Right there.

(The soft SOUND OF BUZZING can be heard)

NAOMI
Oh, the blue? Is that a damselfly, a bluet?

MR. LIBELLULE
No, it's a dragonfly. A Blue Dasher.

NAOMI
How can you…oh, yeah, I see it. It's a male, the metallic green eyes.

MR. LIBELLULE
(Teasing) Don't let it fly around your head…

NAOMI
(Picking up his tone)…or it'll judge your soul! Where is that from? That tale?

MR. LIBELLULE
Sweden, I think.

NAOMI
I think I remember you telling me that. How's Lil doing in summer school?

MR. LIBELLULE
Alright. She wouldn't have to be there if she'd buckle down and stop going out every night.

NAOMI
She doesn't go out every night.

MR. LIBELLULE
She goes out enough to have to attend summer school. She's a lot wilder than you ever were.

NAOMI
I got a D once. Remember?

MR. LIBELLULE
Your sister got Fs, little different. But, yes, I do remember. Honors Algebra.

NAOMI
When I got my yearbook at the end of the year, you said you were surprised they let people who get Ds in the yearbook.

MR. LIBELLULE
I did?

NAOMI
Yes.

MR. LIBELLULE
Do they?

NAOMI
Let them in? Yes.

MR. LIBELLULE
Well, they shouldn't. And you shouldn't've gotten a D. You're the brains, remember? Your sister's the beauty.

NAOMI
Thanks. *(Pause)* I made it up. Passed algebra at J.C. Got a B.

MR. LIBELLULE
Yeah.

NAOMI
What do you mean "yeah"?

MR. LIBELLULE
I heard how you got those grades.

NAOMI
What?

MR. LIBELLULE
Anthony told me.

NAOMI
Anthony…Mendoza? Told you what?

MR. LIBELLULE
About the short skirts you wore to class, showing off your cleavage…

NAOMI
You believed my ex-boyfriend, saying stuff like that?

MR. LIBELLULE
You got good grades, right? You have nice boobs. Whatever you did to get the grades…

NAOMI
I studied to get those grades. I was in class every day and took notes and read all the books to get those grades. I finished every assignment and quiz and test and whatever fucking else…

MR. LIBELLULE
All right, it was just a joke.

NAOMI
It wasn't funny.

MR. LIBELLULE
Maybe I should just keep my mouth shut.

NAOMI
Maybe.

(NAOMI's eyes catch something moving past)

NAOMI (CONT'D)
There's Mom.

(NAOMI wheels away her bike, following the unseen MRS. LIBELLULE)

NAOMI (CONT'D)
Mom! Stop!

(NAOMI exits out of the spotlight. MR. LIBELLULE, disgruntled, follows. NAOMI circles back without the bike and re-enters the spotlight)

NAOMI (CONT'D)
Maybe it wasn't that nice.

MRS. LIBELLULE
(Voice in the dark) What wasn't nice?

(LIGHTS UP on a different hospital room. It is some weeks later. Slightly different arrangement of the same bed, chair [Plus one extra chair], equipment, etc. MRS. LIBELLULE is in different clothes, NAOMI puts on something to denote this is a different time and location from the first scene. MR. LIBELLULE is asleep in the bed)

NAOMI
Nothing. I was just thinking. Sorry I'm late.

MRS. LIBELLULE
That's okay. We're just glad you're here. Where's Lillian? She went out to wait for you.

NAOMI
In the lobby. Is he all done?

MRS. LIBELLULE
As far as I know.

NAOMI
What do you mean, "as far as you know"?

MRS. LIBELLULE
He had some kind of procedure. I'm
not sure.

NAOMI
I thought you were writing things
down. Lil and I told you to write
things down.

MRS. LIBELLULE
Lil's writing them down.

NAOMI
That's not the same thing, Mom.

MRS. LIBELLULE
I know. I'll get out my notebook
next time.

NAOMI
Do you even have one?

MRS. LIBELLULE
Yes. Somewhere.

(MRS. LIBELLULE starts digging
through her overstuffed purse)

NAOMI
Never mind, Mom, it's okay.

MRS. LIBELLULE
I thought I brought it…

NAOMI
It's okay, Mom. Stop looking for it.
Did they do whatever it was they were
supposed to do last week?

MRS. LIBELLULE
I think so. Yes.

NAOMI
What happened last week?

MRS. LIBELLULE
I told you.

NAOMI
No, you told Lil. I can never get you on
the phone.

MRS. LIBELLULE
Oh. That's right. She couldn't take us, so
David drove us down.

NAOMI
Uh-huh.

MRS. LIBELLULE
Well, the stupid doctor told us not
to feed Daddy before the operation,
so he hadn't had anything to eat for
a long time.

NAOMI
They have to do that so he doesn't
throw up under the anesthesia.

MRS. LIBELLULE
I know, but with Daddy's condition…

NAOMI
Did you tell them he's diabetic?

MRS. LIBELLULE
They know that.

NAOMI
But did you tell them?

MRS. LIBELLULE
It's in his chart.

NAOMI
You should always tell them, remind
them.

MRS. LIBELLULE
Well.

NAOMI
You and David got him here. And?

MRS. LIBELLULE
David is so nice.

NAOMI
I know he is. Lil and I have thanked him and his father for taking care of you guys.

MRS. LIBELLULE
His mother too. She made us chili this week and sent David over with it.

NAOMI
That's very nice of them.

MRS. LIBELLULE
They're the nicest neighbors. The ones on the other side…

NAOMI
Mom…

MRS. LIBELLULE
They're a mariachi band. The whole family. Daddy hates all the noise they make. And their kids run all over our bushes…

NAOMI
Okay. Now…

MRS. LIBELLULE
They're in gangs. All up and down our street, the next-door neighbors. Daddy says…

NAOMI
They're in a mariachi band, Mom, not a gang. They play music. Not every Hispanic person is in a gang, no matter what Dad says. Why don't you talk to them, be friendly? You speak Spanish.

MRS. LIBELLULE
Well.

NAOMI
Mom, what happened when you and David got Dad here to the clinic last week?

MRS. LIBELLULE
Oh. Well, they were just about to take Daddy in. The guy brought a wheelchair for him, and he just collapsed.

NAOMI
On the floor?

MRS. LIBELLULE
Yes. Well, David and the guy with the wheelchair caught him, and stuffed him into the chair. They couldn't do the procedure after that.

NAOMI
No, I know. How long were you here after that?

MRS. LIBELLULE
They took him across the street to the hospital, and David and I were there with him until four the next morning.

NAOMI
Four? I called you at one a.m. and you said they were releasing him.

MRS. LIBELLULE
Well. They took their sweet time. Daddy and I are not very happy with these people.

NAOMI
Was it just his blood sugar?

MRS. LIBELLULE
It was down to twenty-three.

NAOMI
Did they just give him glucagon for it, to raise it up? Was it cortisol?

MRS. LIBELLULE
I think so.

NAOMI
Which one?

MRS. LIBELLULE
I don't know. It was at twenty-three.

NAOMI
Yes. But why was his blood sugar so low? He's taking medication.

MRS. LIBELLULE
They don't know, they didn't tell us.

NAOMI
I'm almost sure they had to have, Mom. I'm trying to help you.

MRS. LIBELLULE
I know that.

NAOMI
Do you know how long he has to stay here before we can take him home?

MRS. LIBELLULE
Until he wakes up, I would imagine. Speaking of taking him home, I should go to the bathroom before we leave. *(MRS. LIBELLULE stands and gets her walker)*

NAOMI
You want to go now?

MRS. LIBELLULE
To make sure I do, yes. David had to stop at a McDonald's last time, so I could go.

NAOMI
And so Dad could get something to eat?

MRS. LIBELLULE
(Impishly) Uh-huh. I'll be right back.

NAOMI
Do you need any help?

MRS. LIBELLULE
No. Somebody needs to stay for when he wakes up.

(MRS. LIBELLULE exits. NAOMI goes to MR. LIBELLULE's bedside and looks at him. She strokes his hair)

NAOMI
Dude, McDonald's? You gotta do better than that.

(LILLIAN enters)

LILLIAN
What's taking so long? Where's Mom?

NAOMI
In the bathroom.

LILLIAN
She'll be in there forever. How's he doing?

(LILLIAN goes to MR. LIBELLULE's bedside)

NAOMI
Okay, I guess. The doctor hasn't been by yet. Will they let all of us be in here? I thought two visitors at a time.

LILLIAN
They don't give a shit. God, he looks terrible.

NAOMI
He's a little green. So, he collapsed last time, this time he was okay?

LILLIAN
Yeah, 'cause he actually ate his dinner last night.

NAOMI
He didn't before?

LILLIAN
No. They told him he could eat up until midnight and then have some liquid, broth or something, up to six hours before the surgery. I wrote it out for them.

NAOMI
I know.

LILLIAN
He didn't eat his fucking dinner the night before. That means he hadn't eaten for more than twenty-four hours before he got here. That's why he passed out.

NAOMI
Holy shit.

LILLIAN
Yeah. He keeps doing stupid shit like that. Mom's had to call an ambulance for him a couple of times 'cause he passes out from not eating.

NAOMI
A couple of times? I thought it was just the once.

LILLIAN
Yeah. Dad thought it was funny. He
laughed when he told me he'd fallen
over in the living room and wound up
splashing around in the dog's water bowl.

NAOMI
I don't even understand that. What…?

LILLIAN
He fell, hit his head or something, then
he was so out of it while he was on
the floor, he started feeling around. He
was right by the water bowl and started
sticking his hand in it, splashing around.

NAOMI
For fuck's sake.

LILLIAN
All because he eats like a five-year-old.

NAOMI
His blood sugar was down again?

LILLIAN
To twenty-three.

NAOMI
What are they doing?

LILLIAN
They have no idea.

NAOMI
I keep trying to get a handle on what's
going on, but I can't get a straight
answer. I call Mom, and when she picks
up, I can't get a straight answer. I call
Mom, she tells me one thing, I get a
hold of a doctor, they tell me something
else. I contact another of their numerous
doctors and I only get nurses. They don't
know what's going on or they can't share
any information with me.

LILLIAN
Same here. How was your drive?

NAOMI
Fine. Better than usual.

LILLIAN
Because it's so fucking early. But at least
we got Dad in this time.

NAOMI
And what did they do?

LILLIAN
A PET scan. They need to know how
far the tumor has spread.

NAOMI
If it's not too bad, they'll do that
Whipple thing, right?

LILLIAN
Yeah. They take out sections of the
surrounding organs to make sure they
get everything.

NAOMI
Wow. I thought today was a biopsy. I am
so confused. And I am so tired.

LILLIAN
Did you eat?

NAOMI
Not yet.

LILLIAN
There's a nice cafeteria downstairs.

NAOMI
Doubt they have Chinese. I'm totally
jonesing for Chinese.

(LIGHTS DOWN on hospital,
SPOTLIGHT downstage. NAOMI
walks into light. She's younger than last
time. They're in a pizza parlor)

NAOMI (CONT'D)
I just really want Chinese.

(MR. LIBELLULE, dressed casually,
enters the spotlight)

MR. LIBELLULE
We're not getting Chinese. We're having
pizza. Pick out some pizza. Mom's
going to have Hawaiian. I don't know
why she always gets that. Pineapple

doesn't belong on pizza. We should've just gone to McDonald's.

NAOMI
What about Lil?

MR. LIBELLULE
She went straight to the bathroom.

NAOMI
Do they have just salad?

MR. LIBELLULE
Salad? At a pizza place? Don't be like that.

NAOMI
Like what?

MR. LIBELLULE
A brat. Pick a pizza.

NAOMI
Whatever you have is fine.

MR. LIBELLULE
You don't like pepperoni.

NAOMI
I'll just pick it off.

MR. LIBELLULE
That's stupid. Don't be stupid. Naomi? Naomi. Look at me. Look at…

(NAOMI won't look at him or answer. MR. LIBELLULE smacks her on the side of her head)

MR. LIBELLULE
Pick out a damn pizza!

(NAOMI backs out of the spotlight. MR. LIBELLULE storms out in the opposite direction)

(LIGHTS UP on another hospital room, some weeks later. Same bed, chairs, equipment, etc., in a different configuration. MR. LIBELLULE lies asleep in the bed. MRS. LIBELLULE sits on a chair, her walker close by. LILLIAN sits in the other chair)

LILLIAN
They have pizza downstairs. In the cafeteria.

NAOMI
I'm okay. Why do these hospital rooms all look alike?

MRS. LIBELLULE
Are you sure? I'll give you some money.

NAOMI
I'm good, Mom, thanks. So, another stent?

MRS. LIBELLULE
What? Yes.

LILLIAN
The second one got clogged up, just like the first.

MRS. LIBELLULE
That's why Daddy was having such bad… *(She whispers)*…diarrhea. It was green.

LILLIAN
And eating dinner at McDonald's every night.

MRS. LIBELLULE
We don't go every night. The doctor said Daddy could eat anything he wants. He needs to gain some weight.

NAOMI
That's okay with his diabetes?

LILLIAN
The doctor said he could eat pretty much what he wanted as long as they monitored his levels closely.

MRS. LIBELLULE
We do. We have been.

LILLIAN
Really?

MRS. LIBELLULE
Yes.

NAOMI
Okay, okay. This third stent, how long is
it supposed to last?

MRS. LIBELLULE
Hopefully, longer than the first two.
Daddy's very upset they've only been
lasting a few weeks.

LILLIAN
I don't think the doctors realized how
serious his condition is, Mom.
Dr. Chavez…

NAOMI
That's the same doctor that did the
others?

LILLIAN
Yeah, she said that pancreatic cancer
often causes excessive mucus.

MRS. LIBELLULE
But the doctor also said that it might
not be cancer at all.

NAOMI
Which doctor said that?

LILLIAN
Dr. Newsome.

MRS. LIBELLULE
She told us it might be an autoimmune
disease of the pancreas.

NAOMI
How come I didn't hear about that? I've
been trying to call you, Mom.

LILLIAN
She can't hear the phone.

MRS. LIBELLULE
I can hear it.

LILLIAN
Sure.

MRS. LIBELLULE
Dr. Newsome called a couple days ago.

NAOMI
With the test results?

MRS. LIBELLULE
Those aren't in yet. She called to tell
us that, about the tests, and to say
that Daddy might have autoimmune
pancreatitis.

LILLIAN
Mom…

NAOMI
How would they treat that?

MRS. LIBELLULE
Steroids. Something like that.
Prednisolone.

LILLIAN
Did she say that? Prednisolone
specifically? Did you write it down?

MRS. LIBELLULE
No.

(LILLIAN gets up, angry. She stands far
away from MRS. LIBELLULE)

NAOMI
Was she pretty certain about that
diagnosis?

MRS. LIBELLULE
She sounded like it. I used to
take Prednisone, remember? For
autoimmune hepatitis?

LILLIAN
Yeah, for like, seven years. Remember
that? Way past how long you should
take it.

MRS. LIBELLULE
Yes, Lillian, I know. They thought
I'd developed Cushing's from it.
I remember it.

LILLIAN
And do you actually have Cushing's?
No, you don't.

NAOMI
Lil.

LILLIAN
She doesn't. She doesn't have any of the shit she thinks she's been diagnosed with. She's worn Dad into a little nub. *(To MRS. LIBELLULE)* You did this. Who's going to take you to all your appointments and surgeries and procedures when he's gone? Have you thought about that?

NAOMI
Why don't you go downstairs and get something to eat. Have you eaten? Lil, have you eaten?

LILLIAN
Fine. *(Gathers her things and moves to the door)*

(MRS. LIBELLULE rummages in her purse and holds out some money towards LILLIAN)

MRS. LIBELLULE
Here.

(LILLIAN exits without taking the money)

MRS. LIBELLULE
Maybe I should go with her.

NAOMI
No, Mom, let her go. Give her a little space.

MRS. LIBELLULE
Okay. She gets so angry with us.

NAOMI
You just need to take it easy on her.

MRS. LIBELLULE
You don't get that angry.

NAOMI
I'm not angry. I'm just disappointed.

MRS. LIBELLULE
Disappointed? What do you mean? Why?

NAOMI
I don't know. That's just how I feel. I don't live here. I'm not here all the time. Lil's having to take care of you and Dad and Shasta all by herself.

MRS. LIBELLULE
David and his dad have been taking us to appointments.

NAOMI
Yes, and that's very nice of them, but they're not family. You're our parents. It's…more personal for us.

MRS. LIBELLULE
I suppose. We have to take care of him.

NAOMI
We're trying to. This pancreatitis… I thought he had a tumor.

MRS. LIBELLULE
He does. I think. I'll have to ask.

(DR. SUBRAMANIAN enters, played by same actor as DR. CHAVEZ)

DR. SUBRAMANIAN
Hello, Mrs.…?

MRS. LIBELLULE
Mrs. Libellule. It's French.

NAOMI
Hello.

MRS. LIBELLULE
And this is my daughter, Naomi.

DR. SUBRAMANIAN
Hello. I'm Dr. Subramanian. Dr. Chavez put the stent in for your husband—your father—today, but she wanted me to come and speak with you about the test results that Dr. Newsome sent over.

NAOMI
Have you been taking care of my father?

DR. SUBRAMANIAN
No. I'm an oncologist, on call today. Dr. Chavez had another procedure to perform and she thought it would be clearer anyway if I explained.

NAOMI
Okay. Mom, why don't you sit down?

MRS. LIBELLULE
Okay.

(NAOMI gets out a notebook and pen)

DR. SUBRAMANIAN
Do you have another daughter, the one who was here earlier?

MRS. LIBELLULE
Yes. Lillian just went to the cafeteria.

NAOMI
Maybe for a walk.

MRS. LIBELLULE
Should we wait for her?

DR. SUBRAMANIAN
I'm not sure when I can come back. Let me see if we can page her.

NAOMI
Ooh. Won't that scare her? I mean, whatever the news is, I can write it down and tell her when she comes back.

DR. SUBRAMANIAN
Can you do that? Does that sound all right with you?

MRS. LIBELLULE
Yes. Yes, that's fine.

DR. SUBRAMANIAN
All right. The PET scan that Mr. ...

MRS. LIBELLULE
Libellule.

DR. SUBRAMANIAN
Mr. Libellule took a PET scan in... December. Unfortunately, the tumor in the pancreas has grown and, at this point, it has spread to the liver. It is stage four.

MRS. LIBELLULE
Oh, God.

NAOMI
It's okay, Mom, hold on a second.

DR. SUBRAMANIAN
What's doubly unfortunate is that the size of the tumor, the fact that it has spread, and Mr. Libellule's age and condition combine to rule out the Whipple procedure. I know Dr. Chavez mentioned the possibility of your husband undergoing that procedure, but that avenue is closed, I'm afraid. I'm sorry.

NAOMI
What other courses of treatment might still be available?

DR. SUBRAMANIAN
I think different courses of chemotherapy might be an option. I'm going to send you to Dr. Keats and she can discuss all of that with you.

MRS. LIBELLULE
Dr. Keats?

DR. SUBRAMANIAN
Yes. She's very good. Her office is right across the parking lot. Very close for you.

NAOMI
Good. That'll be easy for you guys to come for your appointments.

DR. SUBRAMANIAN
I'm so sorry, I have another patient to see, but I'll leave you my card and have the nurse set you up with Dr. Keats.

NAOMI
Thank you.

MRS. LIBELLULE
Yes, thank you, doctor.

(DR. SUBRAMANIAN exits)

MRS. LIBELLULE (CONT'D)
Oh, no. She said it was pancreatitis.

NAOMI
They didn't know for sure, Mom.

MRS. LIBELLULE
Now they do.

NAOMI
Makes me feel even worse that I can't seem to be here when he's awake.

MRS. LIBELLULE
That would be nice if you could.

NAOMI
I've been trying. I'd like to talk to him a little.

MRS. LIBELLULE
Your daddy's not a talker.

NAOMI
Yes, I know that. *(They laugh)* I was such a daddy's girl, remember that? In elementary school? Like Laura Ingalls Wilder. Watching *Little House on the Prairie* all the time? I wanted us to be like that.

MRS. LIBELLULE
Well, you were.

NAOMI
Not for long enough. Seems like right when I hit puberty…

MRS. LIBELLULE
He had trouble understanding you.

NAOMI
Why?

MRS. LIBELLULE
You were so…arty.

NAOMI
"Arty." "Overly-dramatic." "Hypersensitive." It's so funny now, because I can't do a thing art-wise. I can't come up with anything, then when I do, it never comes out the way

I imagine. I don't have the heart to make it work. The confidence. The courage. Once, he told me that I was the kind of person who grows up and lives off of others. "That's what artists do."

(NAOMI stands and walks down stage to the spotlight, examining her hair. MR. LIBELLULE joins her, carrying a stool and a brush. He sits on the stool, legs wide. NAOMI sits on the ground between his legs. She is even younger. MR. LIBELLULE starts to brush her hair)

MR. LIBELLULE
You should brush your hair out right when you get out of the shower, honey.

NAOMI
I know. I forgot.

MR. LIBELLULE
Try to remember.

NAOMI
Oww!

MR. LIBELLULE
Sit still, let me get this. Lotta knots in here. They're coming out. Just be patient.

(The brushing gets smoother, easier)

MR. LIBELLULE
See? Little easier now. *(Another sharp jerk as the brush snags.)*

NAOMI
Ouch! I have to get up.

MR. LIBELLULE
There's still more.

NAOMI
I have the fidgets.

(MR. LIBELLULE stops brushing and NAOMI stands up. She wiggles crazily around the space, jiggling and dancing, shaking her hands out. After a bit, she returns to her place in front of her father. The brushing resumes)

NAOMI
Why does my hair always get so knotted up?

MR. LIBELLULE
It's like spider webs. It's so fine.

NAOMI
Is that good for anything?

MR. LIBELLULE
For the fairies.

NAOMI
Why?

MR. LIBELLULE
They like playing in spider webs, dancing around in them. That's why it's such a tangle back here. These are fairy knots.

NAOMI
There were fairies in my bed, messing with my hair?

MR. LIBELLULE
Yep. Looks like they had a great time too. Sometimes they weave the strands together to catch dragonflies.

(Soft SOUND of BUZZING)

NAOMI
So they can ride them around?

MR. LIBELLULE
Yep.

NAOMI
Oww!

MR. LIBELLULE
You got my hair.

NAOMI
Your hair is like spiderwebs too?

MR. LIBELLULE
Mmm-hmm. And your sister has your mom's hair.

NAOMI
Thicker?

MR. LIBELLULE
Thicker, yes. When Lillian was born, she had thick hair, like a bottle brush. Black, like ink. But your sister seems to have gotten everything else from me. She's going to be a looker.

NAOMI
You were skinny like her when you were little, huh?

MR. LIBELLULE
Really skinny. When I met your mom, I was 130 pounds. You, however, got your mom's body. Sorry about that.

NAOMI
How do you know?

MR. LIBELLULE
Stubby legs. Big rear end. My little fatty.

(NAOMI falls silent. A few strokes with the brush)

MR. LIBELLULE
You're gonna look like her when you get older. Bit of a shame.

NAOMI
Are you done?

MR. LIBELLULE
I think so.

(NAOMI stands and takes the brush from MR. LIBELLULE. She exits the spotlight. MR. LIBELLULE sits for a minute, then shakes his head)

MR. LIBELLULE
Shame.

MRS. LIBELLULE
(In dark) Shame.

(MR. LIBELLULE stands, picks up his stool, and exits the spotlight)

NAOMI
(In dark) What's a shame?

MRS. LIBELLULE
(In dark) That you always come when he's sleeping.

(LIGHTS UP on another hospital room, several weeks later. Same bed, chairs, equipment, etc., in a different configuration. MR. LIBELLULE lies asleep in the bed. MRS. LIBELLULE sits on a chair, her walker close by. NAOMI enters)

NAOMI
I know. I said that last time.

MRS. LIBELLULE
You did?

NAOMI
Where's Lil?

MRS. LIBELLULE
Isn't she out there?

NAOMI
I didn't see her.

MRS. LIBELLULE
Shasta called her. Should we go look for her?

NAOMI
No, Mom, I'm sure she's fine. How's Dad?

MRS. LIBELLULE
He's sleeping.

NAOMI
Yes, I see that. I mean, how is his health?

MRS. LIBELLULE
Not good. He has stage four.

NAOMI
Yes. I'm sorry, Mom.

MRS. LIBELLULE
But Dr. Keats said that Daddy was a good candidate for chemo. He's supposed to start next week.

NAOMI
So his knee infection has cleared up?

MRS. LIBELLULE
Enough for chemo, yes. You want to see it?

NAOMI
No.

MRS. LIBELLULE
It's gone way down. You should look.

NAOMI
No. Is this going to affect that? The diabetes? Does it matter with the chemo?

MRS. LIBELLULE
I don't know. We have to get him better. We have to take care of him.

NAOMI
I'm trying. This is the second time I've driven up this week. Was it his blood sugar again?

MRS. LIBELLULE
I think so. He's had… (Whispering)… diarrhea… (Normal voice)…for days.

NAOMI
I thought you fixed that.

MRS. LIBELLULE
We thought so too.

NAOMI
What has he been eating?

MRS. LIBELLULE
He's been eating really good. We had chicken and corn the other night.

NAOMI
That's good.

MRS. LIBELLULE
We've really been trying.

(LILLIAN enters, on her cell phone)

LILLIAN
Okay, I will. Love you, sweetie. I will. Bye. (Hangs up phone) She got in!

MRS. LIBELLULE
Who did?

LILLIAN
Shasta. She got into her top pick.

MRS. LIBELLULE
(To NAOMI) What is she talking about?

NAOMI
Colleges, Mom. Shasta got into college.

MRS. LIBELLULE
Oh, that's wonderful!

NAOMI
Pratt. In New York, right?

LILLIAN
Yep.

MRS. LIBELLULE
Oh, that's far.

LILLIAN
And expensive.

NAOMI
She can probably get some scholarships, she's smart enough.

MRS. LIBELLULE
She's super smart.

NAOMI
What does her dad think?

LILLIAN
Who knows? He's being such an ass.

MRS. LIBELLULE
I think I have to go to the bathroom.

NAOMI
Okay. Do you need some help?

MRS. LIBELLULE
No, I can do it. You stay here with Daddy.

(MRS. LIBELLULE takes hold of her walker and exits)

LILLIAN
I don't know how I'm going to afford it.

NAOMI
College?

LILLIAN
Yes. Levi isn't going to give her anything.

NAOMI
He said that?

LILLIAN
He's been saying for years that once Shasta turns eighteen, he's moving to Mexico. He checked out on her when she hit puberty.

NAOMI
She's still his daughter.

LILLIAN
Doesn't matter. He wants no responsibilities.

NAOMI
What a dick. I'm so sorry.

LILLIAN
Me too. You remember how Grandma and Grandpa gave us money for college?

NAOMI
Yeah, got me through Berkeley.

LILLIAN
How come Mom and Dad didn't set up anything for our kids?

NAOMI
I don't know. I never thought about that.

LILLIAN
They haven't given Shasta anything for college, they haven't set up anything for your girls. They got a lot of money from Grandma and Grandpa, where is it?

NAOMI
I don't know.

LILLIAN
I think Mom wanted her books and
her jewelry and her clothes. Her hair,
her nails. She wanted her perfect house
with its new kitchen, the garden in the
back, her pedigree dogs. That's where
the money went.

NAOMI
No. They couldn't have spent that much.

LILLIAN
How much was it, do you know?

NAOMI
Tom says it was a lot, close to a million
maybe.

LILLIAN
Fuck. And it all went to their
knickknacks and their dogs, their
fucking animals. That stupid kitchen.

NAOMI
That can't be right.

LILLIAN
I'm sure it is. They take those dogs to
the vet at least twice a week for shots,
they get them groomed I don't know
how often. Couple times a month. Have
you seen the medicine drawer below
the coffee maker?

NAOMI
Yes.

LILLIAN
All dog medications. And have you been
back to the house yet?

NAOMI
No, I came straight here.

LILLIAN
They took Boo-Boo in and got that
growth taken off her eyelid.

NAOMI
No. I told them not to. That thing was
harmless.

LILLIAN
Yep. Dad will do anything Mom wants.
She wanted that thing off Boo-Boo's
face. Four thousand bucks.

NAOMI
Oh my God. With all this stuff with
Dad going on?

LILLIAN
She doesn't care. She just wants the dog
to look good. Like her hair and her
nails and her house and herself.

NAOMI
God. I don't want to be here.

LILLIAN
Me either.

NAOMI
I mean, I wanted to be good, be a good
person. Do the right thing. This is the
right thing, isn't it? Taking care of your
parents? Why's it so awful? Why do I
feel so fucking awful? Like I don't want
to be a good person anymore.

LILLIAN
Because they don't care. Not really. I
mean, I'm bitching about the money…

NAOMI
It's their money, though.

LILLIAN
But it's not about the money. It's the
priorities. Why doesn't Shasta mean
more than the necklaces and the rings?
Why don't your girls matter more than
a purebred?

NAOMI
I don't know. Tom makes good money,
maybe they felt the girls didn't need any
help.

LILLIAN
Okay, but what about Shasta? Levi and I
broke up when she was two. They knew
it would be hard financially for me.

NAOMI
They should have.

LILLIAN
But Dad kicked me out of their house after the divorce. He refused to cosign on a loan so I could get someplace to live with Shasta.

NAOMI
Why didn't I know this?

LILLIAN
I don't know.

NAOMI
'Cause I've never learned how to connect, not even with my own family. They never showed us how.

LILLIAN
Yep.

NAOMI
You know what kills me? That they never call to speak to the girls. The past nine months I've been going back and forth to see them and help them out. I leave the girls and Tom and come here, where I don't even know what I'm doing. Dad's never asked about the girls. Not once.

LILLIAN
I'm sorry.

NAOMI
I thought with his grandkids, he'd be different, Mom would be different. This weird half-connection, then disconnect. You think it's all good, then you get punched in the face.

LILLIAN
It wasn't his work, was it?

NAOMI
I don't think so. For Mom, maybe. She was always so afraid she'd piss off her boss. She'd never stay home with me when I was sick. Just picked me up from school, took me home, pulled out

a can of soup for me to make myself, then back to work. I'd be alone, sick, at home. Dad...Dad used to come home fairly early from work. Remember? And I remember him being happy to see me. A long time ago.

(NAOMI moves downstage to the spotlight. She's the youngest she's been)

NAOMI (CONT'D)
Dad! You're home! I'm so glad you're home. I have a picture to show you.

(MR. LIBELLULE enters into the spotlight. He's just returned from work and is dressed as such)

MR. LIBELLULE
Do you?

NAOMI
I drew it myself. It's a princess flying on a peacock. Come see!

MR. LIBELLULE
Okay. But first, I've got something to show you.

NAOMI
Something for me? Did you bring me something?

MR. LIBELLULE
I did.

NAOMI
Where is it?

MR. LIBELLULE
Look in my car. In the back window.

NAOMI
The back window?

(NAOMI goes to the edge of the spotlight, looking into the back window of her father's car)

MR. LIBELLULE
Is he still there?

NAOMI
"He"? I don't see it.

MR. LIBELLULE
Yes. He's right there. See?

(Soft SOUND of BUZZING)

NAOMI
Oh! Daddy, he's beautiful! And he's my favorite color too!

MR. LIBELLULE
Do you know what he is?

NAOMI
A dragonfly!

MR. LIBELLULE
Yes, but what kind?

NAOMI
A Blue Dasher. Pachydiplax longipennis.

MR. LIBELLULE
You remember! Good girl. My little Half-Pint.

NAOMI
You got him just for me?

MR. LIBELLULE
Yeah, I told him my daughter would love to see him and he flew into my car. Sat right there in the rear window, just waiting to meet you.

NAOMI
Thank you, Dragonfly. It's nice to meet you.

MR. LIBELLULE
You're just the right age to meet him. Too much older and you'll be set. Like Jello.

NAOMI
I don't want to be Jello.

MR. LIBELLULE
Yep. Like peachy-orange Jello. You'll get older and have your own ideas. You'll be different. Not my Half-Pint.

NAOMI
I won't. Can I get closer? Will I scare him?

MR. LIBELLULE
We have to be careful. We don't want him to weigh our souls.

NAOMI
How would he do that?

MR. LIBELLULE
He'd fly around our heads, judging us. He wouldn't like children who lie. That's what Swedish people say.

NAOMI
What about adults?

MR. LIBELLULE
Adults too. If grown-ups curse or scold, they don't like that, either. If the person is bad enough, they might stitch up your eyes and your mouth and your ears. Are you scared?

NAOMI
No. I don't lie. Or do those other things.

MR. LIBELLULE
Good. Then we're safe.

NAOMI
We should let him go. He looks too hot in the window.

MR. LIBELLULE
Are you sure? We can keep him. Dry him out and put him in a box so you can look at him anytime you want.

NAOMI
No. That's not fair. He needs to eat the wind. That's what they do, Daddy. They eat the wind to show people how easy it is to be strong and pretty and fly.

MR. LIBELLULE
But you could have him so you can draw him, have your princesses flying on a beautiful blue dragonfly.

NAOMI
No. I don't want to. It's better if he's free.

MR. LIBELLULE
All right. I thought you'd like to keep him. I can never tell which way you're going to go. You're already turning into Jello. I can't get anything right.

(MR. LIBELLULE exits the spotlight. NAOMI captures the dragonfly and holds it in her hands)

NAOMI
Don't worry. I'll set you free.

(LIGHTS UP on another hospital room, several weeks later. The bed is in another position, as are the chairs. There is no more equipment. MR. LIBELLULE is lying in bed, sleeping. MRS. LIBELLULE and LILLIAN are present. NAOMI goes to the bedside and stays there)

NAOMI
When was the last time he spoke?

MRS. LIBELLULE
Yesterday.

NAOMI
His breathing seems alright.

LILLIAN
They took him off the oxygen last night.

NAOMI
You were here?

LILLIAN
The nurse told me.

NAOMI
He's not so yellow anymore. He's more…bluish.

(Soft SOUND of BUZZING that gradually increases in volume until the end of the play)

MRS. LIBELLULE
He started turning that color this morning.

NAOMI
Is it the lack of oxygen? Maybe he needs air.

LILLIAN
I don't think that will help.

(MRS. LIBELLULE cries, then stops.)

MRS. LIBELLULE
I'm sorry. I don't mean to cry.

NAOMI
If you feel like crying, Mom, you should cry.

MRS. LIBELLULE
I know. I just don't want to upset anybody.

LILLIAN
It's supposed to be upsetting. What am I doing here? I'm going to the cafeteria.

MRS. LIBELLULE
What if he dies while you're down there?

LILLIAN
He could die in two weeks, or a month. Am I supposed to stay here twenty-four seven for two weeks, a month? I'll be back.

(LILLIAN gets her bag and exits)

NAOMI
She just needs a break.

MRS. LIBELLULE
She gets so nasty.

NAOMI
We all get nasty. People get nasty with us. It happens. But she's here. That's what she can do. She's here.

MRS. LIBELLULE
What if he dies when she's not here? (Cries, then stops) I'm sorry.

NAOMI
Then he dies, Mom. We've done all we can for him; maybe he knows that,

maybe not. But we know. And we're
still doing everything we're capable of
doing. Lillian's right, though. We can't
be here every second for who knows
how long. You could be here for days,
then go to the bathroom and he could
die while you're blowing your nose. You
can only do your best.

MRS. LIBELLULE
You're right.

NAOMI
(To MR. LIBELLULE) I don't know if
you did your best, if you tried. You were
good for a while, when I was little, for
some of the time. And then you were
mean and petty and gross. For most
of the time. And I don't know why. I
couldn't do anything to stop it. I tried.
I thought if I were special enough,
you'd be a better person. But that's not
how it works.

MRS. LIBELLULE
What are you saying?

NAOMI
Nothing. *(To MR. LIBELLULE)* I
don't know if I can forgive you. Not
for anything big, but for all the little
daily damage you did to me. I'll try,
but that can't be my focus. I've got my
own lovely babies, my husband, and
I'm going to connect with them, even
though I have no idea how to do that.
You really should've taught me, Dad.
You and Mom. But you were your own
thing, the two of you, controlling and
shutting people and each other out.
And that makes me so sad. I'm going
to try. Maybe that's how I'll forgive, by
being better. At least, maybe, I'll be able
to forgive myself for not being special
enough to break you out of whatever
was going on with you. So that's what
I'm going to do. Connect. Love. As
openly as I can, hurting people as little
as I can. Maybe that will free us both.

*(NAOMI opens her hands and a giant
SHADOW of blue and green and black
flies out over the stage)*

ELLEN DOYLE

Ellen Doyle is a Los Angeles–based writer who began her career as a TV animation writer, then had a brief dalliance in sitcoms. After over twenty years of motherhood (and family/dog/house management), she returned to school in her fifties, earning an MFA in Dramatic Writing at NYU Tisch in 2020. She will keep writing plays, and hopes to (one day) open a small theater with a focus on producing works written by women.

Stuck won the Kennedy Center 2020 American College Theater Festival Mark Twain Prize for Comic Playwrighting.

Stuck

A PLAY BY ELLEN DOYLE

CAST OF CHARACTERS

KATE: Fifty-ish. Attractive in a non-fussy way. Likes facts and doesn't have time for nonsense. Tends to cover up with clothing.

JAKE: Fifty-ish. Handsome. Fit. Leans toward irony.

JEREMY SANDAL (Pronounced San-doll): Forty–fifty. French. Charming. Smug. Obscenely good-looking, if possible.

OTTO: Mid-twenties. Easygoing. Inherently sweet. Trustworthy.

SALLY: Sixty-plus. Eccentric. Too brilliant to live on planet Earth comfortably. Has a flair for drama.

FACT CHECKER V.O. / DELPHINE (O.S): Delphine has a French accent, should sound youthful. Fact Checker should sound like a fact checker.

ERIC THE DOG: An older small puppy, like eight months old. Only requirement? Adorable.

TIME
Present day.

SETTING
Cool co-op in New York City. A successful couple (though not wealthy) lives here, so it should be minimalistic with probably some photography and (maybe) a good TV. The living room is attached to an open kitchen. There is also an exterior hallway.

NB: (...) in dialogue indicates a character is thinking, formulating a thought. Like when texting.

SCENE 1

(The stage. KATE sits in a living room chair surrounded by moving boxes, facing the audience. She's wet. Her bare foot is up on the ottoman, elevated. JAKE, also wet, walks onto the stage and hands her a baggie full of ice. She puts the ice on her ankle)

JAKE
We didn't have any frozen peas. Sorry.

KATE
I didn't think we would. 'Cause we don't actually eat peas. Right, Jake?

JAKE
No. We don't. We don't like peas. *(Pause)*

JAKE
(Carefully) Do you think it's broken?

KATE
I have no idea. It's swelling, so...

(JAKE blows out air through his mouth)

JAKE
Can I get you anything else?

KATE
No. Go away.

(He nods...hesitates...then exits the stage)

KATE (CONT'D)
(Direct address) That's Jake. My husband. This morning, I found out he cheated on me. But I didn't find out the usual way, through text messages or a credit card bill, but, rather, when I woke up this morning with sores. Sores on my vagina AND my anus. So what did I do? I freaked out, took an ambulance

to my gynecologist's office (not really, I took an Uber), and she takes one look at—you know—the area, and says, "Oh yes, this is herpes." Of course, my head is fucking exploding, but I'm trying to maintain, and I say to her, "Are you sure? I mean, don't you have to do some kind of test?" And she says, "Of course we'll test it. But this is herpes." And I say, "But how can you be so sure!" And she says, "Because, Kate, I've been doing this for a very long time." I screech, "But how did I get it! I'm MARRIED! For twenty-five years! Can you get it at the gym??? From sitting naked on the sauna slats??" She clears her throat, pats my shoulder, and says, "This is a conversation you may need to have with your husband." I go home—I wait until I'm home—and then I call him. He picks up, says hello, and then I say: "Okay, motherfucker. The jig is up." Yeah. I actually said that. He comes home, admits it right away. That he'd had an affair with a woman at work, but it was over. He had ended it. She's the one who gave it to him. And then he gave it to me. Not on purpose, of course. He was taking anti-viral medicine and thought he had it "under control." Until he didn't, it seems. When I first moved to New York, my uncle gave me a taser. He's a cop. *(She reaches down in the chair and produces a taser)*

KATE (CONT'D)
Just takes a little nine-volt battery.

(She squeezes the trigger twice. It arcs and makes a crackling sound. ZZZZ ZZZZ!)

KATE (CONT'D)
Right?

(She puts it back on the chair)

KATE (CONT'D)
So I grab the taser from the drawer of my nightstand and chase Jake out

the doorway—down the front steps of the apartment building. Pursuing him. But it's raining. The steps are wet. I slip, tumble down—and land at the bottom of the stairs in a heap. In the pouring rain. Moaning. Jake then has to turn around, come back, and help me. I have to put my arm around his neck just to get up the stairs and back inside. Would I have used the taser if I'd actually caught him? Maybe. I'm not sure. Oh, God! I have a shanker on the edge of my asshole. It's pulsating. It's like sitting on a nail. A nail that is being tapped continuously by a ball-peen hammer. Despite the fact that Jake and I have never had anal sex. Can someone please explain that to me? Anal sex. ANAL. That sounds even worse. ANAL. BUTT SEX. ANAL SEX. BUTT SEX. ANAL ANAL ANAL!!!! *(She screams)* AHHHHHHHHH!!!!

(KATE stops. Breathes. Composes herself)

KATE (CONT'D)
I hurt my throat doing that.

(Long pause. KATE motions to the boxes on the stage)

KATE (CONT'D)
We're supposed to move tomorrow. Yup. To a co-op we just closed on. And we have a big mortgage. And it just now occurred to me that we can't afford to live apart. So…yeah…there's that.

(A cautious JAKE walks back on stage with a towel. He extends the towel. She takes it. He stands there)

KATE (CONT'D)
What?

JAKE
(In agony) I don't know. I'm just. So sorry. So, so sorry.

(KATE pats her wet face)

JAKE
Can we talk? Please?

(She grabs the taser, jabs it in his general direction, and squeezes the trigger twice—ZZZZ! ZZZZ! JAKE quickly exits the stage. KATE puts her head in her hands)

KATE
I can't do this.

SCENE 2

(Four weeks later. The new co-op. JAKE is sitting on the couch working on his iPad. KATE enters in an orthopedic boot. She's got the mail with her)

JAKE
Hey!

KATE
(Forced bright) Hey.

JAKE
Need help?

KATE
With the mail? No. I'm okay. Thanks.

JAKE
How'd it go?

KATE
Eh. He took another X-ray, and it's not healing as well as he'd like. Three more weeks in the boot.

JAKE
I still don't get why he won't give you pain meds.

(KATE goes through the mail and takes out the junk)

KATE
Those days are over. The fucking opioid addicts ruined it for everyone.

JAKE
Sorry you're in pain.

KATE
Thanks. It'll be okay. Just…throbs when I sleep. Doctor said to try a pillow under it. (She goes to the kitchen and gets some water)

JAKE
What time's the reservation tonight?

KATE
8:00. Let's Uber. I can't handle the subway again today.

(KATE opens the trash to throw away the junk mail. Something catches her eye. She reaches in and pulls out an aluminum to-go container)

KATE (CONT'D)
(Calling out) Did you eat?

JAKE
I did, yeah. Just a snack.

KATE
Well, what did you have?

JAKE
(Busted) Uh…a burrito?

KATE
A burrito? When?

(She comes from the kitchen with a receipt stapled to a bag)

KATE
4:13 p.m. Chipotle. You knew we were going to dinner at Per Se and you ate anyway? Why would you do that?

JAKE
I'm sorry, honey. I was hungry. I didn't have lunch—

KATE
So you eat a banana.

JAKE
I'll still go to dinner.

KATE
And do what? You won't be hungry. Are you just going to sit there and stare at me while I eat?

JAKE
No, I'll just…I'll eat light.

KATE
It's a nine-course meal! You don't get to
"eat light."

JAKE
So I'll take stuff home in a doggie bag.
It'll be fine!

KATE
Jake. I mean…

JAKE
What?

KATE
I feel like I tried to do something nice
for you and you shat on it.

JAKE
I'm sorry. I didn't mean to shit on
anything.

KATE
It just seems so…inconsiderate.

JAKE
You're right. Totally right.

KATE
Per Se is an event. We've never been and
I thought it would be nice. It was hard
getting those reservations.

JAKE
I know. And I appreciate it. I really do.
(Pause)

KATE
I'm trying to make this work, Jake. I
really am.

JAKE
I know.

KATE
Do you?

JAKE
Of course.

KATE
And you're aware of how hard this is for
me, right?

JAKE
Absolutely. It's hard for me too.

KATE
Wait. What?

JAKE
Oh, God.

KATE
It's "hard for you too"?

JAKE
I didn't mean it like that.

(KATE takes out her phone)

KATE
You know what? Just forget it. I'll cancel.

JAKE
No, no, no, don't do that—

KATE
We'll pay a fee, but it's going to be a
lot less than dinner so we'll come out
way ahead. I'm tired anyway AND MY
FUCKING ANKLE IS THROBBING.

JAKE
But I want to go!

*(She goes into the bedroom and slams the
door)*

KATE
(Through the door) Happy fiftieth
birthday, Jake! Hope you enjoyed your
birthday burrito!

*(JAKE sighs and looks helplessly toward
the closed door)*

JAKE
Don't cancel.

SCENE 3
*(The co-op. JAKE is on his computer
in his sweats. KATE, wearing her boot,
enters with some groceries. JAKE jumps
up and takes them from her)*

JAKE
What?

KATE
There's smoke in the hallway. *(She throws her purse on the couch)*

JAKE
Like…the building's on fire?

KATE
I think I'd be a little more animated if that were the case. Someone's smoking.

JAKE
Weed or cigarettes?

KATE
Cigarettes. *(Beat)* Go smell. Please confirm that I'm not crazy.

(JAKE opens the door, walks out in the hallway, and sniffs. He comes back and shuts the door)

JAKE
I can confirm that you are not crazy.

KATE
Great. Obviously wafting under someone's doorway.

JAKE
That's not good.

KATE
Right? I thought I smelled it last night too. It's much stronger today. *(Beat)* I should find out where it's coming from.

(KATE opens the door, goes back in the hallway, and sniffs a few doors. She comes back and shuts it)

KATE
6D. Have you seen who lives there?

JAKE
No.

(KATE looks at him like, "can't you be more helpful?")

JAKE
Well, I mean, we did know it was a smoking building when we bought it. Maybe it's an isolated incident?

KATE
YES, but on the two—no, THREE times we visited, I sniffed the hallways, the lobby, the elevator—

JAKE
I remember.

KATE
The board interview? I asked. No smoking in public areas, only in your unit. And you're supposed to have an air purifier if you do. *(She scrolls through her phone)* I'm going to call down and report them.

JAKE
Okay.

KATE
What? You think I shouldn't?

JAKE
No. Do it. Definitely.

(KATE dials her phone. We see OTTO at the Front Desk)

OTTO
(Cheerful) Hello, front desk. This is Otto.

KATE
Hi, Otto, this is Kate in 6E.

OTTO
The journalist?

KATE
Oh, nice. You were paying attention.

OTTO
Always.

KATE
So, listen, we're new to how co-ops work. I smell cigarette smoke in the hallway and it's pretty thick. What should I do?

OTTO
(On it) You mean now?

KATE
Yes. And last night too.

OTTO
Any idea where it's coming from?

KATE
6D.

OTTO
D like Delta?

KATE
Yes, D like Delta.

OTTO
Ah. Mr. Sandal. He's been away awhile. Just got back.

KATE
This Mr. Sandal. What's his story? Young? Old?

OTTO
I don't know. About your age? I'm not good at guessing ages.

KATE
About my age? Well, how old do you think I am?

OTTO
Is this a trap?

(KATE laughs.)

KATE
No. No trap. So what do we do?

OTTO
Do you want to make a complaint?

KATE
I do indeed.

OTTO
Okay, so, we give him a letter telling him he has to, you know, mitigate the smoke smell. If he fails to comply, it goes to the board.

KATE
Okay, good. Get the board involved. Good protocol.

OTTO
Okay, then. It shall be done. I'll print it up right now.

KATE
Thank you, Otto. You're competent. I like competent people.

OTTO
Thank you. Me too.

KATE
By the way, have you seen my dry cleaning?

OTTO
Yes, it's here.

KATE
Oh, why didn't you call me?

OTTO
Lack of competency?

KATE
Ha. Thanks Otto. *(She hangs up)*

KATE
You should get dressed. We have Sally.

JAKE
Okay.

KATE
What? You don't want to go?

JAKE
(Carefully) I do. It's just…

KATE
What?

JAKE
It's just…I mean, I'll totally go today, but can we maybe start looking for someone new?

KATE
Why? Because Sally's my therapist?

JAKE
No…I dunno. She eats while we talk. Which, to me is, you know, unprofessional?

KATE
So she eats while we talk. Big deal.

JAKE
But also, she discusses her other clients.
Isn't that kind of…indiscreet?

KATE
So? She doesn't say their names. We
don't know who they are.

JAKE
I know…but I'm pretty sure we could
report her for that.

KATE
Report her? Please. That's ridiculous.
She's an excellent therapist. Albeit
slightly unconventional.

(Pause)

JAKE
Forget it. You're right. I'm sorry I said
anything.

KATE
Sally believes that one of our sicknesses
in society is people feeling isolated. That
if we all just shared more of our struggles,
we wouldn't feel as alone. She feels secrets
are killing us. That's a solid philosophy.

(Pause)

JAKE
I just feel like…is it even helping?

KATE
(Surprised) Yes, it's helping. It's helping
me, anyway. You don't think it's helping?

JAKE
(Sincere) Yes. It is. Absolutely.

*(KATE sighs. Checks herself on being
unpleasant)*

KATE
I mean…any other suggestions, Jake?

JAKE
(Giving it a shot) I don't know. Maybe
you can just forgive me?

KATE
Yeah. No. Doesn't work that way. Sorry
about that…

*(JAKE turns to go into the bedroom then
stops)*

JAKE
This complaint. Do you think it's
anonymous?

KATE
No idea. But I don't care if this guy
knows it was us.

*(There's a knock at the door. KATE
answers it. It's OTTO holding her dry
cleaning)*

KATE (CONT'D)
Oh, hey, Otto, thanks for bringing it up.

OTTO
Of course. I wanted to regain your trust,
m'lady.

KATE
And so you have, kind sir! *(Beat)* Did
you give it to him? What's his name?
Mr. Sandal?

OTTO
Yes ma'am. Just slipped it under his
door.

KATE
(For JAKE's benefit) This complaint.
Is it anonymous?

OTTO
Yes. He won't know it was you.

*(A door behind them in the hallway opens.
It's JEREMY SANDAL. He has only
a towel around his waist. And a piece of
paper in his hand)*

JEREMY
Otto? Did you just leave this under
my door?

OTTO
I did. Yup.

JEREMY
Someone? They have a problem? With my smoke?

OTTO
Yes. Pretty much.

JEREMY
Who was it?

OTTO
Uh, I can't tell you that.

(JEREMY looks at KATE and JAKE)

JEREMY
Was it you?

KATE
Nope! Wasn't us—

JAKE
We actually like the smell of cigarettes.

JEREMY
I have lived here for three years and no one has ever complained before.

OTTO
Well, that's not entirely true.

JEREMY
What do you mean?

OTTO
6F. Remember?

JEREMY
(Rolling his eyes) My God. That guy? Forget it. He was a fucking asshole.

OTTO
Anyway, I better get back downstairs. Read the letter please. Gotta, you know, mitigate the smoke if you don't want any more trouble.

JEREMY
Yes, yes. Fine. By the way, Otto. Let's talk later. I need some supplies.

(OTTO gives him a look, like don't bring that up in front of them)

OTTO
All right, everyone. Have a beautiful evening!

(OTTO gives a wave and leaves. JEREMY turns to KATE and JAKE)

JEREMY
You are new?

KATE
(Pleasant) Yes. We've been here a month. I'm Kate and this is Jake.

JEREMY
Kate and Jake. Your names. They rhyme?

KATE
Kind of—

JAKE
I guess—

KATE
Not really.

(Pause)

JEREMY
D'accord. I will turn on the purifier. And if something bothers you, you can tell me yourself. Be adults. You don't have to tattle on me.

KATE
Well, I already told you, it wasn't us. So.

JEREMY
Mmmm. Right.

(JEREMY turns and his towel falls to the ground exposing his penis. The audience sees his ass).

KATE
(Turning away) Oh my god.

JEREMY
Merde.

(JEREMY casually picks up the towel, goes back into his apartment and shuts the door. KATE closes their door)

KATE
(Whispering for no reason) He did it on purpose? Am I right? He exposed himself on purpose.

JAKE
I don't know, but either way, he's very impressive, don't you think?

KATE
(Laughing) Jesus. Like a baguette. Shit. I'll be frank. I'm scandalized.

JAKE
Finally! A housewarming gift.

KATE
And, I mean, did he just get out of the shower? He didn't look wet. Probably struts around nude all day, just waiting for someone to knock on his door.

JAKE
With his clean, smooth chest and his opulent, wavy French hair.

KATE
And again, that was a very large dick, correct?

JAKE
Yes, indeed. It sure was.

KATE
Probably drags on the ground when he walks.

JAKE
I know. I suffer from the exact same problem.

KATE
Please. You wish.

JAKE
No, you wish.

(KATE and JAKE laugh—then KATE realizes she's laughing with JAKE. She doesn't want to be laughing with JAKE)

KATE
Anyway—

JAKE
Yeah.

(An awkward pause)

JAKE (CONT'D)
I should probably take a shower. Get dressed. For Sally.

KATE
Yup. Good idea.

JAKE
Did you get bar soap, by any chance?

KATE
Yes…in the bag.

(He goes to the grocery bag and gets soap)

JAKE
Thanks.

KATE
Sure.

(JAKE goes into the bedroom and shuts the door)

SCENE 4
(A therapist's office. JAKE and KATE sit next to each other on the couch. The therapist chair is empty. On the coffee table is a toasted bagel with lox and cream cheese)

JAKE
Let's see what she's got today. Lox, bagel. Cream cheese…

(KATE ignores him)

JAKE (CONT'D)
Ooh. She's even got capers, onion. Little slice of lemon…It's a feast! A veritable feast.

KATE
You need to get over yourself, pal. (We hear a toilet flush. Then water running)

JAKE
Come on, I'm just kidding around.

KATE
It's not funny. Who cares if she eats?
Is that what this is about to you?

(SALLY enters)

SALLY
Thank you for waiting.

KATE
Of course.

(SALLY sits down and gets settled. Puts
a napkin on her lap)

SALLY
Would either of you like half a bagel?

KATE
No, I already had lunch. Thank you,
though.

SALLY
Jake? I like sharing…

(JAKE smiles a "no thank you" and
watches her eat. JAKE turns and sees
KATE is watching him watch SALLY
eat. He wilts. SALLY puts down the bagel
and carefully wipes her face with a napkin.
She takes a sip of water. We can hear the
ice clinking. She composes herself. Brushes
a few crumbs off her lap. Then picks up a
yellow legal pad and a pen)

SALLY
So. How was this week?

(KATE and JAKE look at each other and
shrug)

JAKE
Pretty good, right?

KATE
Yeah. I'd say so. We did well.

JAKE
Tuesday was my birthday and we had a
little misunderstanding about dinner. But
we worked it out. Just a little hiccup.

KATE
Not a big deal. We ended up going out
after all. Had a nice dinner.

JAKE
Very nice.

KATE
At Per Se.

SALLY
Per Se? Elegant.

KATE
It is, isn't it? It was Jake's fiftieth birthday.
So. Not sure I'd ever do it again, but it
was a worthwhile experience.

JAKE
For sure. And this week, uh, I guess
it was last Sunday, we also sat on the
couch together for an entire afternoon
and just…read. You know, like next to
each other.

SALLY
(Very pleased) Parallel play.

JAKE
Yes, right. Parallel play. But…it just.
Felt good. Like things are maybe slowly
getting back to normal.

(He looks over at KATE. She gives him a
courtesy smile)

KATE
I don't know about normal. I mean, it
hasn't been that long. Only a month,
but sure. We're making progress.

(SALLY takes a few notes)

SALLY
And how would you define progress?

KATE
I feel like we've had some really good
conversations—

JAKE
(Surprised) Yeah? Like when?

KATE
Oh, like this morning. Remember, Jake? You opened up to me that you feel Sally is indiscreet. And that we should report her.

JAKE
Oh, come on, that's not…Are you trying to get me in trouble? I just said—

KATE
Sally should know how you feel. You want to be honest, don't you? Isn't that what therapy is all about?

SALLY
(*Inquisitive*) What are you referring to, Jake?

JAKE
…

SALLY
…

JAKE
I mean…you're always talking about your other patients and it kinda…you know. Unnerves me.

SALLY
Clients. I'm not a doctor.

JAKE
Clients. Whatever. And it makes me think you're, you know, talking about us. To other people.

KATE
That's what you're worried about?

JAKE
Uh…

SALLY
This concern of yours, Jake. If I were to mention you to someone else, what do you think I would say?

(*They both stare at him*)

JAKE
(*Giving up*) Well, Sally, I really couldn't tell you.

SALLY
Kate. Do you share the same concern?

KATE
No. If you mentioned us it would be anonymous and it would only be used to illuminate our struggle to another client so as to make a point.

SALLY
What do you think I would say? If I were to mention you, that is.

KATE
I'm not sure you even would. We're not special. Just another garden-variety infidelity story. Except in this one, of course, the husband cheats on his wife and gives her herpes. So, on second thought, that does kind of make us special. Maybe you would mention us!

(*JAKE looks up towards the ceiling.*)

(*The lights dim on SALLY and JAKE. KATE turns toward the audience*)

KATE (CONT'D)
Why am I still staying with Jake? Why do I want this to work? These are very good questions and I ask myself these questions every—single—day. All day. If I left Jake, would I date again? How would I even find people? Would I go to a bar? Ask friends to set me up? Use some app? I'm pretty shredded both physically and psychologically. I mean, who would want me after this? I wouldn't. Even contemplating being with someone else is exhausting. I don't want to have to explain myself to anyone new. We keep people around because they know us. And I can't ever have the herpes conversation with a man. No. No way. That would be… Mortifying. I can't even go there. No, I doubt I'd put myself out there again.

Which means I'd be alone. I've never been alone. Jake and I got married right out of grad school. Maybe I'd enjoy being alone. I don't know. Do I still love him? I have no idea. Did I love him before? Yes. I'm sure of that. We've been together twenty-five years. I've been lying next to him in bed at night for twenty-five years. Listening to him breathe. My feet touching his.

KATE
Yesterday, I went almost two hours without thinking about it. But then I remembered and I checked his phone. And his computer. He's not allowed to have passcodes anymore. Jake's actually the one who suggested it. So, you know, he's trying. I'll never trust him again. Or any man, really. Because I realize something now. That for as smart as I am, I am a poor judge of character. I thought I knew my husband, thought I had a successful marriage and, most importantly, how the world was ordered. I was blindsided. I actually know nothing. And that is a very humbling story indeed. Yes, Sally, maybe that's what you'd say if you talked about us. It's a kind of death–of–innocence story. And it's a brutal one.

(KATE turns back toward SALLY and JAKE. The lights come up)

KATE (CONT'D)
This employee you were fucking. Emma.

JAKE
Yes?

KATE
Did she have a pet?

(JAKE looks at KATE. And then SALLY)

JAKE
Look. I'm…happy to…you know… But is it productive for us, from a therapeutic standpoint, to keep going over and over the details like this?

SALLY
Yes. She needs both honesty and transparency. For as long as it takes.

(JAKE folds his hands on his lap)

JAKE
Yes. She had a cat. A tabby. He was very old.

(SALLY turns a page — and writes this down on her pad)

SCENE 5
(The hallway. KATE, wearing her boot, passes JEREMY's door. She sniffs and rolls her eyes—then knocks. No answer. She knocks again, harder. The door opens. JEREMY has a cigarette in his hand)

KATE
(Sarcastic) Oh, hey, you're dressed.

JEREMY
Oui. Does that make you sad?
(He smiles at her. Flirty. Smug)

KATE
Uh…you're making a lot of smoke.

JEREMY
Really? Are you going to report me again?

KATE
I might.

JEREMY
Hmmm. But I thought it was not you?

KATE
Yeah, well, I lied. *(Waves her hand in the air)* Can you please—?

JEREMY
One moment. *(He ducks out of the door frame and comes back without his cigarette)*

KATE
Got that air purifier on?

JEREMY
Oui. Certainement.

KATE
Well, it's not working. What kind is it?

(JEREMY nods behind him. KATE peers over his shoulder into the apartment.)

KATE (CONT'D)
Oh, no. That's not even—remotely up to the task. That's a piece of junk. Why is there almost no furniture in your apartment? You said you've been here for three years.

JEREMY
Why do I need furniture?

KATE
I don't know. To sit? To entertain?

JEREMY
(Sighing) For many years I was very attached to my things. But then I decided they were not making me happy. So I gave them all away. And now I can leave anytime I want with no attachment to people or things. I am free.

KATE
And that makes you happy.

JEREMY
Of course.

KATE
Okay, listen, you gotta solve this problem. Stuff a towel under your door. Switch to e-cigs. I don't care. But I really don't want to get the co-op board involved. I have enough stress in my life as it is. Please? I'm asking you. As one human to another. Can you just solve this?

JEREMY
Fine. What will you give me?

KATE
What will I give you? Nothing. I will give you nothing…What do you mean?

JEREMY
I mean that most of my relationships are transactional in nature and I expect something in return.

KATE
Hmmm. Okay, well, the problem for you is that we live in what's called a co-op…short for cooperative. A place where people agree on common values—

(JEREMY goes back inside, takes a puff of his cigarette and comes back out. He blows the smoke out the side of his mouth, waves it away)

KATE (CONT'D)
What the hell? Are you going to take this seriously or not?

JEREMY
Shhh. Please. Be quiet now. If it means something to you…I will quit. I try to stop for many years but today seems like a very good day to do it.

KATE
(Suspicious) Really?

JEREMY
Yes.

KATE
How do I know you aren't messing with me?

JEREMY
Ho ho! My goodness, Kate, you are cynical! We did not expect that.

KATE
I am? A minute ago you said you were transactional and wanted something in return. You're the cynic!

JEREMY
(He laughs) Yes, I am messing with you. I am not going to quit. But I will "mitigate" the smoke. I will buy a better air purifier. The best money can buy. Made of solid gold, if possible. With tassels.

KATE
Very funny. It has to have a HEPA filter.

JEREMY
A what?

KATE
A HEPA filter. A good one will cost at
least three hundred dollars. I can text
you some links—

JEREMY
Oh no, no, this is all too complicated.
You buy it. Whatever it costs. I will then
pay you back.

KATE
(Brightening) Really? Uh…Okay. That
works. I'll order on Amazon. I have
Prime so, you know, free shipping.

JEREMY
Marveilleux. A rapprochement!
(Taking her hand) Kate.

KATE
(Looking at her hand) What?

JEREMY
I lied. I do want something in return.
(He goes away and comes back with
an adorable puppy in his arms. KATE
practically loses her shit)

KATE
Oh my God! SO CUTE. What's its name?

JEREMY
Eric the Dog.

KATE
Eric? That's fun.

JEREMY
Non. Eric the Dog.

(JEREMY plunks the dog in her arms.
KATE snuggles him)

KATE
(To the dog) Eric the Dog. Ha. You are
so handsome. You're a freaking movie
star. I love dogs. I'm a dog person.
We can't have a dog because Jake has
allergies. (Sniffing the dog) Interesting.
He doesn't smell like cigarettes.

JEREMY
(Offended) Why would he? I put him in
the bedroom when I smoke.

KATE
So you don't smoke in the bedroom?

JEREMY
Non, of course not! Use your head, Kate.

KATE
And what happens to Eric the Dog if
you decide to just leave at a moment's
notice? You with the no attachments.

JEREMY
Mon dieu. I would never leave him.
He is neither a person or a thing.

KATE
Okay, you've piqued my curiosity.
What's the favor?

JEREMY
Can you watch him? Friday afternoon?

KATE
You mean, like, take care of him?

JEREMY
Yes. He whines and is gloomy when I
leave. Yesterday, he vomits. I see him on the
Nest cam. Otto told me you are a writer
and that you work from home. So…

KATE
I mean, surely you must know someone
else in the building.

JEREMY
No one I trust. You seem like, as they
say, a solid citizen. Very straight. Like an
arrow.

(KATE frowns. It doesn't land like a
compliment)

KATE
Wait. You were talking to Otto about
me? Why?

JEREMY
(Rolling his eyes and taking the dog from
her) Forget it. You don't have to watch

him. It is too much trouble—

KATE
It's not that—

JEREMY
I asked him who could possibly watch my dog and he suggested you because you work at home. That is all. Anyway, never mind. I will take him to the doggy day care.

KATE
Well, hold on—

JEREMY
It will be fine. If he vomits I am certain they will comfort him.

KATE
Are you going to work or what?

JEREMY
Yes. To an appointment.

KATE
…What do you do? If I may ask.

JEREMY
I make custom electric guitars. For rock and roll musicians.

KATE
Where? In there?

JEREMY
Oh no. I have a workshop. In Brooklyn.

KATE
Wow. Never heard that before. Custom guitars. Impressive. Have you ever made a guitar for someone I might know?

JEREMY
You? Pfft. Non.

(KATE reacts. Was that a dis?)

JEREMY (CONT'D)
Okay, then. I will see you Friday. At noon?

KATE
Yes. What the hell.

JEREMY
You are wonderful. I have to go. Thank you. I am cooking. *(He shuts the door.)*

SCENE 6
(KATE sits at her desk on her laptop with a glass of wine and her boot on. She stops and looks at ERIC THE DOG who is lying on the couch sleeping. Or running around the stage and playing. Either way it will be cute)

KATE
You okay, buddy? Need some water?

(She picks up the water bowl and puts it near him. She puts a little water on her finger and tries to get him to lick it. He will either drink or not drink)

KATE (CONT'D)
Not thirsty? Okay. Suit yourself. But you must stay hydrated. Nothing's going to happen to you on my watch. *(Picking him up)* Too soon to assume intimacy? Should I back off? I sense you're pulling away from me.

(She snuggles him. Feeling his love and giving it back. This goes on for a bit. There's a knock at the door. KATE crosses and opens it. It's JEREMY)

JEREMY
Bonjour. *(He gives her a kiss on the cheek)*

KATE
Both cheeks. Always. That is the French way. *(She submits to a kiss on the other cheek)* So. Where you been? I texted you. You said you'd be back by three.

JEREMY
Yes. Please, I am sorry. My phone. It died.

KATE
Have you been drinking?

JEREMY
Oui.

(He takes out a cord, looks around for an outlet, and without asking, plugs his phone in. He sees ERIC THE DOG)

JEREMY (CONT'D)
ERIC the DOG!!! MY LOVE, MY ONE TRUE LOVE. *(He scoops ERIC up and twirls him around in his arms)* How was he? A good boy?

KATE
A very good boy. I took him out and we got lots of attention. But I mean. You should have charged your phone or…used someone else's phone. I was getting worried.

JEREMY
Why would you worry?

KATE
I don't know. Like…maybe something happened to you?

JEREMY
Non. Like all Americans, you have a neurotic attachment to time.

(JEREMY nods toward her glass of wine)

JEREMY (CONT'D)
Are you going to offer me some?

KATE
Uh…sure.

(He sits down on the couch and puts his feet up on the coffee table)

KATE (CONT'D)
Hey, make yourself at home.

(KATE pours him a drink. He takes a sip and makes a face)

JEREMY
This is shit. What is it?

KATE
Uh, Kendall Jackson?

JEREMY
Mass-produced wine? This is not wine. I will bring you a good bottle. A French wine.

KATE
I try to keep it under twelve a bottle. Truth be told, I'd probably be an alcoholic if I didn't get buzzed so easy. Two glasses and I'm under the table.

JEREMY
Pfft. I drink a bottle a night. Sometimes two.

KATE
Then you're an alcoholic.

(JEREMY shrugs. Sure, why not? KATE sits down across from him and pours herself another glass)

JEREMY
Are you "buzzed" now?

KATE
A little. Getting there.

JEREMY
Yes! Enjoy your life.

KATE
Question: where was Eric the Dog when you were traveling? Did you take him with you?

JEREMY
Tell me. Who told you I was traveling?

KATE
Otto.

JEREMY
Mmm. Then I see you have talked to Otto about me as well. Perhaps we are both curious about each other. *(He smiles at her)*

KATE
Please. Don't even.

(JEREMY laughs. Happy to get a rise out of her)

JEREMY
My girlfriend. She watches him when I travel.

KATE
Oh. So she couldn't watch him today?

JEREMY
She is no longer my girlfriend. We broke up.

KATE
You broke up? Are you...sad?

JEREMY
Non. Frankly, I am relieved. But I now have a problem on my hands. She wants Eric the Dog. She says Eric the Dog belongs to her. I am refusing of course.

KATE
Oh my gosh. A custody battle.

JEREMY
Yes. It may get ugly. She is sometimes spiteful. And violent.

KATE
Well, I mean, possession is nine-tenths of the law. You have him. How is she going to get Eric the Dog back?

JEREMY
Yes, this is true. But she has a guitar that I made for Bruce Springsteen. I left it at her place. And I need it back. So...as I said. I have a big problem, non?

KATE
Bruce Springsteen? Seriously? Why did you think I wouldn't know anyone you made guitars for?

(He shrugs, not really interested in the question)

KATE (CONT'D)
Anyway, can't you make another one? I'm sure the Boss would understand.

JEREMY
Non. It will take too long. He wants it now. That guy? He is impatient.

KATE
Why'd you break up with your girlfriend?

JEREMY
Forget it. You will not believe it.

KATE
Try me.

JEREMY
Her brother, with whom she is very close—a few months back—was in a terrible motorcycle accident. Slid beneath a car and was, like, how you say, pinned beneath the wreckage. He almost did not survive. We flew to Los Angeles. The doctors removed his leg.

KATE
Yikes. His leg?

JEREMY
Yes, his left leg. Just below the knee. But then, two days later, the doctors, they took the rest of his leg. My girlfriend? She was distraught.

KATE
Of course.

JEREMY
Then they amputated his arm.

KATE
Jesus!

JEREMY
Terrible, yes. She was upset. And I said to my girlfriend, "My god. Pretty soon he will only be a head."

(KATE laughs despite herself)

KATE
That's cold.

JEREMY
She thought so, yes.

KATE
So she broke up—

JEREMY
No, no. We were fine, she saw the humor eventually. But then she came back to me later...very troubled...

and said, "Tell me this. If I was in the hospital and I was just a head, would you visit me?" And I said, "Of course. I would visit you every day. As time permitted." But then she became very serious and said, "But if I were just a head—would you stay with me?"

KATE
You mean, like, stay together?

JEREMY
Yes. And I told her the truth. That I would not.

KATE
Wait. You wouldn't?

JEREMY
Of course not. No one would.

KATE
Not sure that's true—

JEREMY
Oh my God. The tears. The lamentations. You don't really love me. You wouldn't love me if I were only a head. It has been intolerable. For months. The question of the head has taken over our lives.

KATE
Well, why didn't you just say yes? It was a dumb hypothetical question. You would never have been presented with that situation.

JEREMY
Not literally, of course. But it is an important question. And one that we should all think on. And reflect on. *(They both sit there and think about it)*

KATE
How is the brother?

JEREMY
Learning to live without an arm and a leg. *(Nods towards her orthopedic boot)* What happened?

KATE
Oh. I wish it were something interesting, like snowboarding. It was raining and I slipped on some wet stairs. Twisted it. Broke my ankle.

JEREMY
Does it hurt?

KATE
Like a motherfucker.

JEREMY
I am sorry for you.

KATE
Thanks.

JEREMY
Does your husband rub your ankle?

KATE
No.

JEREMY
If you were mine I would rub your ankle. *(Finishes his wine and stands)* I would like to retract my statement. The wine isn't so bad after all. Once the palate has been scorched, of course. *(He heads toward the door and scoops up ERIC THE DOG)* Okay. I must go. Thank you, Kate. Please. One more thing.

KATE
Yes?

JEREMY
Can you watch Eric the Dog again? On Wednesday? I am looking for someone now. The doggie daycares? I go to look. They are all shit.

KATE
Seriously?

JEREMY
I promise. Only one more time.

KATE
(Sighing) Sure. Why not. *(She stands. Obviously a little tipsy)* I'm buzzed. Announcement: KATE IS BUZZED!

JEREMY
Yes! Now you are fun.

(They go towards the door)

JEREMY (CONT'D)
Tell me, Kate, why do you wear so
many clothes?

KATE
Uh…because it's how I dress? It's my
style. *(Beat)* Why?

JEREMY
I think it is a way to protect yourself.
To keep the world at a distance.

KATE
Okay…

JEREMY
You have a beautiful body. Why do you
hide it?

KATE
Oh my God. Get out.

JEREMY
(Laughing) Forgive me. But in my
culture we believe in compliments.
A demain.

*(He gives her a kiss on each cheek then
leaves. KATE stands there. Both surprised
and annoyed to find she is flattered)*

SCENE 7
*(KATE is sitting on the floor playing
with ERIC THE DOG. Tossing a toy)*

KATE
You are so sweet. But you are a whore
for this toy. Your entire life seems
devoted to this toy.

*(KATE's phone rings. She puts it on
speaker and keeps throwing the toy)*

KATE (CONT'D)
Hey.

FACT CHECKER (V.O)
Listen, that poll you cited. Was that a
Pew poll? I can't find it.

KATE
No, Monmouth. Did I—?

FACT CHECKER (V.O)
Uh, wait. You did cite Monmouth. My bad.

*(She throws the toy again. ERIC chases
it. Or not)*

FACT CHECKER (CONT'D) (V.O)
Also, fourth paragraph. The Sanders
Medicare-For-All plan is significantly
more generous than the single-payer
plans run by America's peer countries
such as England blah blah blah…Do
you want to include Germany as well?

KATE
Oh, yes, include them. Good call. Thanks.

FACT CHECKER (V.O)
Will do. Talk later.

KATE
Bye.

*(She hangs up. There's a rap at the door.
She gets up and opens it)*

JEREMY
She is crazy! She is threatening to smash
Bruce's guitar.

(He walks past her, consternated)

KATE
Seriously?

JEREMY
Yes, she says unless I give her Eric the
Dog back, she will destroy it. She will
park beneath my window, lay it down
in the street, and drive over it with her
Audi. And she will do it. Believe me.

KATE
What! That's crazy, all right.

JEREMY
She is a mad woman.

KATE
So call the cops!

JEREMY
And say what?

KATE
That she has Bruce Springsteen's guitar. Say she stole it just to get them over there.

JEREMY
Non. I do not want to get the police involved. She has overstayed her visa. I do not want trouble for her. *(Beat)* Where is the shit wine? I need it. *(Goes into the kitchen and pours himself a glass)*

JEREMY (CONT'D)
What will I do? I will not let her have Eric the Dog. Non. But I need the guitar back.

(A tense JEREMY sits down and takes a joint out of his pocket)

JEREMY
May I?

KATE
No way.

JEREMY
My God, you are a pain. So strict. *(He takes a big sip of wine, then another. Relaxing a bit)*

KATE
(Re: the joint) Did you get that from Otto?

JEREMY
How did you know?

KATE
That time in the hallway. You asked him for supplies. I assumed you weren't talking about office supplies.

JEREMY
Otto. Yes.

KATE
I used to smoke pot in college. Kinda miss it.

JEREMY
So smoke! What is stopping you?

KATE
Well, it's still not legal here. For one.

JEREMY
Was it legal when you were in college?

KATE
No.

JEREMY
So before you were a rule breaker and now you are a rule follower?

KATE
Yes. Because I've grown up.

JEREMY
Then I prefer to stay a child.

KATE
Obviously.

JEREMY
Marijuana is legal in Los Angeles. If you were there would you smoke it?

KATE
Uh…sure.

JEREMY
You have no good basis for denying yourself.

(There's a knock at the door. KATE gets up and opens it up. It's OTTO)

OTTO
Hello. I texted…you have a box. The package room wanted this outta there. Taking up a lot of space.

(He brings in a VERY large box on a dolly and sets it down)

KATE
Ah! The air purifier! Your air purifier is here, Jeremy.

JEREMY
No, my God, no! It's too big!

KATE
Settle down. There's probably a lot of packaging.

OTTO
(Re: the wine) You two having a party?

KATE
Yup. Want some?

OTTO
Nah, can't. I'm on duty. Gotta stay sharp.

(KATE goes over to the giant box)

KATE
Otto. I'll tip you twenty bucks to open this thing and assemble it.

OTTO
You don't have to do that.

KATE
Please. I insist. People should be paid for their labor.

(OTTO opens the box and pulls out a huge monstrosity of an air purifier)

JEREMY
(In agony) No! This is impossible. It is obscene!

OTTO
I think it's…pretty much assembled. You just have to take the plastic off it—oh, wait. I guess I gotta put these wheels on—

JEREMY
WHEELS????

(They watch him unwrap the wheels)

JEREMY (CONT'D)
Otto, I am in trouble. Delphine will not give me the guitar unless I return Eric the Dog to her. She is threatening to put it on the street and drive over it. Below my window.

OTTO
For real? Oh, man, that sucks! Though I'd kinda like to see that. In fact, I'd pay to see that.

KATE
I told him to call the police. But apparently this young woman is not here legally.

JEREMY
How do you know she is young?

KATE
Please.

(JEREMY rolls his eyes)

OTTO
Don't you still have a key? Just go over there and get it when she's not home.

JEREMY
I tried. She told the staff that I am not to be let in. (Pause) Perhaps you can talk with her, Otto. She likes you.

KATE
You know her?

OTTO
Delphine? Yeah, we've all hung out a few times but…I'm not sure I wanna get involved. I mean, she's kinda scary.

JEREMY
Yes, this is true. What about this? You come with me to her building, distract the doorman—and I will slip upstairs unnoticed.

OTTO
Jeremy, man, don't get me involved me in your dumb caper. I'm this close to getting my degree and getting out of here. I don't need any trouble.

KATE
You're in school?

OTTO
Yup. Online. Getting my master's in education. Gonna teach.

KATE
Nice! Good for you.

OTTO
Yeah. Pretty excited. But also…kind of conflicted.

KATE
Why?

OTTO
'Cause I really like it here. Nice people. Job pays decently. Good tips at Christmas. So…yeah. But I wanna teach. Think I might be good at it.

KATE
You would be. I intuit it. And always move forward, never backwards, Otto. Gotta keep moving forward.

OTTO
Yeah. My dad says the same thing basically.

(He finishes putting the wheels on and plugs it in)

JEREMY
(Erupting) I will just give her back the puppy!

KATE
No way! Don't allow this Delphine to blackmail you.

JEREMY
What then?

OTTO
Dude, make nice with her. Play the game! Get back together and then get Bruce's guitar back. You can act, can't you?

KATE
Tell her you'd love her if she was just a head. That you'd stay with her.

OTTO
Oh, the head thing. She's still on that?… So stupid.

(OTTO turns the purifier on. It makes a soft sound. He points a little remote at it)

OTTO (CONT'D)
Check this out. This thing goes all the way up to ten.

(He cranks it. The air purifier is now really LOUD. They all just stare at it)

SCENE 8
(JAKE is on the couch texting. Smiling at the texts. KATE enters from the bedroom and stops. Watches him. He looks up and sees her. Then holds his phone in the air. KATE approaches, takes the phone, looks at his screen — then hands it back to him)

KATE
Thanks.

JAKE
Yup.

KATE
That meme's not funny. Your cousin's an idiot.

JAKE
I know.

(She goes into the kitchen. He goes back to his texts)

SCENE 9
(SALLY's office. JAKE sits across from her. SALLY is eating from a bowl of almonds)

SALLY
How's Kate?

JAKE
Fine. Just a bad cold. She's the one who suggested I come alone.

SALLY
Yes, she emailed me. How are you?

JAKE
Good. You know…trying.

SALLY
Trying how?

JAKE
I mean…trying to show her how sorry I am. Repentant.

SALLY
And are you?

JAKE
Of course. *(Pause.)*

JAKE (CONT'D)
What. You don't think I am?

SALLY
Oh, yes. I'm certain of it.

JAKE
I love her. And I'll do whatever it takes. For as long as it takes.

SALLY
What is love, Jake? That word gets thrown around so much these days. I don't even know what it means anymore.

JAKE
I mean…I guess at its most basic level, love—

SALLY
(Sudden) You had an affair with your employee, correct?

JAKE
Correct. Yes.

SALLY
It was facilitated by secrets and lies. I'm assuming you put much thought into how to cover your misbehavior. Is that how you treat someone you "love"?

JAKE
No. It is not.

SALLY
Love is irrelevant. I don't want to hear that word again.

JAKE
Got it.

SALLY
In all of our conversations, I find you still don't know why you did it. Cheated on her, that is.

JAKE
Well…because I don't know why…I mean. I don't have a good explanation. I was a selfish immature shit.

SALLY
A shit?

JAKE
Yes. And I made really bad choices.

SALLY
Bad choices?

JAKE
(Exasperated) Do you know why, Sally? Because if you do, please enlighten me.

SALLY
Perhaps you're asking the wrong question. Perhaps the right question is—

(She suddenly spits out a nut into her hand)

SALLY (CONT'D)
What the hell? What's a damn cashew doing in there?

(She stands and violently throws it in the trash can. Then sits back down)

JAKE
Do you have a cashew allergy?

SALLY
I prefer not to say. *(Picks up her pad again)* Jake. I have no idea who you are. You have no idea who you are. Because you are leading an unexamined life. And as such, you will continue to make bad choices. And suffer. Suffer terribly. That much I know.

(JAKE looks worried. SALLY's landline on the desk begins to RING. They both stare at it. Waiting for it to go to voicemail. But it doesn't)

JAKE
Do you need to get that?

SCENE 10

(KATE is on her laptop in her robe with a box of Kleenex next to her. ERIC THE DOG runs around — or sleeps. Anything works. JAKE enters from the front door)

JAKE
Hey, how you feeling?

KATE
Better, thanks. I took a decongestant. *(Looks up. She sees his face)* You okay? How was Sally?

JAKE
Yeah. I'm just kinda…it was weird.

KATE
Weird how?

JAKE
I don't know…*(Throws his keys on the entryway table)* I don't really want to talk about it right now. Maybe later?

KATE
Talk about it, don't talk about it. Whatever.

(KATE goes back to her computer. JAKE sees ERIC THE DOG)

JAKE
He's here again?

KATE
Yes. Jeremy still hasn't found anywhere decent. Apparently he took Eric the Dog to one place and they let the other dogs share the special "dejeuner" Jeremy had prepared for him. *(Chuckling)* He was outraged. What a head case.

JAKE
Okay, because…as you know…I mean, I'm sure it hasn't escaped your notice that I'm allergic to dogs.

(KATE looks up)

KATE
Yes, I'm well aware of that, Jake. Which is why we've never had a dog. And I love dogs. So I'm also well aware of my sacrifice.

JAKE
Okay…

KATE
Anyway, you make a solid point. I should have asked. Is he bothering you?

JAKE
No. It's fine. Seems to be okay.

(He sniffs a few times. His nose is clear. He bends down and pets ERIC THE DOG)

JAKE (CONT'D)
Hey, little guy. You are cute. Maybe I got over my allergy somehow. Huh, wouldn't that be great? *(To KATE)* Maybe we could get a dog after all.

KATE
Yeah. Let's get a dog. That will solve all our problems.

(JAKE stands)

JAKE
Kate.

KATE
What?

JAKE
Look at me. Please.

(KATE looks up)

JAKE
You have to be nice to me.

KATE
I was kidding.

JAKE
No, you weren't. A baseline for us trying to make this work is you have to be nice to me. Got it?? You must at least be civil. Otherwise this is all a waste of time. Am I wasting my time, Kate?

KATE
Uh…

JAKE
You said you wanted to stay together, so please start acting like it. I'm tired of the snide comments and the passive aggressive stuff. If you want to cut me loose, tell me now. Please. Tell me now. You would be doing me a favor. You really would. 'Cause I'm trying here and I don't know what else to do.

(Pause)

KATE
No. I don't want to cut you loose.

JAKE
Good. Thank you. And forgiving is active. Not passive. That's from your precious guru, Sally.

KATE
Okay. You're right. I will try harder. To be nice to you.

JAKE
Thank you. That's all I ask.

(JAKE goes into the bedroom and shuts the door. KATE stares at it for a beat— then goes back to work)

SCENE 11
(The front desk in the lobby. OTTO is there alone. KATE approaches in her boot)

OTTO
Hey, how's it going?

KATE
Good. How's school?

OTTO
Excellent. Getting close to the finish line.

KATE
Nice. What grade will you teach?

OTTO
High school. Hopefully, anyway. But I'll take whatever I can get.

KATE
You seem like you might actually like teenagers. Unlike all of my teachers in high school.

OTTO
I do. Yeah. I even admire a little bit of sass here and there.

KATE
So, tell me, what's going on with Jeremy? We've texted a few times but I haven't seen him around much.

OTTO
Oh, yeah. He's back with Delphine. So, you know. He's over there a lot.

KATE
He's back with his girlfriend? Quelle surprise.

OTTO
Right?

KATE
Did Bruce get his guitar back?

OTTO
He did! Yeah. Dog's back. Guitar is back. Crisis averted. Drama all the time with the two of them.

KATE
Cause they're French?

OTTO
Oui. Cause they're French.

KATE
Jeremy still owes me for the damn air purifier.

OTTO
(Typical Jeremy) Jeremy…

KATE
So, listen, Otto. I was wondering if you could procure me some supplies.

OTTO
Supplies? What kind of supplies?

KATE
Uh…the kind you smoke?

OTTO
(Stiffening) Why are you asking me?

KATE
Jeremy said—

OTTO
Mr. Sandal was wrong. He's given you false information.

KATE
Oh. Okay. Sorry. My ankle has been hurting a lot, so…

OTTO
Then it's probably best you consult with your doctor.

(Pause)

KATE
Yes. I guess it is. Thank you. I will do just that.

OTTO
Good luck. And by the way, you have a package in the package room. Sephora, I believe.

KATE
Thanks. I'll go get it right now.

(She gives an awkward wave and walks away)

SCENE 12
(The co-op. KATE is on her laptop. There's a knock at the door. KATE opens it to find OTTO. He's wearing jeans and a t-shirt)

KATE
Street clothes. I almost didn't recognize you.

OTTO
Yeah, I'm off now. Anyway, sorry about earlier. Downstairs. Our boss has security cameras with audio. Sometimes he listens in on us.

KATE
No, it's okay. Took me a minute but I figured something was up.

OTTO
We're not even supposed to discuss personal things with the other doormen.

KATE
Seriously? What do you talk about all day?

OTTO
Sports. And, you know, we gossip about the residents.

KATE
Oh, that's much better. Come on in.

(OTTO steps inside and shuts the door. He holds up a sandwich baggie with a few rolled joints)

KATE (CONT'D)
Oh my gosh. Nice! How much do I owe you?

OTTO
Nah, it's not like that. I'm not a dealer or anything. I just share with Jeremy and he gives me wine. Concert tickets. But I figure you need it for your foot. (Hands her the baggie)

KATE
You're a good guy. Speaking of wine, wanna stay and have a glass?

OTTO
No thanks, I'm gonna work out. Water, maybe?

(She goes to get him water)

OTTO
So, hey, I read a few of your articles online—in the *Atlantic*? I thought healthcare would be, like, you know, dry. But it was interesting. You're a good writer. You make it easy to understand.

KATE
Well, I try. Thank you.

OTTO
Yeah. My dad…

KATE
What?

OTTO
He has lung cancer.

KATE
Oh no.

OTTO
Yeah, and even though my parents have insurance, they're already like…they're gonna have to sell their house. My dad's talking about stopping treatment because he doesn't wanna, you know… saddle my mom with more debt. So…

KATE
You're not alone. Over sixty percent of bankruptcies are tied to medical issues. The majority of them have insurance… I'm really sorry.

OTTO
Thanks.

KATE
That's why it's so important you vote. This stuff really does matter. Do you vote?

OTTO
No. I mean. I did for Obama. First time I ever voted. But 2016? No.

KATE
You need to vote, Otto. I can't stress that enough.

(He nods. She hands him the glass)

KATE (CONT'D)
Sorry about your dad. Is it bad?

OTTO
Stage four. Yeah.

(Pause)

KATE
Can I hug you? May I approach?

OTTO
Yes, ma'am.

(She embraces him)

KATE
I kinda hate your guts for not voting.

OTTO
No, you don't.

KATE
Vote.

OTTO
Okay.

(There's a frantic KNOCK at the door. KATE crosses and looks out the peephole. She opens it to reveal JEREMY holding ERIC THE DOG)

JEREMY
Take him! Quickly.

KATE
Why? What's going on?

JEREMY
Shhh!

(JEREMY thrusts him into KATE's arms and closes her door. We can't see what's happening. We hear JEREMY run back down the hallway and slam his door. Then footsteps coming from the elevator)

DELPHINE (O.S)
JEREMY!! Open the door!

(OTTO crosses and looks out the peephole)

OTTO
Whoop, there she is. Another fight.

(We hear DELPHINE pound on the door)

DELPHINE (O.S)
Ouvrez cette putain de porte!

(She pounds even louder. OTTO puts his water glass down and sighs)

OTTO
Why do I always gotta deal with the nonsense?

KATE
No! Don't go out there. She's crazy.

OTTO
Nah, I have to. It's my job.

(He opens the door, slips past KATE, and closes it. KATE, holding ERIC THE DOG, looks out the peephole)

DELPHINE (O.S)
Otto! He has my dog!

OTTO (O.S)
Okay, come on now, Delphine…let's just calm down.

DELPHINE (O.S)
Non! I will not leave until he gives me Eric the Dog. He is mine.

OTTO (O.S)
All right, but no need to make a disturbance.

(More LOUD POUNDING. We hear JEREMY open his door)

JEREMY (O.S)
Stop—are you fucking crazy? Come inside. Please!

DELPHINE (O.S)
Let go of me!

OTTO (O.S)
Guys. Don't make me call the cops. Come on.

(There's a scuffle)

OTTO (O.S)
Ouch! The fuck!

(Someone in the hallway falls to the ground. KATE gasps. ERIC THE DOG barks. WOOF! KATE covers his snout. Pause)

DELPHINE (O.S)
ERIC! (Beat) THE DOG!!

(DELPHINE POUNDS on KATE's door)

DELPHINECONT'D (O.S)
I know who you are! Open the fucking door, bitch!

SCENE 13
(The rolling air purifier is now in KATE's living room and running on a low speed. JEREMY, OTTO, and KATE are sitting on the couch, feet up, smoking weed. KATE is between the men. They are high. JEREMY looks shell-shocked. OTTO has a bag of ice on his finger)

KATE
Are you sure you don't want to go to urgent care? Looks like it might be broken.

(OTTO looks at his finger)

OTTO
Nah. My insurance is shitty. Thousand-dollar deductible. Plus, the doctor would just tape it anyway.

KATE
Seriously? That's outrageous. Fuck the co-op for not providing you with a better policy.

OTTO
At least I have it.

KATE

(Strident) Seventy-one percent of Americans want universal healthcare. But when you tell them they have to give up their private insurance, that number dips to forty-one percent. So even though everyone basically agrees that healthcare isn't working, why are people so reluctant to abandon their plans? I'm serious. Answer me.

(They each take a drag from the joint and pass it along)

OTTO

Scared of something new, I guess?

KATE

Pretty much, yeah. Change is scary.

(Pause)

KATE (TO HERSELF)

That's deep, Kate. Someone should write that down.

(JEREMY suddenly stands)

JEREMY

I will be sad without Eric the Dog! You were wrong to give him to Delphine!

KATE

What?! What are you talking about?

JEREMY

You should not have opened your door!

KATE

You told me to!

JEREMY

Non. I said no such thing.

OTTO

Jeremy, you did, man. I was there. You said: (Doing JEREMY) "Kate! Open the door! Before she kills us all!"

(JEREMY stops. Runs his hands through his hair)

JEREMY

You are right. I am sorry. Please forgive me. (Sits back down)

KATE

It's okay.

JEREMY

I will be lost without him.

KATE

Me too. He was a good little guy.

(Pause)

JEREMY

Bruce did not like the guitar I made him.

KATE

No fucking way!

JEREMY

Yes. Said he did not like the semi-hollow body when he is the one who wanted it semi-hollow in the first place. He is an asshole. I hate New York. Full of assholes. I hate my life. I hate everything.

(JEREMY puts his face in his hands and begins to cry softly. KATE is surprised. But not knowing what else to do, she takes his hand)

KATE

Sorry friend.

OTTO

Me too. Everything kinda sucks right now.

(KATE reaches over and takes OTTO's hand as well. They sit there for a while as JEREMY cries)

OTTO (CONT'D)

Hey, Jeremy, what are your guitars made of, anyway?

(JEREMY stops and wipes his eyes with his T-shirt)

JEREMY
Maple. Both the body and neck. All one piece. Although sometimes I use the rosewood.

OTTO
Does the wood matter?

JEREMY
Very much. Yes. It changes the tone. Thank you for asking.

(The front door opens, and JAKE walks in, just home from work. He sees them on the couch, all holding hands)

JAKE
Are you guys…smoking marijuana?

KATE
Yup.

JAKE
Oh.

KATE
Why?

JAKE
It's just kinda—unusual. I mean. You're usually so militant about smoking. Of any kind. *(Scratches his head)* So…you're just…hanging out?

KATE
Yup. Hanging out. Smoking pot, holding hands with my neighbors. Cause that's what I'm doing right now. Just living my life.

(Pause)

JAKE
Okay, then, I'll just…go. Away.

(JAKE goes into the bedroom. KATE picks up the remote and turns the air purifier up to ten. It's LOUD. Everyone stares at the air purifier)

KATE
LET'S ALL BLOW SMOKE AT IT AND SEE WHAT HAPPENS.

SCENE 14

(The Front Desk. KATE walks by and sees OTTO. She stops)

OTTO
Hey. What'd the doc say?

KATE
He wants me to try it without the boot. See how it feels. But it's still too tender. I think it needs a little more time to cook.

OTTO
I forget. How'd you break it again?

KATE
Oh, I wish it was something interesting. Like snowboarding. But I slipped on some wet stairs. Broke my fibula.

OTTO
Ouch.

(KATE turns toward the audience)

KATE
Why do I keep protecting Jake? It's my story. I can tell whomever I want. Maybe Jake deserves to be shamed as part of his penance. But more than that, why do I have to keep it all inside? I didn't do anything wrong. Maybe Sally's right. Secrets are killing us. *(Turns back around to OTTO)* Actually, Otto, Jake cheated on me with someone from his office and gave me herpes. When I found out, I went mental and chased after him with a taser gun my cop uncle gave me. I slipped and fell down the front stairs.

OTTO
Whoa! You were actually gonna tase your husband? That's awesome.

(KATE [sort of] starts to see the humor)

KATE
Well, maybe. I don't know. Anyway, sorry about the herpes reveal. Probably more than you wanted to know.

OTTO
Don't worry. I've got HPV. Herpes is probably just around the corner. Probably have it now. Everyone's gonna get it eventually, I figure.

(KATE brightens)

KATE
You think?

OTTO
I do. We're all in this together, man. All of us "sexually active" people, anyway.

KATE
We are, yes. Thanks, Otto. (Beat) You just made my day.

OTTO
You're welcome!

(She taps the desk twice and walks away with a smile. OTTO goes back to what he was doing)

SCENE 15
(SALLY's office. JAKE sits and watches as SALLY drinks a huge lemonade through a straw. And takes a bite of crudité)

JAKE
Can I just get something off my chest?

SALLY
Of course.

JAKE
It bugs me that you eat and drink while we're doing therapy.

SALLY
Why is that?

JAKE
I don't know. Doesn't seem professional, somehow.

(SALLY nods. She gathers her plate and glass then stands)

SALLY
I wish everyone were as honest as you. I learn from my clients. Thank you.

JAKE
No, no, you don't have to put it away— it's fine.

(Too late. She puts the stuff in a mini-fridge, comes back over, and sits)

SALLY
It won't happen again.

(SALLY takes out her pad and pen)

SALLY (CONT'D)
So, then. I was surprised. That you wanted to come back. By yourself, that is.

JAKE
Well, Kate was okay with it—and I'll admit it. Last time left me a little... unmoored?

SALLY
Unmoored. Interesting. Did you cry afterwards?

JAKE
No. (Beat) Was I supposed to?

SALLY
It can go either way.

(Pause)

JAKE
So...last time. You said something about...me not knowing who I am?

SALLY
And you don't know what that means.

JAKE
I don't. No.

SALLY
It's as if you're in a car—but you're not driving. You are the passenger. Which means the car can go in any direction at any time. Like off a cliff. And you, Jake, went off a cliff. An epic one. To know yourself, you must look inward. Why do you do the things you do? What do you want? Ideally, there should be no disconnect between who you are and

who you think you are. If you are ever to have a meaningful life, you must take the wheel. And take it now!

(Pause)

JAKE
Uh, sticking with the automobile metaphor…if I were to do therapy, how long would this…road trip…take me?

SALLY
Who can tell? The best time to do therapy is when you are not in crisis. That's when the real work begins.

JAKE
Seems a little vague. I mean, if I put a trip into Google Maps…I may not drive if it will take too long. Or I might take an airplane. Or some kind of watercraft…

SALLY
Hey. Smart-ass. Cut the shit. I don't appreciate irony.

JAKE
You're my therapist. Are you supposed to talk like that?

SALLY
I'm not your therapist. I'm Kate's. And I'm not sure I even want you as a client.

JAKE
Why?

SALLY
Because you're not interesting to me.

JAKE
Why not?!

SALLY
Because I doubt you're treatable. Or capable of change.

JAKE
What the hell? Is this all because I asked you not to eat your crudité?

(SALLY leans forward, gets stern)

SALLY
Tell me, Jake. How do you view yourself? Are you the villain in this story?

JAKE
Villain? No. I wasn't trying to be malicious or hurt Kate. I did something really stupid and, as you've pointed out several times before, I'm not sure why.

SALLY
So, then. You're like the precocious little boy who took a cookie from the cookie jar even though you knew it was forbidden. And you wanted the delicious cookie so badly you were willing to suffer the consequences if you got caught? You were willing to gamble, so to speak?

JAKE
Uh…yes?

SALLY
NO, JAKE. WRONG. Because a young child is not able to anticipate the consequences of his actions. And like it or not, you're an adult. Marriage is for adults. I think you went unconscious on purpose. And I also happen to believe virtually all ruin in our lives comes from people acting unconsciously. So. Tell me. Why did you commit adultery with this woman?

JAKE
I don't know.

SALLY
I think you do.

JAKE
…

SALLY
…

JAKE
I lied. I've been lying.

SALLY
Oh?

JAKE
There were five in all.

SALLY
Five what?

JAKE
Five women.

SALLY
I see. And when did this begin?

JAKE
About a year ago? Little over a year…

SALLY
What precipitated it?

JAKE
I don't know. I just felt…restless.
Bored. Unhappy with my life? Classic
mid-life…bullshit, I guess. And I
somehow couldn't talk to Kate about it.

SALLY
Did you try?

JAKE
No.

SALLY
Why not?

(Pause)

JAKE
Because I didn't want to be stopped.

SALLY
Now we're getting somewhere.

(Pause)

SALLY (CONT'D)
Why haven't you told Kate the truth?

JAKE
Because that would be the end of us.
And I'm never going to do better than
Kate. I see that now.

SALLY
Do you even want to be married?

JAKE
Of course.

SALLY
Don't just say of course. Think about it.
Carefully.

JAKE
Yes.

SALLY
What will happen if you tell her?

JAKE
She'll leave me.

SALLY
And if you don't?

JAKE
Let's face it. She'll find out eventually.
Somehow. I don't know how, but she
will. I mean…she's a reporter. Right?

SALLY
So. You will be in a perpetual state of
waiting for the other shoe to drop.
Which is its own kind of hell.

JAKE
Yes.

(JAKE puts his face in his hands)

JAKE (CONT'D)
What do I do?

SALLY
Tell her.

JAKE
No. I'm not going to do that.

SALLY
Why not?

JAKE
Because. *(Beat)* I'd rather gamble.

*(SALLY sighs, puts her pen down, and
stands)*

SALLY
I need a snack.

SCENE 16

(The co-op. KATE stands at the open doorway. JEREMY comes down the hallway and gives her ERIC THE DOG on his leash)

JEREMY
He did not do his business this morning. Be alert or you may soon have a stinky surprise.

KATE
What time are you back?

JEREMY
Six? I will bring the wine. Beaujolais and a Syrah?

KATE
Great. Otto is bringing cheese and crackers, I'll do a salad. We'll order pizza. Is Delphine coming?

JEREMY
Non. Sadly, she is no longer my girlfriend.

KATE
Uh oh.

JEREMY
Yes. The question of the head was raised again.

KATE
Aw geez. Delphine…get a grip!

JEREMY
Your husband. Will he join us?

KATE
No, he doesn't care about the Golden Globes. He's an Oscars snob.

JEREMY
Good. One more reason not to like that guy.

KATE
You don't like him?

JEREMY
Non.

KATE
Why not?

JEREMY
Why else? Because he does not like me.

KATE
You're a simple organism, Jeremy. I admire that. Why do you think he doesn't like you? He's never said anything to me.

JEREMY
Because, Kate, I see the way he looks at me. When I am looking at you.

KATE
Oh.

JEREMY
I must go. You are wonderful. I have a lunch. Thank you.

(He smiles at her—and walks down the hallway. KATE watches him go. Then turns toward the audience—and puts both hands on her cheeks)

SCENE 17

(KATE is in the kitchen with her boot on, unloading the dishes. A subdued JAKE enters)

KATE
How was Sally?

JAKE
Good. We are, uh…making progress.

(Pause)

KATE
Do you wanna go to a movie tonight?

JAKE
Maybe. I'm gonna…lie down for a bit. I'm kind of worn out. Can we reapproach in a few hours…?

KATE
Sure.

(JAKE stands there. She turns and sees him staring at her)

KATE
What?

(Pause.)

JAKE
Nothing. I love you. That's all.

(He walks into the bedroom — leaving a perplexed KATE standing there. She goes back to the dishes)

SCENE 18
(SALLY's office. KATE sits across from her)

KATE
There's a guy who lives down the hallway from me. Have I mentioned him?

SALLY
The Frenchman?

KATE
Yes. Jeremy. I want to have sex with him.

SALLY
Because?

KATE
Because he's sexy and uncouth. He's exciting. He has French body odor. I think about him all the time. I saw his penis.

SALLY
His penis?

KATE
It was an accident. His towel dropped.

(SALLY takes a note on her pad)

SALLY
Would this be partially…settling a score?

KATE
(Shrugging) Sure. I suppose. Payback. Why not?
(Pause.)

KATE (CONT'D)
Don't worry about it. I'm not going to act on it. It's just a dumb fantasy.

SALLY
What's stopping you?

KATE
(Laughing) He's…I don't know. He's too loose in the world. Besides, it would ruin things with Jake. There'd be no going back.

SALLY
You would tell him.

KATE
Yes. I would. I would have to. Plus, you know, I don't really wanna have the herpes talk with him. With any man.

SALLY
Must you?

KATE
Yes.

(Pause)

KATE (CONT'D)
Sally, I'm staying. I've decided to forgive him.

SALLY
You're staying.

KATE
Yes. I'm going to get over it. Work harder to get over it. I mean, I'll always be watching him, but whatever. My younger self would have kicked him to the curb. My older self is more pragmatic. I still don't trust him. I've still got a knot in my stomach most days. But maybe I will someday. Like when he's seventy-five and his dick stops working. I don't want to think about it anymore. I'm going to stop checking his texts. His emails. I'm going to will myself to forgive him.

Because thinking about it all the time is no good for me. Mistrust is a poison.

(SALLY stands and heads over to the mini-fridge)

SALLY
Would you like a coffee drink? I have the mocha you like.

KATE
Sure.

(SALLY takes out two bottles, opens a box of bakery cookies, and brings them over. KATE opens her mocha, and they drink in silence for a while)

KATE (CONT'D)
What do you think? Can I do it? Forgive him?

SALLY
Eventually. Yes. *(Beat)* May I tell you a story?

KATE
Please.

SALLY
Years ago, I had a couple come to me for therapy. The husband had committed adultery and she was having trouble forgiving him. Much like you. They were a lot like you two, in fact. He too had given her VD.

KATE
STI. Sexually transmitted infection. Not that it matters. Venereal disease is just kinda…outdated.

SALLY
Thank you, Kate. I appreciate it when you educate me…She was having trouble letting go of the hurt and anger. The suspicion. And why do you think that is?

KATE
(Shrugging) Because it's a process. Because it takes time?

SALLY
Yes and no. You feel mistrust and healing work in opposition to each other. But I believe they actually work hand in hand. Because mistrust can protect you. It is your ally. It allows you to see things you may not want to.

(Silence)

KATE
What happened to the couple?

SALLY
They stayed together.

KATE
So what was your point?

SALLY
She later told me it was a mistake. He was incapable of being faithful.

KATE
Do you think he'll cheat on me again?

SALLY
I have no idea.

KATE
Great.

SALLY
This knot in your stomach. Is this your intuition?

KATE
Probably. Yes.

SALLY
And what is it telling you?

(KATE takes a cookie and chews)

KATE
That something's not right. That he's not been telling the truth.

SALLY
Stay with that.

KATE
Have there been more? More women, that is?

SALLY
I can't discuss this with you. You know that.

KATE
You and I have been together a long time, Sally. Over ten years. Give me a hint. Please.

(SALLY breaks a cookie in half then chews on the corner)

SALLY
Sleep with the Frenchman.

SCENE 19
(JAKE is in the kitchen making dinner. KATE enters briskly)

JAKE
Hey. I was just about to start dinner. Salmon sound good?

KATE
Very good. Love salmon.

(KATE goes into the bedroom. She emerges with her stun gun)

KATE
How many were there?

JAKE
Wait, what?

(She points it at him)

JAKE
Okay, slow down. No, no, no, let's talk about this! Kate!

(She corners him, taps his leg with the stun gun, and pulls the trigger. ZZZZ!)

JAKE
Jesus! AHHHHH!

KATE
How many other women?

(He staggers past her and out of the kitchen holding his leg)

JAKE
Three!

(She chases him and stuns him again. ZZZZ. Holding it longer this time)

KATE
You sure about that?

JAKE
Five. I swear! Five. That's it.
(He collapses on the floor) STOP. PLEASE. NO MORE.

(JAKE lies on the floor moaning)

JAKE (CONT'D)
I'll tell you everything…I will. I swear. Please. Just don't do it again.

(KATE stands there. Catching her breath. Stun gun ready)

KATE
I don't care Jake. The details aren't important anymore. We're done.

(KATE drops the stun gun on his head. It lands with a THUD)

JAKE
Ouch.

(She goes into the bedroom and shuts the door. JAKE begins to cry)

SCENE 20
(The co-op. JAKE and KATE stand by the window)

JAKE
I'm sorry I hurt you. If that even begins to describe it.

KATE
(Weary) I believe you.

(Long pause)

JAKE
How would you feel if I went back to Sally? By myself. To, you know…try and do some real work?

KATE
No. She belongs to me.

JAKE
Right.

(Pause)

JAKE
Is it okay if I take the big suitcase and the two duffels? Come back later for the rest?

KATE
That works.

(He walks into the bedroom and closes the door. KATE sits down, takes off her boot—with lots of velcro ripping—and throws it off her foot. She feels her foot. Rubs it. She gets up, tests it, walks slowly across the room. KATE picks up the boot, opens the closet door, places the boot on the floor—then closes it)

SCENE 21
(A few weeks later. KATE walks down the hallway. She takes out her keys. JEREMY's door opens)

JEREMY
Cá va.

KATE
(Low-key) How's it going?

JEREMY
Kate. I have news. I am leaving. There will be a renter here next month.

KATE
Seriously? Where are you going?

JEREMY
Back home to Lyon. My parents are now old. Plus, it is time for a change. Everything here is bullshit.

KATE
Will that make you happy?

JEREMY
For a time. Yes.

KATE
Can you work from Lyon?

JEREMY
I can work from anywhere.

(They stand there)

KATE
Well, I have to admit, I'm super bummed to see you go. I felt like, you know, we were becoming good friends.

JEREMY
Moi aussi.

KATE
Eric the Dog too.

JEREMY
Oui. He is in love with you.

(They smile at each other)

KATE
Okay…well. Let me know if you need help. Especially with the little guy.

(She puts her key in the lock)

JEREMY
Kate. May I tell you a secret?

KATE
(Turning) Yes.

JEREMY
Quand je me masturbe, je pense à toi.

(KATE laughs.)

KATE
I took French in college. Pretty sure I heard the word masturbate.

JEREMY
You did. Oui.

(She walks back)

KATE
You still owe me for the air purifier.

JEREMY
Merde. Can I please return it to you? I will not need it.

KATE
Sure, why not? I'll have a giant air purifier on wheels to remember you by.

(JEREMY leans over—and kisses her. She kisses him back. It grows in intensity and passion until they're groping each other, making out in the hallway)

JEREMY
Come inside.

KATE
Yes.

(KATE follows him. Then suddenly stops—and comes back out)

JEREMY
What is it?

KATE
(Emotional) Jeremy. Here's the thing. I have herpes. I got it from Jake. He cheated on me. And I'm not having an outbreak or anything but I have a responsibility to tell you. Because I can't really be certain when I'm contagious… and condoms…never a hundred percent. Not sexy. I know. But that's my reality. And I'm just…I'm just not open for business. I'm too…fragile or broken or whatever. And for what it's worth, I'm so attracted to you—but I haven't been with another man in like thirty years and, oh God, this is all just piling up and—I'm sorry. I just can't. Maybe in another time and place. These past few months, I don't know what I would have done without you and your lovely, lovely dog. So, thank you. I mean it.

JEREMY
Kate. Shhh. Be quiet now. Please. (Takes her face in his hands) You are beautiful. And your husband? That guy is an asshole. Come inside. We will be careful. We will protect ourselves from any harm.

(KATE stands there and tries to decide what to do. Then steps over the threshold)

SCENE 22

(Three months later. The co-op is filled with boxes. KATE is almost done packing. There's a knock. OTTO opens the door and peeks in)

OTTO
Hey. The moving guys are parking downstairs.

KATE
Thanks. Come on in.

(OTTO enters)

OTTO
Brought you a little going away present.

(Holds up a baggie with joints)

KATE
Awesome! Thank you. When I get settled, I'll take you out to dinner. Pay you back.

OTTO
What, heck no. You already have. That medical advocate—

KATE
Mrs. Barnes?

OTTO
Mrs. Barnes, yes. She negotiated the bills down, got some of them reconsidered by insurance. Looks like my folks can keep the house. For now, anyway. So, you know, we're all sleeping again.

KATE
Great. That's great. She's the best. We've known each other a long time. She's one of my go-to experts on medical debt. (Beat) How's your dad?

OTTO
I mean…You know. Doing okay. Hanging in there.

KATE
So when do you start?

OTTO
Third week of August. If I'm being real
I'm kinda nervous. You know, all kinds
of anxiety. But like you say, always move
forward. Never backward.

KATE
You'll be awesome. And sixth grade is
the best. My favorite teacher of all time
was my sixth grade teacher. Mr. Castillo.
He was the first person to ever tell me I
should be a writer.

OTTO
Yeah?

KATE
Yeah. You have the power to change
lives. Don't take it casually, Otto.

OTTO
Yes, ma'am. I hear you. And I must vote.
We all must vote!

KATE
Exactly. But only for the right person,
of course.

OTTO
Ha ha. Yes. Absolutely.

KATE
Otherwise just stay home.

OTTO
Right? Just stay home.

(She smiles at him)

OTTO (CONT'D)
Hear anything from Jeremy?

KATE
Yesterday. We FaceTimed. He's in Lyon.
Got a place already. Already has a new
girlfriend.

OTTO
Of course he does.

KATE
He said to say hi. Wants us to come
visit. He sounded drunk.

OTTO
Jeremy…

(Pause)

KATE
So you gonna miss this place?

OTTO
I am. It's a real cool group of people.
And they've been good to me. You?

KATE
No. I won't miss it. *(Beat)* But I'm glad
I came.

OTTO
Yeah.

(Pause)

KATE
Otto.

OTTO
What?

KATE
Do you think Jake would have stayed
with me if I were just a head?

OTTO
That guy? No. No way.

*(She smiles sadly and hugs him. They stay
like this for a bit—then let each other go)*

OTTO (CONT'D)
Hey, where's the little one?

KATE
I don't know, he's here somewhere…
Eric? Eric, come!

*(ERIC comes out of the bedroom.
OTTO bends down to pet him)*

OTTO
What happened to "Eric the Dog?"

KATE
He's mine now. I can call him whatever
I want.

OTTO
He gonna like your new place?

KATE
Yeah. I have a tiny patio where he can leave his little pellet shits. We'll be fine. We'll all be fine.

(Pause)

OTTO
Okay. Well…I'm downstairs. Call if you need me.

KATE
I will. Thank you.

(He leaves and closes the door behind him. KATE turns toward the audience. She picks up the dog and holds him. Breathes him in)

MARILYN MACCRAKIN

I always say that I have been writing my entire life. I began writing plays in earnest as a theatre major in college. I loved reading plays, seeing performances of plays, acting in plays, participating in playwriting courses. I began to wish that I could see more plays written by women and see more plays with female centered characters. I was already writing those kinds of plays, so I continued to attend play readings and play festivals to try to hone and improve my craft. I have learned that the only way to become a better playwright is to keep writing new plays and then to have those plays read out loud so that you can discover what resonates with the audience and what does not. I'm honored that my play *The Venus Verses* is a 2020 ARTemis Arts Wisdom Anthology finalist. My hope is that this brings more opportunities for myself and other women who can continue to develop new plays with strong female characters and themes. In 2019, my play *The Dressing Rooms* was a finalist for B Street Theatres' New Comedies Festival. The Family Tree in 2012 was a finalist in the New Voices Playwriting Contest for Images Theatre.

I am fully committed to creating plays that bring hope and a positive perspective to the world, with a special emphasis on developing compelling female characters that show their strength and their ability to rise above the challenges we all face.

The Venus Verses

A PLAY BY MARILYN MACCRAKIN

CAST OF CHARACTERS

OPAL GREYSON: Seventy-ish. Merebeth's mother, a Bible scholar, and an author.

MEREBETH GREYSON: Thirty-eight-ish. A professional photographer (pronounced like "Meredith").

ELLIOTT WALKER: Twenty-eight-ish. A publisher and photographer.

JASON CORNELL: Twenty-five-ish. A model.

ZOE TAYLOR: Twenty-two-ish. A model.

KATE (KATHERINE) MCKENNA: Thirty-one-ish. Opal's caretaker; used to be a model.

NOTE

Opal Greyson has the beginning stages of dementia. She is a brilliant, older woman who is not used to not remembering things. She is a liberal, intellectual scholar who in her younger years had an almost photographic memory. Now she can brilliantly "cover up" her memory loss by doing and saying inappropriate things. She can "lie" and make up stories to hide her own confusion. Also, in this beginning stage, she has moments of startling clarity—when she realizes that she is losing the attributes of the strong woman she used to be as she fights to make her message heard. Opal is unusual and atypical in the "umbrella" that is dementia/Alzheimer's disease. She is not to be a cliché or a caricature. This is key.

SYNOPSIS

Who would have ever thought that some of the strong women in 1000 BC could have been the first females to evoke the "me too" statement? Opal Greyson, a female divinity scholar, discovers this possibility and is compelled to write a book of biographies compiling the stories of several no-name female heroines briefly mentioned in Biblical histories. Her daughter, Merebeth Greyson, a professional portrait photographer, decides to create authentic-looking, but at the same time edgy and modern photographic portraits of the heroines in the book. Opal suffers a mysterious illness that impedes the finishing of the book, yet Opal creates new chapters inspired by her strange "awake dreams" and visions.

ACT
SCENE 1

(*Lights up dim—smoke-like fog envelopes the scene. There is a fur rug on the floor. A woman [ZOE] with long, flowing hair runs into the scene laughing. She is dressed in a stained muslin undergarment and robe. She is chased by a rugged-looking man [JASON] in battle wear who is shedding gear as he runs. He catches her, and after some playful attempts—they collapse onto the rug on the floor. Flashes of light burst out of the darkness on stage left. The two kiss passionately for a moment, then they seem to freeze. The thick fog dissipates and the lighting changes to a blue lighting. The lights spread out to reveal that the man and woman are inside a tent strung across the stage area with hemp ropes. The man and woman move again, wrestling each other in a sexual way. The woman reaches for a leather flask. She pours wine into his mouth. In a moment, he falls fast asleep. The woman sits on top of the man, straddling him. She rises up, arching her back, and grabs a tent spike—she raises it up like she is going to jam the spike into the head of the sleeping man. But before that happens, the tent, now weakened, falls on top of them and they seem to disappear into the floor. Lights up to reveal a photography studio. MEREBETH appears out of the darkness and enters the area to get closer to the two models. She carries a tripod and professional camera. ELLIOTT WALKER enters from the studio business entrance behind them and watches the scene for a moment. MEREBETH takes the tent off the models, who wait for direction. She arranges the tripod and camera towards the models. She looks into the viewfinder of the camera on a tripod and makes some adjustments. The models arrange themselves in a caress as before*)

MEREBETH
Again, please. From the embrace—with more passion. Stop and freeze in an embrace several times.

(*MEREBETH snaps several photos in rapid mode. Lights still dim*)

ELLIOTT
You need more light.

(*MEREBETH looks out toward the sound blinded by the lights. ELLIOTT moves in a bit closer*)

MEREBETH
Excuse me? I'm sorry, this is a private session.

(*Pause. MEREBETH turns back and takes a few more shots*)

ELLIOTT
But the light is all wrong.

MEREBETH
Actually, I just checked my light meter, so we're all set. Thanks.

ELLIOTT
But the light is bleeding out the shadows?

MEREBETH
Exactly. And may I ask why I have a lighting director all of a sudden?

ELLIOTT
Oh, I'm here about your query—Elliott Walker.

(*ELLIOTT bounds up onto the stage and holds out his hand. MEREBETH turns back to taking photos*)

MEREBETH
Well, you're early. Hold on a sec.

(*MEREBETH takes a few more shots. ELLIOTT moves in and crouches down to see better*)

MEREBETH (CONT'D)
Zoe, lie down by him, put your head on his chest like you're listening to his heartbeat and then rise up, sit on his chest in a dominant position—non-sexual.

(ZOE tentatively sits on JASON's chest. JASON instinctively puts his hands on her hips and smiles)

MEREBETH (CONT'D)
Jason—no smiling or moving—remember, you're dead!

JASON
I'm not dead yet!

(ELLIOTT chuckles. MEREBETH turns as she speaks and gives ELLIOTT a dirty look. She moves right in front of ELLIOTT, he counters)

MEREBETH
Well, you're gonna be—if I see that lecherous smile in my shot!

JASON
Hey, you're the one that told us they probably did more than just sleep!

MEREBETH
(Ignoring his comment) OK, Zoe, now move in for the kill. Aggressive—raise the tent spike high above your head—good, that's right! Good. OK, once again. Arch your back! Good.

(The two models rearrange themselves. She takes several photos, the woman rises up above man arching her back with a tent spike in her hand. MEREBETH snaps more photos, almost tripping over ELLIOTT at one point)

MEREBETH (CONT'D)
OK, I think I got enough. Seems I need to start my interview early, so you two are in luck.

ZOE
Thanks so much for coming early.

Usually, she makes us re-do it a thousand times!

JASON
Yeah, thanks, man.

(JASON and ZOE exit)

MEREBETH
I don't particularly like early birds.

ELLIOTT
I'm sorry. I emailed for an appointment…but I/

MEREBETH
I'm pretty sure in the book of interview etiquette, it says not to tell your potential supervisor how to do her job? Especially in front of the models!

ELLIOTT
I couldn't help it; I was into it—wait a minute—did you say/?

MEREBETH
Did you even read the description online, Mr. Early?

ELLIOTT
It's Walker, Elliott Walker. Yes…of course. But I don't think/

MEREBETH
I don't think creative input was mentioned in the ad and I/

ELLIOTT
(Over in the "ad and I—") Well…I'm a photographer too, and lighting is sort of my specialty.

MEREBETH
(Sighs) Everybody's a critic these days—

ELLIOTT
Do you do performance art here? In this theater, I mean?

MEREBETH
No. And don't get any ideas…It used to be a small theater. But now it's just my photography studio…

ELLIOTT
That's too bad. That would be great publicity/

MEREBETH
Sorry, these little "shows" are really for my eyes only and to help the models get into character.

ELLIOTT
Character?

MEREBETH
I feel if they do a few little "acting" exercises, then their expressions are not "posing." And what kind of photography do you have experience in exactly?

ELLIOTT
My photography? Uhhhh, I mostly do digital art, but I don't know what that has/

MEREBETH
(Cuts him off) You mean photo manipulation?

ELLIOTT
Yes. You say that like it's some kind of a porn star move or something…

MEREBETH
Exactly!

ELLIOTT
Look, I think there's a misunder/

MEREBETH
Use of stock photos?

ELLIOTT
Sometimes…I can't get a clear shot of the Milky Way, so I/

MEREBETH
Fisheye?

ELLIOTT
Occasionally.

MEREBETH
(Like a dirty word)
Bokeh?

ELLIOTT
My specialty!

MEREBETH
Well, then, I'm not really sure/

ELLIOTT
But I'm not sure what this has to do with our collaboration?

MEREBETH
It has everything to do with it! I'm a purist. It's gotta be right out of the camera!

ELLIOTT
OK, I get that but/

MEREBETH
35 millimeter or DSLR?

ELLIOTT
DSLR/

MEREBETH
Humph!

ELLIOTT
Correct me if I'm wrong, but isn't that a Nikon D850 you're using?

MEREBETH
So you're a Nikon guy?

ELLIOTT
Canon.

MEREBETH ELLIOTT
I don't think this will work out unless you/ OK? I think there has been some kind of/ wouldn't mind purchasing a Nikon?/ Misunderstanding here? I don't edit photos.

ELLIOTT
I mean, I will edit the book copy, and I will approve or disapprove the photos— we can negotiate on that—but I will only work with you as a collaborator. I don't think I will be that "hands-on." If you will…

MEREBETH
What on earth are you talking about?

ELLIOTT
I'm here to discuss possibly publishing your book.

(MEREBETH opens her mouth to reply then stops)

ELLIOTT (CONT'D)
I assume you're Opal Greyson, correct?

MEREBETH
Uhhh…Oh! Sorry…yes, the book…the book! Oh…

(Both ELLIOTT and MEREBETH speak at the same time again)

ELLIOTT
We sent you several emails and letters and when we did not receive a response, I volunteered to come out here…

MEREBETH
I thought you were here to interview for my photography assistant that I advertised for?

ELLIOTT MEREBETH
Sorry! What did you say? Wait! What did you say?

MEREBETH
About a book?

ELLIOTT
About an ad?

MEREBETH
Wait—you said a query?

ELLIOTT
Yes, we received your query letter about your book proposal. Did you change your email recently, then?

MEREBETH
That must be it! I…was getting too much spam—so I/

ELLIOTT
That explains it, then.

(Pause—blank look from MEREBETH)

ELLIOTT
Why we had no response from our offer?

MEREBETH
Offer?

ELLIOTT
We received your book proposal and we would like to publish your book in our fall releases.

MEREBETH
Fall? You mean like September?

ELLIOTT
Well, your part actually has to be done by August first.

MEREBETH
In two months!?

ELLIOTT
That deadline was mentioned in several emails I sent you. I'm sort of surprised you didn't receive any—

(MEREBETH crosses to her desk to sort through some papers and photos)

MEREBETH
(Flustered) I'm sorry…there was an emergency…an illness in the family…

ELLIOTT
Oh, I see. I'm sorry…

MEREBETH
And…Well…I think you misunderstood me…I'm not/

ELLIOTT
So, when we did not receive any response, my publisher sent me out here to persuade you…to better our offer of a five thousand dollar advance to a ten thousand dollar advance.

MEREBETH
Oh. Oh! Well, that's good news…I—

ELLIOTT
We wanted to make a better offer in case you were negotiating rights with any other publishers…

MEREBETH
(*Not looking him in the eye*) Oh, yes, lots
of other publishers are interested—

ELLIOTT
That's what we thought…And this is
the resident address that was listed on
your proposal, so—

MEREBETH
That's right. We…I live in the
apartment upstairs.

(*MEREBETH crosses to her tripod to
unlock her camera and fold up the tripod.
ELLIOTT follows her*)

ELLIOTT
So are they better now?

MEREBETH
Who?

ELLIOTT
The family member who was ill?

MEREBETH
Oh, yes! Yes, definitely on the mend!
Well, isn't this a comedy of errors!!
I'm sorry, I also ran an ad for a
photographer's assistant, so I thought
that you…

ELLIOTT
Oh! Yes, well, it just so happens that I
do dabble in photography—

MEREBETH
Dabble?

(*MEREBETH continues to busy herself,
avoiding eye contact with ELLIOTT by
breaking down the set, folding up the fur
rug, taking down a light tree and umbrella
etc. ELLIOTT follows her around, almost
too close at times*)

ELLIOTT
Well, I'm not a professional like you—
So I gather the photos are to be a
part of the book? I don't think you
mentioned that in your proposal…

(*MEREBETH turns and ELLIOTT is
right behind her. She starts to dismantle a
light tree*)

MEREBETH
(*Stops, firmly*) Oh, the photos are a very
important part of the book…my book
and my photography…

ELLIOTT
Interesting concept…You do know
color photos will make the book more
expensive to publish, so I will have to
run this by my boss.

MEREBETH
Oh. Well, I hope that doesn't change
anything…I think the portraits are
integral to—

ELLIOTT
Hence the title: *The Book of Portraits*; I
get it now, of course. So…I will get you
the check, but we will need a draft copy
of the book ASAP. That's why I'm here.

MEREBETH
A first draft? I'm sorry, I'm behind on
finishing…since I was working on the
photos more…

ELLIOTT
Really? In your proposal letter, you said
a first draft was completed?

MEREBETH
Well, we've—I've added more heroines
to the book. (*Beat*) So, you're a
Christian book publisher, then?

ELLIOTT
No. We're sort of an eclectic publishing
company…We think this feminist book
could have a much broader audience
than just ecumenical readers.

MEREBETH
Huh. You do realize that all the female
biographies in the book originate in the
Bible, right?

ELLIOTT
The Bible is still the most widely read book in the world.

MEREBETH
Well, it doesn't have a very good rep for being a "feminist publication."

ELLIOTT
Exactly, correct. And that's why we feel this book is a dynamite idea! And we think the time to publish it is now. Here is a hard copy of our offer. Why don't you look it over and we can discuss it after I update my publisher about the color photos.

MEREBETH
Portraits. The color portraits matching the biographies...

ELLIOTT
Yes, and here is my card with my cell phone number and my email. Please send me an updated draft as soon as possible.

MEREBETH
Oh, of course...I will...

ELLIOTT
OK, great. Looking forward to hearing from you very soon.

(ELLIOT starts to leave, then turns back)

ELLIOTT (CONT'D)
Oh, and good luck with your photos... if you need any advice on how to get the bokeh effect into that tent scene— just let me know.

MEREBETH
Ha ha, very funny...There wasn't any "bokeh" in Biblical times!

ELLIOTT
Oh, I beg to differ! What do you think the "eternal light from on high" was???

MEREBETH
Goodbye, Mr. Walker. You stick to the editing, I'll take the photos.

ELLIOTT
You do understand that I will have to pick and approve each photo for the cover and for the book.

MEREBETH
Really? And you do understand that I have other publishing options? Including self-publishing, where I do not have to acquiesce to a higher power?

ELLIOTT
Ummm. Self-publishing can be very expensive upfront. Especially with lots of color photos.

(ELLIOTT walks back to MEREBETH, who is engrossed, looking at the offer letter, and does not see how close ELLIOTT is to her. He leans in even closer and points to the offer letter. Almost flirtatious)

ELLIOTT (CONT'D)
Read the generous offer, Opal. I'm sure we can work together on this.

MEREBETH
Uhh...Sure. Of course...I'll take a look at it.

ELLIOTT
Thanks. Let me know. Talk soon!

MEREBETH
Holy...crap...

(MEREBETH watches ELLIOTT leave to make sure he is gone. Beat. Yells)

MEREBETH (CONT'D)
Mother!! OPALLLLLLLLLL!!!! Opal Elizabeth Greyson!!!!!!! What in the world have you been up to?

(MEREBETH runs up the stairs to OPAL's bedroom on the second floor. Scene continues upstairs)

(OPAL's ornate bedroom—red velvet bed spread. A large Pieta [framed print] hangs above the bed in the bedroom. Tiffany lamps and large antique furniture. The *bed is on a large platform—you step up to the bed. The platform is large enough to put a chair bedside. OPAL is sleeping propped up with several pillows, her eyes are closed, but her mouth moves silently. MEREBETH comes in and stops for a moment. She takes in a deep breath)*

MEREBETH (CONT'D)
Mom, Mom, are you awake? It's one o'clock in the afternoon!?

(OPAL begins to move fitfully as in a nightmare)

OPAL
(Mumble, mumble)

MEREBETH
Mom, are you dreaming again?

OPAL
Water…!

MEREBETH
Here. Mom, Mom, are you having a nightmare?

(MEREBETH gives OPAL a cup of water. She drinks sloppily, with her eyes closed)

OPAL
Ummm.

(OPAL falls asleep again, MEREBETH gently shakes her)

MEREBETH
Mom, Mom—please wake up. I need to talk to you. MOM!!! WAKE UP!!!

(OPAL's eyes pop open, and she looks at MEREBETH)

OPAL
Merebeth! You don't have to yell.

MEREBETH
(Sighs) Yes, Mother, I do.

OPAL
So, you came to see me for once.

MEREBETH
I'm here every day, Mom. You're not in the hospital anymore.

OPAL
Humph! Good.

MEREBETH
Mom, have you heard from a publishing company—?

OPAL
Where are my pills? I need an aspirin…

MEREBETH
Mom. Do you have a first draft of the new book?

OPAL
Pain! My hand hurts…!

MEREBETH
That's because you banged it against the headboard during a seizure.

OPAL
I did?

MEREBETH
Mother, the doctor said no more aspirin. You overdosed on aspirin!

OPAL
Yes! Because I'm in pain!

MEREBETH
Mom! Where is the draft of your book?

OPAL
What book?

MEREBETH
Mom, your book about the no-name women of the Bible?

OPAL
That's my journal. It isn't a book yet.

MEREBETH
Well, a book publisher wants to make it into a book because you sent them a book proposal.

OPAL
I did nothing of the kind. Why would I
do that?

MEREBETH
Mom, did you contact a Christian
bookseller? With a query?

OPAL
What? Oh. A long time ago...maybe...

MEREBETH
Is last month a long time ago?

OPAL
Hmmm.... Eons...

MEREBETH
Well, I guess in your mind...you said
you were in prison for a year when you
were in rehab for two weeks.

OPAL
Yes! Yes, that's right!! They wouldn't
let me leave my cell!! Just like Paul the
apostle!!

MEREBETH
Right. So before that..."Eons ago," did
you send a proposal, "a letter" about
your book to a book company?

OPAL
I think so...it would be in my journal...
where my book chapters are...

MEREBETH
OK, good! Yes! The book chapters.
Where is your journal?

*(OPAL, more awake now, sits up more in
her bed)*

OPAL
Why do you want it so bad, anyway?

MEREBETH
Mom, I told you a book publisher came
to see you!

OPAL
When? I don't remember that.

MEREBETH
When you were sleeping. I told him
you were ill.

OPAL
A book publisher came to see me, and
you didn't wake me up!! They warned
me about this.

MEREBETH
About what?

OPAL
Elder abuse.

MEREBETH
Oh, good Lord!! That's the last thing
that is happening here! Mom, please, it's
important. Where is your journal?

OPAL
(Rebellious, childlike) I'm not going to tell
you. My hand hurts from writing so much!

MEREBETH
Mom, please don't be a child!
*(Pause. They stare at each other. OPAL
crosses her arms and rubs her hand)*

OPAL
My hand really hurts...

MEREBETH
OK, if I give you one aspirin, will you
tell me where your book is, please? The
publisher said you have a first draft.

OPAL
You were never interested in my book
before.

MEREBETH
Of course, I am! We're collaborating on
all the portraits for the book!

OPAL
Two aspirin, for God's sake, I may act
like a child, but I need an adult dose!!

*(MEREBETH goes to the nightstand
across the room and grabs a bottle, and
gets two aspirin. Walks back and gives it
to OPAL. OPAL takes the aspirin)*

MEREBETH
OK, the book.

OPAL
What book?

MEREBETH
Mother…

OPAL
I have writer's block. I can't find the right pages.

MEREBETH
I gave you a new laptop. So you wouldn't have to worry about the hard copy.

OPAL
Laptop. Crap top!!! I can't use that thing!! It doesn't even fit on my lap!! It keeps falling off!! *(Beat)* I use the computer in my library.

MEREBETH
(Sighs heavily) That ancient PC! It's riddled with viruses!!

OPAL
That's exactly what the doctor said about me!! And you still use me!!

MEREBETH
Mother, I don't use you. Why do you say that?

OPAL
You pressure me to finish chapters in my book, and you steal my ideas!!

MEREBETH
I do not steal your ideas! You inspire my portrait photography!! I give you credit!! *(MEREBETH sits in a chair next to OPAL's bed, softer)* Mom, we did Jael today, like I promised you.

OPAL
Jael, the unsung hero. Page 88.

MEREBETH
No. I did her portrait.

OPAL
Read page 88.

MEREBETH
Mom, how can I read page 88 when I don't have your journal?

OPAL
(Sits up slightly) Under my pillow.

MEREBETH
Mother, you had it there all along?

OPAL
Now I'll have to find a new hiding place. Turn to page 88.

(MEREBETH sighs, turns to a page in a journal)

MEREBETH
(Loudly, under her breath) How can you NOT remember what you had for breakfast, but you remember a page in your journal?

OPAL
(More awake now) Priorities…

MEREBETH
Ha ha. Having a lucid moment, are we?

OPAL
And I had pancakes for breakfast.

MEREBETH
No, you didn't. I asked Katherine, she said you had oatmeal.

OPAL
Well, I told Kate I wanted pancakes.

MEREBETH
You want pancakes every morning.

OPAL
Ummm. And she likes to be called "Kate."

MEREBETH
(Not listening) This is about Ruth, not Jael.

OPAL
Same thing. Same cover-up.

MEREBETH
Cover-up?

OPAL
Read page 88.

MEREBETH
But...

OPAL
Mary-beth...! Page 88!

MEREBETH
OK! Jael and Ruth are similar stories that were whitewashed by the "men" who wrote the Bible.

OPAL
Exactly! Did I write that?

MEREBETH
Yes, Mother, in the margin, you say that the Elders were outraged when you presented your interpretations. You accused the writers of Ruth and 1st and 2nd Samuel of "editing" the truth!

OPAL
(Impersonation of herself) YOU CAN'T HANDLE THE TRUTH!!! You penis-controlled beings of a lost world!!!

MEREBETH
Oh, good Lord! You did not say that!

OPAL
I most certainly did say that! Damn chickens!

MEREBETH
But I'm still not understanding the context...

OPAL
For what?

MEREBETH
Jael and Ruth? You said they are the same in some way?

OPAL
Yes, that's right! In the Ruth story—what do you think "spread the corner of your garment over me" means?

MEREBETH
I take it you don't mean literally...

OPAL
They say it's like a proposal of marriage, which in a sense it is, but in the book of Ruth I say it's a proposal of "let's propose to get it on with the first fruits of the marriage bed!"

MEREBETH
Once again, I wouldn't know what "fruits" you're talking about?

OPAL
Well, you would—if you'd ever gotten married like I told you to!!

MEREBETH
Oh, if it were that simple!

OPAL
I suggested we do an arranged marriage! It usually worked out very well in 200 BC!

MEREBETH
Please! Can we just talk about your book and Jael?

OPAL
Of course. Ruth goes to sleep at the foot of Boaz's bed. Boaz is the rich wheat field owner she wants to become her husband. So, when Boaz wakes up in the morning surprised to see Ruth there, she says, "Spread the corner of your garment over me."

MEREBETH
OK, what does that have to do with Jael?

OPAL
Good! Now you're keeping track. Sisera runs into Jael's tent—not his mother's tent, which was next door, by the way...Why?

MEREBETH
It says here that Jael was waiting for him and invited him in.

OPAL
Yes, exactly. She invited him into her tent and she put a covering over him… check that.

MEREBETH
Yes, that's right. So?

OPAL
(Sighs) So he says to her, "I'm thirsty…" And she brings him milk and honey…

MEREBETH
Nope. No honey.

OPAL
Milk always came with honey in those days. Milk and honey. "Canaan, the Land of Milk and Honey"…?

MEREBETH
And you know that because you lived in the deserts of Israel in a previous life?

OPAL
Perhaps. Besides, milk and honey is a euphemism for the reason she put a covering over him, if you get my drift…

MEREBETH
Mother, you have a dirty mind!

OPAL
(Animated) And everyone thinks the Bible is a prudish book that has no relativity to the modern world. Jael is the heroine who killed Sisera and saved all of Israel from the enemy troops of King…King…Ahaz, no, that's not right, starts with a "J," I think. I'll think of it…later…

MEREBETH
But, Mom, is all this in the book…?

OPAL
What book?

MEREBETH
Your book! The one you wrote a book proposal for and sent to a publisher…

OPAL
I told you I didn't write a "proposal."

MEREBETH
But, Mom/

OPAL
I've been studying these stories my whole life! Don't believe me—read it! Jael…went quietly to him… page 89…or 90…while he lay fast asleep, exhausted…and why was he "exhausted"?

MEREBETH
Because he just came from battle, so Jael gave him some warm milk…

OPAL
Oh, you're as bad as the all-male Bible translators! He ran from a battle that he lost! Badly! He was the sole survivor! He had to pump himself up again! How do men do that, I wonder? What other conquest can they accomplish in a very short amount of time???

MEREBETH
Mother!! No wonder the men kicked you out of the church!

OPAL
They didn't kick me out! I left! So Jael gave him some milk and her honey, and he falls fast asleep! He doesn't hear her sneak up on him and jam a tent peg into his head!! One of the best stories in the Bible.

MEREBETH
That no one knows.

OPAL
And they say the Bible is old-fashioned and out of touch. Jael is the heroine who killed Sisera and saved all of Israel!! Too rated-R for the church.

MEREBETH
You said that already, Mother…

(Pause, OPAL yawns and closes her eyes)

MEREBETH (CONT'D)
Mom, so before you had your seizures,
did you get an email from a publisher?

(OPAL lies back, yawning again, drowsy,
her speech almost slurred)

OPAL
Sleepy little Mary-beth…Mary, Mary,
quite contrary…My little contrary
Mary child…

MEREBETH
Mother, I'm thirty-eight years old…I'm
not a child…

OPAL
God'll get you…every time…
(OPAL yawns)

MEREBETH
Mom. It's time for lunch…not a nap!

OPAL
She…a great one among the Venus
verses…She, most blessed of tent-
dwelling women. He asked for water…
and she gave him milk…Her hand
reached for the tent peg…

(Mumble, mumble)

(OPAL is suddenly tired and she falls
asleep mid-sentence)

MEREBETH
Mom, Mom, are you asleep again?!
Mom…the water??

(MEREBETH examines the pill bottles
on the nightstand)

MEREBETH
Oh no, not again. Damn! Too many
pills!! Only at night! I told her!!

(MEREBETH exits)

(Blackout)

ACT 1
SCENE 2

(OPAL sits at a small writing table in
her bedroom. She opens a leather-bound
journal and finds a blank page. She
reaches for her old leather-bound Bible.
She opens it, flipping through some pages.
She finds a passage with her finger. She
reads silently for a few moments)

OPAL
(Mumbles something then, quietly) No,
no, this is not it. Where is it?

(She looks in her journal a moment. Then
she flips some more pages in the Bible.
She reads with her finger. Then she rests
her hand on the table; her left hand starts
to move like playing a piano. It hops up
in jerking movements. OPAL reaches with
her other hand and slaps it down. Even
though OPAL seems feeble, she has a
booming voice at times)

OPAL (CONT'D)
No, NO!! Stop it! Please stop it!

(She flips the Bible pages some more in a
frantic way—almost tearing the pages)

OPAL (CONT'D)
I know it's in this chapter! Lord, please
help me!

(Mumble, mumble—she looks in her
journal again, flips back further)

OPAL (CONT'D)
I know I wrote it in here! I need to find it!!

(She reads silently. Turns back to the
Bible, finds a bookmark, and lifts it up)

OPAL (CONT'D)
Well, of course, I marked it all along.
It's one of the Venus Verses…

(She sighs. She leans back in her chair,
hand on the Bible, she thumbs her fingers
on the Bible page like playing a piano.
The bedroom door opens, and KATE
leans in to see that OPAL is up at her

writing table and not in bed. She starts to
come in the room but something stops her.
A light beams onto OPAL from above)

OPAL (CONT'D)
(Closes her eyes and quotes loudly) "I
am a Daughter of Zion…an outcast for
whom no one cares…" The song of the
women of the Testaments!

(She takes her journal and pen and writes
furiously. KATE watches her a minute
and then silently shuts the door)
(Blackout)

ACT 1
SCENE 3

(Morning, MEREBETH enters OPAL's
bedroom and sees that she is still asleep,
looks at her watch and crosses through
a door upstairs to a small kitchen where
KATE is making breakfast)

MEREBETH
Katherine!! Katherine! Where the heck
are you?!!

KATE
In the kitchen! Making Opal's breakfast!
(As MEREBETH enters) Please call
me Kate!

MEREBETH
(Enters the small kitchen) It's not
breakfast time, it's lunchtime! And my
mother is still asleep! She sleeps all day
and falls asleep when we are having
important conversations.

KATE
I know. I'm sorry, I/

MEREBETH
Are you giving her too high a dosage again?

KATE
No. I gave her exactly what the doctor
ordered—

MEREBETH
(Interrupts) Then why does she keep
falling asleep mid-sentence!

KATE
That was the last nurse who did that,
remember?

MEREBETH
Yes, the last nurse overdosed her
on purpose because Mother can be
annoying and starts obsessively asking
the same questions over and over, so she
gave her too much medication! So she
would sleep all the time! Are you doing
the same?

KATE
No, I am not.

MEREBETH
Then why is she sleeping so deep in
the day?

KATE
Maybe it's because I catch her talking
to herself late at night, quoting Bible
verses like she's preaching a sermon and
writing pages and pages in her journal
until dawn!

MEREBETH
She shouldn't do that! She needs to be
on a regular schedule! I told you that!

KATE
Have you ever tried to stop your
mother from reading her Bible?

MEREBETH
Uhaaa…

(MEREBETH opens her mouth to speak
and then closes it again)

KATE
Her balance is not good, but her upper-
body strength is amazing! She grabbed
my arm the other night when I tried to
close her Bible and take her back to bed!

MEREBETH
She's not overmedicated, then?

KATE

No, probably in deep REM sleep. Dreaming…And she naps a lot… most patients do after an illness…

MEREBETH

Wait. Did you say she was writing in her journal?

KATE

Furiously. Like she had to write it down before she forgot.

MEREBETH

Oh. *(Pause)* That's good! Maybe she's working on her book. She needs to finish it…

KATE

So, do you want me to try to get her to sleep and go back to bed or work on her novel? So far, I really like this job, so I want to make sure I get this right.

MEREBETH

Look, I'm sorry. You have been doing an excellent job so far…It's just that…after her seizure episodes, they overdosed her with Haldol in rehab…It made her so much worse!

KATE

Yes, that drug can cause hallucinations…not good for older patients…

MEREBETH

Right, that's exactly why I hired you—a vocational nurse—who could keep her medications straight and—

KATE

I'm not a nurse; I'm an accountant…

MEREBETH

You told me you were an accountant and an LVN!

KATE

No, I said I'm an accountant and a live-in.

MEREBETH

So you're not a licensed vocational nurse?

KATE

No. We went over this when you hired me.

MEREBETH

I'm sorry, I interviewed so many home health workers…

KATE

You chose me because I'm a lot cheaper…I charge half as much as an LVN.

MEREBETH

Yes. Well…Mom and I are on a budget now. And I haven't sold many photos lately…But I seem to remember you had a lot of experience…?

KATE

I took care of my grandmother. I told you that Opal reminds me of her—she had her good days when she was back to her old self and then other days… Personally, I think people with dementia get frustrated when they forget things, so they seem to take it out on the people around them most.

MEREBETH

Yes, that's it. That's why I hired you. You "get it."

(Pause. Each thinking a moment)

MEREBETH (CONT'D)

But you were a model too, right?

KATE

Yes, when I was younger.

MEREBETH

Geez, how old are you now? Twenty? Were you a teen model?

KATE

I'm thirty-one. I worked for FaceFresh skincare.

MEREBETH
FaceFresh? That stuff made me break
out with pimples like a teenager!!

KATE
Right. The pimples are getting all the
impurities out. You have to stick with it
until your skin is purified.

MEREBETH
Crap. Really? Does it say that on the
package?

KATE
Yes.

MEREBETH
Why don't you model anymore? I could
use you/

KATE
No. I told you no already. You need
to remember that too. I don't model
anymore.

MEREBETH
Oh, for some reason, I had it in my
mind that you did want to model…

KATE
(Cuts her off) I think that's what you
wanted to hear, but I don't model
anymore. I want to be an accountant—
so I'm going to school to get my CPA
and I need a flexible schedule.

MEREBETH
OK, got it. CPA, not LVN. Used to
model but model no more…

(Pause again. Each thinking a moment)

KATE
So…What is Opal's novel about?

MEREBETH
It's not a novel. It's a nonfiction book
about no-name female heroines in
the Bible, the woman at the well, the
woman with the flow of blood, the
woman caught in adultery…etc., etc.

KATE
Really?

MEREBETH
And also some named ones that no one
has ever heard of like Jael, Deborah the
prophetess…And then all the Marys—
Mary, mother of Jesus, Mary Magdalene,
and Mary of Bethany…

KATE
Deborah is my favorite, the only female
judge mentioned in the Bible. She was a
prophetess and a judge.

MEREBETH
Very good, my mother would be proud
of you! Very few people know that
story.

KATE
Well…a long time ago, I used to go to a
women's study group.

MEREBETH
My mother used to be a guest lecturer
at some women's study groups. She
quit, though, when they told her she
would only be allowed to lecture for
the "all-female" groups! I remember
her getting so mad! "This is exactly
why no one attends church anymore!
Segregation! Are we still back in the
Dark Ages?!"

KATE
Yes, some still feel that way…

MEREBETH
My mother used to be able to lecture
and teach—all without any notes but
she can't seem to collect all of her
thoughts lately…She's getting better,
though…And I'm helping her by
reading her journal to her sometimes.

KATE
That's good. If she has projects that
keep her mind connected to what she
did in the recent past—that helps with
her short-term memory.

MEREBETH
Yes, I think that's why I started creating Biblical portraits for her. When I show her my photos—I can almost see the synapses light up in her brain!

KATE
You show her your photos?

MEREBETH
I take modern portraits of all the heroines she wants in her book. Sort of morphing them into Wonder Woman–like warriors, all based on my mother's insights.

KATE
How awesome! I would love to see some!

MEREBETH
Maybe soon…Hopefully, we can get the photos published in her book.

KATE
Well, then she's got to finish it!

MEREBETH
Yes, that's the goal! And I just found out today that she has a publisher, and he wants a completed draft!

KATE
Does Opal have one?

MEREBETH
I'm not sure…But that may be why she's writing so furiously at night!

(Blackout)

ACT 1
SCENE 4
(Photography studio—KATE on a break is alone reading. She whispers to herself. ZOE sees her and tries to enter quietly but drops a book)

ZOE
Oh, sorry! I thought—!

(KATE jumps up, fearful. KATE grabs a small can of mace from her pocket. It looks like a small hairspray bottle. She points it at ZOE, finger on the trigger)

KATE
Who are you?! You scared me!!

ZOE
Crap! Is that mace?!

KATE
Merebeth said that no one uses the studio at night and no one has keys!

ZOE
Wait! Her models have keys! I'm meeting Jason here…to go over our next photo scene. We're her models! Please…could you put that down!

KATE
Oh. Sure…sorry…

ZOE
Are you a new model?! Merebeth told me I was in this scene!

KATE
No, I am not a model! Why does everyone keep asking me that?

ZOE
Because this is a photography studio, and you're sitting in front of a backdrop behind this tripod, maybe?

KATE
Oh, right, sorry, I was just studying…I didn't even notice…actually.

ZOE
(Still irritated) Studying? Are you the new photography assistant then?

KATE
No. I take care of Opal. I'm on my dinner break. But I just wanted to come down here and study because it's quiet…I'm studying to be a CPA… (Awkward pause. ZOE stares at KATE. KATE turns to go up the stairs)

ZOE
Oh, OK, well, as long as you keep that can of mace in your pocket, you can stay down here, I guess.

KATE
No thanks. I really don't want to be a bother...

ZOE
It's a big area. We call it the stage... Well, actually, it was a stage. Anyway, Jason and I just rehearse our scenes here because Merebeth wants them to be as real as possible, but it's sort of like pantomiming—we don't talk much.

KATE
You rehearse your poses?

ZOE
(Uses the quote signs in the air) Don't let Merebeth hear you call it "posing." "We use real dramatic actions and emotions."

(KATE looks confused)

ZOE (CONT'D)
We don't pose; we act. Like we're "actors" without lines. Merebeth sort of directs us.

KATE
But I still don't understand—why rehearse?

ZOE
I know, it's kind of a pain, really, and rehearsing is very uncomfortable for me...but if Jason and I don't "understand" our Biblical roles—then the photoshoot goes on and on forever because Meredith has to direct us more and explain her interpretation of the stories.

KATE
Huh, maybe I was wrong...

ZOE
Wrong about what?

KATE
I told Merebeth I would never model for her.

ZOE
I knew it! So you are after my job!

KATE
No, no, not at all!

ZOE
From the minute I saw you! And then that little innocent response, (Mimicking KATE) "I'm not a model! Why does everyone keep asking me that?"

KATE
Well, I used to model a long time ago...

ZOE
Ummmm hum...

KATE
No! Really! I won't; I can't. Don't worry. Your job is safe...I just had a momentary lapse in my...vow...not to...

ZOE
It's OK, I'm sure Merebeth will wear you down and dress you up soon! I'm Zoe, by the way...

(ZOE holds out her hand and stares at KATE a moment. KATE is slow to respond. She becomes nervous and uncomfortable because ZOE stares at her)

KATE
No, I shouldn't have said anything. OK, well, my break is over now, so—

ZOE
You know, you do look familiar to me...

KATE
Well, like I said—I modeled a long time ago, lots of magazine ads...for FreshFace, so that's probably where...

ZOE
No, that's not it. Not a photo of you— you look like this girl who came to a meeting I go to sometimes...

KATE
Meeting? No, I don't go out much—

(KATE turns to go up the stairs...but stops when she hears ZOE's words)

ZOE

A VAW meeting—do you ever go to any of those? *("VAW" is an acronym but is pronounced like a word—VAW like LAW)*

KATE

No. Look, I gotta go.

ZOE

Really, it's OK; I just want you to know you're safe here.

KATE

(Turning back) Safe? Really? How do you know if I'm safe here? Models coming in and out—people I don't know! I'll stay upstairs from now on and keep my mace in my pocket!

ZOE

Really…it's just me and Jason—

KATE

(Cuts her off) And how well do you know Jason? And what about the photography assistant? You've never even met that person, right? Are there all going to have keys??

ZOE

OK, OK, you're right. It's hard to feel safe in new places. I know.

KATE

Do you? You seem pretty comfortable. And you seem to pretend you know me. You don't know me at all!

ZOE

You're right. I don't know you but I recognize some symptoms that I've seen in myself in you.

KATE

OK, that's it. I'm going upstairs to study.

ZOE

Sure. But I'd bet you a case of mace that you do know what VAW is, right?

KATE

Yes, of course, it's Violence Against Women, but I—

ZOE

Right. It's a local group in this town that was founded for the prevention of Violence Against Women, but it's known as VAW. It's kind of new here so I'm surprised that you know what VAW means if you haven't been to a meeting?

KATE

(Avoids eye contact with ZOE) I read something about it somewhere…people were complaining that it should be P-VAW because the acronym leaves out the word "prevention"—a very important word for the group anyway…

ZOE

I know. But P-VAW sounds like hee-ha! Like it's a joke! And it's no joke. VAW sounds like LAW because there are people hurting people who are breaking the LAW.

KATE

Yeah, that was what I read…about it… too…

ZOE

OK, I understand…you don't want to talk about it…

(Long awkward pause…neither looks at the other…or moves. As KATE turns to leave, ZOE spits out her words quickly)

ZOE (CONT'D)

Well, I'll share…I was raped when I was seventeen…by a photographer.

KATE

What?

ZOE

I was raped, and he's still out there because I could never prove it.

KATE

Why are you telling me—?

ZOE
(Cutting her off) I didn't report it and I didn't get a rape kit, so he got away with it. Was it a photographer that hurt you?

KATE
NO! I told you that I—NO!

ZOE
I can see it in your eyes, the fear, when I walked in here. And you were there at a meeting one time. I remember your eyes—you had that same fear in your eyes.

KATE
OK, I guess you're not going to drop it. I thought those meetings were anonymous. Sure, I went to one meeting, but I decided to go to a counselor instead.

ZOE
Did it help? Because "counseling" didn't really help me. It was only when I talked to other women and heard their stories that I—

KATE
Well, obviously it did—you're here—you're still a model.

ZOE
Yeah, with a female photographer who does Biblical portraits.

KATE
Well, I can never—

ZOE
Why not? You could model for Merebeth.

KATE
No, NO, I can't!! I can't model anymore.

ZOE
You know, at VAW, they say if you have to keep changing everything in your life just because you were raped, then you don't really have your life back. You're still held hostage by your rapist.

KATE
Well, since you keep prying into my personal life even though you don't know me at all. It wasn't a photographer.

ZOE
I read people pretty well, and I feel like I already know you. You gave up modeling because you were raped, and that pisses me off because I can see what a great model you were and still could be!

KATE
It had nothing to do with modeling! It had to do with me! It was entirely my fault! My stupid fault! Look, I have to go back to work…

(KATE turns to go upstairs, and as she does, she runs into JASON. She pushes him away)

JASON
Wow! What's her problem?

ZOE
She doesn't have a problem—what's your problem?

JASON
I don't have a problem. She was kinda rude, is all.

ZOE
Never mind. You wouldn't get it.

JASON
And why are you always in a bad mood all the time?

ZOE
I'm constantly in a state of PMS, of course!

JASON
Really?

ZOE
No!

JASON
Look, can we talk about this, maybe? We have to work together so…

ZOE
Maybe. But right now I'm trying to get into character. This is a hard scene. It will be hard to get the photos right if we mess this up.

JASON
OK…sure…

(ZOE goes behind a screen and puts on a long muslin dress and a wig with long black hair. JASON puts on a long muslin robe and turns on some music. It's sitar music with a harp, very soothing new-age—yet culturally accurate. They silently collect the props they need to rehearse the scene of Mary of Bethany washing Jesus's feet with her dowry oil and drying his feet with her hair. First, all is silent and in pantomime. At one point, ZOE [as Mary] looks up at JASON [as Jesus] and they just stare at each other. Then a blue light hits them. And a spotlight comes on in OPAL's bedroom. She sits up in bed, wide awake with eyes wide open, staring blindly ahead. She takes a brush from her nightstand and begins to comb her long gray hair methodically. Downstairs—the pantomime becomes real. The music becomes louder more dissonant. As they are staring, JASON pulls ZOE up into his lap and starts kissing her gently at first, then he becomes more aggressive and pulls her closer and won't let her go as she struggles to break free)

OPAL
(Screams) No! No! That's not it!! That's wrong!! That's all wrong!!

(When OPAL screams, ZOE breaks free and runs out)

JASON
Wait. Wait a minute! Zoe!

(JASON stands and stares after her in disbelief. Blackout)

ACT 1
SCENE 5

(MEREBETH is setting up for the photo shoot for Mary of Bethany and Jesus scene. ELLIOTT enters loudly)

MEREBETH
You again?

ELLIOTT
(Flirtatious) Yes, Mr. Manipulator, me. I'm hurt too; you didn't call.

MEREBETH
(Oblivious) You just gave me your card yesterday.

ELLIOTT
Did you read the offer contract? I spoke to my boss—she said a few photos would be OK, but I have to get a contract signed, and I need that completed draft.

MEREBETH
A few photos?

ELLIOTT
Yes, trust me, we can negotiate this all out later. But I really need to get you to sign a contract so I can go back to New York and…discuss the details with …

MEREBETH
What's the hurry? We have two months—I thought you said. I have a couple of rewrites I—

ELLIOTT
I really need more than that. My boss is pressuring me. This is the whole reason I came to California.

MEREBETH
I'm sorry, I really am. This illness has really thrown my schedule for a loop.

ELLIOTT
And I will need to see the photos that you want to go with the chapters and the cover, of course.

MEREBETH
Really? I thought that would be the last thing on your to-do list.

ELLIOTT
Nope.

MEREBETH
Well, that's not good because that's really the reason I was trying to hire an assistant. I have 5,000 photos or more to go through and then choose several—to show my mother—as she will help decide which—

ELLIOTT
You haven't hired anyone yet?

MEREBETH
Since yesterday? No.

ELLIOTT
Ummmm, too many great applicants?

MEREBETH
Yes, but none that share my vision.

ELLIOTT
It's interesting to me how you are trying to blend ancient history into modern technology.

MEREBETH
Is that what you think I'm doing?

ELLIOTT
How would you describe it?

MEREBETH
I create visual scenes based on religious biographies and transcend them into a portrait story in one shot.

ELLIOTT
Biographies?

MEREBETH
My mother's term. Speaking of which, I have a confession to make.

ELLIOTT
You do? Like the fact that you're not Opal Greyson, who is around seventy-two years old, I'd guess, as I found her bio on another book she wrote…a while ago.

MEREBETH
You didn't think I was seventy-two years old? How kind of you. *(Beat)* I should have known that a journalist would do a fact check on me.

ELLIOTT
Actually, how old are you? Old enough to go out for a drink? How about dinner and a drink? I saw this lovely patio restaurant downtown.

MEREBETH
If you're trying to flatter me to get my mother to write more, you can forget it. My mother writes on her own timeline! I don't have any influence on her…

ELLIOTT
I'm not trying to flatter you!

MEREBETH
You know, Mr. Walker, I work with actors and models, I can see right through your ploys…

ELLIOTT
But I'm not—

MEREBETH
(Scoffs) Besides, I'm quite a bit older than the legal drinking age, and as a fact-checker, I'm sure you know exactly how old I am.

ELLIOTT
And I'm twenty-eight, but I've been told that I'm a very old soul.

MEREBETH
Look, I know you are just trying to be kind, but the truth is my mother is the family member who was very ill. Actually, her illness is still undiagnosed, and she has not fully recovered. And I didn't want her to lose this opportunity!

ELLIOTT
I figured as much.

MEREBETH
The good news is that I think she has much of the book written already.

ELLIOTT
Great!! But now I must ask…Are you assisting your mother in the writing?

MEREBETH
No, why would you think that?

ELLIOTT
Well, the chapters you sent me were so…Uhhh…how do I say this…sexual, almost carnal. Did Opal really write them?

MEREBETH
I didn't send you any chapters! Were they emailed to you?

ELLIOTT
From your email, yes. You didn't send them?

MEREBETH
My mother! She works in the middle of the night!! I gave her a laptop with my email on it in a shared drive for the photos! She must have sent them to you! See! She is better!!

ELLIOTT
You sound like you need to be convinced…

MEREBETH
It's complicated…Her illness…is unusual. She now has moments of lucidity combined with these vivid awake dreams. That's why I hesitated to have you meet her because she can vary moment to moment!

ELLIOTT
But you have confirmed that most of the book is written?

MEREBETH
Yes, if I can find it and remove it from her new hiding place…*(Under her breath)* If she remembers where she put it…

ELLIOTT
What?

MEREBETH
Nothing…She has the bulk of the book written, if I can just stop her from adding new things that she hallucinates about.

ELLIOTT
Interesting…Maybe they're visions…?

MEREBETH
Please. She's good, but she's not that good.

ELLIOTT
OK. So we were thinking…

MEREBETH
We?

ELLIOTT
My boss and I—since you seem to have a vivid imagination yourself, it seems like you might be able to assist your mother in finishing her book. Spur her along, perhaps. Maybe even ghostwrite for her…

(Upstairs, a light goes on in OPAL's bedroom; she sits up in bed listening, like she hears voices. Then she stands in her long white silk nightgown and picks up a beautiful white matching robe. She stops as if she is listening to something, and then walks out her bedroom door onto the landing and hears the conversation downstairs. A moment or two. She walks down a few steps quietly, unseen)

MEREBETH
Me? Write? No, I couldn't possibly…

ELLIOTT
Well, you were taking her place, impersonating her. What were you going to do when we found out?

MEREBETH
I fully expected my mother to recover quickly as she has proven by her email to you.

ELLIOTT
In a moment of lucidity.

MEREBETH
Yes, and those are becoming more and more, not less and less.

ELLIOTT
Good! And so I will get to meet with her soon then? And if she cannot produce a good first draft very soon—I will need you to assist her. Possibly be her scribe of sorts and add or edit the draft in a more timely manner. Isn't that what some of the Biblical writers did?

MEREBETH
I suppose I still don't exactly understand your urgency in this matter. Couldn't the book just as well be released in the winter? I mean, I think she has it all together, but her productivity is a little spotty.

(OPAL appears at the top of the stairs. Listens. Unseen by MEREBETH and ELLIOTT)

ELLIOTT
I really hope to meet Opal soon. And have her sign the contract. It's important to get the ball rolling. I mean, as I said, my boss is really putting the pressure on me.

MEREBETH
OK, I will try to set up a meeting very soon—

ELLIOTT
This week, I hope?

(OPAL, looking like Greta Garbo making an entrance, slowly walks down the stairs)

OPAL
How would you like to meet the real author now?

MEREBETH
Mother! I thought you were in bed, taking a nap!

OPAL
And miss my meeting with this handsome publisher! You should have summoned me!

MEREBETH
Mother, you're hardly dressed to meet guests!

ELLIOTT
Why, I think she looks absolutely stunning! Is that gown a Christian Dior?

(ELLIOTT rushes to OPAL to take her hand to help her down the last few steps)

OPAL
Good Lord!! A man after my own heart!! And your name is…? Since my daughter so rudely is not officially introducing us?

MEREBETH
Opal Greyson, this is Elliott Walker, a mysterious and impatient publishing consultant. Although, I've yet to find out what company he works for, the name of which is not even listed on his card! It just says "consultant" with a New York telephone number.

ELLIOTT
I am an independent contractor and I work for…

OPAL
Dante Productions and Literary Publications. I found that listed in an email on my virus-riddled PC, I'll have you know!

ELLIOTT
Very good to meet you, Opal!! I see you are doing quite well!

MEREBETH
(Under her breath) Just wait a few moments…

OPAL
What, dear?

MEREBETH
Nothing.

(ELLIOTT puts his arm gently around
OPAL and leads her into the center of the
room. MEREBETH follows)

ELLIOTT
So, Opal, we were just discussing your
fascinating book! I read some of the
chapter you sent to me on Jael and
Sisera. I also witnessed some of the
photoshoot that Merebeth was working
on yesterday. And although I have not
seen the photos yet, I'm wondering why
you are willing to take the risk of being
so sexually suggestive in your writing
and in the photographic portraits?

OPAL
Suggestive? I do not suggest! I would
say my chapter on Jael is one hundred
percent accurate.

(MEREBETH goes to stand beside
OPAL in camaraderie)

MEREBETH
As are my photographic portraits!

ELLIOTT
Well, it's just in the context that they
are Biblical characters…usually in those
type of illustrations—the characters are
bathed in purity and light—not in a
carnal type of exposure.

OPAL
And that is exactly the problem! My
thesis exactly. People forget, God is the
one who invented sex.

ELLIOTT
Oh, I'm not sure about that.

OPAL
Well, Mr. Walker, I am quite sure you
see—sex is how we know God has a
sense of humor…

(Opal is in and out of her attention span.
She wanders over to Merebeth's desk)

ELLIOTT
(Chuckles) Really? Well, most people
today do NOT have a sense of humor
about sex.

MEREBETH
And that is what's wrong with the
world in a nutshell.

ELLIOTT
Interesting hypothesis…

MEREBETH
Think about it. My mother wrote an
article about it in Christianity Unplugged
magazine.

ELLIOTT
Christianity Unplugged?

MEREBETH
It's a new publication. Her point was
that everyone is so fixated on sex today!
Sexual addiction, rampant pornography,
Viagra—it's all so serious. Like we
couldn't possibly live without sex.

ELLIOTT
Well, in truth, no one would live
without some sex going on.

OPAL
Monks have lived in celibacy for years!
And they are some of the happiest, least
stressed human beings in the world!
Nuns and priests are also celibate…

ELLIOTT
Well, I wouldn't hold nuns and priests
up as a banner for celibacy!

OPAL
Perhaps…I just want to remind
everyone that even people in the Bible
had sex and the problems that go with
it. They weren't that much different
than us, actually.

ELLIOTT
You make it sound like they were real people in the Bible and not just stories.

OPAL
Excuse me, sir!! They very well are REAL people!! Of course, I mean, they were real people!!! Your blasphemy astounds me!!

(MEREBETH moves quickly to take ELLIOTT aside. OPAL sits at the desk and starts swaying a bit in the desk chair)

MEREBETH
Uh oh! Elliott, be careful what you say here. That kind of talk may have my mother pulling out of the book deal altogether.

ELLIOTT
(Loudly) I told you we're not a Christian publisher…

OPAL
Not a Christian publisher! Then who exactly are you?

MEREBETH
It's OK, Mother, they are a…"free speech" type of publisher, they publish all kinds of works…

OPAL
Oh…! I thought Dante was a Christian? …i.e. Dante's *Inferno*, therefore, if you believe in hell, then you have to believe!!

MEREBETH
You know, maybe I should be my mother's agent…Mother, maybe we should shop your book around to other publishers that aren't in such a hurry…

OPAL
(Stands) I don't need an agent!

ELLIOTT
No! Please don't do that! I mean, we really, really want this book…

MEREBETH
(Ignores OPAL) OK, now you're making me curious. If you are not so-called "believers"—why are you so interested?

ELLIOTT
We have our reasons.

MEREBETH
And you're not willing to share them?

OPAL
Yes! I agree with my agent; please share with us.

ELLIOTT
Let me just say that we think the timing is good for a book like this.

MEREBETH
That's rather vague. Actually, now that I think about it; I was completely surprised that you were not a Christian publisher because of the subject matter.

OPAL
Yes, this is very curious…I've always been told that my studies are too racy for the church, but not compelling enough for the secular market?

ELLIOTT
Ummmmm. We are pretty sure we can change that…

MEREBETH
…You're hiding something from us…

OPAL
What she said. Definitely.

(OPAL turns away to the desk and starts to write on a notepad on the desk totally engrossed…She starts humming a hymn loudly. MEREBETH pulls ELLIOT aside and they get very involved in their own little whispered conversation)

ELLIOTT
If I tell you, you have to hire me.

MEREBETH
Hire you as what? A ghostwriter?

ELLIOTT
No, as your photographer's assistant!

MEREBETH
Ha ha. Very funny.

ELLIOTT
Why is that funny?

MEREBETH
You're serious? No. I really need an experienced photographer, not a digital artist. Besides you live in what, New York City?

ELLIOTT
But you said you hadn't hired anyone yet?

MEREBETH
(Loudly) That doesn't make me desperate!

OPAL
(Loudly) Oh, good Lord dear, of course you're desperate!! You're an old maid!

MEREBETH
Mother!

OPAL
(Wagging her finger at MEREBETH) God'll get you every time!

(MEREBETH turns back to ELLIOTT, ignoring OPAL)

ELLIOTT
I'll work for free for the sake of the book! I think I can help you—doesn't that count?

MEREBETH
You're a writer—not a photographer!

ELLIOTT
OK, truth is—I got my MFA at CalArts in creative writing and I minored in photography.

MEREBETH
(Loud) A minor in photography?

ELLIOTT
Yes, at CalArts. Where did you study?

MEREBETH
(Loud) I'm self-taught!

ELLIOTT
(Loud) Well, that explains it!

OPAL
Please! A little less yelling…I'm concentrating on a new chapter!

(OPAL's hand starts moving on the desk like she is playing a piano—it flings up so she presses it down awkwardly)

OPAL
My hand! See my hand is wanting to write! I should…be writing! (Confused) What am I going to write again?? Ruth? No, no that's finished. Esther? Yes!

(OPAL stands and almost falls as she moves away from the chair but steadies herself and begins parading around like on a fashion catwalk)

OPAL
Queen Esther! And the Biblical Beauty Contest! The women walking down the palace runways, parading in front of the king! To become a queen?! Or maybe just another slut in his concubines? What kind of contest is that?!

(OPAL laughs awkwardly and loud. MEREBETH runs to her side)

MEREBETH
Mother! I'll take you up to your room…

OPAL
No! I can take the walk myself! I shall be like Esther!

(OPAL parades herself by MEREBETH and ELLIOTT, going up the stairs carrying her robe like a train, like a beauty contestant. She turns back on a step to deliver her speech; then she starts to walk the rest of the way up and her hand has a small seizure. She sways, almost tumbling.

MEREBETH *runs up to her and takes her up the rest of the way)*

OPAL

Esther! The most beautiful of queen contestants! She takes the walkway of shame in her flowing gown…trying to entice the king into wanting only her! But I have a greater purpose! To save my race!! I was born for such a time as this!! To save…to save my…words!!!

MEREBETH

Mother!! Here let me help you! Elliott, perhaps you should go. I need to make sure she takes her medication now. I'm sorry!

ELLIOTT

No, I'll wait! I need to know she's OK!

(MEREBETH turns back to protest but OPAL almost falls again so MEREBETH guides her up the rest of the way. ELLIOTT watches, then takes out his cell phone and makes a call)

ELLIOTT

Hello! Well, yes, I finally met Opal. *(Pause)* No, she didn't sign the contract…yet. *(Pause)* Well, I'm not sure she can sign anything actually. But I'm sure Merebeth is her power of attorney, will that work? *(Pause)* I think most of it is written…Yes, yes, I will find out. Don't worry. I'll get it done. Yes, yes. OK. Thanks.

(ELLIOTT crosses over to the desk, he looks at some papers on the desk, then he sees the computer is turned on so he starts to look for photos on the screen. Several moments. MEREBETH comes out of the bedroom and starts down the stairs, seeing ELLIOTT)

MEREBETH

If you think you will find any of my photos on there that are not password protected, you will be sadly disappointed.

ELLIOTT

(Jumps up, lying perhaps) Who said I was looking for photos? I'm looking for the book!

MEREBETH

Ha ha! As you know, my mother writes mostly in longhand now in her journal. Then transcribes them to her laptop or the ancient PC upstairs.

ELLIOTT

She emailed me a chapter. She doesn't email chapters to you or anyone to proof?

MEREBETH

Look, I have another photoshoot to set up for…so…you should be on your merry way!

ELLIOTT

Great! Let me help you! What? Get out the tripods, clean the lenses, set up the props?

MEREBETH

I think I told you before. I work alone.

(MEREBETH turns to set up a tripod, ignoring him. ELLIOTT comes up behind her almost whispering in her ear)

ELLIOTT

So sad, you should never be alone…

MEREBETH

You know, Elliott, you're a space invader and a photo manipulator!

ELLIOTT

And you have a wicked sense of humor just like your mother! So tell me, Merebeth, why do you even need an assistant then?

MEREBETH

Because I have a habit of taking too many photos to get the right shot in-camera and I cannot wade through literally thousands of photos on my own…

ELLIOTT
You know why that is—don't you?

MEREBETH
Because I believe the photo should be correct in camera, I told you…

ELLIOTT
No. You don't trust yourself! And you get carried away!

MEREBETH
You wish!

ELLIOTT
So give me a trial.

MEREBETH
You are a trial.

ELLIOTT
(Frowns) A testing period of time. Free labor.

MEREBETH
No…

ELLIOTT
OK, OK, I'll tell you my secret, if you tell me yours!

MEREBETH
Well, since you violate photography copyright, I'm sure you already stole all my photography secrets!

ELLIOTT
Look, my boss says to stay here until we get this done. My boss doesn't just publish books…She's also a producer…

MEREBETH
She?

ELLIOTT
She is an investor in a new movie that is coming out during the January sweeps.

(A brief pause. You can almost see the light dawning in MEREBETH's brain)

MEREBETH
Ahhhh, the dawning of the light. I gather it's that new movie that will cast that new male superstar with the long brown hair—the script is about the supposed relationship between Jesus and Mary Magdalene?

ELLIOTT
Touché—for a woman who is lost in Biblical times most of the day—you keep up.

MEREBETH
By the way, my mother and I have discussed this many times. Those script writers have that storyline all wrong, you know.

ELLIOTT
Really? Do tell.

MEREBETH
Simply put…they have the wrong Mary.

(MEREBETH smiles knowingly at ELLIOTT, who stares back and starts to speak, opening his mouth and then shutting it again. He smiles back at MEREBETH. Blackout)

ACT 1
SCENE 6
(OPAL's room. OPAL is sitting up in bed typing on her laptop. KATE enters in her long cotton nightgown)

KATE
Opal, it's the middle of the night.

OPAL
(Not looking up from her work) I know. The very best time to write. When it's quiet and no one disturbs me…usually.

KATE
I'm sorry, but Merebeth has instructed me to keep you on a regular schedule.

OPAL
Humph! Really now? I'm not a baby that needs to sleep through the night so I won't cry and wake her up, now am I? I might cry if I can't write! *(OPAL looks over at KATE for the first time, she puts her laptop to the side)* Well now I see we have the same wardrobe designer.

KATE
What?

(OPAL stands and they both have very similar white cotton nightgowns. They observe each other a moment)

KATE
Why, yes, we do! How funny!

OPAL
I say we have great taste! Barbizon? Or Christian Dior?

KATE
Definitely Christian Dior.

OPAL
My late husband Thomas bought me this gown…Merebeth found it in storage and brought it to me to wear when I was in the hospital. It was unopened, locked away in a different time…

KATE
So, it's vintage! That's why it's so beautiful!

OPAL
Yes, very vintage…

KATE
I'm sorry for your loss.

OPAL
Loss? For what?

KATE
You said "late" husband.

OPAL
Oh Yes! He was very late! Even late to our wedding…that never happened…

KATE
Oh, I thought you meant—You said he was—

OPAL
Dead? Yes, that too. Merebeth and I got a telegram from London a few years ago that he had died of a heart attack.

KATE
I'm so sorry! Why was he so far away when it happened?

OPAL
He lived there. With his other family. A wife and daughter—just a little older than Merebeth, actually—

KATE
Opal, I'm not sure I'm following…

(OPAL pats the bed gesturing for KATE to sit next to her on the edge of the bed)

OPAL
He was a Bible translator. We met at a conference. I had never met a man who could match my knowledge of the Bible. He completely swept me off my feet. Quite literally, I'm afraid.

KATE
Opal, you don't have to tell me—

OPAL
Why not? You should know that even though I'm a Bible scholar, I'm not perfect! So virgin that I was, I got pregnant of course. Thomas promised to marry me, but he neglected to tell me that he already had a wife and child back in England! So he left me this lovely little heartfelt note tacked on the door of the church where we were to be married!

KATE
Oh how awful!! What a coward!

OPAL
Yes, I suppose, a coward. But you know, I always felt that we had an extraordinary love story, short though it may have been. And it brought me Merebeth.

KATE
You seem so…forgiving…

OPAL
Well, I had to forgive him because Merebeth never could. He never came back to meet her or ever contacted her…until we got that telegram.

KATE
Oh my goodness!

OPAL
He tried to make amends, I guess. He left me a great sum of money and a trust fund for Merebeth. We bought this place so she could use it as her photography studio, and her business really took off after that! And I was able to write my books.

KATE
But Merebeth never knew her father!

OPAL
…Kate dear, can you bring me those papers over there on my desk. I think I will work on my book draft a little more now.

KATE
Now, really Opal, it's after 1 a.m. and I need to rest, so can you please try to rest a bit?

(KATE stands and the light hits her just right. She looks like an angel from another time and place. OPAL stares at her, mesmerized)

OPAL
You…look…are you…?

KATE
What? Opal, are you OK?

OPAL
You…You were in one of my dreams! You're the vision of my…of my…

(OPAL seems to sway a bit and almost falls off the bed. KATE goes to help her onto the bed and tuck her in)

KATE
Opal…I think you need to lie down…

(OPAL falls back against her pillow and starts to fall asleep. KATE takes the laptop away)

OPAL
(Murmuring) Read. Read Martha… Read the Venus Verses…the songs of the…women of the testaments…

(A spotlight hits OPAL who closes her eyes to sleep. The photograph of the Pieta seems to glow in the light but slowly the lights dim. KATE starts to put the laptop away but something catches her attention, so she sits at the end of the bed and holds the laptop and begins to read as the glow of the laptop becomes the only light in the room. Blackout)

**ACT 1
SCENE 7**
(KATE bursts into the photography studio after running down the stairs to where MEREBETH sits at the desk going through some photos)

KATE
I'm sorry, Merebeth! But I quit! Can you write me a check for what you owe me so far? Today?

MEREBETH
What? Why? *(Pause)* Mother! What have you done now?!

(MEREBETH sees her mother coming down the stairs slowly)

KATE
Opal gave me the draft of the book to read and I saw the pornographic photos that you create to go with it!!

OPAL
I confess, dear, I gave her my laptop to read one of my chapters and some of your photos of a beautifully disrobed Jael were in there!

MEREBETH
(Cuts OPAL off, responding to KATE) My photos are NOT pornographic

in any way, shape, or form!! Why do people keep saying that!

OPAL
Well, Kate and I are fashion soulmates now, so she's a little upset with the distressed muslin garb you make your models wear, I guess!

KATE
Right! Scantily clad females on top of a nude man under a fur rug!! Where is that in the Bible?

OPAL
Let's see…Second Samuel, Chapter 3, I believe, or maybe it's Chapter 4…

KATE
(Cuts OPAL off) I'm sorry, but I think you both are making a desecration of the women of the Bible!! I can't be a part of that!!

MEREBETH
Kate, please! Please don't leave your position because you don't like mom's writing or my photos! Those photos might not even be put into the book!

KATE
I don't know. It's not just the photos…

MEREBETH
Kate, you know—this book hasn't even been published yet, maybe it won't be! You should read some of mother's other books that have been published about the miracles and the comforting words of the Psalms before you make any decisions!

OPAL
I assure you my book will be published! Thank you!

MEREBETH
Mother, please let me handle this! You get too excited and explosive when you defend your work! Remember the elders meeting?

OPAL
Hummpf!

KATE
Yes, what did the church elders say! I'd be interested in that!

OPAL
No, you wouldn't! They're all men! They defend the male perspective—the all-mighty male dominance! They stick together like a bunch of bouncers at a strip club!

MEREBETH
Mother, you're not helping!!

KATE
No! This is wrong! I'm no prude, but you can't sexualize Bible stories!

OPAL
My dear little sweet Kate—if that's true, then why can all those men de-sexualize the Bible! Think about it, this has been done for centuries! Mary, the mother of Jesus, was a virgin, but she went on to have other children who were not immaculately conceived. How many people know this? And again, Mary is the only woman in the Bible who is even known worldwide!

KATE
Yes, I understand that. Mary, the perpetual virgin…but…

OPAL
Kate, I have researched this for many years and I believe many things about women were left out of the Bible because writers did not write about sex in those days. And they were all male writers, we must remember. I'm surprised the woman with the flow of blood even made it there!

KATE
But I was taught that you are not to add or take away anything from the Bible. Period.

THE VENUS VERSES

OPAL

I don't add or take away! One small step for womankind and one huge step backward for male chauvinist pigs! If you ask me!!

MEREBETH

Mother, once again, not helping! Kate, you should know that my mother is not alone in this. Many women and also some men think she is correct that the men who wrote the Bible only viewed things from a male perspective. And therefore the opposite is true, the female point of view is completely left out.

KATE

I don't know…I'm still not comfortable with this! (Beat) Oh…maybe I'm just an old-fashioned prude!! I didn't use to be like this…it's so upsetting!

MEREBETH

Please just stay here for a few more weeks…You're helping Mom feel better!

OPAL

Yes, yes, I feel better with you here!

KATE

I don't know…I will think about it… but I'm not sure I can—

(MEREBETH crosses to her desk and opens a couple of drawers looking for one of OPAL's books. She finds it and brings it to KATE)

MEREBETH

Wait! Here. Before you make a decision—read this book that my mother also wrote—a comforting book about the Psalms, (Beat) without any photos…

(Blackout)

ACT 1
SCENE 8

(OPAL's bedroom in a blue dreamlike light. There is a large scrim across the back of the stage. A large stained-glass rendering of the Pieta is projected on it with back lighting so the colors spread out to the stage. A nondescript black shiny casket is center stage on the lower level. Voice of an old fashioned PREACHER [seen only in silhouette] is reciting a eulogy for a funeral. He over-emphasizes and enunciates some of his words. A woman [OPAL] appears in a cloud of fog from the tops of the staircase; she steps down the stairs slowly, once again like she is in a fashion show. She is dressed in a couture-type deep purple dress that is long and form-fitting until it flares out at the bottom [mermaid style]. She wears a "fascinator" black hat with a black netting veil covering part of her face. When she reaches the bottom step, the Preacher begins his sermon. The woman [OPAL] slowly steps forward towards the casket)

THE PREACHER (Elliott's voice)

There was a rich man dressed in purple and fine linen…and at his door was a beggar named Lazarus…longing to eat what fell from the rich man's table…and both the rich man and the beggar died.

(The woman in purple now bends over the casket and sobs writhing with no sound. A man with long hair [JASON] wearing a long muslin cloak with a hood enters and stands next to the woman attempting to comfort her but he does not touch her. Martha [KATE] appears in a tight spot. She wears a muslin robe with a hood / head covering so her face is in shadow. She speaks to the man)

MARTHA (Kate)

Lord, if you had been here, my brother would not have died. But I know that even now God will give you whatever you ask…

THE PREACHER (Elliott)
And the rich man said, "Father…please send Lazarus to dip the tip of his finger in water to cool my tongue because I am in agony in this fire…" *(Beat)* But some say that Lazarus could not help the rich man because at that very moment Lazarus was hearing a different voice…

THE MAN (Jason)
(Yelling) Take away the stone!!

(The woman in purple lifts her head and looks as if she hears the voice. But she looks right through the man and seems to see Mary coming towards her. The man turns towards Mary [ZOE] and meets her in the spotlight. Mary [ZOE] is dressed in a light blue robe enters the scene, she runs to Jesus)

MARY (Zoe)
Lord, Lord, my Lord, if you had been here, my brother would not have died…

(Mary begins to silently cry and Jesus [JASON] wraps his arms around ZOE and cries with her)

THE PREACHER
When Jesus saw her weeping…he was deeply moved in spirit and troubled. And Jesus wept.

(The Man [JASON] turns back to the casket and yells. Martha [KATE] appears near the casket)

THE MAN (Jason)
(Yelling) Lazarus! Lazarus!! Come out!! Take away that stone! So he can come out!"

MARTHA
But, Lord, by this time there is a bad odor, for he has been there four days.

THE MAN (Jason)
Did I not tell you that if you believe, you will see the glory of God? "Come out!! Lazarus come out! Come out and take off the grave clothes!"

(As the man speaks, the woman in purple walks toward the staircase but turns back suddenly and says to the casket)

WOMAN IN PURPLE (Opal)
Thomas!! Thomas! Is that you?! You can't be dead! You can't be!

(The woman in purple crumples to sit on a stair. Her hand starts caressing the top of the stair next to her. She starts to sing and her fingers move like she is playing a piano. Her fingers move more wildly and exaggerated as she sings)

WOMAN IN PURPLE (Opal)
This old man, he play one, he play knick-knack on my thumb with a knick-knack patty whack, give a dog a bone…This old man came rolling…home…Oh Thomas…came rolling home…

(The woman stops singing a moment and walks slowly back to her room. A light from above bathes her face in opal-like radiant glory. A moment. A sudden blackout. The Preacher's voice once again as light comes up low and slowly on the lower part of the stage)

THE PREACHER (Elliott)
Then Jesus said, "Did I not tell you that if you believe, you will see the glory of God?" So they took away the stone. Then Jesus looked up and said, "If you believe, you will see the glory of God! The glory of God! The glory, the glory of God!"

(OPAL is upstairs in her bed like waking up from her dream, back in her white nightgown. Low lights only on her bed high on the platform. She is tangled in the bedsheet—her arm jerks—she untangles herself now—she stands up on her bed and reaches up for the Pieta—the hand she reaches with jerks wildly against the wall and painting. She screams)

OPAL
Saint Vitus dance! Saint Vitus dance!!
Oh Lord, help me! Saint Vitus
dannnnnnnccceeee!!!

*(OPAL screams and crumples to the bed
in an awkward sitting/lying position:
her head against the headboard, her
arm flails wildly and bangs against the
wooden headboard. She cries out in pain.
MEREBETH and KATE run in and see
OPAL. MEREBETH runs to the other
side of the bed to stop her from banging
her hand against the headboard. OPAL
struggles with her)*

MEREBETH
Oh my God!! Kate! She's having
seizures again like she did before!! She
bruised her hand!

*(KATE runs to OPAL's side to feel
OPAL's forehead)*

KATE
She's burning up with fever!

OPAL
Mary-beth…it's Thomas…he's, he's dead…

MEREBETH
I know, Mommy.
*(MEREBETH sits by OPAL's side and
soothes her head. KATE stares and then
turns to leave)*

KATE
I'll call 911!

MEREBETH
Wait! No! Kate! Please don't call 911!
We can help her! She's calmer now. No
need to call 911.

*(OPAL starts to struggle again, looking
around wildly, out of control. Her arm still
bouncing up uncontrolled, she struggles
with MEREBETH. KATE stops but
looks at them, uncertain)*

OPAL
(A weak cry) Thomas? Thomas, are you here?

KATE
But…I think…she's hallucinating…?

*(MEREBETH ignores KATE and speaks
softly to her mother. Then she gently
soothes OPAL's forehead with her hand,
combing her hair away from her wild eyes
in gentle movements like a mother would
soothe a baby. This seems to calm OPAL
and she stops struggling)*

MEREBETH
It's OK, Mommy…it's OK…

*(OPAL looks up at MEREBETH and
whispers like a defeat)*

OPAL
Saint Vitus dance…

(Blackout)

END OF ACT 1

ACT 2
SCENE 1
*(As the end of Act One. KATE brings in
a cup of water into OPAL's room. OPAL
is asleep. MEREBETH is wrapping
OPAL's hand that still jerks a bit even in
her sleep)*

KATE
Did she take the aspirin? I brought
more cold water.

MEREBETH
Yes, she's asleep now.

KATE
I've never seen anything like that! She
was actually hurting herself! Hitting her
hand like that. Maybe you do need a
real nurse!

MEREBETH
This happened before…I took her to
the hospital and they admitted her. And
then they just drugged her up. It made
her worse! I can't let that happen again.

KATE
OK, but if we have to watch her…more closely…

MEREBETH
Yes, no more writing into the night…I think when she doesn't rest much…she has more…
(Pause)

KATE
So, Opal told me about Thomas…She was asking…

MEREBETH
She never got over my father. She acts like she did but she didn't—

KATE
Of course not! There was no closure! Not for her and certainly not for you!

MEREBETH
No, I had closure. I never met him and I never wanted to. Case closed.

KATE
OK, but I think she was having hallucinations and—

MEREBETH
Kate, I promise I'll take her to see her doctor, but she has had awake dreams all her life! She told me she had them when she was a teenager and her mother took her to the doctor and he said it was just her vivid imagination!

KATE
But do they always harm her? Is it some kind of self-punishment?

MEREBETH
No, actually quite the opposite. Opal says her dreams are her creativity working its way to the surface. Then she can write it all down. And she writes longhand so much now. I was wondering if the tremors be a reaction to overuse?

KATE
That's a stretch…But maybe…when Opal was…dreaming…what was she saying? Saint…Vitus's dance? What does it mean?

MEREBETH
I don't know. She said that before. The doctors said it was gibberish.

(KATE searches for her phone or iPad)

KATE
Really? I don't think so. They should have listened to her.

MEREBETH
What? What is it?

KATE
She wasn't speaking in tongues—she was diagnosing herself! "Sydenham's chorea or chorea minor—historically referred to as Saint Vitus's dance—is a disorder characterized by rapid, uncoordinated jerking movements primarily affecting the face, hands, and feet!"

MEREBETH
Really? But how could she know that?

KATE
I looked at some of her books. I read the one about the miracles.

MEREBETH
Her *Miracle Book*?

KATE
Yes, she studied the weird diseases and disorders that plagued people in Biblical times! Lots of the people that Jesus healed were accused of being possessed! Some later commentaries said that those people probably had epilepsy or seizures and the only explanation to the people in that time was that it was from the devil!

MEREBETH

The Miracle Book is the one she was doing research for with my father—when they were together. He was supposed to go back to England after the conference but he stayed here in California for several months to help her…with the book…I've never read it. But it was her most successful book.

KATE

Interesting. Wow! She even has an acknowledgment here for him! It says—

MEREBETH

I don't want to hear it! I said I never read it! I'm sure you can understand why!

KATE

Of course. I'm sorry…

MEREBETH

Did it say when you looked on your iPad what the treatment is for that disorder on that site?

KATE

Not really, anti-seizure drugs, drugs for epilepsy—antipsychotic medications… or rest.

MEREBETH

No drugs…she doesn't do well with drugs.

KATE

Yes, but it doesn't have to be pharmaceutical drugs! Your mom actually did some studies on the medicine of the time. The balm of Gilead…some other things like herbs…and things that I can't remember. I would have to find them in her book again.

MEREBETH

You're thinking something she researched would help her?

KATE

Maybe. I know of some natural sleep aids that might help…

MEREBETH

Yes! Like magnesium or lemon balm? I'm going to make an appointment with her doctor, but let's try this healing balm first. It was in *The Miracle Book*, right?

KATE

Right. But for that…we need… something else…

MEREBETH

What? What else do we need?

KATE

Your mother says in her book that someone with unwavering faith has to pray over the person when they administer the herbs.

MEREBETH

That's you! You said you just found what could help her! And you… you're pure…that's why you don't like mother's book, right? You're like a celestial being, completely pure!!

KATE

No, no, Merebeth, I'm not like that— I'm not pure at all!!

MEREBETH

Please, please Katherine, we've got to try it!! Please, I can't send Mom to rehab again!! You said it—we need a miracle!!

KATE

But I didn't mean that I—

MEREBETH

Kate! Please try for Opal's sake!

(Blackout)

ACT 2
SCENE 2

*(Split scene. Upstairs KATE sits with
OPAL. OPAL sits up in bed with her
laptop in her lap, her hand on the Bible.
ELLIOTT and MEREBETH are
downstairs in the studio)*

OPAL
I can't think of anything to write with
this blank screen staring at me! I can't
create with this bulky laptop. I need my
pencil and my journal…

KATE
You know what Merebeth said. This is
an experiment. We think you use your
hand muscles too much when you
write longhand. So we want you to try
writing with your laptop. Please try,
OK? You need to rest your hands more.
Just a little while longer.

OPAL
Do you know what it's like for me not
to write in my journal? It's how I start
my day! It's how I talk to the Lord and
ask him to inspire me! You two think
the seizures are bad, but not to me!

KATE
You don't think it's harmful to bang
your hand against the headboard? You're
lucky we let you unwrap the bandages
on your hand to use your laptop!

OPAL
Sure, I'm lucky! Now I'll probably get
carpal tunnel syndrome…

KATE
I can help you, Opal. I can be your
scribe. See, here I have a writing pad
and pencil—you just tell me what you
want to write.

OPAL
It's no use. I get inspiration from the
process. I don't think about what I'm
going to write—sometimes my hand
moves like someone else is writing it.

Sort of like the seizures, but in control…
Like the Lord above is helping me.

KATE
Wow! Really?

OPAL
Actually, I think the seizures are from
God…And that's why no one can
diagnose them or cure them. Who can
diagnose what God creates?

KATE
I'm not sure about that…

OPAL
Perhaps to keep me from boasting…
from thinking that I am the author of
my book…of my writing…

KATE
Do you think everything you write is
inspired by God, though?

OPAL
Ahhhhhh, now that is the question,
isn't it? I know you don't agree with
some of my interpretations of my
Bible heroines…

*(OPAL and KATE continue to talk but
in pantomime)*

ELLIOTT
She's had a setback?

MEREBETH
Yes.

ELLIOTT
So, I suppose this means no first draft
any time soon.

MEREBETH
Thank you for your concern.

ELLIOTT
I'm sorry, of course I'm concerned for
Opal's health. I'm just trying to figure
out some timelines.

MEREBETH
Well, the way I see it and Opal sees it, your screenplay writer needs to do some more research and rewrite the screenplay a bit anyway. Won't that change the timeline too?

ELLIOTT
We're completely satisfied with the script, thanks. You haven't even read it, I might point out.

MEREBETH
Bring it. My mother and I would love to poke holes in it, I'm sure.

ELLIOTT
You see, that's why you're not in the movie business. We don't really care if people poke holes in the script or if a controversy arises and there is an outcry about Jesus' relationship with Mary Magdalene possibly being a sexual one! That just brings more free press and more people will buy tickets to the movie including churchgoers and conservatives who want to blast the concept. Yay! That's what we want— lots of press and lots of ticket sales.

MEREBETH
I see. So historical accuracy be damned.

ELLIOTT
This story is fiction. History doesn't matter. Look at Martin Scorsese's film *The Last Temptation of Christ* and Mel Gibson's *Passion of the Christ*. And even *Jesus Christ Superstar*! "I Don't Know How to Love Him"? All big box office hits. And that is also why we love Opal's book and we want to release it right before the film comes out.

MEREBETH
And you think Christians will read it? That it will get reviewed by religious publishers?

ELLIOTT
Yes! Even the secular market will review this book. Especially when you have visual aids through your photography! If I understand what little I've seen and read—you are making accusations that the male writers of the Bible degraded and demoted woman by dismissing them from most stories, keeping them anonymous by not naming them and also kept sexual activity and innuendo completely out of the text, am I right? In this era of "Me too" and women's rights—the idea is explosive!!

MEREBETH
Not many people in the churches agree with my mother's research. Her book with my photos could be panned and banned! I don't think we will change the minds of ministers, pastors, priests! And no one in the Christian right, especially.

ELLIOTT
Perhaps. But you will educate the masses that know nothing about these women! These ARE female heroines! Some that saved the world and quite frankly ultimately saved the Savior of the world! These women were first to go to the grave site; they believed he was resurrected just by seeing an empty tomb and the men had to have proof!! That is HUGE!!

MEREBETH
It is huge. Maybe we should make a movie about that.

ELLIOTT
Maybe.
(Pause, back to OPAL's bedroom)

KATE
Opal, I have a question about your studies.

OPAL
Yes?

KATE
Did you ever study Tamar, David's daughter?

OPAL
"I am a desolate woman…" I cannot love, I cannot marry, I cannot bear children.

KATE
Yes, the Bible says that and also says that she lived her entire life ostracized and alone…So I wondered…I mean, although she may not seem like a female Biblical heroine—she is a heroine to me.

OPAL
Oh my dear child, are you saying…that you…?

KATE
Yes. I feel like I am Tamar…

OPAL
Oh Kate, I'm so very sorry, I will keep you in my prayers…I will…I will…pray…

(As OPAL realizes the gravity, she is overcome, she starts to sway and falls back against the pillows. Kate sits at the desk on the side of OPAL's bed and reads one of OPAL's books. Downstairs MEREBETH tries to go and check on OPAL)

MEREBETH
My mother is really the expert on this. Do you know that she has counted the times that "she" and "her" are mentioned in the Bible? She lectured on it and was going to write a book about but some of the churches got really upset and said they would never buy or promote or use another one of her studies in their classes if she did. All because of her title.

ELLIOTT
Her title? Of a book?

MEREBETH
The Venus Verses. I thought it was rather catchy myself.

ELLIOTT
Yes! Great title!! I love it! Let's use it!!

MEREBETH
But that's a different book…not…/

ELLIOTT
But it still fits!! People will be intrigued! I'm intrigued! What exactly does the title mean? Venus, the goddess, versus Zeus? They will think it is some kind of contest! Some female goddess titan game! This is fantastic!!!!

MEREBETH
Good Lord! That is not it at all! My mother thinks that Venus, the Roman goddess is a good female role model. But once again that got her into trouble with the church because some say that Venus, the goddess of love was promoting promiscuity and was even more carnal than Aphrodite.

ELLIOTT
So we will school them! This will throwback to the bestseller!! Men Are from Mars, Women Are from Venus!

MEREBETH
Actually, Venus is mentioned in the Bible in a roundabout way and this is another derogatory reason not to use the term "Venus."

ELLIOTT
We publishers love it when we can piggyback on past bestsellers!!

MEREBETH
But that would not be a selling point for mother's book! You see, ancient astronomers thought that Venus was two different stars—a morning star and an evening star. In Latin, they were known as Vesper and Lucifer. And further observations of Venus show it to be a very hot and hellish environment.

ELLIOTT
Still not seeing a problem here.

MEREBETH
The Venus Verses might be associated with Lucifer—before his fall from grace into the fires of hell!

ELLIOTT
I LOVE the idea!! That makes it even better!!!

MEREBETH
You would! I think I need to go and check on my mother now...

ELLIOTT
Wait. Now that you've brought this all up. I do have a question for you.

MEREBETH
But I really—

ELLIOTT
So what makes you think we have the wrong Mary?

MEREBETH
That's too long of a story and it's my mother's place to tell it since she pointed it out to me.../

(MEREBETH turns to go up the stairs, but turns back to ELLIOTT by his pleading tone)

ELLIOTT
Please...I want to understand...

MEREBETH
OK, I will tell you but you can't try to dispute it. No arguing...

ELLIOTT
I'll be as docile as a mouse in the church pew.

MEREBETH
Right. So it's hidden in another story, the story of Lazarus...so well hidden, my mother thinks the writer didn't realize...

(A spotlight comes on in OPAL's bedroom. She sits up, eyes closed. At certain times, she speaks in unison with

MEREBETH as these are the words she has taught her daughter. MEREBETH should speak seamlessly throughout)

MEREBETH AND OPAL
I studied the Bible my whole life and one day this one verse just popped out at me.

ELLIOTT
One verse?

MEREBETH
In the Book of John, Jesus asked for Mary of Bethany. Chapter 11, verse 28, Martha says.

MEREBETH AND OPAL
"The Teacher is here and he is asking for you. When Mary heard this, she got up quickly and went to him." Jesus was asking for Mary...

MEREBETH
Mary, the same Mary who washed Jesus' feet with the perfume from her wedding dowry...An extremely intimate moment in front of a crowd who had come to meet with Jesus. The head is usually anointed and not the feet. And she was "wasting" her expensive dowry on a man who she probably knew would never reciprocate and accept her "proposal."

MEREBETH AND OPAL
She was saying, "You're the one I have chosen to give my dowry to."

MEREBETH
And since this was a public moment—if Jesus did not feel the same somehow in his heart, don't you think he would have stopped her—not given her hope?

MEREBETH AND OPAL
Mary of Bethany was special...She was known and fully known by Jesus. They had intimate...moments...

(Spotlight upstairs goes out and OPAL lies back down)

MEREBETH

And before you even ask—I do not think they consummated their relationship. People make too much of consummation! Haven't you ever been in love with someone that you never made love to? Truly, isn't that more noble in many ways?

ELLIOTT

Well, I—I—

MEREBETH

Besides, who's to say whom he loved and whom he didn't love? People who write those screenplays don't study the intricacies of the Bible to find the right hints about Jesus' relationships. They follow the continuing gossip about Mary Magdalene, the forgiven prostitute.

ELLIOTT

Exactly, because it's a proven popular plot line! Look at Julia Roberts and Richard Gere in *Pretty Woman*!

MEREBETH

Sure, I get it! It's a good story to say that Jesus was in love with a prostitute which I don't believe she was, by the way. She was a desperate, homeless woman, so she had to accept the "kindness of strangers," so to speak. But Mary Magdalene was the one who was following Jesus around—lots of female followers were—she probably thought she was in love with him because he treated her with respect and was kind to her. However, and this is key—Jesus sought out Mary of Bethany. And so...

ELLIOTT

And so...

(ELLIOTT moves very close to MEREBETH; they stare at each other. KATE interrupts and runs down the stairs)

KATE

Merebeth! Come quickly, your mother is asking for you—I think she's...she's hallucinating again!! She was resting, then all of a sudden—

MEREBETH

Oh, dear God! What happened now? Elliott, I'm sorry, we'll have to talk more tomorrow...

(ELLIOTT exits. They run up the stairs lights on in OPAL's bedroom. She sits up in bed, completely calm but a faraway look in her eyes like she is blind and she is prophesying)

OPAL

(Very loud) I am Zion, an outcast for whom no one cares!! This is the song of the women of the testaments!!

MEREBETH

Mom, Mom, calm down, you're sweating—Kate, what did you give her? Why is she like this?

KATE

Just aspirin and the lemon balm, that's all!! I don't know what happened!!

MEREBETH

Mom, Mom! Do you feel OK? What's wrong?

OPAL

(Like in a trance) I see them now... they're all coming to me...the women... everyone has a name. Every single one is important. Rahab, Deborah, Esther, Lydia...and Tamar! I left out Tamar!! Merebeth, write this down!! Tamar!! We have to add Tamar to the book!! Please, please don't let me forget!! Please help me Merebeth!! Help me!!

MEREBETH

Mom, calm down! Mom!! I'll write whatever you want but please calm down!!

(OPAL is suddenly quiet. MEREBETH sits at her side, notepad in hand, but then a spotlight hits OPAL from above and she falls back on her pillow. The light dims on everything but her as she starts to dream and sleep fitfully. ELLIOTT the preacher again at the podium, he reads)

THE PREACHER (Elliott's voice)
"In the course of time, Amnon, son of David, fell in love with Tamar, the beautiful sister of Absalom, son of David. Amnon became so obsessed with his sister Tamar that he made himself ill. She was a virgin, and it seemed impossible for him to do anything to her." So Amnon pretended to be sick in bed and he called for his half-sister Tamar to comfort him.

(JASON and ZOE in costume appear on the fur rug bed. ZOE/Tamar stands by the bed with a tray. JASON/Amnon grabs her)

AMNON (Jason)
Come to bed with me, my sister.

(They begin to struggle as he tries to pull her into the bed)

TAMAR (Zoe)
No, my brother, please do not do this wicked thing! Don't force me!

(He continues to struggle with her. The room goes black. ZOE screams. A light goes on again in OPAL's room, OPAL screams and cries)

OPAL
No! No! This cannot be!!

(A spotlight hits KATE downstairs in modern dress)

KATE
I am Tamar. I was raped by a stranger.

(ZOE enters the spotlight now in modern dress)

TAMAR (Zoe)
I am Tamar. I was raped by a friend.

THE PREACHER (Elliott's voice)
"Then afterwards, Amnon hated her with intense hatred. In fact, he hated her more than he had loved her. Amnon said to her,"

AMNON (Jason)
Get up and get out!

TAMAR (Zoe)
No! Sending me away would be a greater wrong than what you have already done to me.

THE PREACHER (Elliott's voice)
But he refused to listen to her. He called his servant and said:

AMNON (Jason)
Get this woman out of my sight and bolt the door after her.

THE PREACHER (Elliott's voice)
So his servant put her out and bolted the door after her. Tamar put ashes on her head and tore the robe she was wearing. She put her hands on her head and went away, weeping aloud as she went. And Tamar lived out her life alone, a desolate woman.

(As the preacher describes this, ZOE in a spotlight acts it out and puts ashes on her forehead, she also takes off her robe and has on modern dress. Another spotlight hits KATE again)

KATE
I am Kate. I was slipped a roofie at a bar and was gang-raped by three men. I don't remember any of it, but I couldn't say no and now no is all I can say...

ZOE
I am Zoe. I was raped by a photographer, my employer, a man who had power over me, but he has power over me no more. But still...I struggle

to take my power back—every day
I struggle…

(A spotlight hits JASON)

JASON (In costume)
I am Amnon. I am aggressive. I think
this is the way to get what I want.

ZOE AND KATE
NO! NO! He can't be here! He can't be
in this dream! No!

(The stage goes dark again)

OPAL
No! No! This can't be! Tamar is the
heroine! Only Tamar…

(A spotlight hits JASON. He is now in
modern dress. He stammers to speak. He
starts to weep)

JASON
No, you see, I too am Tamar. I am Tamar.

OPAL, KATE AND ZOE
NO!! NO! NO!

(Stage goes dark, a spotlight hits JASON,
crumpled on the floor, suddenly younger,
more vulnerable)

JASON
I am Jason. I am thirteen. I was raped
by my uncle…He was aggressive with
me…when I was just thirteen. I told
my mother and father, but they didn't
believe me. No one ever believed me…

(Lights up, JASON is still crumpled on
the floor. ZOE runs to him)

ZOE
Jason, you should have told me!

JASON
I am telling you. I tried to tell you, but
you always ran away from me.

ZOE
Because I was afraid…

(Pause. They stare at each other and
ZOE turns away. JASON turns to
leave and walk away. Then ZOE sees
JASON leaving)

ZOE
Wait! Jason! I believe you. I believe you…

(JASON stops and turns slowly back.
ZOE walks to him and they hug each
other. Blackout)

ACT 2
SCENE 3

(MEREBETH sits at her desk in her
studio looking through new photos.
ELLIOTT enters)

MEREBETH
Hi Elliott.

ELLIOTT
What's wrong? Is Opal OK?

MEREBETH
She's alright but still very weak; I don't
think we'll be able to finish the book in
time for your fall deadline.

ELLIOTT
Oh. That's too bad. Not even if we
helped her?

MEREBETH
Nope. Kate and I took her to the
doctor and they said her heart has
weakened, trying so hard to finish her
book…

ELLIOTT
Well, I have an idea I'd like to run
past you…

MEREBETH
No ghostwriting, no scribe/note
takers here.

ELLIOTT
So, I did some research…

MEREBETH
About?

ELLIOTT
That obscure verse about Mary…about Jesus looking for Mary.

MEREBETH
Wait, did you say you did some research in the Bible?

(ELLIOTT ignores her comment)

ELLIOTT
So, I talked to the screenwriter.

MEREBETH
Really?

ELLIOTT
Yes, he was very intrigued by your idea. Which is kind of amazing because most screenwriters don't take well to you suggesting re-writes to their script.

MEREBETH
It's not my idea. It's right there in the book of John.

ELLIOTT
Right. So here is a question, though, how can you know that from just a little snippet of a verse? We need more "proof," if you will, that Jesus had a thing for Mary of Bethany—more than he did for Mary Magdalene.

MEREBETH
Well, if you put it that way, I don't think he really had a "thing" for Mary of Bethany…

ELLIOTT
But you told me about that verse and said it meant that Jesus loved only her…

MEREBETH
Well, truth be known—the reason I know that Jesus loved Mary of Bethany is because he loved everyone that way. With abandon…

ELLIOTT
So then, that means she wasn't really that special.

MEREBETH
Look, this is just a theory of my mother's that she passed onto me. We know that Jesus called and asked for each of his disciples by name and then he changed some of their names because he was so close to them. He knew them. The twelve. He loved them each like a brother or like a son, unconditionally—even Judas…But as far as I can see, Mary of Bethany is the only woman that Jesus asked for—in a time of great need on his part, for comfort, for companionship, to just be in her company…

ELLIOTT
OK, I'll take your word on that… And you never think that he acted on his passion?

MEREBETH
No.

ELLIOTT
Again, how can you be so sure?

MEREBETH
To put it bluntly—because that would reduce him to being just a man and he had a higher calling than that.

ELLIOTT
And so being "just a man" is a bad thing. I can see why you're still alone.

MEREBETH
Yes, exactly, and I'd like to be alone now if you don't mind. *(Starts to turn away and leave)*

ELLIOTT
Who's Thomas?

MEREBETH
(Turning back) What?

ELLIOTT
In your mother's book—*The Miracle Book*—she has a long acknowledgement to a man named Thomas.

MEREBETH
I really don't want to talk about that.
You could ask my mother when she feels
better, although I really prefer you didn't.

ELLIOTT
Is he your father?

MEREBETH
What!?

ELLIOTT
I take it you didn't have a good
relationship? Maybe that's why you're
still alone?

MEREBETH
Excuse me, but I never even said he was
my father! How can he be my father
when I never even met him!!

ELLIOTT
Well, whose fault is that?

MEREBETH
How dare you!

ELLIOTT
Well, I have an old girlfriend whose
father abandoned her and she spent
years trying to find him…and when
she did—Well, now they have a great
relationship…

MEREBETH
Well, that's just great for her.

ELLIOTT
You of all people—a photographer! You
don't have a bit of curiosity about him?
What he looks like? What his "story" is?

MEREBETH
How did you even figure it out? That
book was written and published years
ago.

ELLIOTT
How old are you? Thirty-eight? And it
was published thirty-seven years ago.
Not too hard to do the math.

MEREBETH
You must have checked it out some
other way! All of Mom's followers—all
of her church friends—none of them
ever even dreamed that was the case!

ELLIOTT
You mother loved him. Still does. I'm
an editor; I can tell from the tenderness
in the writing that the relationship was
very intimate.

MEREBETH
Well, he's dead now—so there's no
visiting him now. And once again, if you
excuse me, this visit is also over!

ELLIOTT
One more question. Actually two.

MEREBETH
You always have one more question.

ELLIOTT
If you believe that Jesus loves everyone
passionately—then why are you alone?

MEREBETH
The way that Jesus loves people has
nothing to do with it!

ELLIOTT
If Jesus loves you so much then
wouldn't he want you to feel that same
kind of love for someone else?

(MEREBETH is momentarily stunned
into silence)

MEREBETH
Elliott, you need to go now. I need to
go upstairs and care for my mother now.
Can you please make sure the studio
door is locked on your way out.

(MEREBETH starts to walk blindly
towards the stairs)

ELLIOTT
Merebeth! What's wrong? I just meant
that you—

MEREBETH
Elliott, please. Just go and please lock the door on your way out...

(MEREBETH keeps slowly walking toward the stairs, her back to ELLIOTT as she says her line. ELLIOTT is dumbfounded. He slowly exits, and you hear the door shut on the way out)

(MEREBETH takes a few steps up the stairs, pauses as she hears the door shut, then crumples down into a sitting position. A quiet sob is released as she sits for a moment. Then she reaches up to the railing; visibly shaken, she pulls herself up and walks up the rest of the stairs. ELLIOTT appears out of the shadows and watches her make her way up the stairs)

(MEREBETH walks into OPAL's room and crawls into bed with OPAL, who is sleeping in almost a sitting position. There is only a small nightlight to light the room. Then the scene turns to blue lighting. OPAL stirs and sits up—she appears much younger and much more lucid. She sees that MEREBETH is curled up like a child beside her. MEREBETH seems younger too)

OPAL
What's wrong with my Mary-Beth child?

MEREBETH
I don't know.

OPAL
Sure you do.

MEREBETH
Why doesn't he ever want to meet me?

OPAL
Oh, I'm sure he does want to...

MEREBETH
I don't believe it.

OPAL
I think he's waiting for you to ask for him...

MEREBETH
But I don't want to!

OPAL
Well, remember this—God'll get you every time.

MEREBETH
Mother, that's your answer for everything!

OPAL
You have to be humble enough to ask for what you want. I loved him. And he loved me too, so I know he would adore you.

(Blue light changes to low light again)

MEREBETH
Mother, what did you say?

(MEREBETH sees that her mother is sound asleep. She rests her head on her mother's shoulder. A change in lighting, from low light to soft morning light. Time has passed. MEREBETH walks out of OPAL's room and down the stairs, which are in low light. ELLIOTT is there sleeping in a chair. MEREBETH sees him and turns on the lights, which awaken ELLIOTT)

MEREBETH (CONT'D)
I could call the police, you know. An intruder in my studio.

ELLIOTT
I work here, remember?

MEREBETH
Not anymore.

ELLIOTT
Right, I guess we shouldn't work together if we are going to be in a relationship.

MEREBETH
What?

ELLIOTT
You didn't let me ask the second question.

MEREBETH
What on earth are you talking about?

ELLIOTT
Last night, I was going to ask you out to dinner to discuss the new script possibilities…but now I guess it would be breakfast.

MEREBETH
I really don't want to talk about that anymore…

ELLIOTT
Just when I was starting to believe that maybe Mary of Bethany was a real person.

MEREBETH
And I'm beginning to think maybe she wasn't…

ELLIOTT
No! You cannot have a crisis of faith now!

MEREBETH
Why not? You're right! If God loves me so much, then why am I alone? And why did my father abandon me? Sure! He was already married and had another daughter, but why wouldn't he want me in his life? He could still keep the secret from his family! I mean, when he died and left us money—that must have been a complete shock to them! What a coward to wait until then!!

ELLIOTT
I'm not sure, but I'd say since he was a very successful Bible scholar and translator, having an affair come out in the media would be a career killer.

MEREBETH
Sure. And that's more important.

ELLIOTT
Well, he did continue to make a lot of money, hence, your trust fund and endowment for your mother.

MEREBETH
Money is rarely a good substitute for love.

ELLIOTT
Another question.

MEREBETH
Really?

ELLIOTT
Did Thomas name you?

MEREBETH
No, of course not! He wasn't even around when I was born!

ELLIOTT
But he knew Opal's…ahh…situation— that she was pregnant before he returned to England, right?

MEREBETH
Yes, I suppose.

ELLIOTT
Have you ever read any of his books?

MEREBETH
No!

ELLIOTT
Has Opal?

MEREBETH
Maybe. She does a lot of research.

ELLIOTT
He mentions you in one of his acknowledgments.

MEREBETH
Now you are just making things up!

ELLIOTT
Nope. I told you I did some research on Mary of Bethany and a book by Thomas Rhoades came up. A commentary on the book of John. Published September 2018.

MEREBETH
He died in November 2018.

ELLIOTT
Yes, his last book was published. You might want to read the acknowledgments.

(ELLIOT *hands her an open book.* MEREBETH *stares and looks up at* ELLIOT)

ELLIOTT (CONT'D)
Maybe you should read it—out loud.

MEREBETH
"An Opal is a very beautiful gemstone. The best Opals have lovely flecks of fire in them. There should be more Opals in the world, I think. So speaking of beautiful gems, I dedicate this Commentary of John to my fiery Opal and daughter Merebeth, who like Mary of Bethany should know that love can surprise you enough to give up your most treasured possessions, but it doesn't always turn out the way you hoped it would. Even so, I pronounce my eternal, transcendent love to both of you."

(MEREBETH *looks up at* ELLIOT)
Mary Beth…my name…My God, I never even…thought…

(*Blackout*)

ACT 2
SCENE 4

(*Whole scene in spotlight as before—* OPAL *in the same nightgown and same chair and table as before. With the leather-bound Bible as before. Low light—She smooths out the journal page. She reaches for her Bible. She opens it and flips through some pages early in the book. She finds a passage with her finger on her right hand. She reads silently for a few moments*)

OPAL
(*Mumbles something then quietly to herself*) No, no, this is not it. Where is it?

(*She looks in her journal a moment. Then she flips some more pages in the Bible. She reads with her finger. Then she reads the Bible and rests her hand on the table, her left hand starts to move like playing a piano, then her hand hops up like jerking.*

OPAL *reaches with her other hand and calms her moving hand with a prayer*)

OPAL (CONT'D)
No, Lord, please, I need to finish… please, dear Lord, not now…

(*She starts to write again. She says each word out loud*)

OPAL
This is the book of their stories. Their portraits…The no-name women in the Bible. Lord, maybe I was wrong about them. Maybe some have no names because they can be any woman and every woman…They can be named Merebeth, Kate, Zoe, and even Opal…

(*Her hand starts to jump wildly again and she covers her hand again*)

OPAL (CONT'D)
They are us!! Lord, help me! They have our infirmities…our sins, our joys, and our successes! They teach us how to survive and how to cope! And, of course, I was wrong to choose my favorites first, we also need the broken ones, Tamar, the desolate woman, the women with the flow of blood, the brave woman at the well…and yes, the old woman with visions and tremors in her hand…My sin is not choosing them is that I thought they might appear weak, and I needed the strength…I needed the strength! (*Closes her eyes and quotes loudly*) "I am the Daughter of Zion, an outcast for whom no one cares…" I chose them!! Because I want people to know them!! I want people to know who they are and to embrace their songs!! Embrace their stories!! The songs of the women of the Testaments!

(*Suddenly, a light appears from above and streams out from* OPAL. *She sits up straighter, her hand stops jerking, and she becomes illuminated in healing light. As she says the names, the streaming light changes* colors, and their portraits appear on the screens on the sides of the stage. The photos are all golden sepia-colored but change by reflecting the colors of the light)

OPAL (CONT'D)
(Softer and calmer) Ahhhhh! And here they are!! I see you now!! You have come for me!! Jael, Mary of Bethany, Martha, Ruth, and Naomi, and Queen Esther…You will lead me to the one I have been, so longing to meet…

(OPAL lays her head back and smiles, still glowing, closing her eyes. One hand on her journal and her other hand falls off the side of her bed, and her pen falls to the floor)

(A moment. Then MEREBETH bursts into the room and sees her)

MEREBETH
NO!!! No, no, no, no!! Kate!! Kate! Oh nooooooooooooooo!

(She runs to OPAL and sees that her left hand is calmly lying on her open journal. MEREBETH starts to cry. Then she sees what OPAL has written)

MEREBETH
Oh, Mother…Oh, my dear, beloved mother…

KATE
What is it? Oh, Merebeth! OH! No! No…

MEREBETH
She has a smile on her face…She was writing…

KATE
Oh! What is that fragrance?

MEREBETH
Isn't that the lemon balm?

KATE
No. It doesn't smell like that. It's the aroma…like an ancient perfume?

(They stare at each other in recognition)

MEREBETH
Do you think? I heard her calling out, saying the names…of the women.

KATE
They were here…to meet her…Just as she would have wanted…

(MEREBETH has picked up the journal and looked at the dedication)

MEREBETH
And she finished it. Here is the dedication—"To Merebeth, Kate, and Zoe. You are my inspiration for the women of the Venus Verses…You all need to tell your stories…You all have names that should be known, so you all need to tell your stories…

(MEREBETH and KATE hug each other in tears)

(Blackout)

Screenplays

REBECCA CUTTER

In my fifties, I awoke one night with the voice of a desperate woman whispering in my ear, "Tell my story." Over time, I felt both irritated and responsible. Why me? What was her story? I was a psychotherapist at the time—used to listening to the lives of others—but this was a foreign experience. She was too insistent to ignore, so I felt compelled to at least try: I named her Lydia, then I took workshops for writing fiction and wrote a novel. The professor's response made evident a native talent I did not know I possessed. Lydia continued to haunt me, so I wrote a screenplay version. I had difficulty taking credit for the work because—at my end—it was more like taking dictation. Each morning I awoke and madly scribbled what I could remember from the night before. I simply got out of her way and listened. Then both versions went into boxes for over a decade, while I wrote a book on the brain, taught "psychopathology in film," and wrote a contemporary screenplay, before switching to essays. It was while writing a memoir, at age seventy-six, that I revisited those boxes and discovered my connection to Lydia. We were both struggling to find the strength to leave a violent husband, she in 1890 and me in 1980.

A Suitable Companion

A SCREENPLAY BY REBECCA CUTTER

FADE IN:

EXT. WESTPORT GARDEN—DAY (SUMMER)

Northwest US. 1890. A majestic tree dominates the garden of an elegant Victorian home. Female laughter leads to a pair of beautiful young women, LYDIA WESTPORT and LAURA CREIGHTON, cradled above in the branches. Sumptuous fabrics and exotic jewelry reflect their wealth. Bare feet dangle. Stockings and shoes lie abandoned on the lawn far below. Lydia's ensemble exhibits a highly iconoclastic style.

They rip their collars open and shove up their sleeves. As much against the suffocating lives they lead as against the heat of summer. Tucked high away from their much older husbands, they freely express themselves. Their passion for life is palpable. Each is reading a copy of Madame Bovary.

LAURA
Can you imagine changing men as often as hats?

Hidden beneath a straw hat, Lydia raises her head, revealing ebony hair, a stunning face, and luminous smile.

LYDIA
Boredom is a poor reason to take a lover.

LAURA
Lydia Westport! Are you speaking from experience?

LYDIA
Of course not! I'm simply saying the answer is not found in regarding men as though they were chocolates.

Lydia tucks her book into the waist of her skirt and descends. Laura stops her as she passes.

LAURA
Why does she choose arsenic? What a horrible way to die!

Laura closes her book and follows.

LYDIA
That's the problem with men writing about women. The wife not only must pay for what her lovers wanted. She must do so in an agonizing manner that guarantees the reader will think twice about her own desire.

LAURA
What about the ending?
When her husband finds the
love letters from Rodolphe, he
forgives her!

They land and put on their stockings
and shoes.

LYDIA
Can you imagine your husband
doing that? Clutching them to
his broken heart? Turning your
bedchamber into a shrine?

LAURA
Howard's far too practical. He
would rent it out.

Laughing uncontrollably, they lie
back onto the grass.

LYDIA
Oh, Laura, What would I do
without you? These months of
reading and talking have been
such a tonic! How can I ever
thank you for all the books?
(whispers)
I keep them locked in a trunk.
Anderson would never approve.

LAURA
He doesn't want his bride reading?

LYDIA
He doesn't want me thinking.

**EXT. MAIN STREET OF TOWN—
DAY (JUNE)**
SUPERIMPOSED: *Five Years Later*

*JESSE WOODS, a ruggedly handsome
carpenter, lopes out of the forest at the
edge of town and joins the stream of
citizens on foot and horseback, in carriages
and carts. A loner, he keeps his head down,
but is friendly to those he encounters. A
man runs to catch up with him.*

MAN
Jesse Woods! Just the man
I was lookin' for!

JESSE
I'll be damned. Figured you'd
left town.

MAN
Wanted you to know I didn't
run out on that job. Sheriff
grabbed me. Just got released
yesterday.

Jesse registers concern, which the
man waves away.

(MAN CONT'D)
Wasn't nothin' criminal. I've
been up north in debtors'
prison.

JESSE
Don't have anything for you
right now. But you're still due
your pay for the days we
worked on the schoolhouse.
Come and see me.

MAN
Appreciate it!

Jesse walks over to BLIND BILLY, a
Native American, sitting on a stool.
At his feet, an upturned hat contains
a few coins. Jesse announces his
arrival and places his hand on Billy's
shoulder.

JESSE
Morning, Billy. It's Jesse. What
are you selling today?

BLIND BILLY
Predictions.

Billy leans toward the hat and cocks
his ear. Jesse tosses a coin in. As soon
as Billy hears the CLINK, he speaks.

BLIND BILLY (CONT'D)

Get ready! Storm's comin'!

Jesse looks skyward, shading his eyes.

JESSE
Don't see a single cloud.
You sure?

BLIND BILLY
Predicting don't got nothing
to do with seeing. It's all about
feeling. She's on her way. And
she's a force to be reckoned
with!

Jesse walks on, checking the sky
again. He doesn't see Lydia Westport
dash out of a shop and directly into
his path. She knocks him off balance
and into the road.

LYDIA
Oh! I'm terribly sorry. Are you
injured?

Jesse looks up to see her silhouette
against the sun. She holds an open
parasol.

JESSE
I don't believe so. Yourself?

Jesse rises and dusts off his pants. He
sees how exquisite she is. Lydia wears
a Parisian dress in stark contrast
to the simple clothing of the other
women passing by.

Smiling, she spins a complete circle.
One sleeve of her dress is folded and
pinned at the waist. She is missing an
arm.

LYDIA
Fit as a fiddle!

Lydia turns and heads up the
street. Jesse watches her undulat-
ing parasol, high above the stream
of shoppers.

He's joined by BUFORD LONG, who
has too few teeth and too much gut.

BUFORD
Keeping company with the
mayor's wife? You know she's
missing a plank or two, don't
you?

Ignoring Bufford's presence, Jesse
continues watching Lydia's parasol. His eyes reflect the disorienta-
tion of a man who's been struck by a
tornado.

INT. PUBLIC LIBRARY—
FOLLOWING WEEK, DAY
*The aisles are very narrow. Jesse is
scanning a shelf when he steps back and
bumps into Lydia. She wears a loose dress
in the fashion of the Aesthetic Movement,
the empty sleeve folded and pinned with
a sterling-silver butterfly. Her hair is
unleashed like a Pre-Raphaelite portrait.
They whisper when they speak.*

JESSE
We keep bumping into each
other.

Lydia smiles, but it's clear she does
not remember him.

LYDIA
Yes...so nice to see you again.

He struggles not to stare at her
missing arm.

JESSE
Have you found what you've
been searching for?

LYDIA
(philosophically)
Does anyone?

Their physical closeness is too much
for Jesse. He quickly steps a few feet
away and studies a shelf.

JESSE
I was thinking Darwin would be good company this evening. His book is usually right here.

LYDIA
Evidently, another patron has found it equally compelling.

JESSE
Must be a newcomer. I have yet to find a man in this town who is willing to discuss anything but politics or commerce.

LYDIA
Emerson would agree with you!

She reaches for a book while reciting from memory.

LYDIA (CONT'D)
There is a prairie beyond your laws. There are two worlds...the post office and nature.

JESSE
Emerson? I've not had the pleasure.

LYDIA
The pleasure is mine.

Lydia places the book in Jesse's hands, smiles, and exits before he can respond. Jesse is again left wondering what hit him.

EXT. BLIND BILLY'S COTTAGE—DAY
Jesse is repairing the front porch of Billy's shack. Billy sits on a stump in the shade. Jesse takes a break and picks up his pack. He pulls out a jar of cider and a book: CU of THE LAST OF THE MOHICANS. *He joins Billy and opens the book.*

JESSE
Where were we? Ah...
(overdramatically)
"Whirling the bloody knife, the victorious Magua uttered a cry so fierce, so wild, and yet so joyous that it conveyed triumph to the ears of those who fought in the valley, a thousand feet below."

Jesse puts the jar in Billy's hand. Billy swigs.

"He shouted, 'The pale-faces are dogs! The Delawares women! Magua leaves them on the rocks, for the crows.'"

BLIND BILLY
That Magua's a real savage! Good thing you're not fixing his porch.

JESSE
I might, if the price was right.

BLIND BILLY
You pale-face dog!

JESSE
By the way, what are you paying me?

BLIND BILLY
The pleasure of my company.

JESSE
Fair enough.

EXT. WHITWELL CLUB COURTYARD— TWO WEEKS LATER, DAY
The Whitwell Club is an imposing structure. Lydia is the only female in the gathering crowd.

A SUITABLE COMPANION

A shimmering jewel floating in a sea of dull suits. Each man she passes tips his hat then turns his back. As the Mayor's wife, she must be acknowledged but nothing more. The group heads up the stairs to the lecture hall.

At the top, Lydia's progress is blocked by a DOORMAN. He's chewing a well-worked cigar and holding a glass of half-finished whiskey.

> DOORMAN
> Hold it, girly! You got pants under there?

The doorman pushes the tip of his dirty boot beneath her skirt, raising it slightly. Lydia stands her ground.

> LYDIA
> The position of doorman means you have no actual power beyond your ability to bully. I know something about bullies, sir, so your tactics do not discourage me.

Jesse is standing midway up the staircase. He recognizes Lydia's voice and pushes his way to her side.

> JESSE
> (to Doorman)
> Do you know who this is?

> DOORMAN
> I don't care if she's the Queen of Sheba. She ain't coming in while I'm on duty.

In the line behind Lydia, impatient men SHOUT complaints.

ELLIOT MINOR, city council member, steps out of the building. He's dapper and sports a mustache waxed into lethal points.

> ELLIOT
> Good afternoon, Mrs. Westport. I see we have a problem.

> JESSE
> Mrs. Westport merely wishes to attend the talk. As do I.

Lydia looks at Elliot, but Elliot stares at Jesse.

> ELLIOT
> You a friend of the mayors?

> LYDIA
> No, Elliot, the gentleman is an acquaintance of mine. This is... Mr.—

Lydia's mouth remains open, but nothing comes out. She's never asked his name. Jesse realizes this, and he shoots his hand out for Elliot to shake.

> JESSE
> Woods. Jesse Woods.

> LYDIA
> We're hoping to be seated as close to the speaker as possible. The longer we remain out here, the less likely that will happen.

> ELLIOT
> I cannot allow you entrance. The bylaws clearly forbid ladies within these walls.
> (to Jesse)
> You are welcome, of course.

Elliot guides Lydia away from the door. His fingers brush her bodice. She jumps back. The three of them stand like rocks in a stream as the crowd flows into the hall.

ELLIOT (CONT'D)
Come now, Mrs. Westport, you understand. It's the way the world is. After all, we wouldn't find gentlemen at ladies' teas, now would we?

JESSE
It's not membership she's seeking.

ELLIOT
(to Lydia)
Membership aside, what you do not seem to grasp is that your presence, alone, is completely unacceptable.

A BURST OF APPLAUSE erupts from the hall. Elliot steps inside and shuts the door behind him. Lydia and Jesse stand in awkward silence for a few beats.

LYDIA
You had better take your seat, Mr. Woods. I wouldn't want you to miss the lecture on my account.

JESSE
To be honest, Mrs. Westport, I'm holding a ticket only because it was given to me. I'm not convinced that Mr. Edison's so-called "progress" is a good thing. Now, I have the gift of an afternoon. My only task is to figure out how to fill it!

Lydia smiles mischievously.

LYDIA
Hmm...so it would be ridiculous to have a gentleman to tea?

She hooks her arm around Jesse's.

LYDIA (CONT'D)
Please do me the honor, Mr. Woods.

She steps down. Jesse does not budge.

JESSE
I'm fairly sure the mayor wouldn't want to find a stranger in his house. Alone with his wife.

Lydia cocks her hip, tilts her head.

LYDIA
It is my house as well.

INT. WESTPORTS' LIBRARY—SAME DAY
Lydia opens the drapes. Sunlight floods the room, illuminating a blue and gold oriental carpet. Opposite the bank of windows is a fireplace. The walls are covered with floor-to-ceiling bookcases, housing volumes of all sizes.

She pulls a cord. MOLLY, the parlor maid, arrives. She is young, plain-looking, with flaming red hair.

LYDIA
Mr. Woods and I will have our tea in here.

Molly is clearly confused by the situation. She cannot take her eyes off the handsome stranger.

LYDIA (CONT'D)
That will be all.

Molly exits with a quizzical look. Jesse walks over to a bucolic painting: CU of a group of fully clothed gentlemen sharing wine and food with plump, nude women whose garments have been flung into the surrounding shrubs.

JESSE
I don't believe I've ever attended a picnic such as this.

LYDIA (O.S.)
They're French.

JESSE
Ah. Well, that would explain it.

Lydia gestures for Jesse to be seated. He chooses a pair of chairs with intricately carved claw feet and a small matching table. Lydia goes to a desk and plucks a newspaper article she has clipped. She paces as she reads it to him.

LYDIA
"A new disease has been discovered, called 'American Nervousness.' People become nervous when they suffer a deficiency of force, the same way Edison's new lights become dim if they receive insufficient current."

Lydia looks up to see if Jesse is listening. He's on his knee, examining the carving on the chair's legs. His face reflects appreciation for the required skill. She clears her throat. His head pops up.

LYDIA (CONT'D)
"The primary cause is the very rapid increase of modern civilization, which is distinguished by these five characteristics: steam power, the periodical press, the telegraph, the sciences, and— the mental activity of women."

Molly enters with a tray of tea and cakes.

LYDIA (CONT'D)
Please close the door as you leave.

Lydia joins Jesse. He's struggling with the teacup's tiny handle and his large fingers. He gives up and holds it like a glass, shifting the hot cup back and forth between his hands.

Lydia watches with amusement, then takes on a more serious mood.

LYDIA (CONT'D)
From the moment you were born, Mr. Woods, you were groomed for exploration and independence. I, on the other hand was discouraged from developing myself beyond the fine art of securing a wealthy husband.

She rises and paces a large circle. As she talks, Jesse studies her face, her neck, the vacant sleeve (captured by a sash at her waist), the grace of her movement, and her feet gliding over the carpet.

LYDIA (CONT'D)
If, in conversation, I challenge the world as it is, I'm stepping beyond acceptable boundaries. In these times, that's a dangerous act.

She stops right in front of Jesse.

LYDIA (CONT'D)
Several women in this very town have done so, and all of them have been declared "stark raving mad." Like poor Bessie McCraw.

JESSE
I know for a fact, Miss Bessie not only wore pants, she wore spurs! She had me construct a rack, so she could hang them by her back door. And, you have to admit, it was a bit odd when she ran for sheriff.

LYDIA
Different does not mean insane.

Lydia steps to the row of windows and sits on the window seat, staring out. Through the window, the remains of a formal garden, abandoned long ago. Death is everywhere. Giant urns overflow with desiccated leaves. Ropes of dried vines hang from arbors flanking the entrance.

Lydia reaches up and touches her empty sleeve.

                    LYDIA (CONT'D)
          I used to garden. Play the
          piano. Ride horseback like a
          horse should be ridden. Now,
          all I have left is mental activity.

She raises the clipping and shakes it.

                    LYDIA (CONT'D)
          The very activity that's evidently
          the cause of civilization's ills!

Lydia's gaze fixes past the garden. CLOSE ON: the magnificent tree that still dominates the space.

                    LYDIA (O.S.)
          It's too late for Laura Creighton,
          as well. Her crime was having too
          much energy for a "proper" wife.
          When Howard could no longer
          control her, he put her away in
          the asylum at Maple Hill.
                  (directly to Jesse)
          As long as wives remain the
          legal property of their husbands,
          we can disappear like that!
                  (snaps)

Jesse joins her on the window seat. Lydia's voice shifts from anger to melancholy. They remain focused on the tree as they speak.

                    LYDIA
          I'm hungry to share books
          and discuss ideas...but I don't
          expect Laura to return.

                    JESSE
          Mrs. Westport, what do I have to
          do with all this? Why am I here?

                    LYDIA
          At the Whitwell Club, you were
          the only man who did not think
          I was ridiculous for wanting to
          attend the lecture.

She turns to Jesse.

                    LYDIA CONT'D
          Mr. Woods, would you be
          interested in joining me in a
          grand experiment?

                    JESSE
          What kind of experiment?

                    LYDIA
          What would you say to our
          becoming...companions?

                    JESSE
          Companions?

He shows Lydia his callouses and scars.

                    JESSE (CONT'D)
          I'm not an educated man, Mrs.
          Westport. I work with my hands.

Lydia gently traces one of his scars. The gesture disarms him. He jumps to his feet and checks his pocket watch.

                    JESSE (CONT'D)
          It's later than I thought. Your
          husband will be—

                    LYDIA
          Please think it over, Mr. Woods.
          We can meet during the Fourth
          of July parade. I'll wait for you
          at the fountain.

She goes to a bookshelf and lifts a book from its hiding place behind two larger volumes.

LYDIA (CONT'D)
I believe you were looking for
this. I've kept it too long.

Smiling, she places the book in his
hand, CU of Darwin's Voyage of the
Beagle.

INT. HARDWARE STORE—DAY

*Jesse enters to find a circle of men sitting
on upturned barrels at the rear of the store.
The group includes Buford Long, Elliott
Minor, TOMMY FINN, and HENRY
COOPER. Tommy, young and brash, does
the Mayor's dirty work. He sports a suit, far
more grand than his position. He's short and
bounces around like a pugilist as he talks.*

*Henry, a former sheriff, is respected by
all as a reasonable man. He has a wind-
blasted face and silver hair.*

*Jesse ducks behind a row of hanging saws
and eavesdrops.*

TOMMY
Balderdash! I'm telling you,
the mayor's going to run for
governor and nothing's going
to stop him!

BUFORD
He don't have a chance with
that wife of his. She ain't got but
one oar in the water, and her
boat's leakin' a mile a minute!

Everyone but Henry hoots at this
remark.

ELLIOT
Henry, you're awfully quiet today.

HENRY
You boys will hear from me
when you've said something
worth responding to.

ELLIOT
(to Buford)
You won't believe this. Last

week she tried to enter the
Whitwell Club!

BUFORD
Her and her high-falutin
ideas. If she were mine, she
would have gotten a good
horsewhipping for that one.

HENRY
Interesting. Under what
circumstances do you expect
Mrs. Westport would ever
consent to be yours?

BUFORD
Consent?

Buford slaps his knee.

TOMMY
When the mayor first talked
about throwing his hat in the
ring, he was up against some
mighty competition, including
Wilbur Drake. Drake hadn't lost
a race in ten years!

ELLIOT
Well, Drake's no problem now.

Tommy smirks and nods.

TOMMY
Thanks to the mayor.

BUFORD
Are you saying Drake ain't got
no bastard son?

TOMMY
I'm just making the point that
when the mayor sets his mind
to something, he succeeds.

HENRY
No matter the cost to someone
else.

TOMMY
That's politics!

HENRY
(to Tommy)
Tell me something, boy. How
does it feel working for a man
who has no principles? I don't
know how you sleep at night,
knowing what he's capable of.

Tommy flashes a junior politician's
smile as he heads for the door. He
turns back to Henry.

TOMMY
I sleep just fine, old man. I sleep
especially fine on payday.

EXT. FOUNTAIN—DAY

*Lydia and Jesse sit on the edge of a
reflecting pool surrounding the base of a
large fountain. The Fourth of July parade
is in progress, a few blocks away. Sounds
of DISTANT BAND MUSIC and
occasional FIRECRACKERS. A wide-
brimmed straw hat filters the sun across
her face. Jesse holds a miniature American
flag. Lydia, draped in patriotic colors, is a
flag.*

LYDIA
May I call you "Jesse"?

Jesse nods, then reaches over and
dunks his bandana into the water.
He cools his face and the nape of his
neck as he speaks.

JESSE
I saw you in the grandstand
sitting next to your husband.
Did you enjoy the program?

LYDIA
Enjoy? I think not. I was playing
the role of "Mrs. Mayor," which
requires things of me that go
against my true nature.

JESSE
Such as?

LYDIA
Keeping my opinions to myself.

She catches her image in the
reflecting pool.

LYDIA (CONT'D)
Everyone assumes I am at my
husband's side, voluntarily.
Truth is, I am yoked by his
position. But I have a secret
for enduring those tedious
ceremonies. I become a prop.
My form is there...pitiful as it is.

She plunges a finger into the water
and, with a single stroke, fractures
her reflection.

LYDIA (CONT'D)
But not my heart.

THUNDER startles her. She recovers
and looks deep into his eyes.

LYDIA (CONT'D)
Have you thought about my
proposed experiment?

JESSE
I've thought of little else. You
deserve an honest answer, and
I've struggled to forge one.

Lydia starts to interrupt. He raises his
hand for her to let him continue.

JESSE (CONT'D)
My best effort will not measure
up, if what you want from me,
I do not possess. I fear that
ultimately you will discover I am
less than you imagine. I've not
known you long, Mrs. Westport,
but I already know that I
couldn't bear to disappoint you.

A CLOUDBURST erupts. Lydia and
Jessie run to the First National Bank
for shelter.

EXT. FIRST NATIONAL BANK—DAY

The bank is closed. Red, white, and blue bunting hangs over the narrow entrance. Jesse and Lydia wedge themselves into the space and watch the storm unleash its furry. LIGHTNING strikes nearby, causing Lydia to jump closer. In the tight quarters, Jesse inhales her perfume and watches a raindrop slide down the nape of her neck.

The storm passes as quickly as it arrived, leaving Lydia energized. She leaps out of the doorway and gestures for Jesse to follow. They stand facing each other, very close but not touching.

> LYDIA
> I accept everything you say, Jesse Woods. I am willing to take the risk that I am completely and utterly wrong about you. Are you willing to gamble as well?

Lydia is animated. Jesse's eyes trace her movements. An exotic butterfly.

> LYDIA (CONT'D)
> True equality will be our foundation! By that, I mean two things. First, I do not want the fact that I am a woman to be a concern. There is no topic that I am unwilling to discuss.

Lydia, breathing hard, is now very close to Jesse. She wipes the rain from her cheeks.

> JESSE
> You said that by "true equality" you meant two things. What is the second?

> LYDIA
> If our experiment is to succeed, we must have mutual respect. We must honor each other's way of being, whether we agree with it or not. Our meetings will

not give us license to intervene in each other's private lives and ...redirect them.

They walk back to the fountain and sit beside each other.

EXT. FOUNTAIN—DAY

> JESSE
> What if I should find you in harm's way? Do you expect me not to take action? That makes no sense. What kind of man would I be?

Lydia unconsciously places her hand on her throat, then, realizing it is there, immediately withdraws it.

> LYDIA
> A man who understands that I wish to be captain of my own ship.

She turns and speaks to their "coupled" image in the reflecting pool.

> LYDIA (CONT'D)
> I want you to join me in my world...not rescue me in yours.

Jesse jumps to his feet.

> JESSE
> I couldn't do that; it goes against my true nature.

Frustrated, Jesse drops back down to the fountain's edge, where they sit with the tension for a couple of beats.

> LYDIA
> Well, it is an experiment. Even if the odds are against us succeeding, I'm game. Are you?

Jesse takes a deep breath and nods. He reaches down and plucks a wildflower growing out of a crack in the road.

JESSE
You're like this flower. It not only manages to survive but thrive, on this well-traveled path. A testament to the hardiness hidden within its delicate structure.

Lydia unsuccessfully stifles a laugh.

LYDIA
I hesitate to point out that by bringing it closer to you...you have, in fact, cut short its life.

Jesse is momentarily horrified at this truth. Lydia refocuses on the task at hand.

LYDIA (CONT'D)
Now, what do you want?

JESSE
Want?

LYDIA
Our arrangement will not be truly equal if only one of us benefits.

JESSE
I assure you, Mrs. Westport, your companionship will not be an unbearable hardship.

LYDIA
Then think of it as a contract. What do you want included in your half?

Jesse looks away, scratches his chin, and rubs his face.

LYDIA (CONT'D)
One more thing. If we are going to be true equals, you must call me Lydia.

The parade is over. People file by in staggered groups.

Some carry musical instruments. Others wave miniature flags. Two ancient widows, in black, whisper to each other when they see Jesse and Lydia. Judgment is etched into their faces.

JESSE
Well...Lydia...what I want from you is your forgiveness.

LYDIA
My forgiveness? I was hoping for something a bit more challenging. Forgiveness for what?

JESSE
I expect I will fail you. I want your forgiveness in advance.

More people pass, SINGING. Jesse and Lydia shout to be heard over them.

LYDIA
That makes no sense!

JESSE
Then we're even.

LYDIA
All right, if you insist.
(earnestly)
I forgive you.

**EXT. MAINSTREET OF TOWN—
SAME DAY**
Lydia and Jesse merge with the boisterous crowd. After walking together for several yards, her name is yelled out from behind.

MAYOR WESTPORT (O.S.)
Lydia!

Jesse turns around to see ANDERSON WESTPORT fifty paces away. The Mayor is an imposing figure. Out of his bushy beard hangs a cigar, which he removes each time he shouts. Unable to get a response from her, he takes off his top hat and waves it like a metronome.

MAYOR WESTPORT
Lydia!

JESSE
Your husband is trying to get
your attention.

LYDIA
Keep walking!

Jesse and Lydia weave at a fast clip
through the mass. The Mayor gains on
them. A FIRECRACKER goes off directly
behind Lydia, startling her. A guilty-
looking boy dashes out of the group
and races out of sight. She stops for a
couple of beats to collect herself.

JESSE
Why are you ignoring him?

LYDIA
Because I did not ask his
permission to leave the
grandstand, and I shall pay for it.

JESSE
But he sees you! Why pretend
you don't hear him?

Lydia glances behind her and takes off
again, this time practically sprinting.

LYDIA
If I go to him, like a dog called
by his master, he'll humiliate
me in front of his cronies and
their silent wives. I prefer to be
shamed in private.

Lydia takes a sharp right, away from
both men, who now—unbeknownst
to them—stand only yards apart,
embedded at the core of the swollen
crowd.

EXT. FREEDOM TOWN—
FOLLOWING WEEK, DAY
*Freedom Town is an area populated
by former slaves at the edge of the city.*

*It's a grid of white-washed huts and
shanties. Adjacent to each, a small sliver
of scratched-out land contains chickens,
vegetables, flowers, or discarded items.*

*Jesse stands at the boundary sign:
FREEDOM TOWN. He runs his fingers
over the text of a large, primitively carved
PLAQUE nailed to an adjacent tree.*

JESSE (O.S.)
In memory of Rev. Robert
Woods and his wife, Savannah.
They dedicated their lives
to the belief that all men
are equal in the eyes of our
Creator.

Jesse is a familiar figure in this patch
of humanity. There's a lot of back-
and-forth greeting as he navigates
the narrow, worn path through the
center. Ahead sits a cottage on a
larger piece of land.

EXT. TAYLOR COTTAGE—SAME DAY
*The cottage is painted every color of
the rainbow. Bottles of all sizes, along
with pieces of scrap metal, hang from an
adjacent shade tree. Each breeze creates a
symphony. A well-tended garden boasts a
variety of flowers and vegetables.*

*Jesse arrives at the gate to find an old
tick hound sunning himself. He reaches
through and pats the dog's haunches.*

JESSE
Hey, Blue.

The dog jumps up and barks his
joy at the reunion. In response, the
cottage door flies open. A large,
elderly Black woman fills the space.
ELIZA TAYLOR wears a dress worn
thin by the years. A bright cloth
wraps her head.

ELIZA
Lordy! Is that my Jesse?

INT. TAYLOR COTTAGE—SAME DAY
Eliza embraces Jesse as he steps into the small but cheery, clean space. The few pieces of furniture are handmade and painted in vivid colors. A large pot sits on a wood stove. She steps over to stir the contents.

ELIZA
I was dying me some dress-up fabric from these here beets. But I can do that anytime. Let me get you some grits.

JESSE
Thank you, Miss Taylor, but no.

ELIZA
You feeling poorly? You don't never turn down my cooking.

Jesse moves around the cottage, picking up familiar objects that comfort and ground him.

JESSE
My mind is overly occupied. You remember what that does to my appetite.

ELIZA
Then lighten your load. Sit and catch me up.

Eliza pushes a chair at him. She drops onto another.

ELIZA (CONT'D)
You know I have a fierce reputation for helping people struck by too many thoughts. You talk, and I'll dig for the root of your ills.

ALVIN TAYLOR enters the cottage with sunflowers in his hand. He is a thin, elderly Black man who carries himself with ramrod dignity. His shirt is soaked with sweat. He reaches under his straw hat, extracts a rag, dips it into a bucket of water, and places it back under his hat.

ALVIN
Wish I had a penny for every time I done did this today. Dries up before I get out the door!

He nods "hello" in Jesse's direction as he sashays over to his wife. He hands the flowers to her.

ALVIN (CONT'D)
(singing)
Some sunshine for my sunshine.

He reaches down to kiss the top of her head. She pretends he's a bother and swats him away like a fly.

ELIZA
Jesse was ready to tell me what's on his mind. Now you come courting me and messed us up. Don't you have nothing better to do, old man?

ALVIN
You want him to tell you his secrets?
(to Jesse)
Look out, boy! She been working me for more years than I can count. Don't have a secret left to my name.

JESSE
(with much affection)
How you feeling, Alvin?

Alvin gingerly lowers his arthritic body onto a chair at a small table next to a window. He looks out at his garden with pride.

ALVIN
Can't complain. Can't complain.

JESSE
Miss Taylor, seems I've gotten
myself into a situation.

ELIZA
You need a charm bag!

She dips into the bodice of her dress
and extracts a cloth bundle the size
of a small apple. She spreads the
contents out onto her lap. Jesse
bends closer.

ELIZA (CONT'D)
That's a cat whisker. Those be
frog bones. These herbs. That's
a piece of quartz. This here's a
dry magnolia petal.

She sweeps everything into a pile,
then slips the bag back into her dress.

ELIZA (CONT'D)
I'll make you one, Jesse. It
might help you with all that
worrying.

JESSE
Next thing I know, you'll be
making me a dress to tuck it into.

ELIZA
Wouldn't that be a sight!

JESSE
(to Alvin)
How's Tobias? I was hoping to
see him.

ALVIN
Our boy's found himself some
work in another county. He
don't get home much.

Eliza moves her chair closer to Jesse.

ELIZA
What's got you all tied in knots?

JESSE
I've gone and made a promise
I'm worried I can't keep.

ELIZA
That's not like you.

JESSE
Truth is, I kind of jumped into it.

ELIZA
Jumped into it? Somebody
must have put some mighty
persuasion on you. It took me
all of two months to get you to
eat my collard greens.

Eliza leans back, closes her eyes, and
reminisces.

ELIZA (CONT'D)
Remember the day our Tobias
brought you home? It was so
cold; you had ice in your hair!
You weren't ten years old.

JESSE
I didn't like that orphanage one
bit. Made my break as soon
as I could. Woke up in a barn,
and there was Tobias. He gave
me a pitchfork and told me if I
helped him, I'd get a meal.

INSERT: EXT. TAYLOR COTTAGE
*Wrapped in a single blanket, the two boys
approach the front steps. The front door
opens a crack.*

ELIZA (V.O.)
When I saw the two of you
coming up the path, I thought,
"What's he doing, bringing a
white boy in here?"

Back to Jesse and Eliza in conversation.

ELIZA
Course that's before I knew who
your people were. They were

brave souls who practiced what they preached. And they paid dearly for it.

JESSE
I try to remember their faces, but they fade as the years pass.

For a couple of beats, they sit silently with their memories. Then Eliza remembers the point she was trying to make earlier.

ELIZA
(nodding toward Alvin)
You sat down right over there. Didn't weigh more than a sparrow. I offered you a hot supper, and you looked in that pot of greens and said, "No thank you, ma'am." Just like that! You were starving, but you weren't about to eat something you'd never seen before.

Jesse rises and heads to the door.

ELIZA (CONT'D)
You leaving already?

ALVIN
Woman, give the boy some room to breathe.

JESSE
I just needed to come home. See your faces. Set myself right.

Eliza embraces him so tightly, he can't break free. This is exactly what he needs. He doesn't protest.

EXT. JESSE'S COTTAGE—EVENING
A simple, well-constructed cottage nestled in the woods.

CLOSE ON the window where an oil lamp shines. Through it, Jesse sits at a table, writing a letter.

JESSE (V.O.)
My dear Mrs. Westport, sleep is impossible, so I take pen in hand. Although I am not keen on lengthy conversations, with your guidance, I shall do my best to keep our exchanges in motion. As you suggested, I will meet you at Thornton Lake on the twenty-first. Sunset. Sincerely, Jesse Woods.

INT. CHURCH—SUNSET
Jesse and DEACON BARNES stand between the pews. Deacon Barnes is pinkish and portly. An adult cherub. With effort, he kneels and inspects the brackets Jesse has just installed. Near him sits Jesse's tool chest with a folded newspaper sticking out. CU: "July 21, 1895."

DEACON BARNES
I want to make sure these are sturdy enough. The...uh... healthier ladies like to sit here near the door. That way they can catch any breeze that might skip through.

The walls of the church are bathed in deepening tones of orange and gold. Jesse attempts to head toward the door.

Toward Lydia waiting at the lake. Deacon Barnes's girth blocks his progress.

DEACON BARNES (CONT'D)
Certain hymns like "Lift Me Up Redeemer" or "Walk With Me All My Days" set the entire congregation into motion. When everyone sits back down at the same time, the whole pew rocks!

JESSE
These new brackets could harness a steam engine.

Jesse looks out the window at the deepening colors. He moves closer to Deacon Barnes.

JESSE (CONT'D)
I need to collect my tools. I'm meeting someone, and I'm already late.

Deacon Barnes does not budge.

DEACON BARNES
(slightly lascivious)
Meeting someone? That sounds promising.

Jesse stares down at him until he steps aside.

JESSE
If only I had a life as fertile as your imagination!

Jesse exits. Close on: a blushing Deacon Barnes.

EXT. THORNTON LAKE—SAME DAY, DUSK
Lydia sits at the end of the dock on a crate, scanning the lake through field glasses. Sounds of: SLAPPING WATER AGAINST PILINGS and QUACKING DUCKS. Jesse steps on a WARPED PLANK, heralding his arrival. Lydia turns.

LYDIA
Good evening. You missed a magnificent sunset.

Jesse sees the hem of her frock is wet, and she is barefoot. She puts down the field glasses and dabs at her feet with a small towel. CU: Her slender ankles. He looks away long enough to collect himself.

JESSE
How long were you going to wait?

Lydia holds up a lantern.

LYDIA
Until you came.

They gaze at each other for a couple of beats before Jesse becomes uncomfortable and shifts topics.

JESSE
I remember swimming here as a child. Now, everybody's abandoned it for that man-made monstrosity on the other side of town. With all the fancy boats for rent and hawkers and peddlers, it's more like a carnival than a lake.

LYDIA
One man's progress. Another man's nightmare. That is, I'm afraid to say...the future.

She slings a leather pouch over her shoulder. He takes her lantern. They walk up the dock to the boathouse.

JESSE
Won't your husband notice your absence?

LYDIA
He's playing faro with that gang of ruffians he calls his staff. That will keep him occupied until well after I return.

INT. BOATHOUSE—DUSK
The boathouse is a weathered clapboard structure with many windows. The fading light of day reveals a bench in one corner with a frayed blanket tucked beneath. Opposite the bench are two wooden chairs. A line of oars are propped against the back wall.

Jesse swings his arms around to clear the spider webs. He shakes out the blanket, covers the bench, and lights the lantern. He opens a window. Sound of CRICKETS and FROGS.

LYDIA
Listen! We have our own Greek chorus to advise us.

JESSE
Maybe they're warning us. Maybe they're saying that by secluding ourselves, we're more likely to become grist for the rumor mill.

Lydia dismisses his remark with the wave of a hand.

LYDIA
I don't speak Greek. In any case, I refuse to allow our precious time to be eaten away by the cancer of innuendo. There will always be those who, unable to find joy for themselves, cannot allow it for others.

Lydia sits on the bench. Bathed in the lantern's light, she rummages through her pouch and extracts a handful of papers covered in notes of indigo script. Jesse watches her lips move as she reads several of them to herself before speaking.

LYDIA (CONT'D)
I've so many ideas, I don't know where to begin. We could talk about philosophy! Discuss suffrage! Art! Or we could take a more serious path and speak of honor or courage.

Jesse pulls a chair over to the bench.

LYDIA (CONT'D)
Is there a topic that you would like to explore?

Jesse leans in and whispers.

JESSE
You.

Lydia leans back.

LYDIA
Me?

Jesse points to the folded sleeve of her dress.

JESSE
Your...loss. What happened? If I may be so bold.

Lydia goes to the open window, her back to Jesse.

LYDIA
Poor judgment.

JESSE
It may be poor judgment on my part, but I am truly interested in everything—

Lydia whips around, her eyes full of pain.

LYDIA
Not you. I lost my arm because of my poor judgment!

She storms out of the boathouse, slams the door behind her and stomps down the dock.

EXT. THORNTON LAKE—DUSK
Jesse finds Lydia at the end of the dock, leaning against the railing. Her hand moves slowly across her body and comes to a rest on the vacant sleeve. She takes a deep breath and stares across the lake, into the distant past.

LYDIA

I waited in the tall grass. For
hours. Waited for a train to
slow down enough for me to
jump on. To finally escape.
When I did, my dress became
entangled...pulling me into the
mechanism.

Jesse is stunned. All he can manage
is a single word.

JESSE

Escape?

LYDIA

Obviously, it was a failed
endeavor.

She omits a deep sigh of profound
disappointment.

LYDIA (CONT'D)

I am still here. I am still
married.

Jesse and Lydia stand side-by-
side at the end of the dock, a few
feet apart. They remain focused
on the opposite bank, as darkness
embraces them.

**INT. JESSE'S COTTAGE—
TWO WEEKS LATER, SUNRISE**

*MORNING BIRDSONG. Jesse lies
nude in bed. All the covers kicked off.
Every window open, the curtains ripple
with an early morning breeze. Jesse sits
up and tries to catch a little as it moves
through the room.*

*A KNOCK splinters the peace. He leaps
out of bed. Grabs his trousers, dressing on
the fly. Opens the door to find Molly.*

MOLLY

May I come in?

Surprised by the unexpected and
unusual guest, he simply nods while
buckling his belt.

MOLLY (CONT'D)

I thought you might be washing
up, so I waited a bit to make
sure you were decent.
(giggling)
Guess I should have waited
longer.

Molly explores the room like a curious child. Jesse follows close behind,
putting on his shirt.

JESSE

Did Mrs. Westport send you?
How did you find me?

MOLLY

Mrs. Westport does not know
I'm here. She sent me to the
hardware store to ask about
locks. The man there told me,
"You want Jesse Woods."

JESSE

Locks?

Molly picks up a hand-carved bird
and examines it closely.

MOLLY

Mayor Westport is gone for the
day, and I can't attend to Mrs.
Westport. He took the key.

JESSE

You're locked out of the house?

She stops at a table on which sits a
small chair with a split leg. She pokes
at the clamp holding the repair in
place.

Jesse pulls on his boots.

MOLLY

No, sir. I'm locked out of her
bedchamber.

JESSE

Are you telling me that Mrs.
Westport is locked in her own
room?

MOLLY
Yes, sir. I lock her in every night.

Jesse grabs his tools and opens the door for her.

JESSE
How can you do such a thing?

MOLLY
I do what I'm told. The mayor is my employer. He says it's for her own safety.

EXT. ROAD TO TOWN—SAME DAY
Jesse and Molly walk at a fast clip.

JESSE
I want to know the whole story, Molly. The train...everything.

Molly does not respond.

JESSE (CONT'D)
Whatever you can remember.

Molly stops dead.

MOLLY
Do you think I could ever forget?

The words pour out.

MOLLY (CONT'D)
Every morning. Every night. Mrs. Westport sits at her dressing table while I brush her hair. And there it is, staring back at us like those mirrors at a carnival. The ones that make people look all shattered and broken.

They resume walking at a much slower pace. A look comes over Molly's face that indicates she has traveled back to that tragic day. At first she is barely audible.

MOLLY (CONT'D)
It was a spring morning. Mrs. Westport was waltzing around the house. Singing at the top of her lungs. Dancing. Swinging her arms.
(voice catches)
I'd never seen her so happy. She asked to have her breakfast served in the garden.

A church steeple rises above the last hill.

MOLLY (CONT'D)
When I brought out her tray, she was visiting each plant and tree, saying, "Goodbye."
(to Jesse)
Why would someone talk to plants, Mr. Woods? Do you think she's...you know...gone in the head, like everybody says?

**EXT. WESTPORT ENTRANCE—
SAME DAY**
A massive Queen Anne pierces a canopy of trees. Jesse and Molly walk through the iron gate, along a serpentine path to a generous wrap-around front porch.

**INT. WESTPORT MAIN STAIRWAY—
SAME DAY**
Molly and Jesse climb to the second floor. CU of large, ornately framed PORTRAITS lining the wide stairway: First, newly elected Mayor Westport stands alone in front of a fireplace. Next, as a youth, he holds a rifle and a dead pheasant.

Last, a portly father and robust mother, elegantly dressed and surrounded by treasures from exotic ports. Between them stands a small boy. Jesse stops to examine it.

JESSE
Ah, the "little mayor." It's safe to say there's a family that was warm in winter. I wonder what it was like to awaken on

Christmas morning to more presents than you could ever put to use?

Molly continues climbing. Jesse leans closer.

> JESSE (CONT'D)
> (sotto voice)
> Let's see what kind of boy grows up to lock his wife in her bedchamber like a common criminal.

The lonely, pained look in the boy's eyes registers deeply within Jesse. Molly calls out from above.

> MOLLY (O.S.)
> Are you coming, Mr. Woods?

Jesse takes a sharp turn to the first landing and stops. Facing him is a single, enormous PORTRAIT of Lydia before her accident. One hand holds a white rose. From the other dangles a basket overflowing with flowers from her garden.

Molly returns to collect Jesse.

> MOLLY (CONT'D)
> That was painted just after they returned from Paris. She—

> MAYOR WESTPORT (O.S.)
> Molly!

Jesse is transfixed by the portrait. He does not move.

> MAYOR WESTPORT (O.S.) (CONT'D)
> Molly! Are you up there?

> MOLLY
> He can't find you here!
> (pushing Jesse up)
> Take the servants' stairs at the end of the hall. They'll take you down to the kitchen and out the back. Go!

Just as Jesse is out of sight, the Mayor bounds up the stairs and practically knocks Molly down. In one hand, he holds a key. In the other, a bouquet of flowers.

> MAYOR WESTPORT
> I was halfway to the capitol when I found the damn key in my pocket! Give these to Mrs. Westport with my apology. I doubt she'll want to see me right now. Can't say I blame her.

INT. VIOLA'S CAFE— FOLLOWING WEEK, DAY
Jesse sits reading a newspaper. The cafe is packed. Henry Cooper enters and joins Jesse.

> JESSE
> Looks like the mayor's campaign for governor is in full swing.

> HENRY
> Why the sudden interest in politics?

> JESSE
> It's just a headline, Henry.

VIOLA, middle-aged and heavily made-up, arrives at their table. Her sleeves are rolled up, revealing a long scar on one arm. She faces Henry as she speaks.

> VIOLA
> What's your pleasure?

> HENRY
> Coffee.

As she turns toward Jesse, CU: jagged scar across her cheek beneath the makeup.

> VIOLA
> How 'bout you, handsome?

JESSE
Same. Wait! Bring me some
cornbread...and apple butter, if
you've got it.

Viola returns to the kitchen.

HENRY
What was it you wanted to talk
about?

JESSE
Need your opinion. You know
me better than anyone else.
I mostly keep to myself. A
creature of habit. That said,
can you see me taking on
something...unusual?

Viola brings their coffee and exits.

HENRY
(chuckles)
Unusual? You haven't gone and
got yourself a fella, have you?

JESSE
I'm serious, Henry. Do you think
it's possible for a man like me
to change?

HENRY
Change? Change what?

JESSE
The way I see the world. The
way I am in that world.

HENRY
I guess it depends on what'll
happen if you don't.

Viola returns with the cornbread and
apple butter. They eat and drink in
silence for a couple of beats. Henry
reaches over and takes a piece of
Jesse's cornbread and dunks it into
his coffee.

HENRY (CONT'D)
I've been meaning to talk with
you about...ah...

JESSE
About what? Speak your mind.

HENRY
Tommy. That runt on the mayor's
staff. He made a comment to me
that didn't sit right.

Henry shakes his head, leans back,
and brushes the whole thing off.

HENRY (CONT'D)
Never mind. There's no
reason to believe anything he
says. I don't know why I even
entertained it.

Jesse's not buying the dismissal.

JESSE
Henry. What did Tommy tell you?

Henry leans forward and whispers.

HENRY
He said early the other morning
he thought he saw you running
out the back door of the
Westport house.

Jesse is fully alarmed now.

HENRY (CONT'D)
I told him he was crazy. Asked
him, "What in the world would
Jesse be doing over there any
time of the day?" He knows how
you feel about the man.

JESSE
It was me. But it isn't what you
think.

HENRY
It doesn't matter what I think.
Where there's talk, there's fire.

Viola returns, fanning herself with her apron.

> VIOLA
> Can I get you anything else, Sheriff?

> HENRY
> I think we're good. By the way, it's "Henry." I'm retired now.

Viola puts her hand on Henry's shoulder.

> VIOLA
> You'll always be Sheriff to me.

Viola exits. Jesse reaches in his pocket and throws some coins on the table.

> JESSE
> You two have some sort of history?

> HENRY
> Back when I was a lawman, Viola was planning to marry a blacksmith. He got this notion she was stepping out on him.

> JESSE
> What happened?

> HENRY
> One night he took to carving on her. I intervened, but it was too late. A real shame. She was a right pretty girl.

EXT. THORNTON LAKE—SUNSET

Lydia is reading beneath a shade tree when Jesse arrives at the shoreline, shirtless. Even though the August heat is oppressive, he puts his shirt back on before approaching her. She smiles at this simple gesture underscoring the dignity of their meetings. Together they spread a cloth and open her picnic basket.

> JESSE
> What were you reading?

> LYDIA
> *Indiana.* It's written by a woman named George Sand.

> JESSE
> George? What kind of name is that for a woman?

> LYDIA
> She's a Bohemian!

Everything Lydia is wearing is a different shade of blue or green. It's as if she has risen directly out of the sea. A sheer scarf is tied around her neck in an unsuccessful attempt to conceal a large bruise.

Jesse stares at the bruise as she talks.

> LYDIA (CONT'D)
> (matter-of-factly)
> It's about an unhappy wife who struggles to free herself from the imprisonment of marriage.

She offers Jesse a fruit tart. He rejects it.

> JESSE
> I'm having enough trouble digesting the reality of your life.

> LYDIA
> The reality of my life is that I choose to speak without censoring myself. This is not always welcomed by others.

She smooths her skirt. Avoids Jesse's eyes. Grabs a book and flips it open.

> LYDIA (CONT'D)
> Emerson invites us to abandon traditional thought. By doing so, he says, only then can poetry and wit "flock to our aid."

Jesse reaches over and pushes down the edge of her scarf.

> JESSE
> What does your Emerson have to say about that?

She pulls away. Tosses the book.

> JESSE (CONT'D)
> Don't you fear your husband?

> LYDIA
> Anyone who doesn't is a fool. But I don't fear him in the way you might think—physically. I fear what he can take from me.

INT. JESSE'S COTTAGE—NIGHT

Jesse hunches over a table, writing by lamplight.

> JESSE (V.O.)
> Dearest Lydia, I am deeply troubled by our meeting today. I can no longer play the blind man, pretending that all is well with you, when it is obviously not. I want to take action with every fiber of my being. But I am hobbled by our "contract."

He runs his fingers through his hair and rubs his neck.

> JESSE (V.O.)
> So, I shall not mention this again without your lead.

He starts to complete the letter, then hesitates. Like a diver before plunging in.

> JESSE (V.O.)
> Were you mine, you would know the proper care you so richly deserve. Sincerely, Jesse.

EXT. THORNTON LAKE—SUNSET

Jesse and Lydia face each other at opposite ends of a rowboat, adrift at the center of the lake. Lydia wears a crisp white skirt. Her jacket is cropped just above the waist.

A miniature bouquet of daisies is tucked in the black band of her wide-brimmed straw hat. She is reading aloud from a book.

> LYDIA
> "Is it so bad then to be misunderstood? Pythagoras was misunderstood, and Socrates and Jesus and Luther and Copernicus and Galileo and Newton and every pure and wise spirit that ever took flesh."

She looks up.

> LYDIA (CONT'D)
> I feel these words so deep in my heart as if Emerson were speaking directly to me! Every day I fight against other people's expectations of what I should be.

She reaches out and touches Jesse's knee.

> LYDIA (CONT'D)
> Except you, Jesse. You don't seem to have any preconceived notions of the "mayor's wife." Why not?

> JESSE
> I'm a carpenter. For most people, that's the end of the sentence. When they see me in the library, they assume something needs to be fixed. So, I know something about being judged.

LYDIA
(returns to book)
"What I must do is all that
concerns me; not what people
think. You will always find those
who think they know what is your
duty better than you know it."

She reaches up and adjusts her hat
against the sun. Her jacket flares
at the bottom exposing a blouse of
lavender lace, through which Jesse
sees tiny patches of flesh.

LYDIA (CONT'D)
Do you understand what
Emerson is saying? He—

The sight sends him over the edge
and into the water to cool off. She's
surprised at the impulsive gesture
and misinterprets it as lack of interest. Jesse surfaces and hangs on the
boat as Lydia continues.

LYDIA (CONT'D)
Perhaps we should not try this
again.

JESSE
Giving up on me already?

LYDIA
No, I mean, maybe we should
try something different. I asked
you to be my companion
precisely because you are not
a slave to someone else's ideas.
You are your own man, yet I
keep ignoring that.

JESSE
What do you suggest?

LYDIA
What if we didn't plan ahead?
What if we simply talked?
Allowed our conversation to
give birth to the topic?

JESSE
Does that mean there's no
more homework?

Lydia is offended for a second, then
laughs, reaches over the side, and
splashes water into his face. He
ducks, swims under the boat and
surfaces on the other side. He signals
for her to stay where she is, so he can
climb back in. He flops onto his back.

JESSE (CONT'D)
Out here. All this space. All this
sky. Makes a man feel really
small. Makes any problems he
has even smaller.

LYDIA
Are you a religious man?

JESSE
When I'm walking on my
property, I find my thoughts
are often directed to questions
of a higher nature. Like, "Why
am I here? What does this all
mean?" What about you?

LYDIA
I think the quest for meaning is
not really meant to be satisfied.
At the end of my life, I may not
have all the pieces, but I will
certainly be thankful for the
puzzle.

He sits up, grabs the oars, and starts
rowing to the dock.

JESSE
What are some of the pieces
you've collected so far?

Lydia fixes on the horizon and
contemplates his question.

LYDIA
I believe my purpose is to greet
each day with amazement. To

witness all the beauty before me. For instance, what a marvelous creature a bird is. It can sing and fly! Imagine that!

Jesse watches the setting sun wash over her face, making it more radiant than usual.

> JESSE
> Do you pray?

> LYDIA
> Not in the sense of asking for something. Mercy, or health, or…a child. No, At the end of the day, my prayer is a simple act. I whisper, "Well done!"

> JESSE
> Well done?

> LYDIA
> Yes. No matter what has happened—separate from any inconvenience or adversity I might have wrestled with—the day was still a magnificent production. Sunrise! Rain! Sunset!…I wish to acknowledge my appreciation.

> JESSE
> Ah! But when you whisper, "Well done," who is it you're addressing?

> LYDIA
> Still debating that one!

BEGIN SERIES OF SHOTS.
THORNTON LAKE. DAY. Jesse and Lydia sit on the dock, feet dangling in the water. She places something in his hand. CU: a small, unusual seashell. He puts it in his pocket.

BOATHOUSE. DAY. Raining. Jesse sits opposite Lydia, watching her read. He holds an open book. She sneaks a look at him. He pretends to read. They repeat this game of cat-and-mouse then break into laughter.

BOATHOUSE. NIGHT. By lamplight, Jesse and Lydia's silhouettes engage in animated debate behind drawn shades.

END SERIES OF SHOTS.

EXT. COUNTRY ROAD—DAY
Lydia is perched on a buckboard, a straw hat tied beneath her chin. A basket of flowers and gaily wrapped packages rests on her lap. Jesse stands in the back, clearing a space.

> LYDIA
> You don't know what this means to me. I feared I would never see Laura again. I had no one to take me.

> JESSE
> Now you do.

> LYDIA
> And on her birthday!

> JESSE
> Tell me about her.

> LYDIA
> We met when we were both newly wed. Like me, she had too much time and nothing to occupy her. Our husbands worked long hours. Each of us had a staff to attend to our immediate needs.

> JESSE
> Sounds like you had a lot in common.

He reaches for the basket and secures it in place.

> LYDIA
> With one exception. She was… is…an extraordinarily gifted painter.

JESSE
Did her husband appreciate
her talent?

LYDIA
In an odd way. Howard
Creighton wanted one thing,
and he used her talent to get it.

**INSERT: INT. CREIGHTON
DINING ROOM. NIGHT.**
*Howard and Laura sit at opposite ends
of a long dining-room table. Guests fill
the other chairs. Several women wear the
latest fashion: aviary taxidermy (stuffed
meadowlark perched on a fur jacket;
hummingbird impaled on a bodice).*

*CU: Laura is deeply engaged in a private
conversation with a dangerously-handsome
man. Howard is trapped between two
elderly dowagers talking his ear off.*

LYDIA (V.O.)
He wanted to cultivate a social
life to advance his position at
the bank. He knew he could
never become a prominent
member of society without
Laura's help. It's her money...
Howard Creighton married up.

EXT. COUNTRY ROAD—SAME DAY
*Back to Jesse and Lydia in the buckboard.
Jesse jumps down and massages the horse's
flank.*
JESSE
What did his social climbing
have to do with his wife's desire
to paint?

LYDIA
She and Howard struck a
bargain.

INSERT: INT. LAURA'S STUDIO. DAY.
Light is abundant. Pitched ceiling.

*Art supplies crammed into every space.
Canvases, with landscapes in various
states of completion, lean against the walls.
Laura—a smock over her dress—puts the
finishing touches on the portrait of one of
the dowagers.*

LYDIA (V.O.) (CONT'D)
He allowed her to use their
attic as a studio. In return,
she agreed to paint portraits
of the wealthy people he was
courting.

EXT. COUNTRY ROAD—SAME DAY
*Back to the buckboard. Jesse joins Lydia
on the seat.*
JESSE
If you don't mind my asking,
what happened? Why is your
friend in an asylum?

LYDIA
Laura kept her part of the
bargain, but not as her
husband had intended.

**INSERT: INT. LOBBY OF FIRST
NATIONAL BANK.**
*Well-dressed, champagne-drinking citizens
pack the space. A draped portrait is about
to be unveiled. Beneath it hangs a plaque,
reading PRESIDENT.*

LYDIA (V.O.) (CONT'D)
Everyone gathered at the bank
for the unveiling of the most
important of all her portraits.

Howard briefly raises his glass toward
Laura, acknowledging her as the
artist. She bows slightly to the gathering. Before she can speak, Howard
turns his back to her and puffs his
chest out, as if he were somehow
responsible. Laura steps behind him.

LYDIA (V.O.) (CONT'D)
The room pulsed with anticipation. As usual, Howard kept as much attention on himself as possible.

Laura pulls the cord, and the velvet drops. The crowd reflects shock, causing Howard to immediately spin around and face the portrait.

LYDIA (V.O.) (CONT'D)
Howard didn't let her speak. But Laura definitely had the final word.

Howard discovers a full-length portrait of the dangerously handsome man, standing before a marble fireplace. Smiling, he is completely nude except for the bowler he holds over his genitals.

EXT. COUNTRY ROAD—SAME DAY
Back to Jesse as he flicks the reigns. They take off for Maple Hill.

EXT./INT. MAPLE HILL ASYLUM— SAME DAY
CU of sign: MAPLE HILL ASYLUM next to a massive door. Jesse carries the basket. Lydia hesitates on the threshold.

The door SLAMS shut, plunging them into a darkened lobby. The only furnishings are a table and chair twenty feet away. A single oil lamp on the table struggles to light the void.

The face of SISTER BEATRICE is in shadow. She wears a white cap in the shape of a large bird in flight. As she speaks, the "wings" dip and swoop. Her voice shakes with age.

SISTER BEATRICE
I'm Sister Beatrice. How may I help you, my children?

LYDIA
Good afternoon, Sister. I am Mrs. Westport, a friend of Mrs. Creighton. This is Mr. Woods. Today is Laura's birthday. Please let her know she has visitors.

The nun opens a large record book and inches her gnarled finger down each column of hand-written entries. She scans several pages while Lydia barely contains her impatience.

LYDIA (CONT'D)
We've spent most of the day traveling. We don't have much time before we must turn around and—

SISTER BEATRICE
"Creighton." Here it is.

LYDIA
Ah! Now, if you would be so kind as to let her know I am here.

SISTER BEATRICE
(still consulting ledger)
I'm sorry, Mrs. Westport. I see that she may no longer receive visitors. Other than her husband, of course.

LYDIA
No longer receive visitors? That can't be possible!

Jesse steps forward and places his arm on Lydia's.

JESSE
What Mrs. Westport means is—

Lydia jerks her arm away.

LYDIA
(to Jesse)
I don't need an interpreter.

Jesse sets the basket down at Lydia's feet and steps back into the shadow, gesturing that she's on her own.

SISTER BEATRICE
Mrs. Creighton's doctor has noted that visitors would be too stimulating for her.

LYDIA
You realize that all her husband has to do is pay a doctor to write that!

Sister Beatrice slams the ledger shut. In response, Lydia shifts to a softer sell.

LYDIA (CONT'D)
Surely you can't object to a brief exchange between dear friends.

Lydia reaches down and picks up the basket, placing it on the table. She pushes it toward the nun.

LYDIA (CONT'D)
I've brought her some baked treats. They'll be good for her spirit.

SISTER BEATRICE
We're well acquainted with what our patients need in order to heal. What they need most of all is for the rules to be followed. Rules provide them with a sense of security. Left to their own devices, they run amok.

LYDIA
Mrs. Creighton did not come here to "heal." Because she was not broken in the first place. If, as you insist, a visit is out of the question, please see that she receives the sticky buns. They are her favorite.

SISTER BEATRICE
How very kind of you, Mrs. Westport, but we have found that sweets cause an increase in activity, which Mrs. Creighton finds disturbing.

Sister Beatrice rises and pushes the basket back toward Lydia.

SISTER BEATRICE (CONT'D)
I'm sure you understand.

LYDIA
What I understand is this. The most dangerous food a woman can eat is wedding cake!

INT./EXT. MAPLE HILL ASYLUM—SAME DAY
Jesse and Lydia step out into the blinding brightness of day.

JESSE
I'm sorry, Mrs. Creighton will never know how strong an advocate you were in there.

Lydia's hand shakes as she removes her hat. Her hair tumbles over her shoulders and blows about. She makes no attempt to capture it. Staring off into the distance, her eyes are wild, full of fear, like a cornered mustang.

LYDIA
I'm not sure I was fighting for her.

EXT. THORNTON LAKE—DAY
Jesse and Lydia sit leaning against the same tree, enjoying sliced fruit and cookies. Her ensemble is East Indian inspired. She picks up a stick and gestures toward the lake.

LYDIA
I declare this body of water to
be Walden Pond.
          (to Jesse)
Tell me about your work.

JESSE
You want to talk about
carpentry?

LYDIA
Well, I'm fascinated by
architecture, which is dependent
on carpentry. Is it not?

JESSE
I'm no architect, but I like
knowing a part of me dwells in
the shelves of the library. The
schoolhouse windows and doors.
The intricate facades and
interiors of finer homes.
          (with caution)
The Whitwell Club.

Jesse relaxes completely. They are
entering his world. He stands and
tosses an apple core high above
the lake.

LYDIA
What challenges do you face
when you are given a project?

It's Jesse's turn to be animated. His
hands poke and slice the air.

JESSE
My work is all about solving
problems. The characteristics
of materials. Configuration
of the structure's parts.
Anticipated stress points in the
assembly.

He checks to see if he still has Lydia's
attention.

JESSE (CONT'D)
The basic frame is all straight
lines, but much of the finish
carpentry involves curves.
Some curves are utilitarian,
while others are decorative.
And, of course, aesthetics must
be considered.

LYDIA
Do you construct around the
design, or design around the
demands of the construction?

He pauses to think things through.

JESSE
It depends. When making
furniture, what might at
first appear stable may not
actually be stable. A piece of
wood might look solid, but—
depending on its exposure to
the elements—it may, in fact,
have a history.

LYDIA
A history?

He drops to his knees in front of her.

JESSE
You can't know what the
wood has experienced. What
pressures it has had to bear.
Until you hold it in your hands.

They hold each other's gaze for a beat.

LYDIA
I never thought of wood as fragile.

JESSE
After a piece is finished, one day
it moves imperceptibly, and the
joint is destroyed.
          (glances at her empty sleeve)
What once fit together
beautifully, is no more.

LYDIA

How can something so slight cause so much damage?

Jesse grabs a cookie and leans back against the tree beside her. Lydia flicks a yellow jacket off her pear.

JESSE

There are things going on deep within the wood, out of sight. On the exterior, it all looks fine. The interior is another story.

Lydia reaches for a book. She blows a yellow jacket off the cover. Jesse swats another away. Dodges a fourth. Sees a swarm arriving. Jumps up. Grabs Lydia's arm and yanks her to her feet. They race off to the shelter of the boathouse.

INT. BOATHOUSE—DAY

Their backs to the door, Jesse and Lydia catch their breath.

He closes a window just as a yellow jacket lands on the pane. Lydia swoons theatrically onto the bench.

LYDIA

My hero!

Jesse bows at the waist.

JESSE

Should I continue?

Lydia nods. He moves to the floor and grabs two wood scraps from a broken chair.

JESSE (CONT'D)

Each woodworking joint is a combination of at least two basic elements that are interlocked...or mated. The way the boards come together determines the type of joint.

He takes the two scraps and forms an "L" at her feet. She leans over to watch.

JESSE (CONT'D)

Miter.
(switches and forms a "T")
Dove-tail.
(places them at an angle)
Beveled.
(makes them parallel)
Tongue-and-groove.

LYDIA

My friend Mr. Burton was an architect. He used the term "mortise and—"

JESSE

Tenon.

Jesse loves being the expert for a change. Completely focused on instructing Lydia. He sets the wood scraps aside, kneels, and uses his hands to demonstrate. He hovers them over her lap. Oblivious to the effect of the "explicit" description.

JESSE (CONT'D)

The pocket, or open slot, of the mortise, accepts a projecting tongue—or tenon. Tenon length should be just under mortise depth.

Lydia fans her neck. Jesse remains earnest.

JESSE (CONT'D)

It's possible to tighten or splay the tenon, so it can't be withdrawn once it's in place. On a wide tenon, a haunch assists against the twisting.

Lydia fans faster. Jesse looks up.

JESSE (CONT'D)

Shall I demonstrate the bridal joint?

EXT. POST OFFICE ENTRANCE—DAY

Jesse leans against a building. On the facade: UNITED STATES POST OFFICE.

> JESSE (V.O.) (CONT'D)
> My dearest Lydia, do you have any notion of what our meetings are like for me? Are you aware of the current that surges through me in your presence?

He removes an envelope from his pocket.

> JESSE (V.O.) (CONT'D)
> The degree of discipline it takes to keep myself in check?

He opens the door, hesitates, then closes it.

> JESSE (V.O.) (CONT'D)
> I do not wish to make you uncomfortable, speaking of such things. Yet it seems right to share them with you.

He turns the envelope over and over in his hand.

> JESSE (V.O.) (CONT'D)
> Since ours is not a traditional arrangement, I am in foreign territory without a map.

He opens the door and allows a couple to exit.

> JESSE (V.O.) (CONT'D)
> Therefore...if you possess similar feelings toward me...I look to you to let me know.

He steps inside.

> JESSE (V.O.) (CONT'D)
> Sincerely, your Jesse.

INT. JESSE'S COTTAGE— MORNING (AUTUMN)

Jesse and Molly converse across his threshold. He shivers against September's chill.

> JESSE
> I'm invited to Mrs. Westport's home this evening?

> MOLLY
> Yes, sir.

> JESSE
> Will there be other guests?

> MOLLY
> Not that I know of.

> JESSE
> You're sure the invitation is for tonight?

> MOLLY
> Yes, sir.

> JESSE
> Come in. I'll walk back to town with you. I've got a full day's work waiting for me.

He ducks into his bedroom. She picks up a spyglass from the window-sill and aims it toward him while he changes shirts. He brings his boots into the front room and puts them on. Molly returns the spyglass to the sill and runs her fingers over a row of books.

> MOLLY
> The mayor says books put notions into Mrs. Westport's head. I think he's right. I don't know how to read, and I don't have the troubles she has.

Jesse waits at the front door. Molly opens a volume with pictures and studies several pages while they talk.

JESSE
Isn't it possible her troubles are
caused by something other
than reading?

MOLLY
(shaking her head adamantly)
He used to strut around with
her on his arm like she was his
queen. They went everywhere
together! Then she started
staying home in the evening to
read.

MOLLY
(to Jesse)
Can you believe that? Choosing
a book over a fancy dinner or a
party?
(back to pictures)
Late at night, when the mayor
returned, they would wake me
up with their arguing.

Molly puts the book back and briefly
glances at another.

MOLLY (CONT'D)
While Mrs. Westport was
healing from her injuries, he
burned all her books. He was
trying to protect her from
dangerous ideas, but she never
forgave him. She moved into
her own bedchamber.
(closes book)
Now, she will sleep alone
forever. With all those scars,
what man would want her?

Jesse's face says it all.

EXT. ROAD TO TOWN—SAME DAY
*Jesse and Molly walk side-by-side. He's
carrying a tool kit. A length of rope is
slung over his shoulder. Molly makes a
bouquet from flowering weeds gathered
along the road.*

MOLLY
You don't say much, do you?

JESSE
That's what I'm told. What
would you like to talk about?

MOLLY
Oh, I don't think anything I'd
say would be very interesting to
you.

Jesse stops to adjust the heavy rope.
Molly hands him a flower. He sticks it
in a buttonhole.

JESSE
(cautiously)
The last time we walked
together you told me about the
morning Mrs. Westport was in
her garden telling her flowers
"goodbye." What happened
after that?

Molly frowns and takes off. Jesse
catches up with her.

MOLLY
I can't!

JESSE
(gently)
I need to know. Please.

Molly sits on a roadside stump and
takes a deep breath. She stares at
her bouquet, plucking and tossing
the dead ones as she speaks.

MOLLY
I returned from the fabric
store. Her friend, Mr. Burton,
was waiting on the porch. He
told me she had not answered
the door. I ran up to her
bedchamber, but she was
gone. The wardrobe was open.
Clothes thrown everywhere! I
knew she was never coming
back.

She tosses the entire bouquet.
Shakes her head slowly, side to side.

MOLLY (CONT'D)
I've never talked about this, Mr.
Woods. Not to anyone. Please
don't ask me to—

Jesse kneels next to her and puts his
hands on her shoulders. He doesn't
want to be cruel, but he's invested in
coaxing as much information out of
her as possible.

JESSE
You're stronger than you know,
Molly. It's just a story now. No
longer real. Just a story you're
telling me.

Molly swallows hard. Her lips move
but nothing comes out the first
couple of tries.

MOLLY
Mr. Burton went to the train
station. He was told that Mrs.
Westport had been there
earlier, checking the schedule.
But she never bought a ticket.

Molly sobs. Great gulps pour from
her as she rocks back and forth,
wrapped in her own arms. Jesse
is flooded with remorse at having
caused her so much pain.

JESSE
I'm so sorry, Molly. You don't
have to continue. I didn't
realize how much—

MOLLY
I don't understand. Why? Why
didn't she buy a ticket? She
had plenty of money.

JESSE
Mrs. Westport did not buy a
ticket, because she did not

want to be found. It didn't
matter which train she chose,
as long as it took her away.
But she knew the man who sold
her a ticket would know her
destination. Later, for a coin or
two of the mayor's money, he
could be separated from that
information.

Molly looks at Jesse but does not see
him. He's opened a gate she cannot
close.

MOLLY
Oh, God! Everything was red!

JESSE
Molly, please stop! I've changed
my mind. I don't want to know!

Molly becomes very still. When she
speaks, it's as if she's in a trance.

MOLLY
Mr. Burton took his dog and
searched along the tracks.
He found Mrs. Westport at
the edge of town. In the tall
weeds. Her body twisted in all
directions. Her arm ripped off.

Jesse leans back against the trunk of
a tree and closes his eyes.

JESSE
That's enough!

MOLLY
Mr. Burton wrapped her in his
jacket, and brought her home
to die. Everything I helped
her put on that morning...her
blouse, her skirt, the ribbons in
her hair...was red.

She rubs an invisible stain off her
skirt.

MOLLY (CONT'D)
Some places a red so deep it was black.

JESSE
Please don't—

MOLLY
In other places, the blood was the color of rust. It made this pattern...just like...just like lace. I remember wondering how something so horrible could be so beautiful.

MOLLY
(to Jesse)
Am I a bad person for thinking that?

JESSE
Things don't always make sense, Molly. Sometimes we—

MOLLY
Mr. Burton put her on the bed and uncovered her. She had been...

Molly grabs Jesse's shirt.

MOLLY (CONT'D)
Mr. Woods, I was raised on a farm. Mrs. Westport had been slaughtered!

Jesse buries his face in his hands and tries to shake the image from his mind.

MOLLY (CONT'D)
Mr. Burton had been in the Civil War. He showed me how to pack the wounds with rags. Then he went for the doctor. Even with all that blood, she looked so peaceful lying there. Like she was sleeping on a giant rose.

Jesse stands and assists Molly to her feet. They continue walking as Jesse asks his final questions.

JESSE
What was the mayor's reaction?

MOLLY
The first couple of days, he stayed in the library, drinking. He didn't eat or sleep. When he was told Mrs. Westport was going to live—when he realized what was in her heart—he ordered me to lock her in at night.

JESSE
But couldn't she make another attempt to escape? During the day?

MOLLY
Not likely. Mayor Westport has a thousand eyes.

Hold on Jesse's face as the truth of this sinks in.

INT. WESTPORTS' LIBRARY— EVENING OF SAME DAY

A fire burns in the fireplace. Jesse walks around the room, again admiring the quality of the furniture. Full of nervous energy. Anticipating Lydia's arrival. He lifts a sheer scarf from the back of the desk chair, inhaling the familiar fragrance. Then turns his attention to the wall of bookshelves. Still holding the scarf, he examines the fine woodworking, not noticing that he is no longer alone.

MAYOR WESTPORT (O.S.)
What do you think of my collection?

Jesse drops the scarf, spins around, and faces Lydia's husband, who shuts the door behind him.

JESSE
I...uh...haven't had time to fully
appreciate it.

The Mayor picks up the scarf. Gets in
Jesse's face.

MAYOR WESTPORT
You've not been in my library
before?

Overhead, the floor CREAKS. Jesse
looks up.

JESSE
Will Mrs. Westport be joining us?

Jesse declines the Mayor's offer of
a cigar. The Mayor takes one and
passes it under his nose, inhaling with
audible appreciation, then lights it.

MAYOR WESTPORT
(exhales toward Jesse)
This is a business meeting, not
a social gathering. If it was, I
doubt your name would have
been on the guest list. In case
you hadn't noticed, we travel in
different circles.

The Mayor lifts a decanter toward
Jesse. Jesse nods.

MAYOR WESTPORT (CONT'D)
You haven't answered my
question. Is this the first time—

JESSE
You've actually read all these
books?

MAYOR WESTPORT
Why read them? Reading is a
passive sport.

JESSE
Then why have them?

The Mayor hands Jesse his drink,
then silently studies him for a beat or
two. He leans in close as he speaks.

MAYOR WESTPORT
Tell me, Woods, what was your
first impression?

The Mayor works his cigar, holds
it out for examination and slowly
exhales toward Jesse.

MAYOR WESTPORT (CONT'D)
Impression is everything. For
instance, a man wouldn't want
to create the impression that
he had no control over things.
He wouldn't want people to
think he was a fool. That kind
of mistake could bring a man
down. End his career.

Jesse drains his glass. His voice
reflects a boldness facilitated by
liquor.

JESSE
Why am I here?

MAYOR WESTPORT
You get right to it. I like that in
a man. Truth is, I have a need
for a carpenter.

Lydia's floor CREAKS again as she
paces behind her locked door. Jesse
looks up as he speaks.

JESSE
Trust me, I'm not your man.

MAYOR WESTPORT
Hear me out.

JESSE
That's going to take more
whiskey.

The Mayor explains while he refills
both glasses.

MAYOR WESTPORT
I possess a wife whose mind
is filled with ideas. Ideas that
lead her to do things that are
unacceptable for a man in my
position. To put it bluntly, she's
a lunatic. When I am unable
to control her, I suffer the most
horrendous indignities. Yet, I
can't put her on a leash, can I?

JESSE
Why are we talking about
Mrs. Westport?

MAYOR WESTPORT
Since I am unable to censor
her, it's imperative that
I prevent my wife from
appearing in public. I have
decided to make several
"alterations" to my property. To
ensure my peace of mind.

JESSE
You want me to make your
home a prison?

MAYOR WESTPORT
"Prison" is a felonious term.
I prefer to think of it as
protecting my wife. From
herself.

JESSE
Locking her up at night isn't
enough?

The Mayor snorts. Jesse realizes
he's revealed too much. He switches
directions.

JESSE (CONT'D)
Aren't you concerned that your
plan could drive Mrs. Westport
further into madness? Wouldn't
that have an adverse effect on
your campaign?

MAYOR WESTPORT
Politically speaking, an insane
wife is preferable to a divorce.
Don't underestimate the power
of the sympathy vote.

Jesse is stunned.

MAYOR WESTPORT (CONT'D)
So, are you interested?

Jesse exits the library. The Mayor runs
to the hallway and shouts after him.

MAYOR WESTPORT (CONT'D)
Name your price!

The front door SLAMS.

**EXT. MAINSTREET OF TOWN—
MORNING, FOLLOWING DAY**
*Jesse searches for Molly among the many
citizens running errands. Identical twins
approach him, their arms linked. They are
NORA and DORA BOWER. As round
as the sweets, they sell.*

JESSE
(preoccupied)
Good morning, ladies.

NORA
Jesse woods! You haven't been—

DORA
—in the shop for the longest time!

NORA
Have you given up candy?

DORA
Or found something sweeter?

The twins laugh as he continues
scanning over their heads.

NORA
Looking for someone?

JESSE
I need to get a message to a
friend as soon as possible!

NORA
Why don't you go to his house—

DORA
—and knock on his door?

Jesse turns to cross the street. The
twins snag him.

DORA AND NORA
(simultaneously)
You're being kidnapped!

They whisk him ten feet to their sweet
shop and push him inside.

INT. SWEET SHOP—SAME DAY

*Jesse hears the distinct CLINK of a lock
behind him. Everywhere sit bins of candy.
Jesse turns to see a twin drop the key into
the bodice of her dress. Irritation replaces
politeness.*

JESSE
(to Nora)
Dora, I can't do this right now!

NORA
I'm Nora.

JESSE
Give me the key!

DORA
You're our guest now. Where
are your manners?

NORA
What's your pleasure?
Peppermints? Licorice?

Through the window, Jesse sees a
flash of red curls go past. He tries the
door in spite of knowing it's locked.

JESSE
(focusing between them)

Nora, Dora, when I return, I'll
buy a pound of each. I promise!

The twins confer, then nod simultaneously.

DORA
A promise from you is as good
as gold.

Dora unlocks the door. Jesse rushes
out and down the street, peeking into
each shop as he passes. At the end
of the block, he turns and looks back
up the street. His face is wracked
with concern.

INT. TAYLOR COTTAGE—DAY
*Eliza is sobbing. Blue goes to the door
and BARKS. Alvin lets Jesse in. Eliza
wipes her face with her apron. Alvin
returns to the chair next to her. Jesse
removes his coat and takes a seat opposite
them.*

ELIZA
I know my Tobias didn't steal no
horse! We raised him right.

ALVIN
If he did, he'll hang for sure.

ELIZA
He just borrowed himself one
for a spell.

JESSE
(to Alvin)
Is that true?

ALVIN
That's what he told us. We went
over to Glover County to pray
with him.

ELIZA
You should see how things are.
He's sleeping on a jail cell floor.
He don't get but one meal a
day, and it's not fit for pigs.

JESSE
Why did he...borrow...a horse?

ALVIN
He told us he was walking back
from church, when a bunch of
White boys started following
him. One of them thought he
had taken an interest in his
lady friend. Tobias said all he
did was nod to her when she
asked if he liked her hat. He
said he was afraid if he didn't
answer her, she'd think he was
being disrespectful.

ELIZA
That bunch of boys closed in on
my Tobias and told him nothing
would put a little life into a
dull afternoon, like a lynching.
They chased him for half a
mile before he jumped a fence,
found a horse, and took off.

ALVIN
Why is he sitting in jail for trying
to save his own life? If those
boys had strung him up, they'd
be out dancing tonight as
usual. What's right about that?

JESSE
I don't have to tell you what's
legal isn't necessarily what's
right. Where's the horse now?

ALVIN
He only rode it till he felt safe.
Sent it right back. Guess it was
the dumbest horse ever born.
Never found its way home.

JESSE
Then they can't prove anything.

Alvin and Eliza shoot each other a
look.

ALVIN
I forget you white until you
say something crazy like that.
Prove? They don't got to prove
nothin'.

Eliza moves to the stove and stirs a
pot of greens.

ELIZA
They say Tobias gonna hang
soon. I explained why he done
what he did, but don't nobody
care.

ALVIN
You live in their world, Jesse.
Must be something you can do.

EXT. THORNTON LAKE—DAY
*Jesse's lone figure walks the shoreline. He's
a portrait of despair. He hammers the lake
with rocks.*

INT. JESSE'S COTTAGE—NIGHT
*Jesse sits at a table, sharpening a tool. His
uneaten supper pushed aside.*

**EXT. ROAD TO TOWN—FOLLOWING
WEEK, DAY**
*Jesse repairs a section of his fence
alongside the main road. Travelers pass on
horseback and buckboards. He struggles
with a stubborn fence post. A carriage
approaches, with Tommy at the reins.*

*Jesse steps into the center of the road and
signals for him to stop. The Mayor pops
his head out the window.*

MAYOR WESTPORT
(irritated)
You a highwayman, now?

JESSE
I need a word with you.

MAYOR WESTPORT
Here?

JESSE

Here.

Jesse turns and walks back to the fence.

MAYOR WESTPORT

You had your chance to talk. Why should I give you another? I'm not accustomed to accommodating.

Jesse keeps his back to the Mayor. The Mayor slams the carriage door, mumbles to Tommy, then stomps toward Jesse. Lit cigar in hand. Jesse points out the trees on his property. They are splendid in their October glory.

JESSE

Welcome to my collection. Pretty impressive, aren't they?

MAYOR WESTPORT

What do you want, Woods? I'm a busy man.

JESSE

About your "security" problem. I've decided to take it on.

MAYOR WESTPORT

Those fine principles of yours buckled sooner than I expected.

JESSE

I got a different angle on things. One I can live with.

The Mayor studies Jesse's face for information. Finding none, he puffs on his cigar.

MAYOR WESTPORT

Everybody wants something. That's the beauty of politics. All you have to do is figure out what that "something" is. Then promise it will arrive immediately after their votes win you an election.

JESSE

You're right. I do want something. But I'm sure as hell not voting for you.

Stung, the Mayor lashes back.

MAYOR WESTPORT

So far, we've established you can be bought. What we haven't established is your price.

JESSE

I don't want to be paid.

The Mayor looks down the road and back.

MAYOR WESTPORT

Let me get this straight. First, you didn't want the job. Now you want the job, but you don't want my money.

JESSE

I don't like the way you get your money. Or the way you use it. So, it wouldn't be right for me to take it.

MAYOR WESTPORT

How I make my money is none of your damn business. And, last time I checked, there was nothing illegal about a man making improvements on his own property.

They stand at an impasse for several beats.

JESSE

Safe to say, your political influence reaches beyond our fair city. I'm needing a favor over in Glover County.

Tommy's restless. He shifts about, kicks at dirt clods and shouts out. His efforts are ignored.

TOMMY
We'd better get going! You've got a meeting to get to.

MAYOR WESTPORT
What sort of favor?

JESSE
A friend of mine is jailed over there. I want him freed.

MAYOR WESTPORT
What's he done? Would I know him?

JESSE
He's accused of stealing a horse. His people live over in Freedom Town.

MAYOR WESTPORT
(spits)
A nigger? I'm running for governor! I can't give the impression I'm a friend to a nigger!

JESSE
Hold on to your hat. There's more.

The Mayor can't believe what he's hearing.

JESSE (CONT'D)
After he's released, I want you to hire him. His folks are getting old. He needs something steadier than I can give him.

MAYOR WESTPORT
You're asking me to help a nigger horse thief get out of jail. Then give him a job. All that in exchange for your labor.

JESSE
That's the deal.

MAYOR WESTPORT
I wasn't planning on paying you that much.

JESSE
Oh! There's one more thing.

The Mayor hoots at Jesse's nerve.

JESSE (CONT'D)
Don't use my name. I want him to think he got the job on his own.

MAYOR WESTPORT
Hell, I can't afford you!

JESSE
Those are my terms.

The Mayor puts his hand out, then withdraws it.

MAYOR WESTPORT
This stays between us, Woods.

Jesse reaches out. They shake. Jesse goes to release, but the Mayor has him in a vice grip.

MAYOR WESTPORT (CONT'D)
If I ever hear a connection between this nigger escaping the noose and my own good name, I'll hunt him down and kill him myself.

INT. JESSE'S COTTAGE— EVENING OF SAME DAY
Still in his clothes, Jesse has fallen asleep, wrapped in a blanket, his head on the table. An oil lamp illuminates attempts to write a letter, scattered at his feet.

CU of one.

JESSE (V.O.)
Dearest Lydia, this will be difficult for you to believe. I have agreed to—

CU of another.

> JESSE (V.O.) (CONT'D)
> Dearest Lydia, in the weeks
> ahead, I will be working on
> a project for your husband.
> My reasons for doing so are
> complex and—

CU of a third.

> JESSE (V.O.) (CONT'D)
> Dearest Lydia, for reasons that
> involve parties outside the
> world you and I share, I have
> entered into a contract with
> your husband. Please have
> faith in me, even though it may
> appear that—

EXT. WESTPORT GROUNDS—DAY

A cold wind whips Jesse and the Mayor as they walk the grounds. The Mayor carries a blueprint.

They stop at a stone cottage. Scattered about are remnants of once being used as a potting shed by Lydia. Now a storage shed, along one side, a collection of lumber, barbed wire, etc., is stashed in a protected area. Jesse pulls a board from the pile and tilts it in one direction, then another, then tosses it.

> JESSE
> Twisted. The ends aren't in the
> same plane.

Repeats his evaluation of others and rejects each one with comment.

> JESSE (CONT'D)
> Bowing. Cupping. Crooking.
> (kicking the stack)
> I won't work with materials of
> inferior quality.

Just as they are about to leave, Jesse spots a large plank bridging two barrels.

> JESSE (CONT'D)
> Now there's a beauty!
> Quartersawn oak. You can
> tell by the growth rings. How
> they're perpendicular to the
> board's width. Once in place,
> this is less likely to shift.

> MAYOR WESTPORT
> Shift?

> JESSE
> Softwood, the kind that comes
> from evergreens—trees with
> needles—shifts slightly. An
> eighteen inch cut of new
> growth pine, once you've got
> it in place, can move as much
> as three-eights of an inch or
> more, than say, a similar cut of
> rosewood.

> MAYOR WESTPORT
> So you can look at a tree and
> tell what it's going to do as a
> piece of lumber?

> JESSE
> It's not all that difficult. Just
> turn around and tell me what
> you see.

Genuinely interested, the Mayor turns around and faces the back of his property.

> MAYOR WESTPORT
> Nothing.

> JESSE
> Nothing?

> MAYOR WESTPORT
> I mean, the trees have lost their
> leaves. So I can't tell what kind
> they are.

JESSE
If they're barren, they're deciduous. Broadleaf. That makes them hardwood. Oak. Maple. Elm. Walnut. Cherry.

MAYOR WESTPORT
Hmm. Well, I certainly don't want any "shifting" going on.

They head for the house. The Mayor opens his blueprint.

MAYOR WESTPORT (CONT'D)
The obvious first step is to heighten the stone wall. What else would you suggest?

JESSE
My job will be overseeing the work. You're the one to decide how many ways there are to corral a wife.

They stop near a garden urn. The Mayor scoops up a cat curled inside. He gently strokes it as he talks.

MAYOR WESTPORT
I don't expect you to appreciate the difficulties that plague me, having never been married yourself.

JESSE
What makes you think I've never married?

MAYOR WESTPORT
Couldn't keep her, huh?

JESSE
It was a long time ago.

MAYOR WESTPORT
Did you fight for her?

JESSE
With everything in my power.

MAYOR WESTPORT
Who did you lose her to? A neighbor?
                    (chuckles)
A riverboat gambler?

JESSE
Yellow fever.

INT. WESTPORT DINING ROOM— SAME DAY

Jesse and the Mayor step into the dining room just as Lydia is sitting down to tea. She wears an exquisite kimono, empty sleeve pinned with a jade dragonfly.

MAYOR WESTPORT
This is Mr. Woods. He will be doing some work around the house.
                    (to Jesse)
This is Mrs. Westport.

Jesse has never been in the presence of both Westports until this moment. Wishing to be invisible, he remains silent but nods at the introduction. The Mayor herds him around the table, behind Lydia, to the other side. As he passes his wife, he offers a snide remark to her.

MAYOR WESTPORT (CONT'D)
I see we're a Geisha today.

Lydia responds by pulling a fan out of her obi and snapping it open. When she speaks, she covers her mouth with it.

LYDIA
Mr. Woods and I have met.

Jesse can't believe his ears.

MAYOR WESTPORT
A reunion! That calls for brandy!

Lydia tucks the fan back in. Her eyes remain boldly on her husband as she speaks.

LYDIA
If I remember correctly,
Mr. Woods, you prefer tea.

Jesse looks everywhere but at the
Westports. He's about to jump out
of his skin. Lydia gestures for him to
take a seat.

MAYOR WESTPORT
He's not a guest, Lydia. He's on
the clock now. I don't mind if
he warms up. But you know my
policy about fraternizing with
hired help.

LYDIA
Really, Anderson, I doubt a few
minutes of civilized conversation
will destroy whatever hierarchy
you've constructed between the
two of you.

The Mayor turns and yanks open
a cabinet door. He takes out a
decanter, pours a drink, and exits.

JESSE
(whispering)
Why tell him we've already met?

LYDIA
Obviously, he knows about us.
Why do you think he chose you
to build my jail?

JESSE
He's told you his plan?

LYDIA
I understand my husband's
thinking. You, however, are a
mystery. How could you—

Lydia runs out.

INT. WESTPORT SECOND FLOOR
HALLWAY—SAME DAY
*The Mayor opens the door to Lydia's
bedchamber. He kneels to examine the lock.*

*Jesse stands on the threshold, regarding the
room like a temple. A shelf holds hatboxes
with familiar hats atop each. At the center
of the highly feminine space sits a plump
bed, a steamer trunk at the foot.*

The Mayor fiddles with the lock on the door.

MAYOR WESTPORT
Let's start by putting something
more substantial on here.

BEGIN "CONSTRUCTION" MONTAGE—
OVER SEVERAL WEEKS—DAY
*WESTPORT GROUNDS. A tent
houses lumber and tools. There's a constant
flow of workers between it and the house.
Some stop to warm their hands over a fire.
Tommy makes sure there's no slacking off.*

*WESTPORT GROUNDS. Workers add
stone to the surrounding wall. In some
places it is now three feet higher. Lydia
watches from her bedchamber window.*

*WESTPORT LIBRARY. Workers are
installing a lock on the door. Lydia stands
on the threshold, looking through them
into the space she and Jesse shared.*

*WESTPORT DINING ROOM.
Workers test bars that roll on wheels to
cover the windows, then slide out of sight
behind heavy drapes. The Mayor gives his
approval.*

*WESTPORT MAIN STAIRCASE.
Workers carry a large wrought-iron gate
up the stairs as Lydia is descending. For a
brief moment she is "trapped" behind the
bars as they attempt to pass each other.*

END "CONSTRUCTION" MONTAGE.

INT. WESTPORT SECOND FLOOR
HALLWAY—DAY
*Jesse arrives at Lydia's bedchamber with
his tool chest and shutters for her windows.
He knocks, but her response comes from
the end of the hallway, near the servants'
stairs.*

LYDIA (O.S.)
Would you mind helping me?

Lydia stands in front of a large oval mirror. She attempts to pin a shawl. It slips to the ground. She holds the pin out toward Jesse.

LYDIA (CONT'D)
I'm afraid this is a two-handed task.

He wipes his hands on his pants. His hands shake. His first attempt fails. Finally successful, he steps behind her. Their framed reflection forms a portrait. They study it silently until they hear workers STOMPING up the stairs.

Lydia points to her bedchamber and takes off. Jesse follows her down the hall, grabs the tools and shutters, and leaps inside. She slams her door behind them just as the two workers reach the top step and enter the hallway.

INT. LYDIA'S BEDCHAMBER—SAME DAY
Lydia stands with her back to the door. She covers her heart as if it were breaking.

LYDIA
Why, Jesse? Why did you—
of all people—agree to cage my soul?

He cannot face her. He grabs a shutter and checks the fit.

JESSE
Last night, I dreamed I was in the middle of Thornton Lake between two drowning people. One seemed closer to shore. So I swam toward the second.

He checks the fit of the other shutter.

JESSE (CONT'D)
After I made sure the first was safe, I went back out for the other.
(turns to Lydia)
I woke up right at that moment. I can't stop wondering if I could have saved both.

LYDIA
Why are we talking about dreams instead of locks and bars?

JESSE
Because I am in the middle of a very deep lake. And time is running out!

He slams the shutter to the floor.

JESSE (CONT'D)
I can't tell you why I'm doing this! You'll have to trust me. I have no choice!

Lydia takes his words to heart.

LYDIA
I have never seen such sadness in your eyes.

They sit with the reality of the situation for a couple of beats. Lydia smiles compassionately, telegraphing her forgiveness. Her smile shifts into a mischievous one. She plops onto her steamer trunk and points to the lock.

LYDIA (CONT'D)
(conspiratorially)
This is where I hide my books!

Her change of attitude is a balm for Jesse. His entire body relaxes as Lydia jumps to her feet.

LYDIA (CONT'D)
Let's have one last adventure!

SCREENPLAYS

JESSE
I won't let it be our last. I'll
make sure—

LYDIA
A day trip!

She dances around the room. She
opens her wardrobe and grabs a
dress. She holds it up to herself in front
of a full-length mirror. Tosses it on the
bed and grabs another, and repeats.

LYDIA (CONT'D)
Anderson is campaigning in
Victorville next week. We'll go
then!

She adds a hat. Exchanges it for
another. Jesse's eyes track her.

JESSE
(laughing)
How about the Perpetual
Motion Exhibit?

INT. HARDWARE STORE—DAY
*Jesse pays for three locks. The clerk shows
him that each comes with two keys. He
slips the extras on a short lanyard. CU: at
the end hangs the shell Lydia gave him at
the lake.*

INT. TAYLOR COTTAGE—NIGHT
*Eliza, Alvin, Jesse, and TOBIAS
celebrate. Tobias is slightly older than Jesse
but shorter and compact like Eliza.*

ELIZA
Glorious day! My baby's home!

Jesse waits until Tobias is free of his
mother's embrace, then steps in and
offers his hand. Tobias takes it and
jerks Jesse into his arms. They hold
each other in silence for a beat or
two. There is joy in Tobias's eyes and
relief in Jesse's.

ALVIN
How'd you get out, boy?

TOBIAS
Just after sunrise, a couple of
men walked in. Unlocked the
cell. Don't nobody say a word.
But I could tell they didn't like
settin' me free one bit.

Alvin passes a jug of his "special
juice" to Tobias. Tobias takes a swig
and shakes his head in response.

ELIZA
Sunrise? Where you be all day?

TOBIAS
Stuck around. Wasn't 'bout to
run out and catch a bullet in
my back. No, sir! Wasn't gonna
let 'em play "runaway nigger."

Tobias passes the jug to Jesse. Jesse
shakes it off. Alvin signals for him to
go for it, Jesse takes a sip and gasps.
The Taylors hoot in unison.

TOBIAS (CONT'D)
Time passed, and they just
ignored me. Then I started
thinking if I stayed any longer,
they might change their minds.
Finally, I decided if they was
gonna shoot me, I'd make 'em
look right at me while they
was doin' it. So I stood up and
backed out.

ELIZA
Why nobody stop you?

TOBIAS
That be a mystery the rest of
my days.

EXT. WESTPORT PORCH—DAY

Jesse pulls a flyer out of his pocket. CU: PERPETUAL MOTION EXHIBIT AT MT. ASH. He dashes up the steps. The door opens to reveal Lydia wearing "widow's weeds," including a long black veil. Both sleeves of her fur coat hang free, giving the impression of two arms.

> LYDIA
> I thought it best if the mayor's wife was not reported seen out of town.

> JESSE
> Ah! The Widow Westport. My prayers have been answered.

INT. EXHIBITION HALL—SAME DAY

Jesse and Lydia study various contraptions. Occasionally he shifts his attention to watching her. They stop in front of the largest one. Their eyes follow the hypnotic movement inside the glass case.

Jesse leans over and whispers to her. She laughs. Reflected in the glass is the scorn of a group of women behind them. Jesse and Lydia run, like naughty children, out the exit.

EXT. EXHIBITION HALL—DAY

Jesse and Lydia stand outside the exit door, then walk over to the nearby buckboard.

> LYDIA
> Evidently, the "widow" was having too much fun.

> JESSE
> I think it was the "dashing cad" they found objectionable. They thought I was wooing you for your inheritance!

> LYDIA
> (as the "widow")
> Then you're not courting me? You have no interest in my vast fortune?

> JESSE
> (dead serious)
> Well, I am courting you. But I don't give a damn about your money.

Lydia's puzzled by his strong reaction. Shrugs it off.

> JESSE (CONT'D)
> When does the mayor return?

> LYDIA
> Late tonight.

> JESSE
> Then we have time for this.

Jesse reaches in the buckboard and lifts out a picnic basket.

He nods toward an empty gazebo in the Exhibition Hall garden. Lydia is so excited, she plants a kiss on his cheek. He's surprised by the impulsive act.

> LYDIA
> I'm so sorry! I don't know what got into me!

Jesse puts his hand to his cheek.

> JESSE
> If ever there was a moment in history that did not require an apology, this would be it.

EXT. EXHIBITION HALL GARDEN— SAME DAY

The gazebo holds a weathered wicker table and chairs. Jesse is deeply preoccupied. Lydia removes her veil.

> LYDIA
> You're a hundred miles away. What's on your mind?

Jesse unsuccessfully tries to shake it off. He randomly tosses the contents on the table. It looks like a tornado has hit.

JESSE
I want something I cannot have.

Lydia steps in and arranges their lunch.

LYDIA
Do you know what Buddhists think?

JESSE
(irritated)
Who?

LYDIA
Buddhists. They live in the Far East.

JESSE
Never heard of them.

LYDIA
I was reading a new publication, *The Buddhist Ray*. It said that they regard all suffering to be the inevitable consequence of wanting things to be other than they are.

JESSE
Then I am definitely suffering.

They eat and sip in silence.

LYDIA
Buddhists believe it's important to embrace the inevitable, rather than struggle against it. They pay attention to whatever life places in their path.
(hand on empty sleeve)
No matter how painful the experience.

Jesse stands and pitches a half-eaten apple against the trunk of a large tree.

JESSE
Life placed you in my path! Now what do I do?

Lydia does not know what to say to that. Jesse drains his glass.

JESSE (CONT'D)
The "inevitable"? How can you be so pessimistic? What about hope?

Lydia jumps to her feet.

LYDIA
Did hope save Laura Creighton?

**EXT. COUNTRY ROAD—
EVENING, SAME DAY**
Jesse and Lydia stand outside the buckboard. She gives an apple to the horse while Jesse checks its hooves.

JESSE
She's getting along in years. Guess this trip was too much for her.

Lydia whispers in the horse's ear, just as Jesse notices the dust cloud of a single rider cresting the hill. As the rider approaches, it's obvious he's having difficulty staying in the saddle. Lydia lowers her veil.

RIDER
Got yourself some trouble?

He starts sliding to the right but manages to grab on before hitting the ground.

JESSE
Our horse seems to be ailing.

RIDER
Maybe she needs somma' this. It'll put him right outta' his mis'ry.

After several attempts, he unties a jug from the horn of his saddle and offers it. Jesse waves it off.

JESSE
We could use a vet. Where are you headed?

RIDER
Not sure. Which way am I pointing?

He tilts the jug until a brown rivulet runs down his chin.

RIDER (CONT'D)
Whoa!

Suddenly, his horse takes off. The rider becomes a dot on the landscape.

JESSE
Damnation!

Jesse throws his hat down, spooking the horse. He reaches over and strokes her forehead, and pats her withers.

JESSE (CONT'D)
Sorry, old girl.

JESSE (CONT'D)
(to Lydia)
Looks like we'll be here aw hile. She needs to rest.

Jesse shivers as he reaches in the buckboard and grabs a blanket, tossing it over the horse.

JESSE (CONT'D)
We might as well hunker down.

He spreads out a second blanket in the back of the buckboard. Assists Lydia up. Climbs in and sits beside her.

LYDIA
Thank you.

JESSE
For what? This mess we're in right now?

LYDIA
For today. It was a great adventure. Believe it or not, I'm still having a wonderful time.

JESSE
For a woman with lofty ideas, your standards for amusement are extraordinarily low.

Her laugh rings out as darkness encroaches.

EXT. WESTPORT PORCH—NIGHT, SAME DAY

The house is bathed in shadows. Jesse and Lydia walk up the front steps, lit only by moonlight. Near the top, she missteps. Pitches out of his reach. Tumbles to the ground.

JESSE (O.S.) (CONT'D)
Lydia!

MAYOR WESTPORT (O.S.)
Leave her be!

The glowing tip of a cigar appears on the darkened porch. Jesse ignores the Mayor's order and rushes to Lydia, sliding his hand under her back.

JESSE
Are you hurt?

LYDIA
(emphatic whisper)
Go! Go!

JESSE
I can't leave you here!

LYDIA
Please! If you truly care about me, go!

Jesse stands. As he turns, he encounters the Mayor blocking his path.

JESSE
She needs a doctor to—

MAYOR WESTPORT
She's not yours to worry about.

LYDIA (O.S.)
I'm just shaken a bit. I'll be fine.

JESSE
I'm not leaving until—

Tommy steps around the corner with a shotgun.

TOMMY
Have we got us a problem?

MAYOR WESTPORT
We've got us a trespasser. But he was just leaving.

The Mayor guides Jesse's arm toward the gate. Jesse snaps it away and heads down the walk. The Mayor calls out to him.

MAYOR WESTPORT (CONT'D)
In case you were wondering, I kept my end of our agreement.

Jesse stops at the gate and spins around. The Mayor walks up to him and whispers in his ear.

MAYOR WESTPORT (CONT'D)
I've hired that nigger friend of yours. So, I'd think twice about any escape plans you might have for my wife.

The Mayor slams the gate behind Jesse.

MAYOR WESTPORT (CONT'D)
He'll come in handy if I get in the mood for a little target practice.

EXT. MAINSTREET OF TOWN—DAY

Jesse and Henry watch a small parade work its way down the street. The Mayor is in the lead, followed by his cronies waving flags and blowing toy horns.

JESSE
Are you going to the celebration tonight at the Westports'?

HENRY
Didn't vote for the man.

JESSE
I want you to go. And take me with you. I need to get into that house and check on Lydia.

HENRY
Lydia?

The last man in the parade is Buford Long. He carries his own sign. CU: VICTRY IS ARES!

Henry turns Jesse toward him and scans his face.

HENRY (CONT'D)
Damn! You're already in too deep.

EXT. WESTPORT ENTRANCE—
EVENING, SAME DAY

The house is lit up like a Christmas tree. Flaming torches line the walk. In addition to random, single horses, all styles of carriages are parked in front. Tobias, bundled against the November cold, shovels manure and throws down hay. Henry and Jesse approach the gate.

JESSE
Tobias! Looks like you got yourself a job!

TOBIAS
Never thought I'd be working for the mayor. Can you believe that? I might even work for the governor!

On the porch, a group of young men SING an inebriated version of "My Darling Clementine." Blind Billy stands just outside the front door, flanked by two very unattractive prostitutes.

HENRY
It's Henry, Billy. I've got Jesse with me. The Mrs. knew there'd be some serious libation tonight. She wanted to make sure I found my way home. Jesse's my chaperone.

BLIND BILLY
Evening, fellas. This is Iris and her sister, Irene. Ain't they beauties? Plenty more inside!

INT. WESTPORT GAME ROOM— SAME EVENING

A deeply masculine space. Hunting trophies mounted everywhere, including a stuffed bear rising above the guests. Someone has stuck a cigar in its mouth. Air is thick with cigar SMOKE. Liquor flows. SHOUTING and CUSSING are punctuated by FEMALE LAUGHTER.

Jesse stays at the back, trying to blend in. Henry steps away to get a drink. Tommy hops onto a billiard table.

TOMMY
Gentlemen! Gentlemen! May I have your attention! I know you're enjoying the liquor and the girls, but let's not forget why we're here.
(raising glass)
To our new governor!

CHEERS erupt as the Mayor enters, cigar in mouth, with a beautiful prostitute on each arm. Stamp of ruby-red lipstick on his forehead. He relishes the response. Lets it wash over him for a minute. He removes his cigar and signals he wants to be heard.

MAYOR WESTPORT
My fellow citizens. By your vote, you've indicated that you don't like the way things are. Well, I'm here to tell you that I'm going to change all that!

The men CHEER and nod in agreement. Jesse is fit to be tied. He shoots his hand into the air.

MAYOR WESTPORT (CONT'D)
You having trouble hearing me back there? Who is that?

JESSE
It's Jesse Woods. I have a question.

The Mayor's demeanor shifts. He's discovered an interloper. The crowd's attention swivels to Jesse. Those near him step out of the line of fire, leaving him fully exposed.

MAYOR WESTPORT
It had better be good. I'm not through with my speech.

JESSE
I was wondering. Since this is a celebration of your victory...why...why isn't Mrs. Westport at your side?

All heads swivel back toward the Mayor. He's busy extricating himself from his female companions.

MAYOR WESTPORT
I don't get your point, Woods. As you can see, none of these men have their wives with them.

Their presence would severely curtail our enjoyment.

He grabs the two prostitutes around the waist as CHEERS bank off the walls. Henry returns and stands by Jesse.

> JESSE
> (shouting above cheers)
> Don't you think she should be here to witness history being made? It isn't every day that a man is elected governor!

The men regard Jesse's words as a signal to CHEER again. The Mayor has to shout above them.

> MAYOR WESTPORT
> You have a point, Woods. But I'm not debating you. The debating's over. I've won!

He jams his cigar into his mouth and pumps his arms above his head like a victorious boxer. The crowd ROARS. He drops his arms. The crowd settles down to hear the remainder of his speech. Instead, he addresses Jesse.

> MAYOR WESTPORT (CONT'D)
> Mrs. Westport is unable to join us tonight. I've sent her to the country.

EXT. WESTPORT PORCH— SAME EVENING

Stunned, Jesse sits on the bottom step. He shivers against the cold. The only sound is that of NEIGHING HORSES. Henry exits the house and joins him. He's carrying a cigar box under his arm.

> HENRY
> You'd better come back inside and have a shot of whiskey to warm you up.

> JESSE
> I think I'll stick with my plan to freeze to death.

> HENRY
> What possessed you to confront the man like that? In his own home!

> JESSE
> He sent her away, Henry! That's what she feared most of all!

He stands and swings his arms against the cold.

> JESSE (CONT'D)
> She told me once that suffering comes from wanting things to be other than they are.

> HENRY
> Maybe she was trying to tell you that if she's accepted her situation, you need to, as well.

Jesse sits back down and puts his head in his hands. Henry sits beside him and pats his back.

> HENRY (CONT'D)
> It's late, son. Time to leave. Right about now, my wife is filling her head with erroneous notions I'll have to defend tomorrow.

> JESSE
> You go on. I'll walk home. Need to clear my head.

Henry holds out the cigar box.

> HENRY
> When I told the Mayor I was leaving, he handed these cigars to me. He said to make sure they got to you.

Jesse pushes them away.

JESSE
He hasn't served a day in his
new office, and already he's
courting my future vote.

HENRY
I'd take them off your hands,
but the wife won't tolerate them
in the house. Calls them "devil
fingers."

They rise to part just as Tobias comes
around from the back of the house.
Jesse leans in and whispers to Henry.

JESSE
Who's the last person Westport
wants smoking these?

Henry hands the cigars to a surprised
Tobias. Up on the porch, two drunken
young men attempt to box. The
victor returns to the celebration
inside. The other staggers over,
plucks a torch out of the ground, and
dashes after him.

Jesse heads home as a light snow
starts to fall. He looks up toward
Lydia's room where, through the
locked shutters, he sees her pacing
silhouette.

INT. JESSE'S COTTAGE— SAME EVENING

*Jesse composes a letter by candlelight. He
reads out loud as he writes.*

JESSE
My precious Lydia: I came
to the victory celebration
this evening to check on
your welfare. I have been
nothing but concerned since
leaving you in the care of your
husband. I pray you are healing
from your fall.

He reaches for a blanket and wraps
it around him.

JESSE (CONT'D)
Do not despair. I am swimming
toward you. I will not accept
that you are beyond my reach.
Eternally, your Jesse.

INT. WESTPORT MAIN STAIRWAY—DAY

*It is early morning. Lydia descends the
stairs in a lush robe with a rabbit fur collar.
Her hair tumbles over her shoulders. Jesse
races up. They meet beneath her portrait.*

LYDIA
Oh! I thought I was alone.

She modestly gathers her robe
tightly around her.

LYDIA (CONT'D)
What are you doing here?

Jesse reaches up and slowly slides
the robe off her shoulder.

JESSE
I've wanted this for a long time.

It falls to the carpeted stairs, revealing a nightgown as sheer as gauze.
Jesse sees in her eyes the permission
he seeks. He removes his coat and
tosses it, never taking his gaze off her.

She grabs the banister and lowers
herself. He wraps his arm around her
and eases her down. They kiss. He
opens the gown and runs his hand
over the crescent of a huge scar.
Lydia snaps her head away. She
cannot bear to watch him seeing her.

LYDIA
No! Please.

Jesse plants kisses all over her
scarred torso.

JESSE
You are more beautiful than
I imagined.

Lydia slowly turns her head back. A tear rolls down her cheek.

LOUD KNOCK.

They ignore the knock. Jesse slides his hand into more pleasurable regions. Lydia arches her back against the stairs and releases a sound of great joy.

INT. JESSE'S COTTAGE—NIGHT

LOUD KNOCK. Jesse lies across his bed, still wearing his clothes from the election celebration. His oil lamp still burns at his bedside. He's embracing his pillow.

LOUDER KNOCK. Jesse jolts awake and realizes he's been dreaming. Henry appears at his bedroom door.

> HENRY
> Get up! The mayor's house is burning! I'm rounding up the volunteers. After the celebration, those firemen aren't fit to put out a blaze. Unless they piss on it!

Jesse dashes to his washbasin and throws cold water on his face. Yanks his coat and hat off a hook.

> JESSE
> What happened?

> HENRY
> One of the torches got inside the house. With all that cigar smoke...and liquor...the fire burned for a long time, before anybody noticed.

Jesse opens the door. Henry grabs his shoulder.

> HENRY (CONT'D)
> It's my duty to recruit you, but I know how you feel about the man.

You don't have to come if—

> JESSE
> Westport was lying to us. She's in that house, Henry!

EXT. WESTPORT ENTRANCE— PRE-DAWN

The home is an inferno. A handful of voluntary firefighters slump near a tree, defeated by the enormity of the task. A crowd has formed. Individual gawkers compete for a closer look. Henry and Jesse push through them to the gate.

> HENRY
> Step aside! Sheriff comin' through!

A deputy stands guard. He pulls Henry aside. Jesse dashes up to the porch. CHARLIE, the Volunteer Fire Chief, stands in the doorway. Behind him, FLAMES lick the walls of the foyer. SMOKE climbs the stairs.

Jesse steps forward. They shout above the ROARING FIRE, BREAKING GLASS AND FALLING TIMBERS.

> CHARLIE
> Can't go in there, Jesse! Too dangerous!

> JESSE
> Is everybody out?

> CHARLIE
> Nobody was home. The mayor left with one of his whores long before the celebration ended. The parlor-maid had the evening off.

Jesse attempts to step around him. Charlie blocks.

> CHARLIE (CONT'D)
> It was like a cattle drive trying to get that bunch of rowdy drunks out of here. But everybody's been accounted for.

> JESSE
> (into house)
> Lydia!

> CHARLIE
> Mrs. Westport's in the country. I heard the mayor tell you himself.

Jesse grabs Charlie's jacket.

> JESSE
> He lied. She's up there!

> CHARLIE
> Even if she was up there, you couldn't get to her. There's an iron gate blocking the stairs. And it's locked!

Jesse pulls the extra set of keys out of his pocket. CU: Lydia's shell dangling at the end. They run inside.

INT. WESTPORT MAIN STAIRWAY— PRE-DAWN, SAME DAY
SMOKE rises in stairway. Choking, Jesse fumbles with the lock on the gate at the top. DEBRIS rains down. Lock opens. Jesse and Charlie dash to Lydia's bedchamber.

INT. WESTPORT SECOND FLOOR HALLWAY—PRE-DAWN, SAME DAY
The key turns, but the door won't open. They throw their weight into it. Won't budge. A smoldering beam CRASHES nearby. Charlie removes his jacket and wraps it around the center.

They lift it and ram the lower part of the door. Hit resistance. Raising their aim, after a couple of tries, they create a hole large enough for Jesse to crawl through.

INT. LYDIA'S BEDCHAMBER— PRE-DAWN, SAME DAY
Immediately, Jesse discovers Lydia's steamer trunk, overflowing with books, has been pushed against the door.

> JESSE
> Lydia!

Charlie kicks out a larger hole in the door. SMOKE prevents Jesse from seeing whether Lydia's there or not. He drops to his knees and feels his way around the room.

> CHARLIE
> Look under the bed! That's where we usually find 'em. Last of the good air.

Jesse crawls along the floor, reaching beneath the bed.

> JESSE
> Lydia! It's Jesse!

He rises. Bumps into her hand dangling over the edge.

> JESSE (CONT'D)
> I found her!

Jesse scoops up her limp body. Charlie kicks out the last board in the door. Jesse straddles the steamer trunk with Lydia in his arms and steps into the hallway.

INT. WESTPORT SECOND FLOOR HALLWAY—PRE-DAWN, SAME DAY
Jesse carries Lydia and follows Charlie back toward the main stairway. Flames roll toward them like molten waves.

JESSE
The servants' entrance!

They head the other direction, with Charlie leading the way.

Charlie kicks open the locked door and heads down the stairs.

The smoke isn't as thick at this end of the hallway. Just before the stairs, Jesse's attention is snagged by the large mirror hanging to his left. Their images are, once again, framed in a portrait. He desperately wants her to be alive, but he knows he has lost her. Charlie shouts up from below.

CHARLIE (O.S.)
Jesse! Get out before the floor collapses!

Jesse studies their "portrait." A thought flickers across his face: Why escape? Everything that matters lies in my arms. He pulls Lydia's body closer and calmly looks down the hallway at the approaching tsunami.

Then, caught in a paroxysm of coughing, the life-force propels him down the stairs.

EXT. WESTPORT GARDEN—DAWN, SAME DAY
Jesse lands on his knees gasping. Still cradling Lydia, he rocks her. Charlie crawls over to them.

CHARLIE (O.S.)
She gone?

Jesse raises his face, revealing the depth of his anguish.

Henry springs toward them. Tobias keeps a short distance. He holds a cigar box. Henry takes Charlie aside and speaks with him. They approach Jesse and Lydia.

Henry kneels and confirms for himself that she is dead. Jesse embraces her for one last time, before Charlie lifts her out of his life forever.

EXT. WESTPORT GROUNDS— DAWN, SAME DAY
The grounds look like a battlefield. In all directions, furniture covers the lawn. Some is charred, some damaged from being tossed out. In between the larger pieces rest items of a more intimate nature: clothing, a jewelry box, framed photographs, a bud vase, etc. Tiny icicles (from the firehose) dangle from everything, creating a cruelly beautiful image.

Henry walks Jesse to Lydia's magnificent "reading tree," beneath which have been tossed the scorched blue-and-gold oriental carpet and claw-footed chairs from the library. The rug's icy coating CRUNCHES as he crosses it. Jesse drops into a chair and strokes the arms, igniting a memory.

LYDIA (V.O.)
Mr. Woods, would you be interested in joining me in a grand experiment?

Henry signals Tobias to take his place, so he can assist a wounded volunteer. After Henry leaves, Tobias reaches into his overalls and extracts an envelope. He hands it to Jesse.

TOBIAS
Mrs. Westport asked me to give this to you. She was a nice lady.

JESSE
When? When did she give it to you?

TOBIAS
Yesterday.

JESSE
I was at the Celebration! Why didn't you give it to me then?

TOBIAS
She say, "Make sure Mr. Woods gets this in the morning." She say, "Goodbye, Tobias. I say, "I ain't goin' nowhere." Then, she say, "No, but I am."

Jesse opens it and reads.

LYDIA (V.O.)
My dearest Jesse. A messenger has arrived in the form of your friend, Tobias. Through him I hope to reach out and comfort you at a time when I know you are grieving. My husband has informed me that tomorrow he is taking me to Maple Hill, as I continue to be a liability. I wanted nothing more than to be "Captain of my ship." Now that ship is sinking. Please do not give a single thought to how you could have saved me. It would not have been possible. More importantly, it would have violated our agreement.

Jesse leans back and looks up into the tree.

LYDIA (V.O.)
I fear you think you have failed me, as you once predicted you would. Nothing could be further from the truth. I want you to know the pleasure our arrangement brought me. Those memories give me such peace in these darkest of hours.

Tobias waits for Jesse to stop. When Jesse does not, he interrupts, holding out the cigar box.

TOBIAS
These is yours too.

Jesse frowns at the box and ignores Tobias. Tobias waits patiently at his side.

LYDIA (V.O.)
Since a wife cannot legally divorce her husband without his permission, I am trapped. There is a Buddhist saying that "Wherever there is a predicament, there is also a gate." My "gate" is in a tiny bottle waiting on my pillow.

Jesse's eyes brim with tears. He stops reading. Tobias pushes the cigar box towards him.

JESSE
Don't want them! Gave them to you!

TOBIAS
Take 'em! They yours.

Again, Jesse ignores Tobias and resumes reading.

LYDIA (V.O.)
Before I leave this world, I have a confession. There were times when I thought we might have made a good "match" I longed for you to ignore my request for proper behavior. I dreamed of you leading us to a more intimate level. As time passed, I could no longer fool myself. If you had held the same feelings, surely you would have let me know.

JESSE
I did!

TOBIAS (O.S.)
You did what?

Irritated, Jesse snatches the cigar box from Tobias's hands. It falls to the carpet, spilling the contents. Among the cigars are small, white envelopes. CU: each is addressed to "Mrs. Anderson Westport."

TOBIAS (O.S.) (CONT'D)
You taught me to read, Jesse.
That there's your handwriting.

Jesse picks up an envelope, then another and another. He turns each over and discovers they are virginal: unopened and unread. He holds them to his heart as Tobias walks away.

LYDIA (V.O.)
I can imagine your surprise as you read this. Without any sign from you, I was hesitant to risk harming the contract we made. Never forget this, my dearest. Our experiment was a great success! Thank you for being a most suitable companion. Eternally, your Lydia.

Jesse lays the letter in his lap. The genesis of a smile appears, as the sun rises on a new day.

FADE OUT.

MIMI AYERS

Mimi Ayers, born in Chicago, raised in St. Petersburg, Florida, has made New Orleans home. Mimi wrote her first play, *Ghetto Fantasy*, a musical, in New York, where she lived for five years and first established herself as a professional actor when she joined Actors Equity in 1975. After almost fifty years, she went back to school and, in 2018, became an MFA Playwriting graduate of the University of New Orleans Creative Writing Workshop (CWW).

Mimi's one-woman show, *Three Women and a Crone,* was presented at the DuSable Museum of African American History in Chicago. Two of her plays workshopped with the CWW have had staged readings in New Orleans: *Man 2 Man* at the Valiant Theatre and *Circus Tails* at the Always Lounge and the Theatre at St. Claude. Mimi wrote *Defending Eulalie*, about the 1840s inheritance trial of a free woman of color, for her thesis defense. A staged reading of the first act was presented at the UNO St. Claude Gallery. Fascinated by the life and times of Eulalie de Marigny de Mandeville, Mimi also wrote a short story and a screenplay inspired by another of Eulalie's slave ownership trials, *Eulalie Mandeville*, F.W.C. The screenplay is a 2020 ARTemis Arts Wisdom Anthology official selection.

Eulalie Mandeville, F.W.C.

A SCREENPLAY BY MIMI AYERS

Caption: In 1815, New Orleans had the largest colored population in the United States and the largest concentration of free people of color. It is twelve years since the Louisiana Purchase of 1803. The code noir (black codes) decrees that non-European women, even free women of color (f.w.c.), must wear the head wrap known as the Tignon.

**EXT. RUE DUMAINE,
NEW ORLEANS—DAY**

Sturdy, graceful white feet of a lady squish through the muddy road leading towards the river. A STEAMBOAT WHISTLE BLOWS in the distance. Bare brown feet and legs of children run across her path. Dark brown feet of her slave, SUZANNE, follow close behind.

Wagon wheels trudge through the rutted road to keep on course. A black man rides one of the four donkeys pulling a wagon almost overloaded with several bales of cotton.

Vendors and people of every color, size, and dress crisscross the road, hawking and buying goods.

EULALIE MANDEVILLE (40) holds up her chin and the hem of her lavender muslin cotton dress higher above her feet. A darker lavender drapes around the bodice. Her pale smooth skin glows. She wears the Tignon like a crown. There's a pencil tucked in a fold of the lilac taffeta fabric head wrap.

Closer to the riverfront a cacophony of calls and greetings in almost every language calls out to Eulalie, "Bonjour," "ça va," and "buenos dias," as she passes. Many give way as she responds and greets them in their language.

EULALIE
Bonjour, ça va?

She rounds the corner walking towards the river.

EXT. RUE ST. PIERRE—DAY
CARRIAGES AND WAGONS pass.
STEAMBOAT WHISTLES blow louder.

Tops of sails and upper decks of boats.

VOICE IN CROWD
Bonjour, Madam Eulalie.

A plainly dressed brown-skinned woman, SUZANNE (30s), carrying a large basket with a smaller one on top, steps from behind Eulalie and stands by her side. She carries two baskets, both filled with rolls of colorful fabrics, with ease.

BETTY (20s), a darker brown-skinned woman in a plain muslin dress and sash, takes a step back from Eulalie.

EULALIE
Bonjour, Betty. Do you have more laces?

BETTY
Oui. Yes, I have many.

Betty displays her laces on the rim of her basket. Eulalie makes a selection.

EULALIE
I will take this and this one and all of this. Cinco pesetas.

BETTY
(pleading)
Madam, seis, six, please? These I made myself.

EULALIE
Betty. Tu le sais, no seis, ils sont cinq.

BETTY
Oui, madam. D'accord. Cinq.

Eulalie hands the laces to the brown-skinned woman behind her and counts out five coins in Betty's open palm.

BETTY (CONT'D)
Merci, Madam.

Betty goes off, hawking in French and Spanish.

BETTY (CONT'D)
Lacets, cordonnes, handmade laces.

EXT. WHARF, MISSISSIPPI RIVER—DAY
Steamboats, paddle, and sailboats, schooners, all kinds of boats splash along the wharf. The sun blazes over black men in chains. They are led down a gangplank of a flatboat by a white man with a whip. Brown and black colored men load bales of cotton onto another flatboat.

EXT. CHARTRES STREET SHOPS—DAY
Stores are open for business, barbers, small cafes and tailors, on Chartres. The street is paved with cobblestones. Eulalie cleans her feet with a cloth she takes from the larger basket. She hands it to the other woman in exchange for her purple leather slippers.

EULALIE
Merci.

HERRMAN KRAUER (35), a short slender German tailor in a handsome suit, taps on the window of his shop.

"Krauer & Sons" is painted in bold letters and beneath in smaller print "Imported Worsted Broadcloths." He steps out to catch Eulalie on the planked sidewalk.

KRAUER
Madame Eulalie.

Taking the smaller basket. She puts some laces in Suzanne's larger basket.

                    EULALIE
                  (to Suzanne)
Distribute these laces to my merchants.

                    SUZANNE
                  Oui, madam.

                    KRAUER
                  (to Eulalie)
Please come in.

                    EULALIE
                  (to Suzanne)
Au revoir. Avant que je...Au revoir.

                    SUZANNE
Au revoir, madam.

INT. TAILOR'S SHOP—DAY
Behind Krauer are neatly stacked dark, dull shades of wool broadcloths. He opens the door wider for Eulalie.

                    EULALIE
Monsieur Krauer, I have some new taffetas.

                    KRAUER
Do you have more of that lilac cross-grain taffeta? Ah. Like your tignon? It is beautiful.

Her hand pats her tignon.

                    EULALIE
Merci. Monsieur Krauer, this is only a remnant. The whole role was gone soon after I showed it to you...first.

                    KRAUER
The whole bolt?

                    EULALIE
Oui, monsieur. You must not hesitate with a bargain. Take a look at these silks. Not as crisp, but fine, no?

Krauer looks through the colorful fabrics.

                    KRAUER
Can you get more like the other?

                    EULALIE
Peut-être, something close, mais très cher, it will cost more. Nothing quite like it anymore in my storehouse.

                    KRAUER
How much more?

                    EULALIE
You know it depends on the weavers and the cost of transportation. Merchants are always charging more.

She takes the pencil from her tignon and figures on the cloth. She shows him the price.

                    KRAUER
I will pay half that and you, madame, may choose some of my fine broadcloth.

                    EULALIE
I have enough broadcloth for now.

She shows him the figure again.

                    KRAUER
Fine. I wish I did not tell my wife about it.

                    EULALIE
Next time, perhaps we can make a better bargain with your cloths. Half now?

KRAUER
Fine.

Krauer puts three large bills in Eulalie's outstretched hand.

EULALIE
Bien.

EXT. DOCK—DAY
Steamboats are unloading tourists.

Heavy boots and bare feet hurry along the planks. SHACKLES CLANGING and CRACKS OF WHIPS are heard in the distance.

PATRICK (21), handsome looks like a European with his light brown hair and fair complexion, but he is a man of color. His jacket hangs on a box next to his easel. It is clean, but the cloth is threadbare. Women pass slowly to look at him. His focus is on the painting. Patrick mixes paints on his palette. He brushes smooth determined strokes on the canvas.

Eulalie mounts the plank with her basket.

Patrick rises from his stool.

PATRICK
Madam Eulalie, bon jour. How good to see you again. It has been a while.

EULALIE
Bonjour, Patrick. Merci. We had some spinning to do. Regardez.

PATRICK
Tres belle.

EXT. WHARF—DAY
PADDLE BOATS SWISH rolling down the Mississippi. WAVES SPLASH against the bows of ships moored and secured with sturdy ropes as they lumber gently in the water.

Activity is all about; birds squawk, and people hawk their wares. "Cailos tous chaud!" "Strawberries!" "Clementines!"

EXT. DOCK—DAY
Eulalie drapes some cloths along her arm.

EULALIE
(lilting, sure)
Madam, regardéz. The finest fabrics from Paris. I have. Come, touch.

She engages with prospective customers.

EULALIE (CONT'D)
Such qualité you will not see anywhere else this fine this side of the ocean.

With the sound of a CARRIAGE approaching, she takes another tack. Stepping up to the covered carriage. It stops a minute.

ALONZO MORPHY (40s), a well-tailored gentleman, leans out of the carriage window.

EULALIE (CONT'D)
Hola, Señor Alonzo. I have acquired some lightweight broadcloth I think will please you.

ALONZO
Venez me oficina mañana.

EULALIE
Acuerdo!

As the carriage moves on, Eulalie pulls out a piece of linen from her bosom, the pencil from her tignon, and writes a note.

That done, she calls out across the road to an older man in his fifties. He wears a long frock coat and a frilly shirt.

EULALIE (CONT'D)
Monsieur, something special for
that special someone. Venez.
Come see. Touch. Ooo la la.
Imagine the shimmer, the feel,
on the bodice of your lady or
the one who gives you love.

The man, without turning, gives her a
signal and walks on.

EULALIE (CONT'D)
Aha, yes.

Eulalie makes another note. She
adjusts her wares, then goes to look
at Patrick's painting.

Patrick makes slow caressing strokes
on the face of a beautiful young
blond with blue-gray eyes on his
canvas.

EULALIE (CONT'D)
You have been dabbling too
long on your pretty young girl.

PATRICK
She is pretty, but not mine.

CUT TO:
EXT. PIER—DAY
*Vessels are lined along the dock, loaded
with passengers and goods coming and
going. Through the crowd, down the pier,
two women stand close side by side. The
taller woman wears a bonnet, the other
wears a tignon and carries a small straw
basket.*

*The tan hand of MARIE (15) squeezes
VICTORIA's pale hand so tight it is
blotched blue and pink.*

*An imposing gentleman, MANUEL
BEAUREGARD (45) gives a
commanding shake of his wolf head
sculpted ivory handle cane at the two
women. He speaks directly to Victoria.*

*VICTORIA (19), the face in Patrick's
painting, nods in rhythm with the ivory-
handled cane. Beauregard puts down his
cane and hands over a money pouch to her.*

BEAUREGARD
And be back at the dock before
sunset.

VICTORIA
Yes, brother. Thank you,
brother.

MARIE (15), lovely in her tignon
of light blue muslin, watches
Beauregard cross over to the Place
D'Armes.

EXT. PLACE D'ARMES—DAY
*The 15 red and white striped 15starred
US flag flaps in the center of the public
square. SLAVE AUCTION CALLS.*

AUCTIONEER (O.S.)
300 for this strong boy, good
for fieldwork, 400...

The St. Louis Cathedral looms majes-
tically in the background. Two matching Spanish-styled buildings on either
side. The Cabildo roof is under repair.
HAMMERING of WOOD and STEEL.

EXT. THE PIER—DAY
Victoria shakes loose Marie's hand.

VICTORIA
Oowww! He wouldn't dare try to
sell you. Here, take this.

Victoria takes off her bonnet. She is
the same girl in Patrick's painting.

Marie shakes loose her hand and
relaxes.

MARIE
You should put that back on.

Victoria waves her away.

EXT. DOCK—DAY
Eulalie hawking her fabrics to the tourists and other shoppers on the dock.

                    EULALIE
          Venez! Regardez. Come see,
          touch my fine fabrics. I have
          laces too.

She stops calling out, seeing a familiar face in the distance strolls over to Patrick painting.

                    EULALIE (CONT'D)
          Ah, regardez, perhaps she will
          come closer this time. Work
          your magic.

EXT. DOCK—DAY
Eulalie completes selling some lace to a modestly dressed WOMAN SHOPPER (30s), in a small sun hat.

                    EULALIE
          Oui. The pattern is my own
          design. Merci.

Marie skips towards Eulalie.

Marie stops just behind Eulalie to call back to Victoria.

                    MARIE
          Au revoir! Avant que je vous
          manque.

Startled, Eulalie whirls around, losing grip on her basket.

Eulalie and Marie both fumble, trying to keep the basket from falling before Marie catches it and Eulalie sets it right. They face each other.

                    EULALIE
          Quelque se dit?

                    MARIE
          I said...

                    EULALIE
          Who taught you to say that?
          Avant que—

                    MARIE
          Pardon, madam?

Eulalie can't stop staring at Marie's piercing green eyes. Marie steps back.

                    EULALIE
          You said, "Avant que je vous
          manque." Where did you learn
          this?

Marie, frightened, looks for help.

                    MARIE
          I was saying goodbye to my
          mistress.

Eulalie follows her gaze to see what she sees. Victoria.

EXT. PIER CLOSER TO DOCK—DAY
Victoria walks towards them. Her focus is on Patrick.

EXT. DOCK—DAY
Marie walks backwards toward the market.

                    MARIE
          Pardon moi, madam. I am so
          sorry.

                    EULALIE
              (shaking the words off)
          Avant que je vous manque...
          before you miss me.

Marie runs inside the market. She is lost in the crowd.

Eulalie starts after Marie but stops when she can no longer see her. Eulalie turns towards Victoria. Victoria, watching Patrick, bumps into Eulalie.

EULALIE MANDEVILLE, F.W.C.

VICTORIA
Madam Mandeville?

Eulalie, recovering, takes a deep breath.

EULALIE
Oui. Bon jour. You are looking for...?

VICTORIA
Cloth. I need fabric for a dress, a gown.

EULALIE
I have fabriques extraordinaire. Some of the finest silks, muslins and taffetas in Nouvelle Orleans.

Eulalie shows off her silks in bright and bold colors.

Patrick slyly looks at Victoria over his easel.

EULALIE (CONT'D)
I have even more special in my place in the market. Come.

Victoria looks to Patrick. He tries to avoid meeting her eyes but eventually smiles and nods.

EULALIE (CONT'D)
Think it over. I must go. My friend, Patrick, has seen my work.

VICTORIA
Yes, as soon as my girl returns from the market.

EULALIE
Your girl? Bien. Ask anyone where to find me.

VICTORIA
She may be a while. She is very picky.

EULALIE
A bientôt! I will find something you are sure to like.

Eulalie picks up her basket and steps off the planks and into the muddy road. She has forgotten to take off her shoes.

EULALIE (CONT'D)
Merde!

EXT. ROAD—DAY
EULALIE spots a WOMAN IN YELLOW TIGNON carrying a basket packed with folds of fabric. Eulalie raises her hand. The woman rushes over to her and puts Eulalie's basket on top of hers. Using the woman's shoulder for balance, Eulalie takes off her shoes.

The woman takes out a rag and cleans and wraps the shoes before putting them in Eulalie's basket.

EULALIE
Merci.

INT. MARKET—DAY
A family of Choctaws sit in a semi-circle on the side of the market. Two of the CHOCTAW WOMEN (20s) have their babies strapped to their backs. A YOUNG BOY (12) holds up colored beads for sale. An OLDER WOMAN (60) draped in a large striped blanket smokes a pipe. In the center are baskets of corn and woven wool blankets.

Eulalie walks around the group into the market.

Marie selects morel mushrooms with care.

Eulalie stays in the shadows behind a vegetable stall, watching Marie bargain.

EXT. DOCK—DAY

Patrick paints, barely glancing at Victoria. As in a minuet, she spirals out and looks towards the market.

She spirals back in towards Patrick. Her dress swirls.

Patrick tries to concentrate on his painting.

> VICTORIA
> Would you like to paint me?

Patrick is caught off guard. Speechless. Avoiding backing into passersby, Patrick manages to maneuver his easel so that she does not see that he is already painting her.

> VICTORIA (CONT'D)
> I have money. I mean, I can pay you.

He gets up, removes his waistcoat from the box, and offers her a seat.

> VICTORIA (CONT'D)
> I prefer to stand.

He lays his waistcoat back on the box.

Patrick holds up his paintbrush and directs her to come closer and turn. He paints in earnest.

> VICTORIA (CONT'D)
> Your friend, Madam Eulalie. Her work is...

> PATRICK
> Exquisite.

> VICTORIA
> Exquisite. Humm. How so?

> PATRICK
> Designed to look like a flowing waterfall cascading to a perfect hemline, barely showing the delicate curve of an ankle.

Rare fabrics fit to frame the softness of her neck...

A vein in Victoria's neck pulsates.

> PATRICK (CONT'D)
> ...in colors sure to highlight the curls of her hair, molded just so, to look as if morning sunshine caressed the bodice of an angel—

> VICTORIA
> Monsieur!

> PATRICK
> Patrick. Mon nom est Patrick.

> VICTORIA
> Monsieur Patrick.

> PATRICK
> Call me Patrick.

> VICTORIA
> Patrick.

CUT TO:
EXT. EULALIE'S SHOP—DAY

Eulalie escorts a stunningly dressed EUROPEAN LADY carrying a huge box out to the road from her shop stall in the market. A footman jumps down from a carriage, takes the box, and assists the lady up the step. Eulalie waves goodbye.

The carriage passes the dock and the Place D'Armes.

CUT TO:
EXT. PLACE D'ARMES—DAY

Shackled, scantily clad slaves are marched up the gallows for auction. BEAUREGARD raises his wolf head handled ivory cane in the background.

CUT TO:
EXT. DOCK—DAY

The SPLASH OF THE WAVES and the KNOCKING OF THE BOATS nearly drown out the AUCTION CRIES.

Patrick's painting is nearly complete. The color of Victoria's dress is now a burnt orange.

> VICTORIA
> May I see what you've done?

> PATRICK
> Not yet.

> VICTORIA
> How much longer?

> PATRICK
> You ask many questions.

> VICTORIA
> Sometimes it is the only way to answers. How long?

> PATRICK
> Not long. I started it when I first saw you stepping off the ferry from Baton Rouge.

They lock eyes.

> VICTORIA
> I saw you too. You stood up so suddenly you startled me.

Patrick goes back to the painting.

> VICTORIA (CONT'D)
> I almost tripped. I couldn't look your way again.

> PATRICK
> You looked as though you commanded the plank to be still.

They both laugh.

> VICTORIA
> How dare it. I am a Beauregard after all.

Patrick starts to wipe and put away his brushes.

> VICTORIA (CONT'D)
> Oh no, now I've ruined it.

> PATRICK (bows curtly)
> Mademoiselle Beauregard...

> VICTORIA
> Please stop. I have been too long conspiring with Marie to meet you.
> (small beat before extending her hand)
> Victoria. Please call me Victoria.

Patrick can't resist her. He stops to wipe his hands with his kerchief and extends an open palm for her hand.

> PATRICK
> Mademoiselle Victoria, I am pleased to make your acquaintance.

She puts her hand in his. He brings her hand to his lips. After an awkward moment, they break away.

> VICTORIA
> You must come to my birthday celebration?

> PATRICK
> (amused)
> I must? I think it would not be proper.

She hands him a small wax-sealed note card.

> VICTORIA
> Two weeks. I must get Marie. Madam Eulalie will be waiting.

CUT TO:
INT. STRAWBERRY STALL—DAY

Marie takes two containers of strawberries from the STRAWBERRY VENDOR.

STRAWBERRY VENDOR
You should buy more at this price.

MARIE
This will do. Thank you.

Victoria comes up to her as Marie hands coins to vendor and puts strawberries in her basket already filled with morels.

VICTORIA
Come. Madam Eulalie is finding the perfect fabric for my gown.

MARIE
I think I saw her pass here.

Marie leads the way through the vendors and shoppers.

INT. SEAMSTRESS STALL—DAY

The space is crammed with baskets and rolls of fabrics, textiles, and notions. TWO SEAMSTRESSES are busy stitching and laying out fabric to cut.

Eulalie drapes the pale gold silk peau de soie cloth over Victoria's shoulder.

EULALIE
This taffeta is perfect. Accent with this silk. Feel. Smooth like water.

VICTORIA
This is nice.

EULALIE
Nice? A burnished gold. It will bring out the lights in your hair.

VICTORIA
Patrick said something like that. Marie, is this not the most extraordinary cloth?

MARIE
Yes, but your papa would be more pleased if it were white.

EULALIE
He would be overjoyed to see his daughter so radiant.

MARIE
You do not know her father.

Eulalie measures and shapes the fabric on Victoria while Marie takes in all the trappings of the shop.

EULALIE
I know fathers, mothers too, want only the best for their children.

VICTORIA
I'm not a child. Patrick could see that.

EULALIE
Patrick. Humm. Turn.

MARIE
Do you have white lace for the top?

EULALIE
(to a seamstress)
White laces.

SEAMSTRESS
Yes, ma'am.

The seamstress brings the box filled with a variety of white lace. Eulalie directs her to give it to Marie. Marie finds just the right one.

MARIE
This one is pretty.

VICTORIA
Too thick. Find something
lighter.

One of the seamstresses assists
pinning the fabric Eulalie has
arranged. Victoria fidgets, trying to
see herself in the mirror.

Eulalie takes over a covered box
to show Marie different laces. She
leaves the box with her.

EULALIE
(returning to Victoria)
Has your girl been with you long?

VICTORIA
For as long as I can remember.
My uncle gave her mother to
my mother—

Marie joins them.

MARIE
My mother was her mother's—

EULALIE
Girl, I was addressing your
mistress.

VICTORIA
Madame, please. Her name
is Marie. Sometimes I have
to remind her of her place.
I'm afraid I've spoiled her.
Oftentimes she is my only
company.

EULALIE
(appeasing)
You are both very pretty.

VICTORIA
Her mother was beautiful.
Yes, Marie?

MARIE
If I may speak...tres belle. Her
emerald green eyes—

EULALIE
A green like yours?

MARIE
Brighter. They sparkled until
the end.

EULALIE
The end?

MARIE
She died having her last child.

Eulalie drops her pencil. Her fingers
shake picking it up.

VICTORIA
Marie, enough.

Marie sulks. She thumps the lace box
like a drum.

VICTORIA (CONT'D)
Patrick seems like a fine
gentleman, even if he would
not show me his painting.

MARIE
You did not come here to see
his painting.

VICTORIA
Shush.

EULALIE
(distracted)
Oui, Monsieur Patrick is an
exceptional artist and a
gentleman.

VICTORIA
In two weeks, I will be twenty.

EULALIE
My first child was born when I
was twenty.

VICTORIA
I must be married...Pardon moi,
madam. I meant no offense.

EULALIE
No matter. Mon père chose for me.

DISSOLVE TO:
INT. ROOM IN MANDEVILLE ESTATE—
EVENING—FLASHBACK—1790

*The comfortable drawing room of
an aristocratic family. A candle brass
chandelier hangs down the center of the
room. Portraits, maps, and tapestries
decorate the walls. The windows are draped
in dark and light fabric overlays.*

*An older couple sits at a small carved
wood table playing cards. A young Eulalie
(17) dressed in the same aristocratic
fashion as the older woman sits by the
window embroidering a piece of woven
fabric.*

*Two officers in the red, blue, and white
military dress of Napoleon's army come to
the entrance.*

*A young EUGENE (20s) with a
recognizable scar over his brow, follows the
older man, PHILLIPE DE MARIGNY
DE MANDEVILLE (40s). Mandeville
signals Eulalie to join them.*

EULALIE
Yes, Father.

She finishes a stitch and puts down
her embroidery before going to him.
The older woman grunts for her to
make haste.

MANDEVILLE
This is Sergeant Eugene Macarty.

Her father takes her hand and gives
it to Eugene.

She is obedient and somewhat drawn
to his rugged attractiveness. She lets
Eugene kisses her hand.

Her father nods his approval.

END FLASHBACK

INT. SEAMSTRESS SHOP—AFTERNOON
The women are chatting.

VICTORIA
You came highly
recommended.

MARIE
Her mother knows—

VICTORIA
(abruptly)
Shush, Marie.

Eulalie drapes different fabrics
across Victoria.

EULALIE
Tell me, Marie...where have you
heard "Au revoir! Avant que je
vous manque?"

MARIE
Madam, I was too anxious to
get to the market.

VICTORIA
Her mother would say that to
her.

Eulalie, agitated, flicks her hand for
seamstresses to bring over various
colored brocade trims. Victoria is
encircled.

Marie places lace here then there.
Eulalie happily works with Marie
making changes. Eulalie shows the
sketch to Marie before she presents
it to Victoria. Victoria is pleased.

EULALIE
I could use someone like your
girl. You will probably marry
soon and have no need for...

Marie is both flattered and flustered.

VICTORIA
Madam! Marie is like family.

EULALIE
My apologies. Have your girl...
Marie...come back for your
finished gown next week.

VICTORIA
What day?

EULALIE
Tuesday or Wednesday.

MARIE
Wednesday.

VICTORIA
Wednesday would be best.

EULALIE
D'accord. Half now and the
balance on completion.

CUT TO:
EXT. DOCK—DAY

*Patrick gives the painting one last flourish
before stepping back to see his work. He
bumps back into EUGENE, now 48,
with the recognizable scar. He's dressed in
aristocratic European gentleman fashion.*

PATRICK
Monsieur Macarty!

EUGENE
Bonjour, Patrick.

PATRICK
Bonjour.

EUGENE
(regarding the painting)
This is marvelous. She must be
someone special to you, yes?

PATRICK
Victoria. Before today, I only saw
her walking around the square.

EUGENE
Ah, Patrick, you have a good
eye. From memory? No...more
from the heart. Bold. A touch
of sun.

PATRICK
Thank you. I'm not sure it does
her justice.

EUGENE
You must do a portrait of
Madame Eulalie. With the
children away, she is gone
much of the day. I propose
a commission for a life-size
portrait of ma cherie.

PATRICK
It would be an honor.

EUGENE
I know just where it should
hang. You are probably the
only one she would consent to
pose for.

PATRICK
Like my Victoria, she will not be
still for long.

Eugene pulls out a currency note
from his vest.

EUGENE
Will this be enough to secure
your service?

Patrick takes the money and gives
Eugene a vigorous handshake.

PATRICK
Thank you!

EUGENE
I will pay...whatever your price
when complete.

CUT TO:
EXT. MARKET—DAY
Eulalie walks out of the market.
Seeing Eugene, she calls out to him.
                EULALIE
Monsieur Macarty, what brings
you here?

                EUGENE
        (whispers to Patrick)
Let us speak no more of this.
I must first convince her.

Eugene meets Eulalie halfway.

            EUGENE (CONT'D)
You, ma chère, I have come to
escort you home. I have news!

                EULALIE
Theo has returned home!?

                EUGENE
No.

                EULALIE
Then we can talk later. I must
speak with Patrick now.

                EUGENE
Humm.

                PATRICK
Yes?

                EULALIE
How did the two of you get
along?

                EUGENE
Us?

                EULALIE
Quoi? No. With Victoria,
Patrick.

                EUGENE
Oh. I've been admiring
her portrait. The textures.
Magnificent.

Patrick turns the easel towards her.

                EULALIE
C'est fini!

                PATRICK
Nearly.

                EULALIE
C'est très belle. It could not be
more beautiful. She posed for
you?

                PATRICK
She was still for a short while.

                EUGENE
Long enough.

                PATRICK
She moves like a dance. I used
to imagine her waiting at the
window for me.

                EULALIE
Pshaw. A woman who waits for a
man will never find happiness. I
think she has come to find it.

                EUGENE
        (taking Eulalie's hand)
Madame Eulalie would have
never waited for me.

Eulalie pats Eugene's hand with one
hand before pulling her other hand
away.

                EULALIE
Mon père did not allow me to
wait. You were not ready.

                EUGENE
You were the one not ready
to settle down. So young and
always so busy. Still, you will not
settle—

                EULALIE
I have no need to settle. You
should go.

EUGENE
What else must you do?

EULALIE
I must take care to make this
gown especially fine.

EUGENE
So busy. Still, you take good
care of me.

EULALIE
That is my duty.

Eulalie takes Eugene's arm and
steers him away.

EULALIE (CONT'D)
One that gives me pleasure.

PATRICK
I think she may find a
suitable mate at her birthday
celebration.

EUGENE
Ah, you think she is looking for
a husband.

PATRICK
It cannot be.

EUGENE
Why not?

EULALIE
Elle est un Beauregard.

PATRICK
She's a Beauregard!

EUGENE
Hummm. Her family may object
to a union with a man of color.

EULALIE
A free man of color.

EUGENE
Even so. The Beauregards.
Hummm.

EULALIE
She knows what she wants. She
spoke of you quite often.

EUGENE
Does she know?

EULALIE
Who could tell? Patrick, did you
tell her?

PATRICK
We just met.

EUGENE
The color or lack of color of
your skin is no matter to me. I
hold all Madam Eulalie's friends
in high esteem.

It is well then they are so few.
More free people of even some
little color are moving away to
start une nouvelle histoire.

A light-skinned man passes.

EUGENE (CONT'D)
Is he or is he not?

He looks to Eulalie, then to Patrick for
an answer.

EUGENE (CONT'D)
No matter.

Patrick begins to pack away his
painting gear.

EUGENE (CONT'D)
Ma cherie, if your father had
not placed your hand in mine,
I would have begged to make
you mine.

EULALIE
Pshaw. I know it was the dowry
from mon père that sealed the
bargain.

EUGENE
Eulalie!

EULALIE
I also know not to even nod
to your mother, La Madam
Macarty, when I see her on the
street.

EUGENE
If not for that damn Code Noir,
you know you would be my
legal wife.

Women in bonnets and fashionable
hats and women in stylish tignons
pass back and forth. Sometimes you
only can tell who are colored by the
tignon headwraps.

EULALIE
No matter. Enough of us.
Patrick, what is your plan to win
her hand?

PATRICK
I have no such plan...She has
invited me to her birthday—

EULALIE
She spoke of her birthday cele-
bration cruise. She invited you?
This is good.

EUGENE
Will you tell her? She should
know.

PATRICK
I will not deceive her. Maybe I
should not go.

EULALIE
You can not disappoint her.

Patrick looks down at his clothes.

PATRICK
This is my only—

EULALIE
I will make you a handsome outfit.

PATRICK
What have I to offer her?

EUGENE
Your talent. Your artistry is
remarkable.

EULALIE
And your devotion. No more
excuses!

PATRICK
I will go. I will finish her portrait
for a gift.

EULALIE
It will be an exquisite present!

EUGENE
Your work is sure to be admired.
You will be in great demand.

PATRICK
You are both dreamers.

EULALIE
Mon ami, you must dream a
grand dream for yourself.

Patrick finishes packing up his painting gear. Takes one last look at the
portrait before securing it to go.

PATRICK
Au revoir.

EUGENE
Au revoir.

EULALIE
A bientôt.

PATRICK
Yes, soon. And no lace, a
simple shirt, si vous plait.

EXT. RUE DUMAINE—EVENING

The sun has begun to set.
UNIFORMED GUARDS patrol the
streets along the two-story houses down
Dumaine street. Few people are out.
DOORS AND SHUTTERS CLOSE.
Cries of "BELLES CHANDELLES."

EULALIE walks behind a dark and lean
MALE SLAVE (50) carrying a lantern
to light the way.

INT. SEAMSTRESS SHOP—EVENING— MONTAGE

The male slave sits guarding the open
entrance to Eulalie's stall. Two lanterns
light the space.

Eulalie gathers the skirt and bodice pieces
of Victoria's dress. She lays out other
fabric pieces on a table.

Eulalie hand stitching the skirt, the
bodice, the trims, and lace around the
neckline.

She admires her handiwork, a work of art.

She smooths the inner lining of a man's
suit vest. It's the same gold fabric as the
dress. The shirt beside it is plain with a
simple fold down the center.

EXT. PLACE D'ARMES—DAY

Eugene in his usual aristocratic garb and
Eulalie, in a simple dress made of rich
indigo blue muslin and gold rope trim,
walk along the square towards the market.

> EULALIE
> Mademoiselle Beauregard's
> girl. She's there.

> EUGENE
> She?

> EULALIE
> Her name is Marie.

BEAT.

> EULALIE (CONT'D)
> She is my sister.

> EUGENE
> Sister? Why do you say this?
> How do you know this?

> EULALIE
> She's my mother's child. I
> know it. She described her, our
> mother. Her bright green eyes.
> Not just green, emerald green.
> And she said…"Au revoir! Avant
> que je vous manque."

> EUGENE
> Hmmm, you heard her say that?

> EULALIE
> Yes.

> EUGENE
> Your peculiar farewell? Back
> before you miss me. Hmmm.
> The children still missed you.

> EULALIE
> It was comforting to hear ma
> mere say it. "Avant que je vous
> manque." Before she was sold
> to the Beauregards…I doubt
> if Marie knows anything of our
> mother's early life…Make note
> of her, her character, her eyes,
> but do not let her see what you
> now know.

> EUGENE
> As you wish.

> EULALIE
> I must find a time, a way to
> bring her into my life. My
> mother would have wished it so.

Eugene puts his hand out to escort
her across the road.

> EULALIE (CONT'D)
> How do I look?

EUGENE
Beautiful as always. This is why
you're wearing my favorite dress?

She takes his arm.

DISSOLVE TO:
EXT. EULALIE'S HOUSE—DAY

*A green and white house curves around
a street corner. Similar Spanish-styled
two-story brick houses are on either side.*

*Patrick taps the door knocker. Marie,
beside him, wears a plain beige and white
dress. She carries a tapestry bag.*

*Eulalie opens the door. Her hair is pinned
up in a twist. She wears a short-sleeved,
squared neck, high-waisted plum and blue
striped dress. She welcomes them in but
Patrick shakes Eulalie's hand. He pats
Marie's shoulder farewell and turns away.*

They watch him walk away.

EXT. MUDDY ROAD—DAY

*Patrick's scuffed boots follow the toe prints
and shoe and boot imprints of those who
have passed before.*

DISSOLVE TO:
EXT. BEAUREGARD CEMETERY—
EVENING

*Beyond a black wrought iron gate, there is
a mausoleum and ornate tombstones. Some
as tall as the young live oak trees.*

*Rain beats against a mahogany casket.
Dark shadowed human forms follow.
Patrick leads the procession. Water drips
down his face.*

DISSOLVE TO:
EXT. EULALIE'S HOUSE—DAY

*Eulalie opens the door wide and reaches
out to welcome Marie into her home.*

*Marie walks past Eulalie clutching her
belongings up close to her.*

*Eulalie composes herself and briskly leads
the way.*

EULALIE
Your room is this way.

CUT TO:
INT. EULALIE'S PARLOR—DAY

*Eulalie's portrait hangs on the wall behind
a round table.*

*The rich detail and boldness of Patrick's
portrait of Eulalie, in Eugene's "favorite
dress," her hair in a braided upsweep is
striking. It's the focus of the sturdy wood
furnishings and brocades on the parlor side
of their home.*

*Eulalie, in a simple lavender muslin dress,
descends the spiral wooden staircase.*

*JEAN PIERRE (27), a tall black man in
short black pants and a white shirt, calls
from a door off the parlor. He speaks with
a French Caribbean lilt.*

JEAN PIERRE
Bonjour Madam Eulalie. Pardon
moi. Marie désirér—

EULALIE
Good morning Jean Pierre. We
must speak the language of the
Americans. What does Marie
want?

JEAN PIERRE
She wants to know if you and
Monsieur Eugene, Eugene,
Mister, Master Eu—

EULALIE
Monsieur Eugene will do for now.

JEAN PIERRE
Do you want café or chocolat...
late with your breakfast?

EULALIE
We'll have coffee, thank you.

He gives a slight bow and returns to
the kitchen.

CUT TO:
INT. KITCHEN—DAY

Marie stops shaping dough in the small, but fully equipped kitchen long enough to give Pierre a kiss.

> MARIE
> Coffee, oui?

> JEAN PIERRE
> Yes.

> MARIE
> She will out American les Americans.

INT. PARLOR—DAY

Eulalie unrolls the fabric an unusually colorful patterned fabric laid on the coffee table.

> EULALIE
> And this is my present. Pretty. But...what is this?

Her smile quickly disappears. She takes the roll to the shop side of the house.

INT. SHOP IN HOUSE—DAY

The shop is set up on the other side a center spiral staircase. Stacks of fabrics line the walls, baskets of textiles, and notions are on the floor.

Eulalie slams down her hand to stop the roll on the long table. Notions and thread fall on the rug.

The colorful and finely woven fabric begins to show signs of unraveling and mishmash weaving as it flattens out.

> EULALIE
> Eugene, allez! Eugene, come see the cloth you picked out for me. Regardez, c'est incroyable. The weave! Ackh!

EXT. COURTYARD—DAY

Eugene, closed eyes, sits feet up on a chaise under a flower laden magnolia tree.

INT. EULALIE'S PARLOR—DAY

Eulalie unrolls and slams, unrolls and slams her hand finding more rough patches in the fabric.

> EULALIE
> Eugene! Worthless. Come see... Eugene, do you hear me?

BIRDS CHIRPING temporarily drown out Eulalie's shouts as

Eugene enters from the outside. He is somewhat disheveled.

> EUGENE
> Eulalie, all la Rue de Dauphine hears you.

> EULALIE
> I thought you were still upstairs.

> EUGENE
> I was outside. Did you not hear me?

> EULALIE
> In the courtyard in this heat!

> EUGENE
> I was trying to enjoy some peace under the shade of the magnolia.

> EULALIE
> Peace! If only I had time to just sit and -

> EUGENE
> You could if you would stop for just a moment. Come join me.

> EULALIE
> Look at this fabric.

Eulalie points out the twisted weave in the fabric.

EULALIE (CONT'D)
See what your French fabricator has sold you. Fornicator!

EUGENE
Carbonnaire? No.

EULALIE
Oui. Monsieur Carbonnaire with the fabrics "extraordinaire," has sold you goods that are not. How much did you pay him?

EUGENE
He assured me it was from a special order by the Emperor himself.

EULALIE
An Emperor so desperate for capital he would sell the moon for a star if he could. You should have laid the fabric out and checked it.

EUGENE
What do you know of the moon and stars? I can not get you to sit and gaze on either.

EULALIE
I know enough. More than you do of fabrics.

EUGENE
It was so unusual. Jean Pierre thought you would like it too.

EULALIE
Jean Pierre was with you? And Marie?

EUGENE
She had gone off to the market.

EULALIE
My Marie would have known to check it. You must take it back.

EUGENE
That is not possible.

EULALIE
Why not?

EUGENE
We have made an agreement.

EULALIE
An agreement with a liar cannot be valid.

EUGENE
Perhaps, but...I can't. Eulalie waits. Eugene is stuck.

EUGENE (CONT'D)
Carbonnaire's schooner sailed down to Florida last week.

EULALIE
So...we are cheated.

Eugene looks over to the portrait of Eulalie on the wall.

EUGENE
(to the portrait)
Where is my daring belle?
(to Eulalie)
Put that away for now. Come, sit with me.

EULALIE
Not now, Eugene. I must prepare the fabrics for my vendors.

EUGENE
The magnolia is in full bloom.

EULALIE
Eugene...I am not.

EUGENE
Some flowers need some shade to maintain their bloom. We can take time now for ourselves...enjoy the things we've worked for.

EULALIE
We can not all stop to enjoy a
life of leisure.

EUGENE
You given me six beautiful
children. If not for the plague
all their lives would be well
taken care of.

EULALIE
Emeriste has at least married
well. Isi and Theo have good
business sense. But I will not
have our younger ones left to
the mercy of the courts.

EUGENE
Their future is secure—

EULALIE
You can not be sure of that.
Their future is what I work for. I
will not have them left no better
than slaves.

EUGENE
Eulalie, enough!

Eulalie returns her attention to the
fabric.

EULALIE
(calling out)
Marie!

INT. KITCHEN—DAY
*Marie heaves a sigh but continues to put
together a tray of coffee and beignets.*

EUGENE
Eulalie, Please, come sit with
me...for a while. Plenty of
shade.

Marie enters the parlor with the tray.

EULALIE
We have so little control.
(to Marie)
We should stock the baskets
now, but first take a look at this
fabric my Eugene has bought
and see if anything can be
done with it.

Marie puts the tray on the coffee
table then goes to the long table on
the shop side.

INT. SHOP SIDE OF HOUSE—DAY
*Eulalie and Marie stand side by side
rolling out the fabric.*

MARIE
Pretty. But oooh...

EULALIE
Aha! You see it too.

Both feel the uneven weaves. They
push, pull, and point out flaws in the
fabric.

CUT TO:
EXT. EULALIE'S HOUSE—DAY
*A small black carriage rounds the corner
in front.*

*A hand reaches for the knocker hanging
below a shiny black lion-faced knob in the
center of the door.*

INT. SHOP SIDE OF HOUSE—DAY
Eulalie and Marie roll up the fabric.

*LOUD KNOCKING from the outside
door.*

*Eulalie gives a firm squeeze to Marie's
hand. Marie's hand goes limp.*

EULALIE
I'll get it. Go sit outside,
Eugene. Smell the magnolias.

Marie throws Eugene a sympathetic look.

EULALIE (CONT'D)
I'm coming. Un moment.

Eulalie disappears into an alcove.

EULALIE (O.S.) (CONT'D)
And I have never been daring!

Eugene picks up his coffee and talks to the portrait.

Eulalie's tight lips in the portrait reveal an intense, impatient woman.

EUGENE (V.O.)
Ma belle Eulalie. Why do you feel you have to work so hard, as if I did not matter?

CUT TO:
EXT. EULALIE'S HOUSE—DAY
ARMED GUARD in full blue and white military dress stands beside a DEPUTY SHERIFF in a crisp black suit. He hands Eulalie a rolled parchment.

Eulalie unrolls paper, reads, and shakes her head no.

EULALIE
I have the bill of sale.

DEPUTY SHERIFF
I have orders for her to come with us.

INT. EULALIE'S PARLOR—DAY
Eulalie nearly staggers back to the parlor. Her shaking hand crushes the parchment.

EUGENE
Eulalie?

She tries to speak.

EUGENE (CONT'D)
What is it?

EULALIE
(gaining composure)
C'est impossible. Marie, take the tray back to the kitchen.

Marie does as she is told.

EULALIE (CONT'D)
Read this.
(handing over the document)
Beauregard lies.

EUGENE
Beauregard! What now?

EULALIE
Manuel Beauregard has got an order of Sequestration to take her away.

EUGENE
Take her?

EULALIE
"Forcibly detained." You have it there in your hand. Read it.

Eugene skim reads some parts aloud.

EUGENE
Sequestration...Marie?! They accuse you of keeping her here "by force...illegally!"

EULALIE
Oh my, Marie. Mon Dieu.

EUGENE
But look.

On the paper, his finger points under the H of "Hulalie."

EUGENE (CONT'D)
This is not your name. "Hulalie." H-U-L-A...They have made a mistake.

EULALIE
Yes, they have. Beauregard! Ack!

EUGENE
Sequestered until ownership is
established.

EULALIE
Can they do that? Just take her?

EUGENE
Who delivered the order.

EULALIE
The deputy sheriff with a guard.
They are outside.

EXT. EULALIE'S HOUSE—DAY

A uniformed guard sits in a carriage seat.
IMPATIENT HORSE HOOVES
SHUFFLE. Deputy Sheriff paces in
front of the door. He BANGS THE
DOORKNOB.

INT. EULALIE'S PARLOR

Eulalie and Eugene look at the paper
together.

EULALIE
I told him I have the deed. She
belongs to me.

EUGENE
I will go to our solicitor. We
cannot keep the deputy waiting.
You must prepare Marie.

EULALIE
What should I tell her? What
can I say to her?

EUGENE
Tell her the truth.

CUT TO:
INT. KITCHEN—DAY

Marie sits across the table from Eulalie.
Eulalie holds Marie's hands. Marie is
becoming impatient.

EULALIE
There is a deputy sheriff at the
door.

MARIE
What have I done?

EULALIE
Nothing. There has been a
mistake. You must go with him.

MARIE
To jail?

EULALIE
Just until Manuel Beauregard's
suit is proved false.

MARIE
What suit?

EULALIE
I am your lawful owner.

Marie pushes away from the table.
She stands and looks down at Eulalie.

EULALIE (CONT'D)
I must tell you / something.

MARIE
Sell me to Jean Pierre. He
would buy me. He would give
me my freedom.

EULALIE
It is not so simple. It must go
to the courts now. This will be
settled soon.

MARIE
How soon?

EULALIE
I don't know for sure.

MARIE
You're not sure of something?

EULALIE
Get your shoes. The Deputy's
waiting.

Marie tears off her apron and throws
it on a chair. She slips into her shoes.

She grabs her scarf off a hook on the wall and wraps her hair as she goes. She doesn't look back.

Eulalie stands looking at the closed door. She starts after Marie, stops, then starts again.

Eugene swings open the door.

> EUGENE
> She's gone.

Eulalie picks up Marie's apron and holds it.

> EULALIE
> I couldn't tell her.

> EUGENE
> What stopped you this time?

> EULALIE
> I tried! The longer I wait, the harder it is. She would leave me.

> EUGENE
> Of course, like our children. Marie is grown now too.

She hangs up the apron, giving it one last stroke.

> EULALIE
> I know. She asked me to sell her to Jean Pierre.

> EUGENE
> Why don't you just give her—

> EULALIE
> I'll tell her when she comes home.

> **CUT TO:**
> **INT. EULALIE'S PARLOR—DAY**
> *Eulalie helps Eugene button his waistcoat.*

> EUGENE
> I will see where they take her.

> EULALIE
> Hurry. Don't let them put her in a cell. She's done nothing wrong.

> EUGENE
> (running out)
> Morphy will get this sorted.

> EULALIE
> Beauregard has no right. I have the deed.

> **CUT TO:**
> **EXT. LA CABILDO—DAY**
> *ALONZO MORPHY (40), wearing a black solicitor's robe and white wig, rushes out of La Cabildo, the government office. Eugene catches up with him on the pavement in front.*

> EUGENE
> Esquire Morphy.

Morphy takes Eugene by the arm and has him walk with him.

> MORPHY
> Ah, mi amigo. Esquire? You have need of my legal services?

> EUGENE
> Yes, a matter of utmost importance.
>
> Please take a look at this.

Eugene makes him stop and hands him the parchment.

> MORPHY
> I was just on my way to my—

> EUGENE
> You must see about this now. We have just received a judge's order of Sequestration. They mean to hold her.

> MORPHY
> Sequestration? Madam Eulalie?

EUGENE
Of course not. She is a free woman. It's for Marie, her... Madam Eulalie has a deed for her, but Manual Beauregard is suing for custody.

MORPHY
Come with me, my friend. We will talk in my office.

CUT TO:
INT. MORPHY'S OFFICE—DAY
Morphy, court robe off, in his suit pants and shirt, reads while Eugene paces.

MORPHY
This names Hulalie Mandeville.

EUGENE
It is probably written as they call her. They have no regard. We are sure it is meant for Eulalie.

MORPHY
Ah.

EUGENE
Alonzo. I must post bond. We cannot let them keep Marie locked up.

MORPHY
She is in the Calaboose?

EUGENE
Not yet. She's locked in a cell behind the Cabildo. Give me your counsel.

MORPHY
Do you have the deed?

EUGENE
At home. Eulalie has it.

MORPHY
Get it at once and meet me at the Sheriff's office. I will need the deed to file an answer.

CUT TO:
INT. EULALIE'S PARLOR—DAY
The shutters are closed, the curtains are drawn.

A key opens the top doors of the armoire. She gets out some deeds from a drawer. And something else.

EULALIE
Ha. This will settle it. Deed? No, this is...the bill of sale. Where is the deed?

She pulls out more documents and compares them. It's a bill of sale, not a deed like the others. She looks at the portrait.

EULALIE (CONT'D)
Patrick, don't make me look at myself. Where is the deed? Mon cher Patrick. You did give me the deed? Where is it? What the Beauregards did to you, I do not know. Merde! I will have justice.

DISSOLVE TO:
INT. PARLOR—DAY—EARLY MORNING
The shutter windows are wide open. The parlor is well lit with the early morning sun.

Eugene enters, followed by Beauregard.

EUGENE
Have a seat at the table.

Eugene puts a document on the table and hands him a quill. Beauregard sits.

Eugene gets the inkwell from the top drawer of the armoire and sets it beside the document.

BEAUREGARD
Your...woman is not home?

EUGENE
She is upstairs.

Beauregard studies the document.

BEAUREGARD
Your rates are higher than
usual.

EUGENE
You knew my discount.

BEAUREGARD
Yes, I thought you might
reconsider.

EUGENE
(goes to take the paper)
Perhaps I should.

Beauregard stands, takes hold of the
paper and signs it.

BEAUREGARD
There.

He extends his hand. Eugene takes
the paper and blows it dry and starts
upstairs.

EUGENE
Have a seat.

Beauregard sits and looks long at
Eulalie's portrait.

BEAUREGARD
That style looks familiar.

He gets up to look closer. Up close
the portrait is vibrant with colors and
texture

Eugene returns with a smaller piece
of paper, a check.

EUGENE
The loan is due in sixty days.

BEAUREGARD
(reading the check)
It has her signature.

EUGENE
It's her money.

BEAUREGARD
Something about that painting.
The style?

Eugene maneuvers to get him out of
the house.

EUGENE
Come, I'll see you to the door.

DISSOLVE TO:
INT. EULALIE'S PARLOR—DAY
The portrait looks on the darkened room.

*Eulalie stuffs the deeds back in the
armoire top drawer.*

EULALIE
(to portrait)
Beauregard knows your child
does not need Marie. I need my
sister with me. Is he trying to
use your little one for bait? He
wants...

Eulalie pushes in the drawer with
sudden awareness.

EULALIE (CONT'D)
He has no shame. He means to sell

Marie. Mon Dieu! That's it. L'argent.
Money. It is always about the money.
He must find another way to pay his
debts. I must get my sister out of this
mess.

She takes the bill of sale and runs up
the stairs.

CUT TO:
EXT. STREET ON SIDE OF EULALIE'S HOUSE—DAY

Eugene runs up to the house. A horse and carriage clacks away farther down the road.

INT. EULALIE'S HOUSE—PARLOR—DAY

One of the doors to the armoire is open. The drawer with the deeds is unlocked.

> EUGENE
> Eulalie!

Eugene rummages through papers.

He calls again at the stairwell.

> EUGENE (CONT'D)
> Eulalie, The deed. I need the deed.

CUT TO:
INT. CARRIAGE—DAY

Eulalie, dressed for business in a tailored dress and jacket, looks at the bill of sale. She folds and puts it in her bag.

INT. SHERIFF'S OFFICE FOYER—DAY—LATER

Morphy holds out his hand. Eugene shakes his head.

> MORPHY
> The deed? Do you have it?

> EUGENE
> Eulalie must have taken it. I thought she may have come to you.

> MORPHY
> No. It is getting late. Marie is still here.

Marie sits in a small brick room behind the gated door.

> EUGENE
> You saw her?

> MORPHY
> I told her it would not be long.

> EUGENE
> What must she be thinking?

> MORPHY
> That I lied.

> EUGENE
> I mean Eulalie. What has she done with the deed?

INT. NOTARY OFFICE— EARLY EVENING

Eulalie steps into a small office just as the NOTARY CLERK (30s) takes out his door keys from his waistcoat

INT. SHERIFF'S OFFICE FOYER— EVENING

> MORPHY
> Did you not tell her you were coming to me?

> EUGENE
> Yes...I think. We were in such a hurry.

> MORPHY
> I'll speak to the Sheriff, see if suitable arrangements can be made for the night.

> EUGENE
> (horrified)
> The night?! Can you do nothing else? I have money to post bond.

> MORPHY
> There's nothing to be done without the deed. You could get a copy from the Notary. But no, they will have gone for the day. Come to my office tomorrow morning with the deed. I will be there early.

INT. NOTARY OFFICE—DAY

Gold lettering on the dark wood office door: Christoval Armas, Notary Republic. The door opens as she reaches for the doorknob.

The notary, ARMAS (45), is done for the day. His pocket watch says he should have left earlier, but he invites her in.

Eulalie paces in front of the Notary's desk as he writes, quill pen to parchment.

> NOTARY
> Madam, please sit down.

> EULALIE
> I can not sit. Please hurry.

> NOTARY
> If I had hurried before, I would be eating my supper now—

> EULALIE
> How much longer? All is in order, oui? I must get the deed to the...

He stops and looks up at her. She plops down in a chair, exasperated.

> EULALIE (CONT'D)
> It is urgent.

The notary, with agonizing slowness, continues to complete the document. Eulalie can't sit. The quill moves faster across the document.

CUT TO:
EXT. IN FRONT OF CABILDO—EVENING

A guard outfitted in a cocked hat, deep blue frock coat, black leather breast straps supporting cartridges and a bayonet scabbard takes a torch to the lanterns in front of the government building. The bricks glow, reflecting the light.

Eulalie jumps out of the carriage before Jean Pierre can assist her.

INT. THE CALABOOSE—EVENING

A long wooden bench is the only furniture in a small gray brick-walled room. An older GUARD (30s), equipped with a musket and short sword in a scabbard, stands in front of a steel bar door.

> EULALIE
> Here, I have what is needed.

Eulalie thrusts the deed up to the guard's face.

> GUARD
> Get away with that before we lock you up too.

> EULALIE
> Can I at least see her? She's my...I have the deed.

The Guard comes toward her.

> GUARD
> The sheriff will return in the morning.

> EULALIE
> Do you know who I am?

> GUARD
> Eulalie Mandeville. Would you care to wait here while we check your vendor status?

> EULALIE
> That is no concern here.

> GUARD
> It has been brought to the attention of the sheriff's office—

> EULALIE
> I will return with our solicitor.

The Guard adjusts his belt and watches her leave.

She pulls open the heavy iron-enforced wooden door. It SLAMS SHUT.

CUT TO:
INT. EULALIE'S PARLOR—LATE EVENING
The parlor is dark save for a red glow through the window.

Eugene sits fuming in a parlor chair. Eulalie knows he's there but starts up the stairs.

EUGENE
Where have you been?

She can't climb another stair.

EUGENE (CONT'D)
More important. Where is the deed?

EULALIE
I have the deed.

EUGENE
I should have taken it with me. Morphy needed the deed to release Marie.

EULALIE
Oh...

She makes a big effort to control herself. Eugene comes to support her.

EUGENE
Why didn't you let me handle it?

EULALIE
I thought I had all that was needed.

She loses control.

EUGENE
Where is the deed?

EULALIE
I have it now. I only had the bill of sale. I did not trust it was enough.

EUGENE
Nor me?

EULALIE
Mon cher, je suis trés désolé. The notary prepared a copy of the deed.

EUGENE
Too late. Now Marie must spend the night sequestered in the calaboose.

She breaks down and sobs. He embraces her.

EULALIE
My fault. I should have waited for your counsel. I should have...

EUGENE
Shuss...I will get it to Morphy at first light. She will be home soon.

CUT TO:
INT. EULALIE'S KITCHEN—DAY
The kitchen lacks sunlight, and gloom has set in.

Marie and Jean Pierre sit solemnly at the table.

MARIE
We should not just stay here. We could—

Eulalie enters and dismisses Jean Pierre. Marie reaches for him. Eulalie waves him out.

EULALIE
You must be tired. I've seen to clean bedding for you. We'll be fine without you today.

MARIE
Will you?

EULALIE
Yes. This will be settled soon.

Eulalie goes to Marie and sits her down. She brings a chair close.

EULALIE (CONT'D)
Marie, I must tell you. You are
my sister.

MARIE
What!! What nonsense!

Marie doesn't know what to make
of such a ridiculous statement.
She starts to put the dishes away.
Anything but listen to another word.

EULALIE
I've known since the first day we
met.

MARIE
Why would you say something
like that?

EULALIE
Your mother was my mother.

MARIE
Oh, I know why you say this.
Because I told you about her
green eyes.

EULALIE
Yes, and the way she said
goodbye.

MARIE
Avant que—

MARIE (CONT'D)
je vous manque.

EULALIE
je vous manque.

MARIE
(shaking her head)
No, I have heard others say that.

EULALIE
Me. I remember that of our
mother.

MARIE
(slowly)
And your children...Why tell me
this now? After all this time.

EULALIE
I didn't know how to tell you.
After awhile, it became a secret
I didn't dare share.

MARIE
That was a secret you should
have kept to yourself.

Eulalie follows Marie as she finds one
thing to do then another.

EULALIE
I wanted to tell you.

MARIE
I thought you were trying to
make me your friend. Ha! My
owner, my friend! Why do you
keep me your slave?

EULALIE
Only on paper. You're under my
care. You're so young.

MARIE
I was young when I came to
you. I'm a woman now.

EULALIE
You're still only eighteen. It is
my duty to protect you.

MARIE
From what?

EULALIE
Slavers! Other masters might
have taken advantage of you.

MARIE
You're a slaver.

EULALIE
People under my roof are under my protection. No one is bound. Some of my vendors pay off their debt to be freed.

MARIE
And me. Why can I not work to be free?

EULALIE
Free to do what?

MARIE
To be away from you.

EULALIE
I am your sister.

MARIE
You are my mistress. Why not let me earn my freedom?

EULALIE
You must not think of yourself as a slave. I do not.

MARIE
You have the papers. How else can I think of myself? I am a slave.

EULALIE
Only on paper.

MARIE
Paper you keep—

Eulalie stands abruptly.

EULALIE
Marie, I will not argue with you. Go to your room. You should rest.

MARIE
(bitterly)
Yes, mistress.

Marie storms out.

INT. PARLOR—DAY
Jean Pierre and Marie cross paths at the stairwell. He tries to catch Marie's hand.

EULALIE (O.S.)
Jean Pierre, venez, si'l vous plait!

MARIE
Our mistress calls.

Marie yanks open the side door to the courtyard and goes out.

INT. KITCHEN—DAY

EULALIE
(to Jean Pierre)
Have Suzanne prepare the breakfast.

CUT TO:
EXT. BEAUREGARD GARDEN—DAY
BLACK MEN, Beauregard's slaves in light muslin shirts and rough short broadcloth pants, work to maintain a courtyard of neatly trimmed hedges and rose bushes on trellises. Flowers and trees in every hue of green are all around.

A brick-paved path in the center of the garden leads to the Italianate style mansion.

CUT TO:
INT. BEAUREGARD HOME STUDY— MORNING
The room is filled with dark wood study furnishes. Ivory statues are on tables, mantels, and Beauregard's desk.

Beauregard and his attorney, F. H. SUMNER (40), a would-be imposing man, if not for his client, review court documents. Beauregard bangs his ivory handled cane on his desk to command another document.

BEAUREGARD
So, the wench will be
sequestered again?

SUMNER
Yes, as soon as the judge signs
the order. Eulalie de Mandeville
de Marigny. Psst. She thinks too
highly of herself. You spelled
the name like it sounds, yes?
With an H?

SUMNER
Yes, though that may not be to
your advantage.

BEAUREGARD
That was the name on the deed.

SUMNER
The deed? You said that she
had no deed. I cannot support-

BEAUREGARD
She does not have it. I pay you
enough to follow my orders, not
question them.

SUMNER
As your legal representative,
I cannot advise you—

BEAUREGARD
Stop telling me what you
cannot do.

Get me that girl back. The wench
Marie belongs to my dear, orphaned
niece.

SUMNER
Of course.

CUT TO:
EXT. EULALIE'S HOUSE—DAY
*The police carriage pulls away as Jean
Pierre looks on from the front door.
Eulalie puts on her gloves comes out of the
house. Her eyes follow the police carriage
down the road.*

EULALIE
Get our carriage.

JEAN PIERRE
Should we not wait for Monsieur
Eugene?

EULALIE
No. He is out collecting debts. I
have a debt to settle on my own.

JEAN PIERRE
I could find Monsieur Eugene.
I am sure he would want to be
with you.

EULALIE
Do you want Marie to spend
another night in jail?

JEAN PIERRE
No.

EULALIE
Then get the carriage.

JEAN PIERRE
Right away.

He leaves.

CUT TO:
EXT. THE BEAUREGARD MANSION—
DAY
*A large decorative B is in the center of an
arched iron gate.*

*Eulalie's carriage pulls up to the pathway
to the Beauregard courtyard and mansion.*

EULALIE
Jean Pierre, wait here.

Eulalie adjusts her gloves. She gets
down from the carriage on her own
and walks towards the house.

Beauregard steps out the door.
He's without his jacket but carries
his cane.

BEAUREGARD
(walking slowly)
Stop there.

EULALIE
We can speak as well here as
anywhere.

BEAUREGARD
Everything that needs to
be said will come from my
attorney.

EULALIE
You are ill-advised to think you
can win this case.

BEAUREGARD
My appeal will succeed this
time.

EULALIE
You know your claim is false. I
bought Marie—

BEAUREGARD
At an illegal Sheriff's sale!

EULALIE
Patrick sold her to me with a
notary. It was a public auction.

Jean Pierre dismounts the carriage
and stands at Eulalie's elbow.

BEAUREGARD
He had no right!

EULALIE
You have no right!

As the argument escalates, voices
rising, Beauregard's two gardeners
come from behind the house. One
man carries a shovel, the other a
rake.

BEAUREGARD
Your friend, Patrick, deceived
my sister.

Jean Pierre seeing the gardeners,
takes a stand between them and
Eulalie. The men dig around a tree.

EULALIE
You did not know Victoria well.

BEAUREGARD
Get out. You have no business
here.

EULALIE
Oh, but I do.

BEAUREGARD
You—

EULALIE
Shhhh. You have spies in your
house. Word of your treachery
has reached my ears. You think
your sister did not know Patrick
was a man of color? I am sure
she did not.

EULALIE
I am sure she did.

BEAUREGARD
You should not even be here. I
could have the courts lock you
up as well.

One of the gardeners starts to rake
leaves in closer.

Jean Pierre steps towards him. He's
bigger. The other gardener keeps his
distance.

EULALIE
What would you have done if
your sister's child did not look
white? Would you have done
away with her daughter the way
you did, Patrick?

BEAUREGARD
His death is not on my hands.

EULALIE
Aha! I did not mention his death. J'accuse.

BEAUREGARD
Enough with the French. We speak plain English now. You have no right to accuse me of anything.

EULALIE
We still have some civility in La Nouvelle Orléans.

BEAUREGARD
New Orleans will change!

EULALIE
Not before this case is done. And I will have plenty to say of your dealings with the English en francais et anglais.

BEAUREGARD
You have no proof.

EULALIE
Give up this suit, and I will say nothing of the debts you paid them.

BEAUREGARD
Your master—

EULALIE
I have no master. But if you are referring to Eugene, he is my partner. I know all his dealings and yours.

BEAUREGARD
Concubine of a usurer!

EULALIE
Murderer!

Jean Pierre gently touches her elbow.

BEAUREGARD
Try to prove it. No one in the court will take the word of a colored person over mine.

EULALIE
A free person of color is still allowed to speak. Do you want them to hear what I have to say?

BEAUREGARD
(to Jean Pierre)
Take your mistress away.

EULALIE
I have proof—

JEAN PIERRE
Madam Eulalie, we should go.

BEAUREGARD
Your slave has more reason than you.

EULALIE
He is not my slave.

BEAUREGARD
Whatever he is—

The gardeners move in closer. Jean Pierre takes Eulalie's elbow.

JEAN PIERRE
Madam, we should go.

He firmly escorts her to the carriage.

EULALIE
I will have justice.

BEAUREGARD
My attorney will hear of this!

EULALIE
So will mine!!

The carriage drives off.

Eulalie sits fuming inside the carriage.

CUT TO:
EXT. CABILDO—DAY
The massive door of the Calaboose SLAMS SHUT.

Marie follows Eugene down the steps. He turns and brings her to walk beside him. Stains on her blue dress and her pride.

INT. EULALIE'S KITCHEN—DAY—LATER
Marie, in a clean dress, sits across the table from Jean Pierre. She holds his hands with a fierce intensity.

> JEAN PIERRE
> I'm just glad to have you home.

> MARIE
> Not home.

> JEAN PIERRE
> Wherever you are is home to me.

Marie turns to look at him.

> MARIE
> Let's go away.

> JEAN PIERRE
> Where?

> MARIE
> Anywhere. West. I can't stay here.

> JEAN PIERRE
> It would be hard to travel without free papers. Talk to her.

Marie shakes her head in despair.

INT. EULALIE'S HOUSE— VARIOUS ROOMS
MONTAGE as Marie avoids Eulalie going and coming from one room to the next. If Marie is there when Eulalie comes in, Marie leaves. If Eulalie is in a room, Marie finds something else to do somewhere else. Their outfits change day to day.

END MONTAGE

INT. EULALIE'S PARLOR—EVENING
Eulalie paces around the table. She changes direction each time she goes to the kitchen door.

> EUGENE
> Let her be for a while. She has been through a lot.

> EULALIE
> So have I. Why can't she see I did it for her?

> EUGENE
> She is very unhappy.

> EULALIE
> Do you see me smiling? This back and forth has not been easy on me either. I just wanted us to be together. I wanted to protect her.

Eugene comes to her and guides her to a chair.

> EULALIE (CONT'D)
> Mon cher, what can I do? She won't even look at me. We used to talk all the time while we worked together. I miss my sister.

Eugene can only sit with her.

> EULALIE (CONT'D)
> Why does she not understand? She has seen what they do to slaves who have no protectors.

Eulalie pushes herself out of the chair and heads again towards the kitchen.

> EULALIE (CONT'D)
> I could make her come to me. She is my slave. Oh, Eugenie, I did not mean that. I didn't. What must I do? What must I do?

Marie enters the parlor.

MARIE
Madame Eulalie...

Eulalie goes to embrace Marie but is stopped by her hard glare.

EULALIE
Yes, Marie?

EUGENE
Come sit with us.

MARIE
May I speak with you?

EULALIE
Certainment.

EUGENE
You two should talk. Marie, come, take my chair.

EULALIE
That would be—

MARIE
No thank you, Monsieur Eugene.

EUGENE
Marie, you are at home now. No need for formalities.

MARIE
Merci, Monsieur. This is not my home. May I speak to the madam in private?

EUGENE
Hummm, I will leave you two.
    (He starts out)
Eulalie, hear her. You both must come to an understanding.

EULALIE
Of course.

Eugene guides Marie towards the chair but she refuses to sit. He goes to the kitchen. Eulalie rises to face her.

EULALIE (CONT'D)
You can say anything to me. I am your sister.

MARIE
My owner. We only have the same mother.

EULALIE
I have tried to make you understand. You are my slave in name only. It's a piece of paper. Please sit down.

MARIE
A piece of paper indeed.

Marie takes her time to sit in the chair.

MARIE (CONT'D)
When Mr. Leonard told me you had bought me. I was glad. I thought Miss Victoria would be happy it was you. I kept their secret too from Master Beauregard—

EULALIE
He is not your master.

MARIE
Miss Victoria was my mistress.

EULALIE
She was.

MARIE
It was a hard birthing for Miss Victoria. When the baby finally came and showed no signs of color, I could see Mr. Beauregard was relieved. He must have known.

EULALIE
Perhaps—

MARIE
I had no choice, but I was
happy to stay if Mr. Patrick
needed me there for the baby.
Mr. Patrick knew he wasn't
wanted. He and his baby were
going to live with his family
here in New Orleans. I thought
I was going to be fine living
with a free woman of color.
I would work hard to buy my
freedom. A free woman would
understand.

Eulalie shakes her head. She wants
to understand.

MARIE (CONT'D)
I was happy you let me talk
about my mother.

EULALIE
I too was happy to speak of
our—

MARIE
(cutting her off)
When you finally told me, just
before the second time, they
took me to jail, I began to hate
you.

Eulalie catches herself and leans on
the back of the chair.

MARIE (CONT'D)
Sisters! You kept me a slave.

EULALIE
Patrick needed the money. He
did not want you to be at the
mercy of the Beauregards.
From the first day I met you,
I wanted you to be with me. I
never wanted you to feel like a
slave. I treated you fairly, more
like an equal. I treated you like
a sister.

MARIE
You should have freed me,
gave me my free papers to
show me I was your equal. That
would have been fair. Dear
SISTER, you should have freed
me, done it for OUR mother.

EULALIE
I did it to protect you.

MARIE
You keep saying that. Who
were you protecting me from,
the Beauregards? I would be a
slave to whoever bought me?
It matters not if it were the
Beauregards or the Mandevilles
who would "protect" me. Did
you never know what it felt
like to belong to someone, not
yourself? Did our mother never
speak to you of such things?

Eulalie pulls herself up. Some of the
following conversations overlap as
they to make their points.

EULALIE
I was just a child. Would
you rather be with the
Beauregards?

MARIE
Of course not. But Miss Victoria
treated me more like a sister
than you ever did.

EULALIE
She was not your sister.

MARIE
When she died, it was like
my sister had died. I never
expected you to be anything
more than someone who would
at least understand the need to
be your own person, to belong
to no one.

EULALIE
And where would you have gone? Belonging to no one and no one to protect you? What trade did you know except to be a servant?

MARIE
I could sew. My mother taught me to sew and cook too.

EULALIE
But I taught you the finer skills of the needle and—

MARIE
Hah. You think you were more skilled than I. I had been praised for my needle work as well. I only pretended to let you "teach" me. It made you feel good. You never thought of me as your equal. You're free!

Eulalie sits defeated. Tears flow behind closed eyes.

SMASH CUT TO:
EXT. THE SKY—DAY—HIGH NOON
Blast of sunbeams.

Sunlight radiates over a light blue sky. A ball reaches its pinnacle and floats down.

EXT. THE MANDEVILLE PLANTATION—DAY
A white monstrosity of French Victorian opulence. The mansion has white and gold ring-topped colonnades on both stories.

Off the side of a circular dirt path driveway, a young golden-toned WOMAN (15) is playing with a white looking CHILD (4). The child's wavy brown curls bounce as she almost catches the ball. She giggles and runs after the rolling ball.

Sounds of a HORSE DRAWN CARRIAGE in motion.

TWO DARK BROWN MEN grab the woman. She's kicking and screaming.

The child drops the ball and rushes to her mother.

The woman's sparkling emerald green eyes are flooded with tears. She reaches out for the child.

WOMAN
Mon enfant!

CHILD
Maman.

WOMAN
Let me say goodbye.

CHILD
(crying)
Maman!

The child runs around, reaching out, trying to get close to her mother.

CHILD (CONT'D)
Non. Non! Non.

WOMAN
(to her captors)
Let me go. Let me hug my child.

A man's figure appears in the window of the mansion.

WOMAN (CONT'D)
Au revoir...

CHILD
Le dit. Avant que...Maman, le dit Avant que je vous manque... Avant que...

The child cries too hard to say more. The woman continues to struggle as the men drag her away.

CUT TO:
INT. MARIGNY DE MANDEVILLE DRAWING ROOM—DAY

A YOUNG WHITE WOMAN (23) in a long flowing floral dress comes to the door of the drawing room.

She holds out her hand to the man and pulls him away from the window.

CUT TO:
EXT. THE MANDEVILLE PLANTATION—DAY

The child cries on the lawn alone. An OLDER WHITE WOMAN (60s), richly dressed, takes the crying child by the hand.

A white wolf handle cane taps the window of the carriage. The carriage drives off.

The child looks back and tries to pull away.

> CHILD
> (sobbing)
> Avant que...avant que...

DISSOLVE TO:
INT. EULALIE'S PARLOR—EVENING

Eulalie turns to face Marie. Marie stands firm.

> EULALIE
> Did you never feel like...

> MARIE
> Like your sister. No. I felt closer to you when I did not know. I was grateful.

> EULALIE
> At least not fearful.

CUT TO:
INT. COURTROOM—CABILDO DAY

Three judges sit behind a long heavy wood carved bench. JUSTICE MARTIN, the presiding judge, with his smooth forehead and rolls of vertical wrinkles below the eyes, sits in the center. Clerks sit at desks on either side of the judge's bench.

Morphy approaches the podium centered in front of the bench.

Beauregard sits alone in the row behind his new young attorney, MARVIN ARGOTE (28), looking silly in his attorney's white wig. Two of his older familiars greet and take seats in the row behind him. Eugene and another gentleman sit in seats behind Morphy's table. A common-looking MAN TAKING NOTES (25) sits apart from them.

Morphy opens his portfolio on the podium.

> MORPHY
> Honorable judges of the court...
> Alonzo Morphy, representing the defendant Eulalie Mandeville of New Orleans. In as much as the lower first district court and the court of appeals of the City of New Orleans have found in favor of the defendant, Eulalie Mandeville, we pray this final appeal to the Supreme Court of the State of Louisiana, which was granted on the fifteenth day of November 1820, by Judge Joshua Lewis, will disavow any further action by the plaintiff, Manuel Beauregard against my client and finally, put to rest his unjust and unlawful claims to the negro slave, Marie Louise.

As he adjusts his papers, the screen splits.

On the RIGHT screen, Morphy and the court are in session.

On the LEFT screen, a montage of Patrick's trials and tribulations.

MORPHY IN COURT ON THE RIGHT

> MORPHY (CONT'D)
> Document A and Document B en francais, presents the decision of the father, Patrick Leonard with family and friends after deliberation in a meeting in New Orleans, on May 25, 1816. It was their opinion that due to the state of the affairs of the said Minor Adelaide, it was necessary for the father to dispatch all of, including a negro wench named Marie Louise, the property of the said minor. It was thereafter directed that after the usual publication, the slave should be sold.

The documents before the court show the order for the advertisement for the sale of said slave in the city of New Orleans. Thereafter, the plaintiff, Eulalie Mandeville purchased said slave in good faith. It was not for my client to know whether the proceedings before the Judge of probates were regular or irregular. The law will protect her in her title.

As Morphy returns to his seat, two of the judges look over to the plaintiff's table. Argote nods with a polite smile.

PATRICK'S LIFE MONTAGE SEQUENCE ON THE LEFT

A man's fingers sliding a ring on a smaller, lighter hand.

Patrick and Victoria kiss and embrace on the deck of a ship. Their shadow is cast in the moonlight on the water.

WAVES CRASH against the hull of a ship.

Victoria is sweating and groaning.

Patrick and Beauregard hover outside the door where SCREAMS are heard. They avoid eye contact.

A baby cries.

Patrick holds a tiny bundle wrapped in a white blanket. Strands of light brown hair frame the pale INFANT. Beauregard looks on.

SILENCE

Victoria lies lifeless in bed. Marie stands stricken in the corner of the room.

Blood curling scream reverberates.

> PATRICK (V.O.)
> Noooooooooooooooooooo!

A gavel bangs.

END SPLIT SCREEN SEQUENCE

CUT TO:
INT. EULALIE'S PARLOR—NIGHT
A globe encased candle on the table gives a dim light to the room.

Eulalie blows out fire from a long stick.

> EULALIE
> You have grown up. So, what now?

> MARIE
> Give me my freedom, my sister.

Eulalie sits in her chair and closes her eyes.

A RUSH OF WIND. A THICK SWELL OF DARK MISSISSIPPI GREEN WAVES splash on a pier. A STEAMBOAT WHISTLE echoes in the distance.

CUT TO:
SPLIT SCREEN
Court in session ON THE RIGHT
Patrick montage ON THE LEFT

INT. COURTROOM—DAY

ARGOTE
The court records show that
the minor Adelaide Leonard
and the father, Patrick Leonard
were residents of Baton Rouge.

Argote leaves the podium. As Argote
takes his seat, Morphy takes his portfolio to the podium.

MORPHY
That sale was judged to be
good and valid in law and that
the plaintiff had no right to the
said slave Marie Louise.

Before your honors, Document C,
is the deed of sale executed by
Christoval de Armas, Notary Public in
this City under a decree of the Judge
of Probates for which there was no
appeal.

PATRICK'S LIFE MONTAGE
CONTINUED ON THE LEFT

*Beauregard knocks on a door. He is
received in.*

Visuals of time passing.

*Patrick knocks on the same door. He is
turned away.*

This repeats at different doors.

*Slashes paint over and destroys an
unfinished painting clearly in his colorful
textured style.*

*Patrick with his FAMILY in white to
dark golden hues.*

FAMILY V.O
(voices distorted)
Come! Venez! This is your home.

Come back to New Orleans. We
will take care of you and your
baby.

Eulalie joins the Family.

The FAMILY and Eulalie surround
Patrick in a dream-like embrace.

Marie hands over the baby to an
OLDER WOMAN. She takes the baby
inside the circle.

Patrick signing papers.

Eulalie signing papers.

Eulalie gently lays her hand on
Patrick.

END SPLIT SCREEN SEQUENCE

CUT TO:
INT. EULALIE PARLOR—DAY
*Eulalie takes a deep breath before opening
her eyes.*

EULALIE
You have always been free to
come and go as you please.

MARIE
As you please. Where have I
ever gone where you did not
know? Where have I gone
without your bidding?

EULALIE
Je ne sais pas! I do not know.
You could have gone—

MARIE
Where? To the market? To the
docks to check out what's new
in fabrics?

EULALIE
I did not hold you captive. I was
glad Jean Pierre was there to
look after you. It was impossible
to do anything else. Je t'aime,
ma souer.

Marie begins to pace about the
room. Eulalie follows her every move.

MARIE
Ma souer, if you want to show
me your love, set me free.

**CUT TO:
SPLIT SCREEN**

ON THE RIGHT INT. COURTROOM—DAY
*Beauregard's two gentlemen friends have
left the courtroom.*

MORPHY
That sale was judged to be
good and valid in law and that
the plaintiff had no right to
the said slave Marie Louise.
The court further stated that
in the interest of the child,
the child of Victoria Leonard,
deceased, and Patrick Leonard,
now recently deceased, have
been neglected, it is due to the
fault of her tutor, Manuel J.
Beauregard. In as much as the
appellant "humbly" believes
the judgement of the district
court and court of appeals to
be erroneous, we, most humbly
pray that the Honorable
Supreme Court of this State will
concur with the lower courts
and once more find in favor of
my client, Eulalie Mandeville.

ON THE LEFT
*Beauregard, MUFFLED VOICE, talks
to men in the shadows.*

*Eulalie and Marie (earlier scene repeated)
watch Patrick walking away from Eulalie's
house. Men in the shadows.*

*A corner pub lights flicker off. Patrick lies
dead on the side of the road.*

END SPLIT SCREEN SEQUENCE

CUT TO: INT. EULALIE'S PARLOR—DAY
EULALIE
Jean Pierre was charged to look
after you wherever you went.

MARIE
We have been nowhere where
you or Monsieur Eugene has
not bade us to go.

EULALIE
It is true. You have been discreet.

MARIE
Discreet. I have had enough of
secrets. I have been too much
back and forth and back and
forth in the jails and barracks of
New Orleans.

Eulalie rises from her chair and walks
towards Marie.

EULALIE
Pardonne-moi!

MARIE
Not pardon. Freedom.

EULALIE
Je suis très désolé. I don't know
what to do.

MARIE
Sister, you always know what to
do. Do what is right. Do it for
our mother.

Eulalie takes Marie's hands in hers.
Marie lets her.

EULALIE

I will do it for you. My father sold our mother. That can't be undone. I hope I have not waited too late to make amends. Please, forgive me.

Eulalie kisses Marie's hands.

She goes to the door and calls out.

EULALIE (CONT'D)
Eugene! Eugene, venez.
(to Marie)
Get Jean Pierre. We have family business to discuss!

Marie runs to the door but comes back to embrace Eulalie.

Eulalie hugs her tight before pushing her towards the kitchen.

CUT TO:
INT. EULALIE'S PARLOR—DAY—LATER

The Armoire is converted into a desk with the slat between the doors, and the drawers pulled out. Eulalie dips the quill in the inkwell and continues writing. A florid but steady script:

"She is entitled to be free."

CUT TO:
COURTROOM. INTERIOR—DAY

Thereafter, your honors, the documents show Eulalie Mandeville femme de libre de couleur demuran en cette ville in presente et acceptitan—

One of the judges clears his throat.

JUSTICE MARTIN
Mr. Morphy, we do not all speak French.

MORPHY

I beg your pardon your honors. The documents show Mademoiselle Eulalie de Mandeville, a free woman of color, presented herself and accepted the offer to purchase the slave in question by order of a certified Court. All was done and signed by the notary Christoval Armas on May 25, 1815.

The associate judges look over to Sumner. Morphy returns to his table. Sumner rises.

MORPHY (CONT'D)
Yes, your honor, the father of the child did reside in Baton Rouge. He lived there with his wife until her death. However, his home was here, with his family in New Orleans, where he had planned to return with his child. It was only his death that prevented him from doing so.

Argote looks down at his papers.

Eugene watches as all the judges turn to Beauregard.

Morphy's confidence fades as the judges turn to him with blank stares.

Justice Martin bangs his gavel.

CUT TO:
EXT. LA CABILDO—DAY

Eugene shakes hands with the gentleman who sat beside him in the courtroom. The doors to the Cabildo are closed. He paces under the portico.

MUSIC of brass instruments and a violin. MUSICIANS and VENDORS attract some passersby while others saunter past.

INT. NOTARY OFFICE—DAY

Eulalie and Marie sit on a bench in the small notary's outer office. There is an empty reception desk and chair. Marie opens and closes her tapestry bag. She is continually relieved to find the next thing she seeks, a comb, a shawl, etc.

> EULALIE
> It should not be much longer.

> MARIE
> Even if the case is decided in your favor. Jean Pierre and I will leave.

> EULALIE
> I know.

Eulalie reaches in her small bag and begins to occupy herself embroidering a handkerchief.

> MARIE
> What is he doing that takes so long?

> EULALIE
> He has notarized my letter granting you freedom. Now he must make sure there is no lien.

> MARIE
> Lien?

> EULALIE
> He's making sure I don't owe anybody anything. Checking court records. We must trust the notary abides by the decision of record and give us the papers.

> MARIE
> I do not trust the outcome of this latest appeal.

> EULALIE
> Nor do I.

Marie gets up and looks out the window on the road below.

> MARIE
> This is why we're here, yes? Just in case.

> EULALIE
> Yes.

> MARIE
> We would leave without it.

> EULALIE
> I know. But no need to.

Eulalie puts down her needlework and joins Marie at the window.

People, carriages, and wagons seem to drag on.

> EULALIE (CONT'D)
> This is taking a long time.

> MARIE
> What if the sheriff comes for me?

Marie puts her ear to the notary's door.

> EULALIE
> Come away from there.

Marie plops down beside her.

> EULALIE (CONT'D)
> I think I can now sense when they're coming long before the knock on the door. Still, I wish he would hurry so we can be on our way.

She goes back to her needlework.

CUT TO:
EXT. THE CABILDO—DAY

Eugene paces under the portico. He stops whenever someone comes out of the courthouse. He checks the time on his watch. Still no Morphy.

Jean Pierre joins him. He carries a small canvas bag.

JEAN PIERRE
Monsieur Eugene.

EUGENE
Jean Pierre! Court was adjourned over an hour ago. They already have all the documents. How can they not uphold our cause?

Morphy comes outside with his head hung down.

EUGENE (CONT'D)
What?

MORPHY
It is bad news.

EUGENE
This I can see. What happened? I thought you said it would be a simple matter... upholding the decision of the lower courts.

MORPHY
It should have been. But Beauregard's attorneys...

EUGENE
Were better than ours.

MORPHY
They knew the judges better.

EUGENE
Beauregard.

MORPHY
I think the chief justice knew Beauregard personally. It was as if they were in one accord from the beginning.

EUGENE
Is that fair?

MORPHY
Justice is not always fair.

JEAN PIERRE
You call this justice?

EUGENE
There should have been nothing but justice. What now?

Morphy just shakes his head.

EUGENE (CONT'D)
Can you protest? Can we appeal?

MORPHY
No. The State Supreme Court was the final appeal for both sides.

He rips the wig from his head.

EUGENE
What will I tell Eulalie?

MORPHY
Tell her the truth. Tell her that justice was not served in this case. Our cause was just. Tell Marie she must flee.

EUGENE
What?

MORPHY
"You must flee." The message given to me is not from me.

EUGENE
What are you saying? Are speaking in riddles?

MORPHY
I am an honorable member of the Court. I am not saying something the courts would not allow.

EUGENE
Morphy, as my friend, what do you advise?

MORPHY
Marie must flee. You must get the message to her as soon as possible.

EUGENE
How soon? Surely not today. Will they send the sheriff?

MORPHY
Maybe. I don't know.

EUGENE
What nonsense.

MORPHY
I did not expect this.

EUGENE
(to Jean Pierre)
Are you ready?

JEAN PIERRE
For our just-in-case plan, if all did not go well?

EUGENE
Yes.

JEAN PIERRE
I was hoping we could leave with good news to take on our journey.

EUGENE
Have they returned home?

JEAN PIERRE
No. I am to meet Madam Eulalie and Marie at the office of the notary.

MORPHY
You must hurry.

EUGENE
Go there and tell them—

Morphy inches away. He puts his wig back on and covers his ears.

MORPHY
I must go. Excuse me.

Morphy rushes off.

EUGENE
Excused, not pardoned. Jean Pierre, our attorney has failed us. You must hurry to deliver the message.

JEAN PIERRE
"Marie must flee"?

EUGENE
It is not such a strange message. Hurry.

JEAN PIERRE
I will.

Jean Pierre turns to go. Eugene stops him.

EUGENE
You have everything you need in your bag?

JEAN PIERRE
We had plans to start our journey after she got her free papers. We were going to the market first.

EUGENE
No, go to them now. I will get some provisions for your travel.

JEAN PIERRE
Sir, pardon my saying so, but you know nothing of shopping.

EUGENE
I will do my best.

JEAN PIERRE
Thank you. I am sure that will be good enough.

EUGENE
We will meet at the apartment. They will not think to look there, I'm sure.

JEAN PIERRE
Who can be sure of anything?

EUGENE
Hurry, let's not take any chances.

They go off in different directions.

INT. NOTARY OFFICE—DAY
Marie listens at the Notary's door.

MARIE
It is quiet in there. Is there another exit?

EULALIE
I think not. You worry too much. You will soon be free, on paper and indeed.

Eulalie puts away her needlework.

MARIE
Free to be my own person.

EULALIE
You have always been your own person. And you will still be my sister.

Marie comes to sit beside her.

MARIE
Wherever I am, I will still be your sister. A very grateful sister. Thank you.

EULALIE
Do not thank me. It is something I should have done long ago. Will you forgive me for my selfishness?

MARIE
Oui, ma souer. And will you forgive me for my unkind words?

EULALIE
It was I who was unkind. Holding on to you. Holding you captive.

They sit in silence, holding hands.

EULALIE (CONT'D)
My children are grown and gone. And now you.

MARIE
They write. And so will I.

EULALIE
Only if it is safe.

MARIE
Do you think they will ever return from Cuba?

EULALIE
The laws keep changing. Even a free person of color has no certainty of their future. It may be better if they never returned. I am content enough knowing they are well and free. They have always found a way to assure me of that. They are good boys.

MARIE
Good men.

EULALIE
Yes, they have proven themselves to be admirable men.

MARIE
Much like their mother. Very determined.

EULALIE
And like their father. Very resourceful. Though sometimes too trusting.

MARIE
It is good they have made good choices and can afford to be independent.

EULALIE
Oh. You will be fine.

Eulalie takes out a reticule from her bag and hands it to Marie.

EULALIE (CONT'D)
For you. You can be independent too.

Marie feels the weight of it.

EULALIE (CONT'D)
You have earned it. For the work you have done for our business. Your skills have been much appreciated.

Marie unloosens the drawstring and looks inside.

MARIE
Ma souer! It is full. Merci, merci.

We will make a grand new start.

EULALIE
Where do you think you will go?

MARIE
Maybe north.

Eulalie in a sudden panic, grabs Marie by the shoulders.

EULALIE
Not just across the lake. You must go much farther North or West.

MARIE
First, you can't part me. Now you want me far away?

She pulls in and knots the strings of the reticule. She puts the small purse in her bag. She changes her mind and puts it inside her dress.

MARIE (CONT'D)
Jean Pierre could not stand cold for long.

EULALIE
This waiting is starting to make me nervous.

MARIE
We have talked of California.

EULALIE
West. Yes, far away from les Americaines.

MARIE
It is far. But we will find a way to be together again.

EULALIE
California. I would rather never see you again than have you someplace...not safe.

MARIE
They speak Spanish in California.

EULALIE
Its good we have had to speak so many languages here. French then Spanish, more French and now so much English. Aak, it's hard on the tongue.

MARIE
And so many more languages on the docks. Some even harder. Guten tag.

EULALIE
Ciao.

They laugh hard enough to remember the moment.

EULALIE (CONT'D)
You should probably speak
Spanish there all the time.

MARIE
Yes, we both can speak that
well enough. We may slip
into our French when we find
ourselves alone.

EULALIE
Try to blend in wherever you
decide to go.

Eulalie goes to the notary's door
and knocks. No answer. She turns
the knob. It's locked. She goes to
the window. Stares, puzzled at the
locked door.

EULALIE (CONT'D)
Where is Jean Pierre?

Marie joins her at the window and
looks out.

MARIE
He is to meet us here with our
belongings. We will not travel
with much. Eugene has already
given him his freedom. Did you
know?

EULALIE
He only told me yesterday when
he told me he had arranged
this meeting with the notary
for us. Almost two years ago—
he did this and never told me.
Maybe it had...

MARIE
Jean Pierre asked him not
to. He thought it better if you
thought of us working together
as equals. As /

EULALIE
As slaves no more.
          (shaking her head)

That's so like him, mon cher
Eugene, to honor the trust of
those he holds dear.

EXT. STREET—DAY—LATER
*Few carriages pass. More wagons are
empty going the opposite direction than
going towards the more densely populated
buildings.*

*Jean Pierre jumps off a wagon. Waves
goodbye to the driver and runs down
the road.*

**EXT. WINDOW OUTSIDE NOTARY
OFFICE—DAY**
*Marie smiles inside the window frame.
She waves.*

INT. MARKET—DAY—LATER
*Vendors are packing up the remainder of
their produce and goods for the day.*

*Eugene hurries from vendor to vendor,
gathering fruits, nuts, and dried meats.*

CUT TO:
INT. NOTARY OFFICE—DAY

JEAN PIERRE
We must go.

EULALIE
Pour quoi? What has
happened?

MARIE
We must go now?

JEAN PIERRE
Yes, now. It is not good news I
bring.

EULALIE
Eugene sent you? The decision
is final? It was not in our favor?

JEAN PIERRE
I'm afraid not. Your attorney
gave us a message.

MARIE
Tell me.

JEAN PIERRE
Marie must flee.

MARIE
That's it?

JEAN PIERRE
In haste.

EULALIE
Yes, but, Marie, you must not
go without your papers.

She raps impatiently at the door.

EULALIE (CONT'D)
(whispering)
We must not wait for Señor
Armas to get the news. Jean
Pierre, delay anyone who even
looks like they may be bringing
bad news.

JEAN PIERRE
All right, but we must hurry.

EULALIE
(still whispering)
Yes, yes. Let us go in with a
calm visage so as not to alarm
him.

As Eulalie knocks, the door opens.
Armas is coming out with the document in his hand.

EXT. COURTYARD—EVENING
*A marble nymph TINKLES in the
small fountain in the corner of Eulalie's
and Eugene's courtyard. They sit in a
wicker chaise enjoying the shade of the
magnolia tree.*

EUGENE
I will miss those two.

EULALIE
I miss this now. Especially my
sister.

EUGENE
You like saying that.

EULALIE
My sister. Yes, I wish I had said
it more.

EUGENE
Now she too is free.

EULALIE
I am a colored woman, no
different than any of my slaves
or merchant vendors. My
mother's blood makes me a
mulatto.

EUGENE
You are a free woman of color.

EULALIE
How much longer will that
matter in the eyes of the law?
No matter the color of my skin.
I can not deny my blood.

EUGENE
Red, the same as mine.

EULALIE
But we are not the same, cheri.
I will never be free like you are
free.

EUGENE
Without the Tignon, no one
would even guess.

EULALIE
En Nouvelle Orléans? Everyone
knows me here.

BEAT

EUGENE
Where do you think they are now?

EULALIE
Not far enough. A new life.
Where the color of their skin will
matter less.
(She laughs)
They almost refused a
marriage certificate.

EUGENE
Time. You insisted, of course.

EULALIE
Oui. She let me have that last
command.

They both laugh.

EUGENE
They should be far away by
now.

EULALIE
Oui, très loin.

EUGENE
Very far. All is well.

EULALIE
C'est bon.

BEAT.

EULALIE (CONT'D)
The magnolias are in bloom
again.

EUGENE
All is in bloom again.

BEAT.

EUGENE (CONT'D)
Will you be all right without
Marie?

EULALIE
She will be safe.

EUGENE
In California?

EULALIE
Better there than here.

The outside knocker is heard.

EUGENE
Juan Carlos will get it.

EULALIE
Ahh. What a pleasant breeze.

EUGENE
Not too hot?

EULALIE
It's a nice warmth.

Knocking is louder, heavier.

EULALIE (CONT'D)
That's the sheriff.

EUGENE
Such rude knocking.

EULALIE
Very rude.

EUGENE
What shall we tell them?

EULALIE
A lie.

EUGENE
Agreed.

Eugene pulls Eulalie up from the
chaise. They kiss.

He watches her casual stroll across
the courtyard.

He has to laugh seeing her change
her gait to rush in the house
pretending to be agitated.

EULALIE (V.O.)
Did you not get my message?
She has gone!

CUT TO:
EXT. ROAD—DAY

Marie and Jean Pierre sit in the back of an open wagon, their backs to the couple in the buckboard seat. They hold hands, leaning against their meagre possessions and provisions.

The city of New Orleans fades in the distance.

THE END

ROSEMARY FRISINOTOOHEY

Writing was always a major joy in my life—early on, it was poetry and stories—but my first career was in radio news. I was on the air in Baltimore, San Jose, Boston, New York, and Washington, DC. As my four children came along, I shifted to part-time work on radio, but the writing went on in the background. I finished one novel, started a second, and finally turned to plays. My first script was produced off-off-broadway.

The kids grew, and I went back to a five-day-a-week shift on the air in Washington, but a hit-and-run accident at four a.m. turned my life around. As I recuperated, my husband and I decided I should devote all my time to playwriting. I did so and finished my first full-length play. Since then, I've had more than 300 productions of my work in forty states and on four continents. In London, my comedy was Audience Favorite in the British Theatre Challenge. In New York, I won the Next Generation Playwriting Contest, and in 2019 I tied as Gold Medal Winner in the Italian American Theatre of Chicago's First Playwright Competition. I've also won the Baltimore Playwrights Festival three times and the Oglebay Towngate Theatre Competition twice. Nine of my comedies are published and three of my dramas have been honored with artist grants from the Maryland State Arts Council. I'm a member of the Dramatists Guild of America and SAG/AFTRA. There's more at www. frisinotoohey.com

Lady Volcano is one of two screenplays I've written. I created the main character after seeing a news story about a woman who, because of a simple misunderstanding, held police at bay for days. My heroine is like many of my friends...she's vital, intelligent, talented, and nowhere near ready to be sidelined just because she's over sixty-five.

Lady Volcano

A SCREENPLAY BY ROSEMARY FRISINOTOOHEY

FADE IN:
EXT. ROUGH COUNTRY—DAY

Steep hills, plunging canyons, no sign of civilization.

The ROAR of a motorcycle, distant, then louder.

The bike crests the top of a hill and tears down into the valley. We catch a glimpse of boots, jackets, helmets.

It roars up another hill, down the other side, and races along a dirt road, pulling up in front of a squat, beat-up building, next to half a dozen other motorcycles.

It's a bar, but it's too cool to have a sign.

The biker—seen only from the rear—is short. She pulls off the helmet and a mass of brown hair streaked with gray tumbles to her shoulders. She pushes open the grungy door with a bang.

INT. BIKER BAR—DAY

Guys on bar stools, some young, some old, turn toward her, nodding with respect as she strides toward the back where the biggest, raunchiest biker greets her with a grin.

> **RAUNCHY BIKER**
> Nettie, baby. How the hell are you?

NETTIE smiles up at him. It's not a young face but it's full of life and a ballsy sort of confidence.

> **NETTIE**
> Les, you old son of a bitch.

And just as they high-five it...

INT. BEDROOM—NIGHT

Nettie awakens from her dream and sits up in bed. She looks at her husband, who's snoring. And then she lies down, eyes wide open.

INT. SCHOOL PRINCIPAL'S OFFICE—DAY

Nettie faces the smiling female PRINCIPAL, 40s.

> **PRINCIPAL**
> Sorry, Nettie, the answer is no.

> **NETTIE**
> I was hoping for another year.
> I love teaching the volcano unit.

PRINCIPAL
And I hate to lose a good
science teacher, but it's the
county rule. Sixty-four, and
you're out the door. Hey, that's
a poem, isn't it?

She erupts in laughter. Nettie smiles
politely.

PRINCIPAL (CONT'D)
Think of all the things you'll
have time for now that you're
retired.

NETTIE
Sure. Cleaning out the
basement...

PRINCIPAL
Oh, Nettie, you're such a riot!

INT. KITCHEN—DAY
*Nettie lugs a laundry basket. Phone
RINGS. She picks up.*

NETTIE
Hello.

INTERCUT—KITCHEN/MISSY'S KITCHEN
*At her neighbor MISSY's house, the
NOISE from the kids' video games is
deafening.*

MISSY
Nettie, it's your pesky neighbor
again. My sitter's got the flu.
Can you watch the boys? It's so
lucky for me you're retired now!

NETTIE
Yes, isn't it? Sure, I can do it.

Nettie smiles wanly and hangs up. A
car horn BEEPS outside.

EXT. FRONT YARD
*GWEN, 30s, is pulling folding chairs out
of her car.*

GWEN
Hi, Aunt Nettie. Thought I'd
drop these off for the family
reunion. It's so sweet of you to
hold it here again. Ta-ta, got to
run.

Gwen drives off as MRS. J, 70s,
approaches with a clipboard.

MRS. J
You need to sign my petition,
Nettie. Those new people on
Sutter went and painted their
shutters kelly green.

NETTIE
That's a pretty shade.

MRS. J
What? Exterior trim must be
in the original colonial colors.
It says so right there in the
covenants.

She tries to hand Nettie her clipboard. Phone RINGS inside.

NETTIE
I...think I better get that.

MRS. J
All right. Catch you later.

Mrs. J trots off as Nettie goes inside.
She stops at her door and looks down
the street. All the houses look exactly
alike.

**INT. INTERCUT—
KITCHEN/POLLTAKER'S CUBICLE**
She grabs the phone.

NETTIE
Hello.

POLLTAKER
We're conducting a survey on
email use. May I ask you a few
questions?

                    NETTIE
Okay.

                    POLLTAKER
First, I have to qualify you.
Stop me when you hear your
age. Are you between 18 and
29? 30 and 39? 40 and 49?
50 and 59? 60 and above?

                    NETTIE
That's me.

                    POLLTAKER
Thanks for your time, ma'am.

                    NETTIE
Aren't you going to ask me
anything?

                    POLLTAKER
Sorry, but we're only interested in
the opinions of people under 60.

CLICK of the receiver. SOUND of the
doorbell.

            INT. LIVING ROOM
*Nettie opens the door. Missy's boys enter
without looking up, lost in their hand-held
games.*

        INT. BASEMENT—NIGHT
*A model train runs around an elaborate
layout as ROY follows its every move.
Nettie comes down holding travel
brochures.*
                    NETTIE
Roy...

                    ROY
Yeah, hon.

He's pleasant, but he's fixed on his
trains.

                    NETTIE
What if we took a trip to Italy?

                    ROY
Italy? Mmm. Kind of far, isn't it?

                    NETTIE
But wouldn't it be great to
roam around over there for
two or three weeks? See Mount
Vesuvius...

                    ROY
Well, you can go for a couple of
weeks, you're retired.

                    NETTIE
But you have vacation time
coming.

                    ROY
Yeah, but what if something
happened, and I needed those
days?

                    NETTIE
A week then. Couldn't we just—

Phone RINGS upstairs.

                    NETTIE (CONT'D)
I'll get it.

                INT. KITCHEN

                    NETTIE
Hello...yes, he's here.
(calls downstairs)

                    NETTIE (CONT'D)
It's for you. Klamath Falls.

Roy comes upstairs.

                    ROY
Is it my brother?

She shakes her head no and hands
him the phone.

                    ROY (CONT'D)
Roy Lowery here...what?...

He sags against the wall and turns to
Nettie.

ROY (CONT'D)
It's Ray...a heart attack.

NETTIE
Is he...?

Roy nods and turns back to the phone.

ROY
I was telling my wife...yes, of course. I'll fly out tomorrow.

Nettie opens a drawer and stuffs the travel brochures inside.

EXT. AIRPORT—DAY

Nettie pulls up to the curb. Roy jumps out of the car and grabs his bag.

She watches him rush into the terminal and then drives off.

INT. HOME OFFICE—DAY

Nettie, at her computer, is connecting with a NURSE at a nursing home via Zoom.

INTERCUT—HOME OFFICE/NURSE'S STATION AT A NURSING HOME

NETTIE
Hey, Jean. How are you?

JEAN
Good, Ms. Lowery. He's waiting for you. Have you set up in a minute.

INT. NURSING HOME CUBICLE—DAY

SOUND of a respirator. PHIL, a very old man, lies in bed. A Christmas tree sits on a table, and a wreath hangs at the window. The nurse wheels in a computer.

INTERCUT—HOME OFFICE/NURSING HOME CUBICLE—DAY

NETTIE
How's my favorite uncle?

PHIL
It's a nonstop party, babe. How goes it with you?

NETTIE
Same here. I see you got the tree.

PHIL
It's a beaut. The nurses all sang "Jingle Bells" when it came.

NETTIE
Wish I'd been there.

PHIL
Me too, doll. Would you believe some guy down the hall complained? He said it didn't make sense to sing Christmas songs in June.

NETTIE
I hope you gave him a piece of your mind, Uncle Phil.

PHIL
Can't do that, don't have much of a mind left. Anyway, he's just one more unhappy person in the world. Which reminds me, have you done something special for my favorite niece today?

NETTIE
Not yet, but I'm working on it.

PHIL
No excuses, darlin'. Remember, if you don't make yourself happy, who will? And you can take that to the bank.

INT. BASEMENT—DAY

Nettie comes downstairs into the storage area. She looks at boxes and cabinets and then takes down a dusty cardboard box from a shelf.

Inside are faded blue ribbons and trophies. She pulls them out one by one: "Top Target Shooter," "Best Junior Sailor," "Senior Year Marching Band."

She opens an old album and sees herself as a laughing, happy kid, swinging off a rope at the end of a pier, holding a BB-gun, playing snare drum in the band, grinning at the wheel of a boat.

Phone RINGS upstairs and she runs to get it.

INTERCUT—KITCHEN/EXT. GAS STATION

Roy's on his cell. Under his arm is a big box.

NETTIE
How did it go, Roy?

ROY
Okay. His friends had a lot of nice things to say about him.

NETTIE
What time does your plane get in?

ROY
Hon...I don't want to fly back. I know this sounds crazy but ...Ray hated planes and I just can't bring him back that way, his ashes, I mean.

NETTIE
You mean you're going to drive all the way from Oregon?

ROY
Yeah. I want to make a few stops.

NETTIE
What kind of stops?

ROY
Once upon a time, he and I were going to go cross country and see the sights. I thought I'd do that and leave a little bit of him here and there.

NETTIE
Is that legal?

ROY
I'll be careful. Look, I...I just need to do this. Okay?

NETTIE
Sure, Roy. Okay.

ROY
See you in a couple of weeks.

EXT. GAS STATION—DAY

Roy pockets his phone. A young garage MECHANIC approaches.

MECHANIC
She's all ready.

Sitting there is a big old hog of a motorcycle.

ROY
Think she'll make it back East?

The mechanic shrugs.

MECHANIC
Everything's a crapshoot, mister.

Roy puts the box in a bag on the back of the bike.

MECHANIC
You...ride bikes a lot?

It's a fair question. Roy does not remotely look like a biker.

ROY
Think I don't know how?

MECHANIC
Easy, man. Just askin'.

Roy gets on, revs it up, and the motor ROARS to life.

The mechanic shouts above the noise and points.

> MECHANIC (CONT'D)
> Kickstand.

Roy kicks it up. The mechanic watches as Roy roars away.

EXT. BARREN FIELD—FOGGY NIGHT

A soldier with a rifle, World War II vintage, walks a patrol, and executes a sharp turn. It's Nettie.

As she strides in the other direction, a MAN emerges from the fog. She levels her rifle at him.

> NETTIE
> Who goes there?

> MAN (PIERRE)
> It is I, Pierre LeVeaux.

> NETTIE
> Pierre?

> PIERRE
> Annette?

They rush toward one another.

> PIERRE
> Annette, ma petite choufleur!

And just as he takes her in his arms...

INT. BEDROOM—NIGHT

Nettie wakes up from her dream. The clock says 4:20.

Restless, she gets up, puts on her turquoise chenille bathrobe and heads to the basement.

INT. BASEMENT—NIGHT

She pokes around and finally unearths a long, dusty box. She opens it, takes out a

BB-gun and holds it fondly.

She loads it, aims at an old calendar, but misses.

She tries again and does better.

LATER INT. BASEMENT—DAY

Sunshine pours in the window, and Nettie, still in her bathrobe, has set up a mini rifle range.

She aims and fires, hitting a can which falls onto a dish strainer which knocks loose potatoes which roll down a drainboard into a bowl on a kitchen scale.

That triggers the on switch of a music box and little penguins skate around a plastic lake.

Nettie grins and records her hit on a chart.

SOUND of the doorbell.

INT. LIVING ROOM—DAY

She peeks through the curtain and sees Mrs. J, determinedly RINGING the bell. Nettie tiptoes away from the door.

EXT. FRONT PORCH—DAY

But nosey Mrs. J has spotted her through the curtains. Miffed, the woman marches off.

INT. BASEMENT—DAY

It's a new day. And the rifle range is even more elaborate.

Nettie, again in her bathrobe, prepares to shoot.

EXT. SIDE YARD—CONTINUOUS

Missy's boys (unseen by Nettie) watch through the window.

INT. BASEMENT

Nettie fires. The BB ricochets off a can, hits a bottle, and spills a liquid into a papier-mache volcano which causes a bubbly substance to "erupt" down the side. She pumps the air.

EXT. SIDE YARD—CONTINUOUS

The boys, still unseen by her, scamper away.

MONTAGE—NETTIE IS DOING WHAT SHE WANTS

INT. KITCHEN—DAY

She's eating a big bowl of ice cream, but then she stops, looking critically at the plain, white walls.

Now she's painting the walls apple red, looking happy.

INT. LIVING ROOM—NIGHT

She brings in boxes, opens them, and pulls out Christmas lights, a wreath, and a giant inflatable Santa.

EXT. FRONT PORCH—NIGHT

She's just finished stringing Christmas lights along the edge of the porch. She steps back and admires her work.

END MONTAGE

EXT. STREET—DAY

Mrs. J and Missy stroll down the street.

MRS J
I know she was in there. And she refused to open that door. As if I had the black plague or something.

MISSY
My boys saw her shooting a gun.

MRS. J
Good gracious!

MISSY
Jeremy said it looked like she was making some kind of a bomb.

MRS. J
I swear I don't know what's come over that woman.

Missy looks startled and stops in her tracks.

MRS. J (CONT'D)
What's the matter?

Speechless, Missy points to Nettie's house.

A Christmas wreath hangs on the door, lights along the porch are blinking and Santa is on the grass next to the flowers.

MISSY
Oh, Lord, we better call somebody.

INT. LIVING ROOM—NIGHT

Nettie, in her comfy bathrobe, her trusty BB-gun at her side is eating popcorn and watching an old Western on TV.

ON TV: EXT. OUT WEST—DAY

A wagon train is under attack. And it doesn't look good.

The hero is trying to hold off the Indians. He takes an arrow in his arm and grimaces in pain.

A woman leaps to his side. It's Nettie.

NETTIE
Wade, you're hurt!

WADE
Don't worry about me, babe.

She rips a piece off her petticoat and expertly bandages his wound as more arrows rain down.

Then she grabs his gun, shoots, and the Indian chief falls spectacularly off his horse.

She fires a few more shots but the tide has turned, and the Indians gallop away.

WADE (CONT'D)
You're one hell of a shot, Nettie!

The MUSIC swells and Wade is about to manfully conquer his pain and take her in his arms when there's a KNOCK at the door.

EXT. FRONT PORCH—CONTINUOUS
Police Officer BUCKLEY, very young, KNOCKS again LOUD.

> BUCKLEY
> Anybody home?

INT. LIVING ROOM—NIGHT
Nettie instinctively picks up her BB-gun and peeks through the curtains at her bay window.

> NETTIE
> What do you want?

EXT. FRONT PORCH—NIGHT

> BUCKLEY
> Open up, ma'am. Officer Buckley, Northeastern District.

INT. LIVING ROOM—NIGHT

> NETTIE
> I'm busy. I don't want to open up.

With her BB-gun she moves the curtains back.

EXT. FRONT PORCH—NIGHT
Buckley spots the gun barrel and goes into red alert mode. He backs up, pulling his own gun.

> BUCKLEY
> Put down your weapon and come out with your hands up.

INT. LIVING ROOM—NIGHT

> NETTIE
> What? For pete's sake, it's only a—

EXT. FRONT PORCH—NIGHT

> BUCKLEY
> I repeat...lay down that firearm and come out with your hands up.

INT. LIVING ROOM—NIGHT

> NETTIE
> I'm telling you, it's just a—

She accidentally pulls the trigger. The gun goes off with a THUNK and there's the SOUND of breaking glass.

EXT. FRONT YARD—NIGHT
To the newbie Buckley, it sounds like a real gunshot. Startled, he falls backwards off the porch.

INT. LIVING ROOM—NIGHT— CONTINUOUS
The BB has punctured a small window on the side of the bay. Nettie studies the broken pane and the glass on the floor.

> NETTIE
> Oh, nuts.

EXT. FRONT YARD—NIGHT
Buckley crawls across the yard as if he were under attack.

INT. LIVING ROOM—NIGHT

> NETTIE
> Now, what's Roy going to say when he sees that?

Nettie puts the gun down and heads to the kitchen.

EXT. FRONT YARD—NIGHT
Buckley grabs his radio.

BUCKLEY (ON RADIO)
Unit twenty-six, ten-thirteen!
Officer in need of assistance!
914 Hawthorn! I repeat,
ten-thirteen!

INT. KITCHEN—NIGHT—CONTINUOUS
Nettie fishes around inside the broom closet.

EXT. FRONT YARD—NIGHT

BUCKLEY (ON RADIO)
Shots fired! 914 Hawthorn.
Suspect inside. I repeat,
ten-thirteen!

EXT. STREETS—NIGHT
SIRENS WAIL as police cars race through the streets, lights flashing.

INT. KITCHEN—NIGHT
Nettie emerges from the closet with a broom and a dustpan.

EXT. STREET OUT FRONT—NIGHT
SIRENS WAILING, police cars squeal to a halt outside.

They aim their bright lights at the front door just as...

INT. LIVING ROOM—NIGHT
Nettie opens the door, holding a broom and dustpan.

She blinks, seeing police cars and flashing lights, and quickly shuts the door.

EXT. STREET OUT FRONT—NIGHT— CONTINUOUS

OFFICER #1
Is that the suspect?

OFFICER #2
Was she holding a gun or what?

INT. LIVING ROOM—NIGHT
Startled and breathless, Nettie leans against the inside of her door, not really believing what has just happened.

SEVERAL DAYS LATER

EXT. STREET OUT FRONT—DAY
SOUND of music: The song "Second Hand Rose."

And it's LOUD.

The Christmas wreath and the giant Santa are still there, but police crime scene tape is now strung across the street.

Competing with the MUSIC is the SOUND of police walkie-talkies.

Cops crouch behind cars. Neighbors peer from their windows.

Down the street, TV mobile units are parked every which way. Near one of them, a TV reporter finishes her makeup.

REPORTER (GERRY)
Ready, Bob?

Bob nods, hoists a camera to his shoulder, and they head to a spot on the street. The reporter flashes a megawatt smile.

GERRY (CONT'D)
Hi, there, Officer. Can we get that music turned down, please?

The cop obliges, the music fades, Gerry takes a breath and launches into her standup.

GERRY (CONT'D)
Gerry Shane here for WXVR-TV-real-life-real-people-news. We're just down the street from the home of Annette Lowery, the woman who's held police at bay now for four whole days. Her neighbors say she's always been a very caring person.

INT. NEIGHBOR ANNIE'S LIVING ROOM—DAY

ANNIE, 70s, sits with her husband, George.

ANNIE
When I was sick, Nettie brought George his dinner for two straight weeks. Even baked him a pie. Banana cream wasn't it, George?

George nods solemnly.

INT. MISSY'S KITCHEN—DAY

The boys race around nonstop.

MISSY
When my sitter can't make it, Nettie is the first person I call.

EXT. STREET—DAY

GERRY
But now they say they're puzzled by her bizarre behavior.

INT. ANNIE'S LIVING ROOM—DAY

ANNIE
Santa Claus on the lawn in June? What on earth does it mean?

George shakes his head, trying to grapple with this mystery.

INT. MISSY'S KITCHEN—DAY

MISSY
You put your trash out next to somebody you figure you know them. But we hear she's got guns, maybe even explosives. Who would have thought it?

(to the kids)

Put that down, Jason!

EXT. STREET—DAY

A TV NEWSMAN (JIM) with a mike, is doing his standup nearby.

NEWSMAN (JIM)
Police have blocked off the street and that means her neighbors are virtual prisoners inside their own homes.

INT. NEIGHBOR MARIE'S DINING ROOM—DAY

MARIE, late 40s, is completely unglued.

MARIE
My daughter's wedding is this week and we don't even know if we can get to the church! Could a mother's heart be broken anymore?

DIANE, 20s, the bride-to-be, sits next to her, weeping.

EXT. STREET—DAY

NEWSMAN (JIM)
And the big question is, why would a responsible citizen choose to defy the entire police department?

GERRY
What transformed this motherly homemaker, a retired schoolteacher, into a gun-toting criminal?

INT. ANNIE'S LIVING ROOM—DAY

ANNIE
George thinks it's all those cellphones. Radio waves flying all over the place, what's it doing to people's brains?

A solemn nod from George.

INT. MARIE'S DINING ROOM—DAY

MARIE
Eighteen years we've lived here and she does this the week of my daughter's wedding! How vicious can this woman be?

A fresh gush of tears from the bride-to-be.

EXT. STREET—DAY

NEWSMAN (JIM)
Four days into this standoff and police have set up a command post at Glenville Elementary.

INT. COMMAND CENTER—DAY

Officers talk on phones, work at computers. Officer RUGGIERO, Lieutenant HOAG, and Chief JACKSON stare at a map on the wall.

JACKSON
No way to get a clear shot?

HOAG
She's got curtains at every window, Chief.

RUGGIERO
Looks like she's the Martha Stewart of barricade subjects, Chief.

Jackson gives Ruggiero a sharp look.

HOAG
The state police psychologist keeps calling her, but she won't talk.

INT. KITCHEN—DAY

Phone RINGS. Nettie, in her trusty turquoise bathrobe picks up the phone and immediately hangs up without listening.

INT. COMMAND CENTER—DAY HOAG

The doc thinks maybe the family can get through to her. That's her niece over there talking to Weams.

Hoag nods toward Sergeant WEAMS, 40s, talking with Gwen.

GWEN
I can hardly believe it, Sergeant. Aunt Nettie wouldn't hurt a fly.

WEAMS
Right. Let's head on over there.

EXT. STREET—DAY

Weams and Gwen walk toward the house.

WEAMS
Have you contacted her son?

GWEN
We don't know where Tommy is. All I know is he's somewhere in Mexico.

EXT. BEACH—DAY

It's deserted except for a run-down beach house.

TOMMY, late 30s, pries the cap off a beer bottle, pitches it onto a mound of caps behind him, and drinks his breakfast.

EXT. STREET—DAY

WEAMS
And what about the husband?

GWEN
Uncle Roy went to Klamath Falls to pick up his brother's ashes.

WEAMS
Ashes?

GWEN
Like when somebody dies and
they get cremated? It gives me
the creeps just talking about
it but it seems like nowadays
everybody wants to end up in
little boxes instead of great big
boxes.

Weams & Gwen navigate the wires
from the TV mobile units.

WEAMS
Drove all the way out there, did
he?

GWEN
No, he flew out, but he's driving
back because Ray didn't like
airplanes.

WEAMS
Who's Ray?

GWEN
His brother. The one who died.

Weams gives Gwen a look as he
takes all this in.

EXT. DESERTED HIGHWAY—DAY
*The motorcycle sits on the shoulder as
Roy peers at a map.*

GWEN (V.O.)
Uncle Roy said he just didn't
feel right flying back with the
ashes.

Roy folds the map, pats the box
behind him and rides off.

EXT. STREET—DAY
*The reporters are wrapping up their
liveshots.*

GERRY
Four long days and there's no
end in sight to this standoff.

NEWSMAN (JIM)
Last night police fired tear gas
into the house, but somehow this
woman managed to stay inside.

WEAMS
(calling)
Kowalski! Get these people out
of here!

NEWSMAN (JIM)
This is Jim Van Buren for WYNC...

GERRY
Gerry Shane here for WXVR-
TV-real-life real people—

WEAMS
Now, Kowalski!

KOWALSKI
(to reporters)

Folks, could you please...

JIM
Just doing my job, Sergeant.

Kowalski ushers Gerry and Jim away
as Weams leads Gwen to a camera
set up in the street.

GWEN
You mean I'll be on television?

WEAMS
It's only closed circuit.

GWEN
I don't know if I can do that!

INT. HOME OFFICE—DAY
*Nettie's at her computer, calling Uncle
Phil's nursing home.*

INTERCUT—HOME OFFICE/NURSE'S STATION AT THE NURSING HOME

NETTIE
Can he talk to me?

NURSE
Sure, Ms. Lowery, give me a minute.

INTERCUT—HOME OFFICE/NURSING HOME CUBICLE—DAY

PHIL
Hi, darlin'. What's up?

NETTIE
I was just trying to make myself happy, Uncle Phil, but there's kind of a problem. And the police—

PHIL
Police? What's going on?

INT. INTERCUT—COMMISSIONER'S OFFICE/COMMAND CENTER—DAY

The COMMISSIONER is on the phone with Chief Jackson.

COMMISSIONER
We've got to end this mess, Sam. The mayor wants to announce his run for governor, but he can't do that because the TVs keep leading with Annie Oakley.

JACKSON
Commissioner, the sharpshooter's all set up, but he can't get a clear shot. We need more time.

COMMISSIONER
You haven't got more time. Call me when I can give the man some good news. And it better be soon.

The commissioner hangs up with a bang.

INT. COMMAND CENTER—DAY
Jackson makes a face at the phone.

OFFICER #2
Can you pick up on line five, Lieutenant?

HOAG
Lieutenant Hoag here. Who's this?

INTERCUT—COMMAND CENTER/ MARIE'S DINING ROOM—DAY

MARIE
My name is Marie Falco. I live in Cape Cod with the perfect landscaping we just paid beaucoup bucks for. Lieutenant, our daughter is getting married and tonight's the rehearsal dinner.

HOAG
Ms. Falco, I don't have time to—

MARIE
You've got time for her over there with the Santa Claus in the yard. My taxes pay your salary too!

HOAG
Ma'am, you've got five minutes.

MARIE
What? She gets four days of the sitting and the waiting, me, you're giving five whole minutes? Where is the justice here?

HOAG
The clock is ticking, Ms. Falco. What can I do for you?

MARIE
All right, all right. Four
bridesmaids, the matron
of honor, who's six months
pregnant, five groomsmen, my
mother, who's eighty-three and
the groom's parents who came
all the way from Eau Claire,
Wisconsin, all these people
are supposed to come to my
house. But they can't get here
because you won't let anybody
down the street!

HOAG
We are dealing with a disturbed
individual. For her safety—

MARIE
The safety of miss high and
mighty over there does not
particularly concern me right
now!

INT. INTERCUT—HOME OFFICE/
NURSING HOME CUBICLE—DAY

PHIL
It must be a misunderstanding.
Tell them you want to be left
alone.

NETTIE
But what if they come in here
with their guns blazing?

PHIL
They can't do that, Annette.
Police can't just bust in on you
unless they've got reason to
believe you've got stolen goods.

NETTIE
They fired tear gas in here last
night.

PHIL
I'm telling you, every man's
house or woman's house in this

case is his or her castle. That's
the law going back to 1604. You
just have to go talk to them.

EXT. STREET—DAY

WEAMS
(on a bullhorn)
Mrs. Lowery, please turn on
channel seven on your TV.
We're trying to communicate
with you. Channel seven. Please
turn on—

Nettie's front door opens a crack,
something is placed outside, and
quickly the door closes.

Police crouch near their cars, peering at it.

INT. INTERCUT—COMMAND CENTER/
MARIE'S DINING ROOM

MARIE
My brother is commander of
the American Legion, and he
says we can have the dinner at
their hall. It'll only be Styrofoam
plates instead of my mother's
de Havilland china, but if we
can get there—

HOAG
Ma'am, you cannot drive down
the street.

MARIE
But we could put the minivan in
neutral and drift—

HOAG
There will be no drifting, no
driving, no movement of any
kind. Your street is locked down.

An officer rushes up to Hoag.

OFFICER
Lieutenant, she put something outside the door!

HOAG
Ms. Falco, I have to go.

He hangs up.

MARIE
What? Did you just hang up on me?

EXT. STREET—DAY

WEAMS (ON HIS RADIO)
Can you tell what it is?

RUGGIERO (V.O.)
Looks like a boombox, Sergeant.

WEAMS (ON HIS RADIO)
You think it might be wired or—

NETTIE (O.S.)
Hello, out there.

Her voice echoes down the street.

INT. LIVING ROOM—DAY
Nettie sits on her sofa in front of the TV, holding a mike.

NETTIE
Can anybody hear me?

EXT. STREET—DAY
Weams steps before the closed-circuit TV camera.

INTERCUT—STREET/LIVING ROOM

WEAMS
We hear you, Mrs. Lowery. Have you got something to say?

NETTIE
Yes, I do. Can you all just go away?

WEAMS
Be happy to do that, ma'am, but first I've got to ask you a few questions.

NETTIE
To whom am I speaking?

WEAMS
Sergeant Chuck Weams of the Parkersburg Police. To begin with, are you holding a weapon?

NETTIE
If I'm in my own house, Sergeant, what business is it of yours, whether I'm holding a weapon or not?

WEAMS
Mrs. Lowery, I'm just trying to assess the level of danger.

NETTIE
There is no danger. I'm sitting in my living room. Why you people are out there, I have no idea.

WEAMS
Now, we both know this whole thing started because you fired a gun at a duly authorized officer of the Parkersburg Police.

NETTIE
It was an accident. Besides, I didn't hit him.

WEAMS
No, but you scared him half to death.

NETTIE
It's only a BB-gun.

WEAMS
Ma'am, until we can verify that, we're not leaving. Besides, it's

against the law to fire a BB-gun in this city.

NETTIE
Inside my own house?

WEAMS
Yes, ma'am. Your house is inside city limits.

NETTIE
Why was he pounding on my door in the first place?

WEAMS
Your neighbors called and complained about the Santa Claus.

NETTIE
That's silly.

WEAMS
It's your neighborhood, not mine. There are restrictions on when you can display seasonal décor. They're also worried about your safety.

NETTIE
For heaven's sake, why?

WEAMS
Conduct which runs counter to an individual's established mode of behavior could indicate a problem.

NETTIE
Let me get this straight. I hung a Christmas wreath on my door and put Santa Claus on the lawn, and that's why the whole police force is camped out there?

WEAMS
It's just the tactical unit, ma'am.

NETTIE
And what does the tactical unit do?

WEAMS
Tactical covers high-risk operations, hostage situations, home invasions, and the like.

NETTIE
Then you're wasting your time. There are no hostages here, and my home has not been invaded. Now, why don't you all just go away?

WEAMS
Like I said, until you put that gun down, nobody's going nowhere.

NETTIE
That's a double negative, Sergeant.

WEAMS
Mrs. Lowery, we will not abandon our position until we have determined you are not in danger.

NETTIE
I never was in danger.

WEAMS
We also have to make certain that you will not endanger any member of the community. Now, if you want to end this thing, all you have to do is come out, unarmed, with your hands up.

NETTIE
That's ridiculous! I'm not a bank robber!

WEAMS
Nobody said you were. We just
don't want anybody to get hurt.
We're very concerned for your
welfare.

NETTIE
Is that why you fired tear gas in
here last night?

WEAMS
You want to tell me how you
could stay in there with the tear
gas going off?

NETTIE
I put lotion on my skin and
stuck my head in the freezer.
The cold and the lotion prevent
the skin's pores from absorbing
the gas.

WEAMS
I heard you taught science.

NETTIE
For twenty-seven years, Sergeant.

INT. CITY HALL—DAY
*Downtown, the MAYOR is wrapping up
a news conference.*

MAYOR
...and that's the linchpin for the
light rail system. Any questions?

REPORTER 1
Your honor, what about
that barricade situation on
Hawthorn Circle? It's been
going on now for four days.

MAYOR
The police have it under control.

REPORTER 1
A lot of people might disagree
with you on that. The residents
of twenty-three houses have
had their lives completely
turned upside down over there.

MAYOR
I know it's frustrating, but it's a
very delicate situation.

REPORTER 2
How many cops does it take
to deal with one woman in her
sixties?

MAYOR
You've got to understand. The
subject in question is armed.

REPORTER 3
What's the next step? You
going to call out the National
Guard?

A few chuckles among members of
the press.

MAYOR
Some of you may find this
amusing but I assure you
there's real danger there.

REPORTER 4
What's she got? A pea shooter?

More laughter.

REPORTER 2
I heard it was a slingshot.

REPORTER 4
Hey, it could be water balloons.

The room erupts in laughter as the
mayor does a slow burn.

INTERCUT—STREET/LIVING ROOM—DAY

NETTIE
What about that music you've been blaring at me day and night?

WEAMS
We're trying to maintain a friendly atmosphere. Your niece said "Second Hand Rose" is your favorite song.

NETTIE
Well, it used to be. But who in their right mind wants to hear it twenty-four hours a day? Why can't you just leave me alone?

WEAMS
As I said, we'll be glad to do that once we've ascertained you are not a threat to yourself or anybody else. Now...can you ...put your weapon...down?

NETTIE
Of course, I can put it down.

Weams takes a deep breath.

WEAMS
So. Have you done that? Can you verify that you are no longer holding a gun?

Tense looks from the police, the TV reporters, the neighbors. Everyone's frozen, hanging on her answer.

NETTIE
No, I cannot verify that.

WEAMS
Mrs. Lowery, you just said you were going to lay that gun down.

NETTIE
I did not.

WEAMS
Okay, I know you're tired. You're having trouble making up your mind.

NETTIE
I am having no such thing.

WEAMS
Ma'am, you just said—

NETTIE
You asked me if I could put the gun down, and I said I could. That means I am capable of putting it down; there is nothing preventing me from putting it down. The thing is...I don't want to! Would you like to know why?

WEAMS
If you'd like to tell me.

NETTIE
Sergeant, I am in my own house, which happens to be my castle in the eyes of the law, and there is no reason on earth for me to alter my behavior to please you or anybody else. If I want to sit here until doomsday holding this gun, that is my prerogative. Are we clear?

WEAMS
Yes, ma'am. We are clear.

KOWALSKI
Sergeant, her brother's here.

WEAMS
(to Kowalski)
Send him over.

WEAMS (CONT'D)
(to Nettie)
Okay, Mrs. Lowery, we are at an impasse. And I know you know what the word means. Is there anything you want?

NETTIE
Such as what?

WEAMS
Do you have a list of demands?

NETTIE
No, I don't have...wait! Ice cream. I'm all out of ice cream.

WEAMS
Any particular flavor?

NETTIE
How about a butterscotch sundae?

WEAMS
All right. You come out with your hands up, and I'll get you the best butterscotch sundae you ever had.

NETTIE
That's not fair!

WEAMS
We are in negotiations. You make a demand, and I counter with—

NETTIE
Oh, keep your old butterscotch sundae!

HAROLD, 60s, approaches Weams. He looks confused. It's pretty much his natural state.

WEAMS
Thanks for coming. Harold, is it?

HAROLD
That's me. What should I do?

WEAMS
Just talk to your sister, nice and calm. Try and get her to come out of the house.
(to Nettie)
Mrs. Lowery, your brother's here.

NETTIE
Has he got a butterscotch sundae?

Weams steps away, Harold steps up to the plate and waves.

HAROLD
Hi, Nettie. Alice said to tell you, you need to cut back that juniper bush next to the porch. She says it looked awful overgrown last night on the eleven o'clock news.

Nettie rolls her eyes in exasperation.

NETTIE
Tell her I'll get right on it.

EXT. MARIE'S BACKYARD—DAY
Marie, the angry mother of the bride-to-be, and her overweight hubby, JOE, are stealthily moving from one bush to the other in their yard headed toward the back fence. Joe's got a ladder.

JOE
Did you call Mrs. Amrhein?

MARIE
All I'm going to do is walk through her yard, Joe. Is that a crime?

JOE
I don't know what's a crime anymore, Marie.

EXT. STREET OUT FRONT—DAY
Nettie's door opens a crack.

The police now see a thin slice of her turquoise robe.

RUGGIERO (ON HIS RADIO)
She's at the door!

INTERCUT—STREET/LIVING
ROOM—CONTINUOUS

Nettie stands just inside, one eye on the TV, holding her mike.

HAROLD
Alice wants to know if this whole thing is about our Christmas card?

NETTIE
What Christmas card?

HAROLD
Last year's. The one you didn't get because we ran out of stamps for my side of the family. Anyway, Alice said I ought to give you our holiday greetings in person.

He pulls a Santa Claus hat from his pocket and puts it on.

HAROLD
She wanted me to put the whole suit on, but I said it was too hot.

WEAMS (ON HIS RADIO)
Can we get a shot?

INT. NEIGHBOR'S UPSTAIRS
BEDROOM—DAY

A TACTICAL OFFICER focuses a high-powered rifle on the turquoise sliver of Nettie's robe at the door. He talks with command on his radio.

TACTICAL OFFICER
It ain't great.

HOAG (V.O.)
It may be all we're gonna get.

INT. NEIGHBOR MRS. AMRHEIN'S
DINING ROOM—DAY

MRS. A, 80s, sits at her window talking on the phone.

MRS. A
It's all so crazy, Myrtle.

Suddenly, she sees Marie's head pop up over her back fence.

MRS. A (CONT'D)
Now, somebody's on top of my fence.

EXT. MARIE'S BACKYARD—
DAY—CONTINUOUS

Joe's ladder leans against the stockade fence. Marie is nearly at the top, but she's terrified.

MARIE
Oh, Joe, the ground is so far away.

JOE
I tried to warn you, Marie.

She climbs down the ladder in tears.

MARIE
All I want to do is give our daughter a wedding. Is that too much to ask?

INT. MRS. A'S DINING ROOM—DAY

MRS. A
I swear to god, Myrtle, I just saw somebody's head over my back fence.

EXT. MARIE'S BACKYARD—DAY

JOE
Look, I'll climb up, swing over, and then you just follow me, okay?

Joe starts up the ladder.

EXT. STREET OUT FRONT—DAY

Harold, Santa hat on his head, launches with gusto into...

                    HAROLD
          Holidays, jolly days, me-oh-my-
          oh-golly days.

**INT. MRS. A'S DINING ROOM—
CONTINUOUS**

Mrs. Amrhein sees Joe straddling her back fence.

                    MRS. A
          Now, somebody else is out
          there!

EXT. STREET OUT FRONT

                    HAROLD
          What's our wish for you this
          season? We don't even need a
          reason.

EXT. MARIE'S BACKYARD

Joe is perched on top of Mrs. A's fence but he looks queasy.

                    MARIE
          Are you all right, Joe?

INT. NEIGHBOR'S UPSTAIRS BEDROOM

The sharpshooter fixes Nettie's robe in his gun-sights.

EXT. STREET OUT FRONT

                    HAROLD
          We just want to say, merry
          Christmas, happy new year...
          and have a nice day!

INT. MRS. A'S DINING ROOM

Mrs. Amrhein sees Joe fall off the fence.

                    MRS. A
          Good Lord, Myrtle! He fell into
          my yard!

EXT. STREET OUT FRONT

Ear-splitting SCREAMS from Marie echo from the backyard.

                    WEAMS
          What the hell was that?

Nettie disappears inside and slams the door.

                    WEAMS
          Go check it out, Kowalski.

Cops scurry to the back of the Falco house.

Harold takes off his Santa hat and scratches his head.

                    HAROLD
          I didn't think it was all that bad.

                    WEAMS (ON RADIO)
          What have you got back there?

                    KOWALSKI (V.O. ON RADIO)
          Need medical assistance,
          Sergeant. A man fell off the
          fence.

                    WEAMS (ON RADIO)
          What was he doing on top the
          fence?

                    KOWALSKI (V.O. ON RADIO)
          Haven't determined that.

                    WEAMS (ON RADIO)
          All right. We'll get the EMT's
          and an ambo back there.
                    (to himself)
          Of all the goddamned, idiotic
          pain in the butt...

INT. 1ST FLOOR HALL—DAY

Nettie looks frustrated as she slowly walks down the hall.

She passes her sewing room, where a wire dressmaker's form on a stand catches her eye. She stops and studies it.

EXT. LONELY ROAD ALONG A BEACH—DAY

A beat-up cab comes to a stop. BRAD, 20s, gets out. He crosses the sand toward Tommy's beach house.

Tommy is passed out on the porch with a beer in his hand.

> BRAD
> Excuse me, sir, are you Thomas Lowery?

Tommy opens one eye.

> BRAD (CONT'D)
> I'm from WYNC-TV, and we—

> TOMMY
> Don't have a TV.

> BRAD
> Sir, we're willing to pay all your expenses including roundtrip—

> TOMMY
> Go 'way.

Tommy turns away. But Brad comes at him from the other side.

> BRAD
> Roundtrip airfare, first-class accommodations, all meals included. All you have to do is tell us—

> TOMMY
> You want to...fly me somewhere?

> BRAD
> To Parkersburg. WYNC wants the exclusive rights to your story.

> TOMMY
> My story?

> BRAD
> Yessir. WYNC wants to hear from a member of the Lowery family.

There's a faint glimmer in Tommy's half-opened eyes.

> TOMMY
> Any particular reason?

> BRAD
> I can tell you all about it on the way to the airport.

INT. LUXURY CAR IN TRAFFIC—DAY

RICHARD and JOAN are mid-50s. He wears nice threads; she's decked out in gold jewelry, the real thing.

He drives, talking on his cell.

> RICHARD
> He flushed the retainer down the john? Well, try to fit him in Thursday...just re-schedule the Vogel twins...so check with the lab and get back to me.

Richard pockets his phone.

> RICHARD (CONT'D)
> I cannot believe that girl has a college degree.

> JOAN
> Calm down, Richard. You're just upset because we're missing our cruise.

> RICHARD
> Damn right, I'm upset. We're losing, every dime we paid for it, Joan.

> JOAN
> Next time, buy the travel insurance.

RICHARD
I don't even know why we're going to Nettie's house.

JOAN
The police want the family to talk to her. Maybe we can help.

RICHARD
Well, where in the hell is Roy?

JOAN
Gwen said he's taking his dead brother's ashes to the Grand Canyon.

Richard gives her a look.

JOAN (CONT'D)
Don't look at me. This is your family.

INT. MOTEL LOBBY—DAY
Way out west, a motel CLERK is watching a TV story on Nettie.

ANNOUNCER
...four days now with no end in sight. Tear gas was fired into her living room but somehow she managed to avoid...

Roy enters, holding his big box.

ROY
Can I get a room?

The clerk kills the TV sound and hands Roy a card to fill out.

CLERK
One night?

Roy nods, writing as he cradles the box.

CLERK (CONT'D)
Want to put that on the floor?

ROY
No thanks, we're fine.

Roy pats the box affectionately.

ROY (CONT'D)
Would you happen to know if there's a bowling alley around here?

CLERK
Sure. There's one about ten, twelve miles up the road. Canyon shopping center.

ROY
Thanks.

INT. NETTIE'S BEDROOM—DAY
Nettie has changed into black slacks and a dark top. She stuffs a backpack with a few clothes and zips it up.

Now she studies herself in the mirror. But she's not happy.

Then she snaps her fingers. Another idea. She rummages in a drawer and pulls out a short silver blonde wig. She fusses with it, puts it on, and checks the mirror. Success. She looks different.

EXT. STREET—DAY
Kowalski leads Richard and Joan to Weams.

KOWALSKI
Mr. and Mrs. Gerber, Sergeant.

WEAMS
Thanks for coming, folks. You're her cousins, right? You two were about to go on a cruise?

JOAN
Oh, yes, we have a standing order with the travel agent. Europe in the fall, the Bahamas in the spring, every year.

RICHARD
Every year but this year.

WEAMS
You're a dentist?

RICHARD
Orthodontist. Speaking of
which, Sergeant, you know
it wouldn't take much to get
those two teeth you got on
the side there lined up.

JOAN
And since we're not on the
cruise, Richard has openings
this week.

WEAMS
Thanks, I'll...think about it.

INT. LIVING ROOM—DAY

*Nettie wraps her robe around the wire
dressmaker's form and carefully moves it
near the window, arranging the curtains
to hide the "head." She steps back and
admires her handiwork.*

*Richard and Joan are now on the TV. Joan
waves cheerfully.*

JOAN (ON TV)
Yoohoo! Richard and Joan are
here! On the street where you
live!

RICHARD (ON TV)
Yeah, we canceled our cruise
to be here, Nettie. But don't let
that worry you.

Nettie pulls money out of a drawer
slips on the backpack, looks around
one last time and heads for the
basement.

INT. BASEMENT—DAY

*She pulls a chair over to a window, gets
up on it, opens the window, and peeks out.
The coast is clear.*

*She puts her backpack outside, boosts
herself through the window and closes it
behind her.*

EXT. STREET—DAY
JOAN
And the cruise wear was so
attractive this year, I over-
bought! Imagine!

Joan erupts into peals of laughter.
She elbows Richard.

JOAN (CONT'D)
(whispering)
Come on, Richard, laugh.

Richard forces a laugh.

RICHARD
(through his teeth)
We sound like idiots.

EXT. YARD—DAY

*Nettie creeps along her fence to an overgrown
bush. Hidden by the bush, she pulls a couple
of loose slats from the fence and inches
through. Now she's in Mrs. A's yard.*

*She steals along Mrs. A's fence toward the
street.*

**EXT. STREET IN FRONT OF
MRS. A'S HOUSE—DAY**

*Mrs. A stands with some neighbors.
They're watching ATTENDANTS put
Joe into an ambulance.*

MRS. A
This used to be such a quiet
neighborhood.

A neighbor nods sagely.

JOE
Can somebody go check on
my wife?

ATTENDANT
Has she broken both legs too?

Everybody watches the ambulance pull away. As it does, Nettie slips onto the street and heads in the opposite direction.

She turns at the next corner. Coming toward her is a kid with a skateboard.

> NETTIE
> What'll you take for that?

> KID
> Huh?

> NETTIE
> The skateboard.

She pulls out three twenties and hands them to him.

> NETTIE (CONT'D)
> Deal?

> KID
> Ahh...yeah.

He pockets the cash. Nettie, a little clumsy, balances herself on the skateboard with her backpack and heads off, leaving her neighborhood behind.

EXT. STREET OUT FRONT—DAY

> JOAN
> Now, Nettie, don't you give our trip a second thought. We are here for you.

> WEAMS (ON RADIO)
> She's standing at the window. If he's got a shot, let's take it. We might not get another chance.

INT. NEIGHBOR'S UPSTAIRS BEDROOM—DAY

The tactical officer is struggling to get Nettie—actually, it's Nettie's robe—in the crosshairs.

EXT. STREET—DAY

> JOAN
> Now, Nettie, we know something must be bothering you. Let me tell you about my friend Carla. She was married to a urologist who left her after she gave him the best twenty-six years of her life. The woman was a total wreck, but then she took this course.
> (to Richard)
> What's it called?

> RICHARD
> Anxiety reduction through vowel intonation.

> JOAN
> Yes, so now when she gets upset, she sits and intones the vowels. We were at Lord and Taylor's last week when something triggered her hostility. Well, she sat right down in the middle of men's furnishings started her vowels and you could just see the anxiety flowing away from her body.

> RICHARD
> Show her, Joan.

Joan sits cross-legged on the street, elbows together, with her hands outstretched on either side of her face. She takes a deep breath.

> JOAN
> (chanting)
> A...A...A...A...

INT. MAYOR'S OFFICE—DAY

The mayor looks worried. He's with a CONSULTANT in a pricey designer suit.

CONSULTANT
You know, mister mayor,
ending that standoff is not your
problem. It's how you end it
that matters.

MAYOR
But people are tired. They want
action.

CONSULTANT
What kind of action?

MAYOR
We've got a sharpshooter set up.

CONSULTANT
Great. So, some cop with a
high-powered rifle takes out
a little old lady in a bathrobe.
How's that going to play on the
eleven o'clock news?

The mayor frowns and drums his
fingers on his desk. Then he reaches
for the phone.

INT. NEIGHBOR'S UPSTAIRS
BEDROOM—DAY
*The tactical officer has shifted. Nettie's
robe is clearly framed in his sights.*

EXT. STREET—DAY

JOAN
Of course, when she's really
stressed, she moves on to the
next two vowels.

(chanting)
EEE-III...EEE-III...EEE-III...

INT. NEIGHBOR'S UPSTAIRS BEDROOM
*The officer's fingers start to squeeze the
trigger. Suddenly, his radio crackles.*

HOAG (V.O. ON RADIO)
Stand down! Do not fire!
I repeat, stand down.

The sharpshooter relaxes.

INTERCUT—STREET/COMMAND
CENTER—DAY
Weams grabs his radio.

WEAMS (ON RADIO)
What the hell happened?

HOAG (ON RADIO)
City Hall says no guns.

WEAMS (ON RADIO)
But he had a damn clear shot!

HOAG (ON RADIO)
You want to take it up with the
mayor, Weams?

EXT. STREET OUTSIDE THE
NEIGHBORHOOD—DAY
*Nettie's gotten the hang of the skateboard.
She's moving along at a good clip. In the
distance ahead are the tall buildings of
downtown.*

INT. AIRPLANE CABIN—DAY
*Tommy's cleaned himself up for the flight
to Parkersburg.*

Now he's baring his soul to Brad.

TOMMY
See, being a poet is not some
wacko career choice. It's
reaching down into the depths,
pulling up the muck, the
detritus that emanates from
this cesspool we call life.

STEWARDESS
Care for a beverage, sir?

TOMMY
(without missing a beat)
Scotch, up.

Tommy pulls out a dog-eared
notebook.

TOMMY (CONT'D)
See this? This, my friend, is the product of seventeen years of toil and pain. But is some publisher going to spend a few bucks to get it into print? Hell, no.

STEWARDESS
Five dollars, please.

Brad fishes out the cash as Tommy downs the drink in a gulp.

BRAD
Think we can make our connection to Parkersburg?

STEWARDESS
No promises on that, sir, because we left so late. But the pilot's doing his best.

INT. BOWLING ALLEY—DAY

Roy awkwardly cradles a professional, highly polished bowling ball. He drops it and watches it roll into the gutter.

He picks up another ball and tries again. Same result.

Three middle-aged guys in the next lane are watching him. One guy strolls over as Roy's first ball returns.

BOWLER #1 (JOE)
Mighty nice ball you got there.

ROY
Thanks.

Bowlers #2 and #3 come over to Roy's lane.

BOWLER #2 (DAVE)
That there is a Urethane Ebonite sixteen-pounder.

ROY
So they tell me.

BOWLER #1 (JOE)
Is it...new?

BOWLER #3
Come on, Joe, does it look new?

JOE
I only meant...

ROY
I know. You can't figure out what a guy like me is doing with a ball like this.

JOE
Well, yeah. Kind of.

ROY
It's my brother's. He passed away.

BOWLER #3
Died at the bowling alley, right?

ROY
How did you know?

BOWLER #3
A guy owns a ball like that, you can bet the alley was his home.

JOE
What frame was he in?

ROY
Eighth, they tell me, working on a spare. They say he just went down.

BOWLER #2
Didn't cross the foul line, did he?

JOE
Dave! Show some respect.

DAVE
Sorry, mister. I didn't mean nothing.

ROY
They said Ray never crossed a foul line in his life.

JOE
And he sure wasn't about to do it in death.

BOWLER #3
Your brother was lucky. That's how we all want to go. When the time comes, of course.

DAVE
I bet he's up there right now at that big bowling alley in the sky, rolling one three hundred game after another.

ROY
You guys know a lot about bowlers.

DAVE
We ought to. We're in here four times a week.

JOE
Five. I'm in a traveling league.

ROY
My brother's friends said I ought to have his ball since it was so important to him. But ...I'm no bowler. Just doesn't seem right it won't ever roll another strike.

BOWLER #3
Maybe we could help you out.

ROY
Would you do that?

DAVE
It would be an honor, mister.

INT. AIRPORT—DAY
Tommy sits looking out the window. Brad's texting.
TOMMY
Never been to Atlanta before.

BRAD
We're not in Atlanta. We're at the airport in Atlanta.

TOMMY
But how about that sky? Take a look at that gorgeous—

BRAD
I don't want to, all right? Look, I'm trying to get us on another flight but there is no other flight, so we're probably going to have to spend the night on these friggin' plastic chairs. Now maybe that's okay with you, but me? Not so much.

TOMMY
I just thought you might want to see—

BRAD
You want to look at the sky, knock yourself out. Just leave me alone.

Brad goes back to texting. Tommy gives it a minute and then launches into

TOMMY
Purple haze was in my brain, lately things don't seem the same, actin' funny, don't know why, 'scuse me while I kiss the sky. You know who wrote that?

BRAD
Man, did I just tell you—

TOMMY
That, my friend, was the late, great Jimi Hendrix.

Exasperated, Brad sags in his chair.

INT. BOWLING ALLEY—DAY

Roy and his new buddies are drinking beer and sharing nachos.

JOE
So you never bowled with your brother?

ROY
No, we were into motorcycles. I'll never forget the day he went West on his hog. He said when I finished high school he'd come back and get me. We were going to ride cross country on his bike, just him and me. See the sights.

BOWLER #3
Like EASY RIDER.

ROY
Yeah, only before EASY RIDER. Then, the night I graduated, he calls me up. Said he was tired of riding the thing. Told me he sold it. Man, was I ever angry.

DAVE
So you didn't go West?

ROY
I didn't even talk to him for a year. I took some college courses for the hell of it and I did okay. Next thing you know I had a job, a girl, we got married...

JOE
And you never went out there?

ROY
No. We'd talk on the phone sometimes, but we were never close after that. I know it sounds dumb, but I couldn't forgive him for selling that bike. I didn't believe he could do it.

Roy shakes his head.

ROY (CONT'D)
Turns out I was right.

BOWLER #3
What do you mean?

ROY
When I flew out there for his funeral, guess what I found in his garage?

EXT. DOWNTOWN WATERFRONT PLAZA—DAY

Nettie strolls along, taking in the sights. A crowd watches a juggler. A banjo player and a fiddler are playing country.

She walks past a three-masted old-time sailing ship. A sign reads "Avast maties! Come aboard for a pirate cruise!"

A cute REDHEAD, 20s, on crutches, puts a smaller sign next to it: "Female Pirate Wanted. Must be experienced sailor."

Nettie continues on but then stops and looks back. She settles her backpack and approaches the redhead.

NETTIE
Can I try out for the pirate job?

The girl looks her up and down.

REDHEAD (AMY)
You sail?

NETTIE
I used to. A lot.

REDHEAD (AMY)
Come on in.

INT. PIRATE TOUR TICKET OFFICE

Nettie follows the redhead into the back room. JACK, 30s, in a pirate costume, is buried over some papers.

REDHEAD (AMY) (CONT'D)
Jack, maybe we've got a
replacement.

Jack sizes Nettie up. He's not
impressed.

JACK
I don't know, ma'am. I'm not
sure that...

REDHEAD (AMY)
But she knows how to sail.
And we've got that tour group
coming. Be a shame to cancel.

JACK
Come on, Amy. A silver-blonde
pirate?

Amy grabs a big pirate hat and
plops it on Nettie's head.

AMY
How about that?

He's still not convinced.

JACK
Can you handle a schooner?

NETTIE
I used to win prizes for it.

JACK
What's your name?

NETTIE
Ann...Annie.

AMY
The tour group's coming at five.

JACK
Well...I guess we could try it.

INT. BOWLING ALLEY—DAY

ROY
My father was out of the picture
so Ray was big brother, dad,
and Superman rolled into one.

BOWLER #3
But why did he say he sold his
bike when he didn't?

ROY
I've been thinking about that
for the last thousand miles.
My mom wanted me to go to
college, and I bet Ray figured
if I hooked up with him, that
would never happen. So he just
told me a big, fat lie.

JOE
And gave you a future.

Roy nods in recognition.

DAVE
At least you got his ball. That's
the best part of a bowler, you
know.

Suddenly, there's a commotion at
the bowling alley door. A couple of
reporters and TV cameramen burst
in. They stop just inside, studying
everybody in the place. Then, one of
them spots Roy.

CAMERAMAN
There he is!

They make a mad dash across the
lanes.

All the bowlers stare open-mouthed.

One reporter slips and lands in a
gutter.

A woman races past him but slides
partway down lane four.

ALLEY MANAGER
What the hell are you, people
doing?

A guy gets to Roy first, a microphone
in his hand.

MALE REPORTER
Are you Roy Lowery?

EXT. STREET—DAY
On the street in front of Nettie's house, things are at a standstill. Officer Ruggiero goes to Weams.

RUGGIERO
Sir, can I see you a second?

WEAMS
What's up?

RUGGIERO
I don't get it, Sarge. She's been standing stock-still at that window now for over an hour.

WEAMS
Think it's some kind of trick?

RUGGIERO
Well, why doesn't she sit down, or get a sandwich or go to the john? Something's funny.

WEAMS
Maybe you're right. We need to get inside. But we need a distraction.

Weams goes to Gwen.

WEAMS (CONT'D)
This is serious, ma'am. How about talking to your aunt?

GWEN
Well, I guess I could try. If you think it'll help.

EXT. BACKYARD—DAY
Six tactical cops in body armor move stealthily toward Nettie's house, three on one side of Mrs. A's fence, three on the other.

EXT. STREET—DAY
Gwen stands nervously in front of the camera.

GWEN
Hi, Aunt Nettie. Just thought I'd stop by and say hi. So...hi.

EXT. BACKYARD—DAY
Three officers are at the steps leading to the kitchen door. The other three are outside the basement window.

One notices the window is unlocked. He signals to his partners, opens it, and peer inside.

EXT. STREET—DAY

GWEN (CONT'D)
When I saw you last week, I had no idea you were planning on staging a shootout with the police. The big question is right now, we don't know whether to go ahead and hold the family reunion or not.

INT. BASEMENT—DAY
The three cops squeeze through the window into the basement and silently mount the stairs.

EXT. STREET—DAY

GWEN
But we want you to know that we're all here for you. All except Aunt Iris, that is. She's having that procedure today. Not that I want to tell the whole world about it.

INT. KITCHEN—DAY
One cop opens the kitchen door, and the other three enter. All six are now inside.

EXT. STREET—DAY

GWEN
I could bring you some food, but I can't imagine you're

running out, you being such a
great canner and everything.
You know everybody loves your
chowchow.

INT. HALL—DAY

*The officer in charge gestures to three of
the others to check out the upstairs. They
mount the steps. The other three move
down the hall. Guns drawn, they peer
around every corner.*

EXT. STREET—DAY—CONTINUOUS

GWEN
The sergeant's real nice, Aunt
Nettie. Won't you please think
about coming out?

INT. LIVING ROOM—DAY

*Finally, the cops move into the living
room. The TV's on but the only sign of
Nettie is her robe.*

*One pulls the robe off the dress form and
holds it at arm's length, shaking his head.
The guy in charge grabs his radio.*

TACTICAL OFFICER (ON RADIO)
Sergeant? You're not going to
like it.

EXT. STREET—DAY

Weams clicks off his radio.

WEAMS
(to himself)
Now where in the hell is she?

EXT. HARBOR—DAY

*The pirate ship sails into view. Tourists fill
the deck. Jack is at the helm. A couple of
other guys, all in costume, hang off the lines.*

*Suddenly, a small schooner sails up close
to the big ship. A LONE PIRATE is on
deck. He calls out to Jack.*

LONE PIRATE
Ahoy there, Black Bart! You've
got our gold from the Spanish
ship.

JACK
And you're a thief and a liar.

LONE PIRATE
You're the same. Give us
our share or sleep with the
Spaniards.

JACK
It's you who'll be doing the
sleeping.

Jack fires his gun at the schooner.
There's a puff of smoke, and the lone
pirate falls, blood pouring onto the
deck.

Nettie, in full pirate regalia, steps out
of the schooner's cabin.

NETTIE
Who gave you leave to kill my
son, Black Bart?

JACK
And who might you be?

NETTIE
Anne Bonny, you murderer.
Now you have to deal with me.

She pulls a gun from her skirt, aims
at Jack, and fires. He ducks, but she
jumps to the wheel and pulls the
boat about.

Two more pirates appear on Nettie's
deck and the battle, mostly noise
and smoke is now in full swing.

The tourists are loving it.

One of Nettie's shipmates is wounded.
She shoots at a pirate high up in the
big ship's rigging and he falls spectacularly off his perch into the water.

The crowd cheers.

Nettie shoots at Jack, and he drops his gun.

NETTIE
Give us the gold, Black Bart, or you won't see tomorrow.

JACK
Here, take it, you witch.

Jack throws a bag of loot at Nettie's feet.

JACK (CONT'D)
Good riddance, Mistress Bonny. We'll settle up in Tortuga.

Nettie laughs and bows mockingly in his direction.

NETTIE
Say your prayers on that one.

She wheels the schooner about and sails away. The tourists cheer.

EXT. STREET—DAY
But nobody's cheering in Nettie's neighborhood.

A grim-faced Chief Jackson, flanked by Weams and Lieutenant Hoag stands before a bunch of microphones.

JACKSON
Yes, the subject is free right now, but I guarantee she won't be free for long. Every police officer in this state and every law enforcement agency in the region is hunting her down.

TV NEWSMAN JIM
You consider her armed and dangerous?

JACKSON
That would be an affirmative.

TV NEWSWOMAN GERRY
Any idea how she got away?

Jackson is clearly steamed about it.

JACKSON
That's...under investigation. Now, if you'll excuse me...

JIM
Chief, we're talking about a little lady in her sixties. How could she—

JACKSON
Don't glamorize this woman. Her age is irrelevant. She is a threat to the peace and stability of this city. And I assure you the men and women of this department will not rest until she's in handcuffs.

The police hurry off. Gerry turns to face her camera.

GERRY
Keep it with WXVR-TV real-life-real-people news for the latest on the hunt for Nettie Lowery.

INT. PIRATE TOUR TICKET OFFICE—DAY
Jack, Amy, and Nettie are high-fiving it.

AMY
And you thought she couldn't do it!

JACK
So I was wrong. What else do you do?

NETTIE
What do you mean?

AMY
Are you musical at all?

NETTIE
I used to play drums.

AMY
Perfect! She could do tambourine.

NETTIE
Tambourine?

JACK
We've got a band. I play keyboard, Amy sings, but there's supposed to be five of us, and we're one short.

AMY
My sister plays the fiddle, but we were in a car crash, and she got banged up worse than I did.

JACK
Thing is, we've got a gig tonight, and the guy who owns the bar is a real jerk. If only four of us show, he won't let us play.

NETTIE
But I don't know your music.

AMY
All you have to do is keep time.

NETTIE
Can I wear the hat?

AMY
Sure. We're the "Band of Pirates."

INT. BAR—NIGHT

It's a grungy establishment with a handful of people at some tables near a small stage and a couple of guys at the bar.

Jack, Amy, and two other guys are putting their all into some recycled Led Zeppelin. Nettie's holding her own with a tambourine.

BAR PATRON #1
Does that woman look familiar to you?

BAR PATRON #2
Come on. You think every redhead you see looks familiar.

PATRON #1
Not the redhead. The other one.

PATRON #2
Her? What have you got? A mother fixation?

PATRON #1
I didn't say I liked her; I just said she looked familiar. Like I've seen her somewhere.

PATRON #2
Maybe your grandmom's nursing home.

PATRON #1
No, I...look. There.

He points to the TV over the bar. There's a picture of Nettie without the wig and the hat.

"Police hunt goes on for Annette Lowery."

Nettie doesn't see it.

PATRON #1 (CONT'D)
She's that woman they're looking for. Maybe there's a reward.

He pulls out his cell.

EXT. PRISON EXERCISE YARD—DAY

The sky is gray, and so are the drab dresses on the women prisoners.

A fragile young BLONDE cowers in a corner. Prisoner #1 (MAXINE), 40s, and Prisoner #2 (CRYSTAL), 30s, approach.

LADY VOLCANO

PRISONER #1 (MAXINE)
Need you to do somethin' for me sweetcakes.

BLONDE
What?

PRISONER #2 (CRYSTAL)
Get on your feet when Maxine's talking to you.

The blonde stands, terrified.

BLONDE
What do you want me to—

MAXINE
Just hang on to my phone. I don't want 'em to find it in my cell.

BLONDE
But if they find it on me, they won't let me have visitors.

PRISONER #2 (CRYSTAL)
Aw, poor baby! Is Brad Pitt coming to see you?

BLONDE
My mom's bringing my little boy on Sunday. If they find your phone—

MAXINE
She's not getting it, Crystal.

CRYSTAL
Look, babydoll, Maxine's not askin' you, she's tellin' you.

Maxine slips her cellphone into the Blonde's pocket.

BLONDE
Oh, please don't make me—

CRYSTAL
I guess you don't hear so good. I'm gonna have to—

Suddenly Crystal gasps. A hand is squeezing the back of her neck in a vise-like grip.

NETTIE (O.S.)
Maybe you don't hear so good.

MAXINE
Who are you?

NETTIE
The name's Nettie. Now take your phone back.

Crystal grimaces in pain as Nettie squeezes harder.

NETTIE (CONT'D)
Come on, your pal's hurtin'.

Maxine retrieves her phone and Nettie releases Crystal.

MAXINE
You might want to be careful who you make enemies with, hon.

NETTIE
That's my worry, hon. Now take off.

Maxine and Crystal slouch away.

BLONDE
Gee, thanks. Is there anything I can do for you?

NETTIE
Not really. Unless you got a butterscotch sundae on you.

INT. POLICE INTERROGATION ROOM—DAY

Nettie's daydream ends as police psychologist PAXTON, 40s, puts an ice cream sundae in her hand.

She wears a Department of Corrections jumpsuit.

PAXTON
Figured you might want a
sundae for breakfast.

NETTIE
Thanks.

PAXTON
Feel like talkin'?

NETTIE
I guess.

PAXTON
Want to tell me why you did all
this?

NETTIE
I guess...I just got fed up. I was
tired of being hot and cold
running Nettie.

PAXTON
Hot and cold...?

NETTIE
Like a faucet people turn on
when they want something.
Plus, the whole retirement thing
got to me. Hey, this is good.

She takes a big spoon of the sundae.

NETTIE (CONT'D)
But I'm glad it's over. Time
for everybody to get back to
normal. Whatever that is.

INT. CHURCH—DAY
ORGAN MUSIC: "Here comes the bride."

Mother-of-the-bride Marie sits up front,
tears of joy running down her cheeks.
At the back of the church, Joe's face is
wreathed in smiles.

But...he's in a wheelchair. With both his
legs in casts stretched out before him.

The wedding guests smile as he's wheeled
up the aisle next to the radiant bride,
Diane. Marie gushes more tears.

EXT. STREET—DAY
Gerry stands on neighbor Missy's porch
holding her mike.

GERRY
Now that the manhunt for
Nettie Lowery is over and she's
in custody, we thought we'd
check in on her neighbors.
We've been invited to a
counseling session at the
home of Missy Donahue.

Gerry and her cameraman step into
Missy's house.

INT. MISSY'S LIVING ROOM
Missy and half a dozen women
smile nervously at the camera. A
COUNSELLOR, 40s, sits in the
center of the sofa.

GERRY
Thanks for letting us in, ladies.

COUNSELLOR
Let's begin by sharing our
feelings about what happened.
Anyone like to start?

An uncomfortable silence.

COUNSELLOR (CONT'D)
I'm sure you all have ideas,
ladies.

WOMAN #1
Well, it was awful. We were
prisoners! In our own homes!

Sympathetic looks all around.

WOMAN #2
It was like being under attack.

WOMAN #3
As if somebody dropped a bomb!

WOMAN #4
Devastating. Simply devastating.

Several women dab at their eyes.

MISSY
I'll say this. She sure got
everybody's attention.

WOMAN #5
But who gave her the right to
wreck everyone's life?

WOMAN #6
Exactly. Why was it "her turn" to
make herself happy?

COUNSELLOR
Let's go down that road a little.
Would you perhaps like it to be
...your turn? To make yourself
happy?

WOMAN #6
Like that's ever gonna happen.

WOMAN #4
Yeah. Fat chance.

GERRY
Can I jump in here?

COUNSELLOR
Be our guest.

GERRY
Why won't it happen? Why
don't you get to be happy?

WOMAN #5
We're too busy making
everybody else happy.

WOMAN #2
And if we stop, we're facing the
big G.

GERRY
The big G?

WOMAN #2
Guilt. Look, it's all in here.

She picks up a woman's magazine
off the coffee table.

WOMAN #2 (CONT'D)
You're holding down a job, plus
you have to have the perfect
house, perfect kids, and put
perfect meals on the table.

WOMAN #1
You forgot the perfect body.

Groans all around.

WOMAN #4
You know what's in men's
magazines?

WOMAN #3
Blondes in string bikinis.

WOMAN #4
Yeah, but mostly it's...relax,
take it easy, have a beer. Oh,
and once in a while, build a
birdhouse.

Lots of laughter.

WOMAN #3
You know what, though?
Sometimes I wonder what it'll
be like when the kids are gone
and the job is history.

WOMAN #1
What do you mean? You'll
finally have some time.

WOMAN #3
Yeah, but...when all that stuff is
over...what's left for me?

COUNSELLOR
Do you think maybe that's how
Nettie felt?

MISSY
Could be. Maybe she just
wanted to stop the carousel.

WOMAN #6
No, she didn't want to stop it;
she wanted to get on and have
a ride.

WOMAN #5
And get a shot at the brass ring.

COUNSELLOR
Is there something wrong with that?

The women look from one to the other.

INT. POLICE INTERROGATION ROOM—DAY

PAXTON
So, bottom line, you want more out of life than a butterscotch sundae.

NETTIE
Well, I still want to do something meaningful. But I'd also like to have some fun. What's the point of being sixty-four if you don't know what makes you happy?

Noise on the other side of the glass gets their attention. Two officers are bringing in a couple of teenage girls.

OFFICER #1
Come on, honey, behave.

GIRL #1
Like I told you. He's my boyfriend.

OFFICER #2
And that's why you hid the stuff for him.

GIRL #1
We need money. We're gonna get married and—

OFFICER #1
What's he gonna tell his other girlfriends?

The second girl sees Nettie through the glass.

GIRL #2
What you lookin' at, Miss Thing?

GIRL #1
Isn't she a little old for this racket?

GIRL #2
Hey, she's got ice cream. I want ice cream!

The cops hustle the girls into another room.

NETTIE
So young. What's going to happen to them?

PAXTON
Most likely, they'll end up at the Girls Juvenile Detention Center.

NETTIE
What's that like?

PAXTON
It's nowhere near as well-equipped as the boys' center. But boys outnumber girls five to one in the system so the boys get the gym, the ball field, and all the teachers and counselors they need. The girls get what's left.

NETTIE
That's not right.

PAXTON
No. But it's how it is.

NETTIE
They need teachers?

PAXTON
Yeah, but like I said, they don't have much of a budget.

NETTIE
Would they take a volunteer?

PAXTON

I can put you in touch with the administrator. Which reminds me, I better go check your status.

INT. AIRPORT—DAY

Brad, tired, and unshaven, walks through the Atlanta airport, talking on his cell.

BRAD

...but is there any point in bringing the literary genius all the way there if his mom's already in custody?...okay, I'll be in touch.

As he hangs up, Brad sees Tommy ahead of him in the middle of a crowd. Tommy's reading something aloud and the people around him are listening.

TOMMY

The sky pivots like a bowl on a wheel, each side first coming near, then going far.

A couple of teens, an old guy in a wheelchair, a mom with a baby, all seem to be mesmerized.

TOMMY (CONT'D)

Ribbons of clouds arch over the earth, billowy banners spiral out like the downy hair on a baby's head.

The mom beams as if the pope had just blessed her child. A businessman is rushing by, but he stops, caught by the words.

TOMMY (CONT'D)

Is there some kind of answer for us in the wavy threads that spin off the spine of the globe?

A woman stops working on her laptop and looks up, thoughtful.

TOMMY (CONT'D)

Some wisdom for the weighted down? A signal for the burdened, the harried, the hurried, the worried?

A guy takes off his bluetooth and tunes in.

TOMMY (CONT'D)

Clouds sweep over the mountain, bringing the breath of a breeze.

Settle down, say, take a break. Only if we listen...can we get the gift ...of nature's peace.

Silence.

Then the old man starts to clap. One by one, the crowd joins in, applauding enthusiastically.

Tommy blinks, basking in the glow.

The AIRPORT MANAGER, FRED, 40s, strides up to his female ASSISTANT, 30s.

AIRPORT MANAGER (FRED)

Why did you call me down here? What's so important?

She points to Tommy.

The people around him call out: "More!" "Give us another!" "What else have we got going on?"

Tommy launches into another poem and the crowd goes quiet.

TOMMY

So here I am, waiting in the waiting room and my time is up to you. That's how it seems to be, we both agree, but in reality, it's just not true.

Fred shrugs.

AIRPORT MANAGER (FRED)
So?

ASSISTANT
Fred, thirty minutes ago, we
had a near-riot down here.
2318 and 379—

FRED
I know. Both in second delays.

ASSISTANT
Now, look. People are relaxed;
they're smiling, all because
this guy's doing poetry. Maybe
that's the answer.

FRED
The answer to what?

ASSISTANT
To making people forget
they're sitting on plastic chairs,
eating lousy food, listening to
boring announcements. What if
it's art?

Fred still doesn't get it.

ASSISTANT
We hire entertainers. Poets,
like him. Or painters, dancers,
actors.

And the light finally dawns.

FRED
You mean, the bad news is your
flight's delayed, but the good
news is...

ASSISTANT
You get a free show! We call it
a festival, a fair, a circus! And,
we'd be supporting the arts.

Tommy continues to enthrall the
crowd.

TOMMY
This day of mine is not your
plaything. You cannot make it

so. Yes, you own the clocks, the
things that tick and tock. But
me? Oh, no. That's not so.

FRED
Corporate would love that.

ASSISTANT
Right. Now, how we pay for it...

FRED
The airlines could ante up when
they're late. They floated that
idea at the last regional. Might
even boost on-time departures.

TOMMY
All those numbers on all those
screens will never rob me of
what's mine. I am who I was
when I walked in. And you don't
own my time.

The crowd erupts in laughter and
cheers. Fred and the assistant high-
five it.

EXT. CITY HALL—DAY
*A crowd of women CHANTS "LET
NETTIE GO! LET NETTIE GO!"*

*Some carry signs: "NETTIE LOWERY-
OUR HERO" "NETTIE FOR
MAYOR."*

Police try to keep them behind barriers.

Newsman Jim has his mike in hand.

JIM
So why are you here today, ladies?

WOMAN #4
We've decided Nettie was right.

WOMAN #5
You bet she was.

WOMAN #1
She was just tired of missing out
on all the good times.

WOMAN #3
We know what that's about.

Voices from the crowd: "You said it,"
"When's our turn?"

WOMAN #4
She didn't hurt anybody, so why
is she locked up?

WOMAN #5
Right. We want to see the
mayor.

WOMAN #2
We want her to run for mayor.

WOMAN #3
Exactly. Any woman who can
hold down a job and run a
house can run City Hall.

The crowd erupts into CHEERS.

INT. MAYOR'S OFFICE—DAY
*The CROWD NOISE is audible inside
the mayor's office.*

He's on the phone. And he's not happy.

MAYOR
Look, I've had enough of this
broad...I know she's in custody
but I don't want to look at TV
like I'm doing right now and see
her damn picture...well, think of
something.

He slams the phone down.

**INT. POLICE INTERROGATION
ROOM—DAY**
Paxton comes in.

PAXTON
Got some news. You're free to
go. You've been declared not
criminally responsible.

NETTIE
That makes me sound like I'm
crazy.

PAXTON
No, it just means you bear no
responsibility. No responsibility,
no crime. They can't keep
you without charging you.
Bottom line, they don't want to
prosecute.

NETTIE
I bet Sergeant Weams would
like to.

PAXTON
He'll get over it. Look, you're
in a lose-lose situation for City
Hall. They just want you to go
away. Now, you could demand
to see a lawyer, go before the
magistrate, make a fuss...

NETTIE
I've had enough of a fuss.

PAXTON
Okay, then. You get to go
home. But it's got to be tonight,
after the eleven o'clock news.
Unmarked car, no lights, no
sirens, and everybody's happy.
Deal?

EXT. STREET—NIGHT
*A car pulls up silently in front of Nettie's
house. There's a single light on in the
kitchen.*

*Nettie gets out, still wearing the jumpsuit.
She watches the car pull away and goes
inside the gate.*

*As she closes it, Roy opens the front door.
And then he's down the stairs and across
the yard to her.*

NEXT DAY
INT. KITCHEN—DAY

Roy's at the table with a cup of coffee, phone in hand.

ROY
(into phone)
Of course, we'll come see you... that's terrific. What are you calling it?...yeah, I like "Runway Rhymes"...

Nettie comes in, towel-drying her hair.

ROY (CONT'D)
(to Nettie)
Tommy.
(into phone)
She's fine. I'll tell her...okay. Talk to you later.

Roy hangs up.

NETTIE
How is he?

ROY
Sounds great. He wanted to talk to you, but he had a poetry reading to run to. And get this, the airport's going to help get his poems published.

NETTIE
So I guess he likes Atlanta?

ROY
Sounds like it. How you feeling?

NETTIE
Okay. Better.

She looks out the window.

NETTIE (CONT'D)
Is that a reporter out there?

ROY
Yeah, he must have found out they let you go.

She sits and takes a breath.

NETTIE
Roy, I'm sorry.

ROY
For what?

NETTIE
Everything. Him out there.

ROY
Take it easy. Sooner or later, he'll get tired and go home.

NETTIE
What about the broken window?

ROY
I can fix it.

NETTIE
But I embarrassed the whole family.

ROY
They'll get over it.

NETTIE
I spent the night in police custody.

ROY
I'm glad you were safe.

NETTIE
So you're okay about all this?

ROY
Well, I have to admit I was kind of surprised when the TV people caught up with me and told me what was going on.

NETTIE
Surprised?

ROY
Okay. Shocked. But look...right now, I got enough guilt of my own.

NETTIE

Ray?

Roy nods.

ROY

All those years. Why the hell didn't I go see him? Man, nothing tastes as rotten as regret.

NETTIE

Take it easy, Roy. Most of us never do what we really ought to do.

ROY

That's no damn excuse.

NETTIE

At least you re-connected with that wild biker guy inside.

ROY

Oh, I don't know how wild he is.

NETTIE

You just drove cross-country on a motorcycle. That's pretty wild for a guy in his sixties.

They chuckle.

ROY

Hey, I'm not the one who held the whole police force at bay.

NETTIE

It was just the tactical unit.

ROY

Come on, wild woman, you got me beat, you know you do.

They laugh.

ROY (CONT'D)

Oh, I almost forgot. This came. Special delivery.

He hands her an envelope. She opens the letter, reads it, and drops it on the table.

NETTIE

The school board "declines" to reconsider my retirement. Guess you can't blame them. Nobody wants a gun-toting schoolteacher.

ROY

So you'll do something else.

NETTIE

Maybe. County schools aren't the only place they need teachers.

INT. INSTITUTIONAL HALLWAY—DAY

Peeling paint, ancient light fixtures, it's pretty drab.

Nettie, carrying bags and books, walks down the hall with Ms. MARX, 40s, a juvenile detention facility administrator.

MARX

These girls have been through some horrific things. Neglect, abuse, even rape. That's why they're so defensive.

NETTIE

What about their families?

Marx shakes her head.

MARX

Some of the parents are incarcerated themselves. Or they're sick, deceased, or just out of the picture. The only family some of these kids have is a sister who has her own kids or maybe a grandmom.

Marx opens the door of a classroom.

MARX (CONT'D)
Our girls aren't easy, Mrs. Lowery.
Ask for help if you need it.

INT. CLASSROOM—DAY
Nettie goes in, puts her things down and sizes up the dingy room and the beat-up desks. She moves with purpose to the window and raises the shades.
LATER
INT. CLASSROOM—DAY
Eight bored, disdainful teenage girls slouch at the desks. One looks asleep; one is doodling another's doing her nails.

NETTIE
And the inclined plane makes seven. That's it. Any questions?

GIRL #1
Can we go?

NETTIE
Soon. Time's not up yet.

Girl #1 makes a face and slouches farther down in her chair.

NETTIE (CONT'D)
Okay, so maybe the seven basic machines are not the most exciting thing you've ever heard about.

Derisive laughter.

NETTIE (CONT'D)
But I'm going to try to make science more interesting. It'll help if we get to know one another. Anything you want to ask me?

One girl rolls her eyes, another pops gum.

NETTIE (CONT'D)
I've never seen so many girls with nothing to say.

GIRL #2
We got stuff to say. We just don't want to say it to you.

NETTIE
Because..?

GIRL #3
We don't need you reportin' us.

NETTIE
Who says I'm going to report you?

GIRL #4 (JASMINE)
Don't give us that shit.

GIRL #5
Easy, Jasmine. It's a trap.

JASMINE
I ain't afraid of her. I ain't afraid o' nothin'.

NETTIE
What do you want to say, Jasmine?

JASMINE
I wanta know—

GIRL #5
Jesus fuckin' christ.

JASMINE
Shut your face, all right?

JASMINE (CONT'D)
(to Nettie)
I want to know why you white bitches think you can come in here and boss us around. 'Cause, it ain't gonna work. Not with me, it ain't.

NETTIE
I didn't come to boss you around. I came to teach you science.

GIRL #6
That's what they payin' you for?

NETTIE
Nobody's paying me.
I volunteered.

GIRL #7
You workin' for free? What are
you, some kind of reject?

Laughter.

GIRL #5
Just like always. We get the
garbage.

GIRL #6
Why you workin' for nothin'?

GIRL #7
Like I said, she's a reject.

NETTIE
I've been a teacher a long time
but when you hit sixty-four
they won't let you teach in the
county schools.

GIRL #8
Sixty-four? That's older than my
grandma.

GIRL #5
She a reject too?

GIRL #8
Shut your fuckin' mouth about
my grandma.

JASMINE
So you gonna come here every
day...for nothin'?

NETTIE
I like to teach.

Looks of disbelief, mistrust.

GIRL #5
Yeah, sure. 'Til you get sick of us.

The door opens and a woman
looks in.

YOUNG WOMAN
Time for your group sessions,
girls.

As they leave, Nettie smiles at
Jasmine.

NETTIE
See you tomorrow, Jasmine.

Jasmine gives her an icey look and
slouches out the door.

**SEVERAL DAYS LATER
INT. CLASSROOM—DAY**
*Nettie places a small rubber ball on her
desk.*

NETTIE
So. A body remains at rest
unless it is compelled to change
by an outside force. Which
means...

She looks at the girls, all of whom
ignore her.

NETTIE
That unless I pick up that ball,
or knock it off the desk, it will
stay there forever. Right?

No response.

NETTIE
Good. Glad you agree. Of
course...

She takes another ball from her
pocket and tosses it from one hand
to the other as she strolls around the
room.

NETTIE
...a strong gust of wind could
blow through the window. Then
what?

She tosses the ball to one of the girls,
who is so startled she catches it.

GIRL #6 (LATOYA)
I...I don't know.

NETTIE
Think about it. The wind roars
in. What happens to the ball?

GIRL #6 (LATOYA)
I...guess it falls on the floor.

NETTIE
Good guess. Can I have my ball
back?

Latoya tosses it and Nettie catches it
neatly.

NETTIE
Thanks, Ms. Dennis.

GIRL #5
(sarcastically)
"Miss Dennis."

LATOYA
My name's Latoya.

NETTIE
Do you mind if I call you
Ms. Dennis?

Latoya shrugs "who cares?"

NETTIE
Of course, a strong wind is not
the only possibility. We might
have an earthquake. Then
what?

Nettie tosses the ball to another
girl, but this one makes no move to
catch it.

GIRL #7 (CLINTON)
(defiant)
We don't have earthquakes
around here.

NETTIE
You're right, we don't. Not often.
Want to get that ball for me?

Girl #7 rolls her eyes.

NETTIE
Okay, Ms. Clinton.

Nettie takes another ball from her
pocket and strolls as before.

Clinton grabs the other ball and
throws it at Nettie who catches it and
starts juggling both balls. The girls
are surprised. Nettie juggles as she
talks.

NETTIE
But if we did have an
earthquake and the desk got
upset, what would happen to
the ball? Ms. Rivera?

JASMINE
Who gives a fuck?

Several girls laugh.

NETTIE
You know, Ms. Rivera,
somebody with such a beautiful
face shouldn't let words like
that come out of it.

GIRL #8
Ooh! She's got a beautiful face.

JASMINE
Shut the fuck up.

Nettie focuses on the balls as she
tosses them higher and higher.
The girls are watching them too.

NETTIE
Does it make you feel good to
talk that way?

JASMINE
It's how I talk, okay? And who
cares about whether the friggin'
ball falls off the friggin' desk.

NETTIE
It's science, Ms. Rivera.

JASMINE
What the hell good is science?

NETTIE
Yes! Thank you!

Nettie pumps the air and puts the balls down.

I've been waiting all week
for that one. Science, ladies,
is knowledge. Knowledge is
power. And to know something
is to be strong.

GIRL #5
You sayin' we're not strong?

NETTIE
I'm saying you can be stronger.
Stronger up here.

She taps her forehead.

JASMINE
What the fuck for?

NETTIE
For when some guy tells you he
wants you to "make him feel
good" and then he disappears
when you get pregnant. Or
when he says he needs you to
"hang onto stuff for him" and
he promises you won't get into
trouble and then—

GIRL #2 (JERMAINE)
Well, you don't always—

GIRL #8
Geez, Jermaine.

NETTIE
So you hide the gun or the drugs
or the money and then you get
caught. And where is he?

GIRL #7
You talk like all the guys we
know are no good.

LATOYA
Yeah, and all we have to do
is learn science and shit and
everything 'll be fine.

NETTIE
I didn't say that.

LATOYA
Then what—

NETTIE
I'm talking about thinking for
yourself, taking charge of your
life.

JASMINE
There's nothin' wrong with my
life! Maybe it don't suit you, but
I'm fine with it, okay?

NETTIE
Okay, Ms. Rivera.

JASMINE
And stop saying my name like
that!

NETTIE
It's a polite way of addressing
a young woman. Which is what
you are. And if you're happy
with your life, that's good. If all
of you are happy, that's great.

She looks each one in the eye.

NETTIE (CON'T)
But if maybe, just maybe, you
want things to be different...if
you'd like to have nice clothes
or a nice place to live and if
you don't ever want to come
back to a place like this...then
maybe it's time to start using
what's inside. Up here.

She taps her forehead. The room is
dead quiet.

NETTIE
That's why I'm teaching you science. To make you think. To put you in the driver's seat. To change your life.

NEW DAY
INT. CLASSROOM—DAY

Nettie's desk is covered with plastic bags, rock salt, ice, half and half, strawberries, sugar, and a bottle of vanilla.

NETTIE
Ladies, today we're going to do an endothermic experiment. Can you say endothermic?

The girls look bored, but they're watching her, curious.

No takers? Well, if you can't say it, you can't eat it.

LATOYA
Eat what?

NETTIE
The ice cream we're going to make.

CLINTON
What kind of ice cream?

NETTIE
Vanilla for starters. But then we'll try some strawberry.

She holds up a bag of strawberries.

JERMAINE
How you gonna make ice cream?

NETTIE
As I said, it's an endothermic process. We put half and half and sugar in this bag and rock salt and ice in this one. But I'm going to need help mixing it. And if you don't help me—

Latoya gets up.

LATOYA
I'll help.

NETTIE
Great. Now hold this bag while I put in the ingredients.

MONTAGE—NETTIE BREAKS DOWN BARRIERS WITH THE GIRLS

INT. CLASSROOM—DAY

Latoya mixes the contents of one bag. Girl #8 works on the other bag as Nettie explains the process. Then the girls enjoy the ice cream.

EXT. A STREAM NEAR SOME TREES—DAY

Nettie scoops up water from a shallow stream pointing out pond life. The girls sit on the bank. A few wrinkle their noses at the smell of the water. Nettie pulls out a worm and dares one of them to hold it. Clinton takes it, teasing the others.

INT. CLASSROOM—DAY

Boxes of spaghetti are everywhere. Several of the desks have been pushed together and on them are two bridges made of dry pasta. The girls watch as Nettie carefully puts a small weight on one of the bridges. It holds. Jermaine puts a weight on the second bridge and it holds for a second but then…collapses. The girls laugh.

EXT. A LOW ROOF—NIGHT

Nettie shows the girls the moon up close through her telescope. Jasmine marvels at the sight.

END MONTAGE

INT. CLASSROOM—DAY

It's noisy with the girls' chatter.

Papier-mache volcanos are erupting on several desks.

LATOYA
Look at mine!

CLINTON
My colors are better than yours.

GIRL #3
Look how high hers goes!

Ms. Marx and Roy are out in the hall, seen through the glass door. Roy sports a full beard.

One of the girls goes to Nettie.

GIRL #1
Ms. Nettie, Ms. Marx wants to see you.

Another volcano erupts to squeals and screams as Nettie steps out into the hall.

INT. INSTITUTIONAL HALLWAY—DAY

NETTIE
(to Roy)
What are you doing here?

ROY
Thought we ought to celebrate your last day of school.

NETTIE
My last day this session, Roy.
I told Ms. Marx I'll be back.

MARX
You better come back.

Marx turns and heads up the hall.

NETTIE
So what do you have in mind?

The noise continues from inside the classroom.

ROY
How about we take a trip?

NETTIE
Where to?

ROY
Oh, somewhere in the country.

He hands her an envelope.

She takes out some tickets, looks startled, and looks at him.

Another volcano erupts in the classroom to cheers and laughter.

EXT. HILLY TERRAIN—DAY
Two gloved hands rev up a motorcycle and it roars to life.

A second pair of hands guns a second bike.

Roy turns to smile at Nettie and she snaps the band on her helmet.

They take off and barrel along a rough road, passing lots of stone work.

Soon they come to a sign. "VESUVIO" it says, with an arrow pointing ahead.

Both bikes tear around a bend and the volcano looms into sight.

They roar toward Mount Vesuvius as we

Fade to black.

CPSIA information can be obtained
at www.ICGtesting.com
Printed in the USA
BVHW092157091221
623709BV00011B/411